D0899910

A STUDY OF HEGEL'S LOGIC

A STUDY OF HEGEL'S LOGIC

BY

G. R. G. MURE
WARDEN OF MERTON COLLEGE, OXFORD
HON. LL.D. ST. ANDREWS

OXFORD
AT THE CLARENDON PRESS
1950

Oxford University Press, Amen House, London E.C. 4
GLASGOW NEW YORK TORONTO MELBOURNE WELLINGTON
BOMBAY CALCUTTA MADRAS CAPE TOWN
Geoffrey Cumberlege, Publisher to the University

PRINTED IN GREAT BRITAIN

PREFACE

To very many modern philosophers modern philosophy seems pretty well sufficient unto itself. It could, indeed, surprise no serious historian of philosophy to find an alliance of empiricism and logical analysis indifferent or hostile to most thinkers of the past. Yet there may still be some students of philosophy, young as well as old, who feel a sense of oppression and sterility when they attempt to labour in the confined atmosphere of modern philosophic thought. They may wonder whether where there are no roots there can be any fruit. To them it may still seem that 'there is a world elsewhere', and that the wider fields in which great thinkers used to range and sow have long enough lain fallow or been but sparsely cropped. They may even fear that, unless those fields are once again vigorously tilled, not professional philosophy only but all civilization is threatened with a very terrifying return of the dark ages. To them, I have thought, a book on Hegel might not come amiss.

In that hope I published *An Introduction to Hegel*.[1] A great part of it was historical; the rest was mainly an attempt to explain Hegel's general conception of logic as a clue to his system. The present work is designed as a sequel, and I have throughout it presupposed the detail of my *Introduction*.

Chapters II–XVIII contain an outline exposition of Hegel's categories in which the main course of the *Encyclopaedia*, Part I, is slightly modified and supplemented from the *Wissenschaft der Logik*. I have tried to display as clear a thread of thought as I believed I could disentangle from the two versions together, but I have ignored entirely certain sections of the larger Logic where the dialectic is so difficult and so seemingly minute that, even if I were sure I understood its transitions, I should hesitate to treat of them in a work which is intended to be of some assistance even on a first reading of Hegel. A comparison of Table I on the one hand with the Table of the *Encyclopaedia* categories given in Professor Stace's *Philosophy of Hegel*,[2] and on the other with

[1] Clarendon Press, 1940.

[2] Macmillan, 1923.

the Table which accompanies the English translation of the *Wissenschaft der Logik* by Messrs. Johnston and Struthers,[1] will show the middle course which I have taken. I have added some comment, but if one accepts Hegel's conception of truth[2]—and unless one did one would scarcely be interested to write about him—one cannot suppose that the effort either to attack or defend his argument in minute detail will bring much profit. For when Hegel's dialectic fails, it is not incorrect but arbitrary. Hence the tasks proper to a critic of Hegel's Logic are first to analyse the constituent materials from the history of philosophy which went to its making and to question his use of them, and secondly to ask what progress in the understanding of what thought is has been made in the years since Hegel. The latter task I have not much attempted, though in the chapters of this *Study* which do not directly expound the Logic I have offered certain tentative views of my own on the subject. To the former I have tried to contribute by amplifying Hegel's own comments on his predecessors, and, as I did in my *Introduction*, I have laid the main stress on Aristotle and Kant.

These chapters expounding Hegel's Logic were more or less finished when war broke out in 1939. I have since realized that in my *Introduction* I have, by confining myself too closely to sympathetic exposition of Hegel's system, given the impression that I accept its detail to a far greater extent than I do, and I perceived that my exposition of the Logic might well have the same effect. I therefore tried to think out and set down more precisely than I had ever before done my own reaction to Hegel's philosophy. The result appears first in Chapter I. There I have raised my doubts in the course of discussing Hegel's theory of language, a discussion which seemed in these days an appropriate approach to his Logic. In Chapters XIX–XXII I have tried to develop them into a definite line of criticism. I have not found the task easy, and I know that I have left it very far from complete. If the reader finds obscurity and repetition, one cause, I must admit, is that I was too often in two minds.

[1] George Allen and Unwin, 1929.

[2] Which I have discussed in the two last chapters of my *Introduction*.

For the purpose of expounding Hegel I have found helpful the summaries of doctrine contained in Kuno Fischer's *Hegel's Leben, Werke, und Lehre* and in Professor Stace's *Philosophy of Hegel*. I must confess that I have never seemed to find inspiration or safe guidance in any work of J. E. McTaggart on Hegel. Among works devoted to Hegel's Logic I have found Stirling's *Secret of Hegel* stimulating and Dr. Marcuse's *Hegel's Ontologie* (Frankfort, 1921) extremely instructive. To Wallace's excellent, though free, translations of the *Encyclopaedia* Logic and Philosophy of Spirit, and to his all too brief accompanying notes, I owe, in common with every English student of Hegel, a very great debt. But I have learnt far more from my author and far less from his commentators than has been my fortune in the study of any other thinker. This may seem a poor advertisement for a fresh work on Hegel, but I think my case is universal, and to try to conceal it would deceive no serious Hegelian student. I have allowed it to serve as an excuse for providing no bibliography. If one is required, the most complete I know is Benedetto Croce's,[1] although it is more than thirty years out of date.

In such views of my own as I have put forward the influence of the Oxford idealists will be easy enough to trace. My rough sketch of a philosophical method, or policy, may recall the conception of a scale of forms which R. G. Collingwood works out in his *Essay on Philosophical Method*,[2] and behind his metaphor of philosophic travel by the double method of compass and dead reckoning[3] lies essentially the same thought as I have tried to express in distinguishing the *a priori* and empirical sources of dialectic.[4] Yet I should always desire to stress the truth that forms, categories, principles, laws of thought—however we name them, and whatever precedence our titles are meant to convey—are no degrees upon a static scale; that they live only because they are, one and all, phases in the activity which thought is; and that for the same reason none of them can possess

[1] Appended, I think, to the first edition only of *What is Living and what is Dead in Hegel's Philosophy*. It appears in the French translation of that work.

[2] Clarendon Press, 1933.

[3] Ibid., p. 223.

[4] See Chapter XX, especially § 7·2.

eternal finality in the shape in which it works in human experience.[1]

The list of abbreviations on p. x is repeated from my *Introduction to Hegel*, and for my use of capital letters I must refer the reader to what I said in § ix of the Preface to that work. Besides the Table of Categories which I mentioned above, I have included for the reader's convenience a second Table to cover the main forms of Nature and Concrete Spirit given in Parts I and II of Hegel's *Encyclopaedia*.

My thanks are due to Professor H. J. Paton, Mr. W. H. Walsh, and Dr. J. L. Beck, who have all read portions of this *Study* in manuscript and given me the benefit of valuable comment. Dr. Beck has also been kind enough to read my proofs.

G. R. G. M.

OXFORD

12 December 1948

[1] Not that I mean to suggest that Collingwood was in the least blind to this truth.

CONTENTS

ABBREVIATIONS

JE: Jubilee reprint of the 1832–45 edition of Hegel's works, edited by Hermann Glockner; Stuttgart 1928–39.

Phän.: *Phänomenologie des Geistes.*

LL: 'Larger Logic': *Die Wissenschaft der Logik.*

Enc.: *Encyclopaedie der Philosophischen Wissenschaften*, ed. 3.

EL: Part I (*Logik*) of Encyclopaedia, ed. 3.

ΦN: Part II (*Naturphilosophie*) of Encyclopaedia, ed. 3.

ΦG: Part III (*Philosophie des Geistes*) of Encyclopaedia, ed. 3.

ΦR: *Philosophie des Rechts.*

ΦH: *Vorlesungen über die Philosophie der Geschichte.*

HΦ: *Vorlesungen über die Geschichte der Philosophie.*

KRV: Kant, *Kritik der Reinen Vernunft.* The first and second editions are referred to respectively as A and B, and the original paging is kept.

IH: The author's *Introduction to Hegel*, Clarendon Press, 1940.

All references to Hegel's works are to JE (which preserves the paging of the 1832–45 edition as well as its own) unless otherwise stated.

I

LANGUAGE AND HEGEL'S LOGIC

1. In *An Introduction to Hegel*[1] I sketched very broadly Hegel's conception of logic in relation to the rest of his system, and in the opening sections I wrote of how hard it is in any philosophical discussion to say what one means. The sense of this difficulty returns upon me with heavy weight as I face the task of expounding Hegel's logical categories in some detail.

1·1. Among contemporary philosophers of a certain way of thinking the use of verbal language, even the construction of new languages, for philosophical purposes, is a dominant topic; but the general nature of language is by most of them more commonly taken for granted than critically examined. This unsatisfactory reluctance to penetrate below the surface and make clear what language is before attempting to determine what can be done with it contains, as it seems to me, a warning that it may be well before tackling afresh the linguistic problem of expounding Hegel to seek help from his own theory of verbal language.

It seems to me, too, that a brief preliminary sketch of that theory, which is set out in ΦG, §§ 458–64, as a part of Hegel's treatment of Presentation (*Vorstellung*), might also at a later stage help us to criticize Hegel's general conception of dialectical movement.

2. Presentation is a phase, more precisely a triad of phases, in Hegel's dialectic of Subjective Spirit, which is itself the first main phase, the main thesis, of Concrete Spirit.[2]

In Hegel's view, Concrete Spirit[3] is a single self-reconstitutive activity. In every phase of its whole dialectic—in its emergence from Nature as Subjective Spirit, in its transition to and manifestation as Objective Spirit, and in its self-completion through the stages of Absolute Spirit—it is a concrete attitude of subject to object. In any one given phase

[1] Clarendon Press, 1940; see Preface to this *Study*, p. v.

[2] See Table II and IH, ch. viii, which is presupposed in this discussion. Cf. also Reyburn, *Hegel's Ethical Theory*, ch. v.

[3] See IH, ch. viii, §§ 3·1 ff.

of it the proximate lower phase as a totality has been sublated[1] to become the object or content of the subject, which has thereby come to exhibit a fresh attitude to an object which is also fresh, but fresh only in the sense that it is the subject's whole self of the previous phase developed by becoming object or content.[2]

2·1. Concrete Spirit, beginning in Subjective Spirit to distinguish itself from Nature, takes shape as a developing series of modes of experience; a series which exhibits the difference of cognitive and practical attitudes but also their unity, the unity out of which they differentiate themselves, and the unity into which they synthesize only again to diverge and again to synthesize. As modes of experience—states of mere feeling, forms of consciousness, mental functions, and so forth—these earlier phases of Concrete Spirit belong to Subjective Spirit. The phases of Objective Spirit display spirit in the more concrete shape of moral and social institutions,[3] and take their names largely from these; but the modes of Subjective Spirit cannot be named in terms of the object or content, for that at their level is still too natural, too incompletely spiritualized, to provide distinctive characterization for forms of spirit. We can designate them as modes *only*; as modes, that is, which, although they vary with their contents or objects, yet do so only formally, because they are not fully and completely the forms *of* their contents. We cannot name them except in terms of the subject.[4] On the other hand, they are not subjective in any sense of the word which would abstract them from all content and any object. Spirit in Subjective Spirit distinguishes itself from Nature, but it does so only inasmuch as it emerges

[1] *Aufgehoben*; see IH, ch. xi, § 5·01.

[2] I say 'object or content' because what the subject is aware of may at different stages be a mere felt content, a definite and 'detached' object, or a content in which the subject finds full self-expression. The 'or' thus indicates a difference of emphasis and not mutual exclusion; it is *vel* and not *aut*.

[3] Cf. ibid., §§ 6 and 6·1.

[4] When Subjective Spirit reaches the stage of Theoretical Mind the subject comes gradually to attain that view of its object as Nature which it elaborates in natural science. But that is a view of Nature as a 'detached', essentially non-spiritual object (see ibid., § 5·1), not an object which could legitimately provide a name for the phase of spirit to which it belongs.

from Nature by gradually reconstituting itself out of Nature.[1] Every phase of Concrete Spirit, Subjective and Objective alike, is a total concrete attitude of subject to object, a mode of experience which, using the term in a broad sense, is always self-consciousness.[2]

2·2. The main dialectical triad of Subjective Spirit is Soul, Consciousness, Mind.[3] The main triad of Mind is Theoretical Mind, Practical Mind, Free Mind; and it is in the course of the development of Theoretical Mind—Mind, that is, as cognitive and not yet volitional[4]—that verbal language emerges.

2·3. Soul (*Seele*) is more than natural life. A living organism has its objective existence as something self-external; it is what it is not for itself but for us;[5] it is only implicitly subject. But Soul is not self-external nor objectively existent merely for us. It therefore belongs to Subjective Spirit, although only in Consciousness will the distinction of subject and object begin to emerge. Soul is the immediate *prius* of that distinction, the dim, quite unindividualized basis or material of feeling from which Consciousness is aware of having risen and constituted itself. Because it is the first phase of Concrete Spirit, it is a mere subjective mode, and its content is still natural. It is a first faint spiritualizing of the features of the living organism and of the influences of race and natural environment. These are transformed in it to obscure feelings which, when we reflect upon them from a self-conscious level, we generalize and call the instincts and innate characters, the moods and temperaments, of individuals; but Soul considered abstractly as the first subjective mode of spirit is a bare universality neither yet manifested in individuals nor itself a single subject. Hegel suggests that it is the passive *νοῦς* of Aristotle, which is potentially all things.[6]

[1] It is perhaps unnecessary to remark that the development is primarily logical and not historical; cf. ibid., § 7.

[2] Cf. ibid., ch. viii, § 3·1.

[3] *Geist*. I have arbitrarily translated this overworked word by 'Mind' instead of 'Spirit' in order to mark the restricted, subjective sense in which it is used here.

[4] Although in Soul and Consciousness spirit has already passed through implicitly volitional phases which as Theoretical Mind it contains sublated.

[5] Cf. IH, p. 69.

[6] Not, be it observed, Aristotle's *ψυχή*. It seems also to be much what F. H. Bradley means by 'feeling'.

Hegel's conception of Consciousness, which does not differ greatly from Kant's save in that Hegel stresses far more strongly than Kant its inner process of development, will become tolerably clear if we look back to it from the level of Theoretical Mind.

2·4. Theoretical Mind subdivides into Intuition (*Anschauung*), Presentation (*Vorstellung*), and Thinking (*Denken*), and we must here begin to follow the movement more closely, remembering always that in every phase the subject has for its object its own lower self, the proximate preceding phase of itself, whereof in its present phase it is the development and the higher truth.

3. Hegel's Intuition, which is a reconstruction of Kant's sense-intuition, is immediate and still based and bodied in sense; but because it belongs to Mind it is the beginning of intellection. It contains surpassed within itself the phases of Soul and Consciousness. It is not the mere sensuous feeling of Soul in which the distinction of subject and object is only implicit, and it is also more than Consciousness in which that distinction becomes fully explicit. The object of Consciousness becomes in the transition from the immediate certainty of Sensuous Consciousness to Sense-Perception a given, 'external' world which the subject finds confronting it, a rudimentary and perpetually altering world of endlessly multiple sensuous *qualia*[1] developed out of the feelings and sensations of Soul; but it is only when these *qualia* have shown themselves as things with sensuous qualities, and when contradiction has broken out between the thing and the quality, the rudimentary universal,[2] that the subject overcomes the mutual independence of subject and object which distinctively characterizes Consciousness. The contradiction is solved (at this level) when the subject takes the universal moment, the qualities or properties of the *percepta*, as what its perceived object-world essentially is; when, that is, it finds its object to be after all not merely given and external

[1] Cf. IH, ch. xi, § 4. The object of Sensuous Consciousness is a mere somewhat (*Etwas*), for which see ch. ii, § 4·2, below.

[2] Between 'this' and 'such' (cf. IH, ch. v, § 2·3) or, as Bradley analyses it, between the 'that' and the 'what' which slides beyond it (cf. ibid., ch. xiii, § 4·61).

but the rational content of its own intellection. It is only at this point, at the first dawning of intellect and the universal in sense, that Consciousness passes into Theoretical Mind, of which Intuition is the first phase.[1]

3·1. Intuition is immediate, but it unites two moments: (*a*) a selective attention of the subject whereby it fixes the object as its own proper object and no longer an independent external, and (*b*) an object fixed as a 'this here and now' in a context of space and time, which are the essential forms of Intuition. 'When intellect (*Intelligenz*) reaches a concrete unity of the two moments, when, that is to say, it is at once self-collected (*sich erinnert*) in this externally existing material and yet in its self-collectedness sunk in the self-externality, it is Intuition.'[2]

3·2. This account of Intuition becomes clearer if we again compare it with Consciousness. The term 'sense-perception' tends in current usage to imply a more developed mode of experience than does Hegel's *Wahrnehmung*. The object-world of Hegel's Sense-Perception is an endlessly altering world of sensuous *qualia*, but it is not yet spatio-temporal; the *qualia* have no places, and the 'altering' of what, following Hegel, I have proleptically named 'things with qualities or properties' is not for the conscious subject a process in time but a mere oscillation of *qualia* too indeterminate to preserve their characters against one another. Accordingly, the object-world of Sense-Perception is not strictly a world. It has still something of the self-externality of Nature.[3] It possesses no periphery and no centre to constitute a focus for the subject. The subject in Sense-Perception is correspondingly

[1] I have greatly abbreviated the dialectic, describing it in purely cognitive terms. In fact Consciousness does not pass into Theoretical Mind until the self-consciousness which begins as bare, abstract universality when the subject finds its universal in its perceived world has developed through rudimentary phases of appetite and the recognition of other selves. Only through self-assertion in appetite and the logically subsequent recognition of a plurality of other selves does the subject begin to become aware of itself as truly and not abstractly universal, as a universal principle manifested without loss of singleness in different individual selves. This rudimentary self-consciousness, though it emerges in a practical phase of Concrete Spirit, contributes, sublated, to every further phase and therefore to Intuition.

[2] ΦG, § 449. See also § 5·2 below.

[3] Cf. IH, ch. viii, § 4·21.

dispersed; it is not self-possessing, not able to fix and make its own any definite element in its object. But in Intuition, which although immediate in contrast to Presentation is itself a dialectical movement, the subject first finds the 'detached' object of Consciousness to be after all not 'detached', and feels it[1] as its own stuff and content. Then by selective attention within this content, which was the scarcely determinate field of Consciousness, the subject at once collects and concentrates itself and thereby constitutes its object a 'this here and now'. Whereas in Consciousness the subject passively endured modification as its object varied, in Intuition the subject begins in active attention to constitute its object in detail as its own object. It begins, that is, to idealize its object; for Intuition is the first stage of Theoretical Mind, and the last stage of Theoretical Mind is Thinking.

Thus in Intuition, if I have followed Hegel, the subject becomes aware of itself as an individual among other individuals[2] apprehending as its own stuff and content a 'this here and now'.

3·3. The kinship between the Hegelian and Kantian doctrines of intuition is obvious, but the deep difference, too, is worth noting.[3] For Hegel as for Kant the content of intuition is in some sense the individual 'this here and now', and spatio-temporal intuition is the matter for the form of thinking. But Kant's forms of intuition inform a sense-manifold passively received from the thing-in-itself, whereas Hegel's Intuition has a matter immanent in it, a lower self which its activity consists in transcending and intellectualizing. It is true that in order to justify *a priori* synthesis in mathematics Kant offers his forms of intuition as at once and in one pure forms and pure spatio-temporal contents (manifolds), but how for purposes of empirical experience this pure spatio-temporal form-and-matter should inform a sense-manifold which is passively received from the thing-in-itself and presents, so to say, no credentials, remains a sheer mystery. The content of Hegel's Intuition, on the other

[1] This 'feeling' is to be construed in the general sense of immediacy; it is not the feeling of Soul or the immediacy of Sensuous Consciousness; see ΦG, § 446, and IH, ch. viii, § 4·21.

[2] Cf. footnote 1, p. 5 above.

[3] Compare what follows with IH, ch. ix, §§ 5·13 and 5·2.

hand, traces a legitimate descent back to Nature through the continuous self-development of Concrete Spirit.

Between passive and active, particular and universal, sense and thought there may be chasms which philosophy can never finally cross, but the demand that they be bridged is of the very essence of philosophical thinking, and Hegel—though of course with Kant's help—came far nearer to fulfilling it than Kant. His dialectical treatment of spirit may restate the question, but so does any fresh solution of a philosophical problem which does not manipulate it into nonsense.[1]

4. Before we pass from Intuition to Presentation it is worth while to prepare the way by considering an aspect of the dialectic of Subjective Spirit which is apt to escape the reader's notice and perhaps sometimes escaped Hegel's, too. Every phase of Subjective Spirit is, as we have seen, the proximate truth of its immediately preceding phase, of its own lower self which it sublates. Spirit, that is, is in each successive phase more real, more truly possessed of the nature which it claims for itself or, in phases which are not explicitly self-conscious, for its object.[2] It follows that in any given phase the immediately preceding phase is incompletely sublated: it persists, subserving its successor but not fully absorbed by it. Indeed, since every phase is thus defective, in any phase all the preceding phases must be present imperfectly sublated.[3]

4·1. This is paradoxical. We seem compelled to say either that spirit is at once in more than one phase, or that any one phase is in fact not one but more than one. Yet this paradox, a reminder that the dialectic of Concrete Spirit is primarily logical and not temporal, is common experience. Every man is familiar with the contradiction of apparently experiencing in at least two modes at once. The paradox is perhaps most evident in practical experience, with which we are not here concerned; but when we perceive with our senses and also

[1] Hegel's debt to the *De Anima* of Aristotle, whom Kant had not much studied, is also conspicuous throughout his treatment of Subjective Spirit; cf. IH, ch. v, and Preface, § iv, para. 3.

[2] Cf. ibid., ch. i, § 2·01 and xiv, §§ 1–4.

[3] This applies ultimately to the whole dialectic of Concrete Spirit, and *mutatis mutandis* to Nature and even to the logical categories, the realm of pure thought, as well.

think, we do not simply perform two successive and separate acts; rather the sense-perception and the thought are two phases of a unitary act, for it is the perceived object, and therewith our consciousness, that in thinking we reconstitute. Yet the unity of the act is imperfect, for it is inherent in our thinking, when we think upon a perceived object, that we do not succeed in fully reconstituting that object and therewith our own consciousness. We fail to pass completely from the one mode of experience to the other, and we still depend upon that which we strive to supersede.[1] Sense, which thought should surpass, remains as an expletive to thought.

4·2. The fact that experience is a self-transcending activity, any stage of which is incomplete not merely because there is more to come but because a previous stage adheres to it, so to say, imperfectly digested, may prove a key to many problems if it is understood; but misunderstood it is the very source and fount of error. To confuse one level with another is fatally easy if one never is unambiguously at one level of experience. Hegel often charges Kant with this mistake:

'The Kantian philosophy may be most accurately described as having viewed spirit as Consciousness, and as containing the features of a phenomenology, not a philosophy, of spirit. The subject (*das Ich*) Kant regards as reference to something away and beyond, which in its abstract description is termed the thing-in-itself; and it is only from this finite point of view that he treats both intellect and will.'[2]

Hegel's point, as I understand it, is that Kant, deceived by the fact that consciousness is a phase never wholly overpassed in experience, regards the differentia of consciousness, viz. the subject's attitude of detachment from an alien object, as still persisting to characterize what are in fact more developed phases of spirit which possess their own differentiae.

5. Presentation is the phase of antithesis intermediate between Intuition and Thinking. In Thinking the universal will be explicit, though still in a measure abstract and subjective. On the one hand, the universal will be at once the subject's own content, the content of the subject's active thinking, and at the same time the essential nature of the object. Yet, on the other hand, the subject's appropriation of its object will still be incomplete, and the subject's essen-

[1] Cf. IH, ch. viii, § 3·3 and ch. v, § 2.

[2] ΦG, § 415.

tial nature will not exhaust but at once complement and contradict its apparent nature. In other words, the development of Theoretical Mind through Intuition and Presentation will have vitally modified, but not completely overcome, that 'givenness' which made the object of Consciousness alien and 'detached'. We have now to trace this modification.

5·1. The dialectical transition from Intuition to Presentation takes place, if I do not misunderstand Hegel, as follows. Intuition is the subject's rational certainty that its object is its own self, but that certainty is still a claim to be made good. The universal is at present quite rudimentary; it is only implicitly or potentially the Notion, the universal developed through particularization to true individuality.[1] The object of Intuition is an individual 'this here and now' one with the intuiting subject, and 'this here and now' necessarily implies a spatio-temporal context. But this context is a mere felt background[2] out of which the attending subject selects a mere fugitive 'this here and now' and appropriates it as explicitly its own. By virtue of this selective and appropriative act the 'this here and now' ceases to be *in pari materia* with the background context upon which it is still, nevertheless, based and partially dependent. Intuition now therefore must develop itself as more completely a subject one with its own content. It must more fully sublate its lower self, the prior phase of 'feeling' out of which it emerged by selective attention. Intuition, that is to say, becomes Presentation, though in Presentation Intuition will itself still persist not wholly sublated.

5·2. Presentation has three main phases: Recollection (*Erinnerung*), literally 'internalizing', which, in the sense of the subject's appropriating the recollected content, Hegel takes to be the true significance of recollection; Reproductive Imagination (*Einbildungskraft*); Verbal Memory (*Gedächtnis*).

In Recollection the content of Intuition is internalized as an image (*Bild*)[3] of the thing recollected. The content is thus

[1] For Hegel's conception of the universal see esp. chs. xi and xii below.

[2] Cf. footnote 1 on p. 6 above.

[3] 'Image' or *Bild* should not suggest that Presentation any more than Intuition is visual to the exclusion of the other senses, though Hegel, like most other psychologists except Croce, often talks as if it were.

freed from its immediacy, and the subject bestows on it its own space and time. When one recollects something, that is to say, the space and time in which it is then presented is peculiar to the recollection; the thing is not contained in the space and time of the original intuition. Moreover, some of the features of the original intuition are lost, and the image is so far arbitrary and contingent. On the other hand, the image is still more or less fugitive. It tends to do what may equally well be described as (*a*) becoming generalized, implicitly universal, or (*b*) lapsing into an unconscious or subconscious, merely potential state, in which it is owned but not fully possessed by the subject. In fact, Recollection proper may equally well be described as (*a*) the occurrence of a fresh intuition which is subsumed under, recognized as an instance of, the generalized image, or (*b*) the re-emergence, re-actualization, of the generalized image as a fresh intuition. In that potential, subconscious state the image does not of course exist like a picture forgotten in a cellar: it has become an element in that implicit universality which must form a context of possible experience to the focus of the subject's actual experience.[1]

So Recollection in its full sense is the synthesis of the generalized image and the fresh intuition. The image, in Recollection developed and internalized by the subject, becomes distinct both from the blank night of its potential state and from the actual intuition: it becomes more definitely universal. It has its existence in the intellect to, or for, which it is presented. But that brings us to the second main phase of Presentation.

5·3. The subject, now actively appropriating its presented

[1] Hegel attributes the erroneous view that ideas or presentations (*Vorstellungen*) are preserved localized in particular areas of the cerebral cortex because they are particulars, to the inability to grasp that the *Vorstellung* is an implicit universal (ΦG, § 453). To localize corporeally the universal, which belongs to the mind, and not even simply to this or that mind, is obviously absurd. On the other hand, local affections of the cortex in some sense correlated with mental function appear to be an indisputable fact. These affections are clearly not any sort of ideas, but to admit such a correlate at the physical level is no more inconsistent with Hegel's conception of the relation of mind and body than to admit that we see with our eyes or flush when we are angry.

content, is Reproductive Imagination, and as imagination develops the subject produces images from its potentiality which have less and less reference to actual intuition. The individuality of the image is now constituted by the subject; its original individuality, that of the singular 'this here and now', is dissolved.

This reproductive imagining develops by freely combining its presentations and becomes creative imagination, as in symbolism, allegory, or poetry. In creative imagining the mind, though its original material is intuition, needs no help from fresh intuitions. To the extent that its presentations are produced out of itself, it may be called self-intuiting. It actually reclothes with imagery the universal content, and its effort is now towards expressing or 'uttering' itself, giving itself being as the objectively real.[1] Nevertheless, its presentation, even if it be in a measure self-presentation, is not yet fully real; it is still the presentation *of* an object. The subject's possession of it, or unification with it, is incomplete—Hegel calls it merely formal—for spirit in its theoretical activity seeks *truth* in its object, and the image does not present a *knowable* object.

5·4. The subject has so far appropriated, internalized, universalized—they are the same thing—its presented image that this image becomes for the subject first a symbol (*Symbol*) and then a sign (*Zeichen*) of a content. In a symbol the sensuous features of the presentation as it is intuited are more or less identical in essence with the content symbolized, whereas a sign has no natural connexion with its meaning.[2]

The intuited symbol or sign is thus relatively external to the internalized or universalized meaning, but these two are simply two moments of the *Vorstellung*, two phases of spirit, the one imperfectly sublated in the other. Sign and symbol differ only because in the sign the sublation is more complete. Hegel's teaching thus contrasts sharply with any

[1] 'Sich selbst zum Sein, zur Sache zu machen.' ΦG, § 457.

[2] Cf. Bradley, *Principles of Logic*, ch. i, § 5. Bradley's 'idea' is precisely Hegel's *Vorstellung*, and these sections of ΦG throw much light on the early chapters of Bradley's Logic. I have tried to compare his position with Hegel's in IH, ch. xiii, §§ 4 ff.

empiricist and realist doctrine of ideas such as Locke's, and the contrast is enlightening. Hegel's *Vorstellung* is already universalized. The universal is still abstract, because the sensuous phases of spirit are imperfectly sublated in it, still adhere imperfectly digested; but the universal is genuinely developing out of its lower sensuous self. On the other hand, the representative idea, which is assumed to be impressed on, or in some other way produced in, a blank mind by a presupposed real entity, could obviously never develop significance and universality.

5·41. The Kantian doctrine of intuition and imagination abandons the realist assumption of Locke and furnishes the mind with its own forms for its experiencing, but by making the unknown thing-in-itself the source of that manifold which the human mind informs, Kant precluded the possibility of any development through sense to thought and, in Hegel's view, achieved a purely subjective idealism. This is not to deny that Hegel owed a great debt to Kant's view that there is an *a priori* factor in imagination and in particular to Kant's triple synthesis of imagination, viz. apprehension, reproduction, recognition.[1]

5·5. This sign-creating activity of the mind, says Hegel, may be called 'productive memory' (*Gedächtnis*),[2] and he thus makes it clear that he takes the essence of *Erinnerung* and *Gedächtnis* to be not so much the recalling of the past and its retention (the ordinary meanings respectively of these two words in German and of 'recollection' and 'memory' in English) as the persistence and development of the intuited content upon which such reproductive recall and retention depend.[3] But we cannot pass immediately to the synthesis of *Erinnerung* and *Einbildungskraft* in *Gedächtnis*, for at this point in the dialectic originates verbal language.

5·6. An intuition used as a sign exists only as sublated, and more truly as a temporal than as a spatial existent sublated: it is more truly a 'this now' than a 'this here'. For time is the

[1] See KRV, A, pp. 98–104.

[2] ΦG, § 458.

[3] Hegel connects *Gedächtnis* with *Denken* and in *Enc.* ed. 2, ΦG, § 458, closes with a sentence noting the difference in his own use of *Gedächtnis* from the customary meaning of the word; see Lasson's ed.

negative, vanishing moment of the spatio-temporal,[1] and therefore, Hegel concludes, the sign *par excellence* is the vocal sound.

Thus the vocal sound is in the first instance an individual intuition which the subject produces from its potentiality. As such it is, like any other 'this now', relatively external to, only formally possessed by, the subject. But in so far as the vocal sound is a word with a meaning, that external moment is present only as sublated.[2] The subject, articulating vocal sound as spoken language, makes its presentation linguistic. That, if I follow Hegel,[3] is to say that its presentation becomes now not merely (*a*) the meaning, the significant universal content, to which the sign as original relatively external existent adheres not perfectly 'digested', but also and further (*b*) the meaning expressed *as* speech. The word is (*a*) an audible noise internalized as a sign with a universal meaning which has no natural connexion with it, but it is also (*b*) the outward utterance of the meaning, the self-expression in which the mind, so far as is possible at this stage of its development, gives itself being as the objectively real.[4]

6. The complete fusion of the word, the internalized sound, with the image-universal is the synthesis of Recollection and Reproductive Imagination, namely, Verbal Memory. When memory (in Hegel's sense of the term) is fully developed, we think (though the word 'think' is still proleptic) in words without any intervening image. The word is fused in one *Vorstellung* with its significance. The externality (the sound) has vanished, and the single presentation is abiding and universal. It is a presentation still, but it is almost thought proper. 'Given the name "lion"', says Hegel, 'we need neither the actual vision of the animal, nor even its image: the name alone, if we understand it, is the unimaged simple presentation. We think in names.'[5]

[1] Cf. ΦN, §§ 257 ff.

[2] Though never quite completely sublated; cf. §§ 4 and 4·1 above.

[3] See ΦG, § 459.

[4] Cf. § 5·3 above. The reality which the mind thus gives to itself is reality in what Bosanquet calls 'the objective world or world of meanings'; see Bosanquet, *Logic*, ed. 2, Introduction, pp. 4 ff. Bosanquet's whole discussion of meaning and naming in these pages is closely based on Hegel.

[5] ΦG, § 462.

We still, however, do not in the full sense think, because there is still for the subject a difference between the meaning and the reality meant. When we think in names it is an act of reference, not an activity of full self-identification with the object. The mind still has an object or content which is subjective with the subjectivity that infects all phases of Subjective Spirit. The objective reality which it has given itself in verbal self-expression is not complete reality. The mind is not yet fully what it claims to be.

The nearest approach of Mind in Presentation to objective reality is Verbal Memory, which is for that reason, when perfect, mechanical. 'A composition is not thoroughly memorized until one attaches no *meaning* to the words', says Hegel.[1] His point is that we here reach not something meaningless but something more than meaning, a phase no longer involving reference away to an object: the last remnant of the subserving sensuous phase is vanishing as we pass from Presentation to Thinking.[2]

7. Thinking and its dialectical subdivisions (Understanding, Judgement, Syllogism) are outside our immediate interest. Suffice it to note that Thinking as a phase of Theoretical Mind is the thought of the Understanding and not philosophical thinking. It is still a phase of Subjective Spirit, and it is prior to Practical Mind and to what Hegel calls Free Mind.[3] Its object is its own universal content, but it determines the features of that content only implicitly. Mind even as Thinking has still to develop in phases which are formal modes.[4]

With this development we are not directly concerned. There are, however, certain further features of Hegel's theory of language which it may be worth while to touch upon before we try to apply it to the problem of expounding his logic.

7·1. Benedetto Croce, whom no idealist discussion of language can ignore, extends the meaning of the term to cover

[1] ΦG, § 462.

[2] Mechanical recitation is not a phase of the dialectic; it merely illustrates what Hegel is trying to stress, viz. the sublation of the phase of reference and of the word as the means of reference as we approach Thinking. Mechanical memory is an analogue of Habit, a phase of Soul and an indispensable *prius* to all further activity of spirit; cf. ΦG, §§ 409–10.

[3] See Table II.

[4] Cf. § 2·1 above.

far more than speech. To Croce language is intuition-expression, the aesthetic first moment of theoretical activity. It is prior to thought, innocent of any distinction between reality and appearance, fact and fancy, and yet autonomous. It is in fact identical with aesthetic experience.[1]

With this wide conception of language Hegel's theory has features in common. Like Croce, Hegel treats language as logically prior to thinking, and the Hegelian categories of Being, although they are *Denkbestimmungen*, determinations of thought, operate *par excellence* in sensuous experience. They are immediate, presenting no such distinctions of real and apparent, inner and outer, &c., as emerge in the categories of Essence.[2]

Yet Hegel's conception is narrower than Croce's. He conceives language only as verbal language, and only as that which makes thinking possible. 'Language', he says, 'is the work of thought; hence nothing can be spoken in language which is not universal.'[3] In ΦG the creative imagination of the poet is only mentioned in passing; it appears as something of a loose end. No phase of Subjective Spirit is specifically aesthetic. Hegel's view of language as self-expression might perhaps have been developed to reach much farther back through the earlier phases of Subjective Spirit, and by such a Crocean modification his not particularly satisfactory theory of art might have benefited. It is, moreover, true that, since language to Hegel is sensuous and the sensuous is immediate, one may easily over-emphasize Hegel's insistence that what is spoken is universal; as perhaps does Croce himself.[4] For no philosopher has yet succeeded in stating unambiguously the precise relation of sense to thought, and if we remember that to Croce aesthetic intuition, though it is not thought, is theoretical, the Crocean intuition may seem after all to be not so very far from the kind of awareness which Hegel's categories of Being are intended to define. Nevertheless, the main difference remains: Hegel did not identify this immediacy of Being with aesthetic experience, and his theory

[1] For a brief general discussion of Croce see below, ch. xxi, §§ 6·1–6·8.

[2] See following chapter, especially §§ 1·2 and 1·3. [3] EL, Introd., § 20.

[4] See *What is Living and What is Dead in Hegel's Philosophy*, Eng. trans., pp. 124 ff.

of language is not Croce's identification of linguistic with aesthetic.

7·2. It has, on the other hand, nothing in common with mathematically influenced views of language as the expression of thought. Hegel, it is true, maintains that as language becomes a more efficient aid to thought so it loses its sensuous features, discards the superabundant wealth of its more purely symbolic stage. As it develops grammar simplifies, and a mass of trivial distinctions which originate in direct symbolism vanish as the symbol becomes a sign.[1] Accordingly in script, which is a borrowing by speech of spatial intuition for practical purposes of communication, the hieroglyph, like the onomatopoeic word, is primitive, and alphabetic language marks the advance of civilization. Leibniz, Hegel holds, in advocating a universal hieroglyphically written language to promote international intercourse, was quite unpractical, because the progress of thought continually changes the nature and the relations of the objects of thought. Constant renaming would be necessary, and the universal language would be perpetually obsolescent. Although sensible objects do on the whole admit of permanent symbols, yet the nomenclature even of these does change, as, for example, in chemistry and mineralogy. Thus progress in language, which is progress towards thinking, is progress from symbol to sign and from hieroglyphic to alphabetic script. But this obvious truth is no foundation for semantics. The goal of this progress from symbol to sign is not a set of fixed languages, traditional terminologies found ready-made or languages created *ad hoc*, which may be selected as alternative vehicles to express a problem, and then by some strange miracle to solve it, or better still to show that it was an illusion which sprang from defective language. On Hegel's view language logically precedes thought, although it survives and subserves thought as its expression. It belongs to the final stage of Presentation, to Presentation as that develops into Thinking. If you try to separate a problem from the alternative languages in which it might be expressed, conceiving it as a naked body which you may clothe with alternative garments, you invite the question, What is

[1] See ΦG, § 459, from which most of this section is drawn.

the problem before you select the language? And there is no answer, because there are no naked problems.[1]

7·21. You may, indeed you must, examine what other men have said to help you solve a philosophical problem; and you will with luck discover how certain persons formulated and answered a question at least sufficiently akin to your own question to make your examination worth while. The persons concerned may be your English contemporaries, or they may be men long dead who spoke another tongue. They may be philosophers, or they may be ordinary people educated in varying degrees. In every case you will with varying success be reaching their thought through its linguistic expression. But language logically precedes thought as well as expresses it. You will find that by that fact their language is shaped in its peculiar meaning, which you will not succeed in penetrating and possessing unless you can penetrate and possess their prior stage of coming to think-and-express their peculiar question and answer. If you prefer to construct your own language or metalanguage, you will not be weaving a fabric undetermined by the problem which you are already struggling to formulate and solve; you will not be fashioning a brand-new instrument of criticism. If you do succeed in stating a problem and its solution better than it was stated by Plato, then you will have thought better than Plato, and in natural consequence your language will be an improvement on his. But you will not have bettered Plato's thought by any independent syntactical simplifications.

7·3. The general view which I have criticized tends to suggest that the final stage of language as the expression of thought would be a set or sets of quasi- or even actually mathematical symbols. But that again receives no support from Hegel. In his view the symbol becomes the sign, and sensuous diversity disappears; but the sign is not arbitrary in the sense of originating fortuitously and possessing no

[1] Wittgenstein (*Tractatus*, § 4·011) is completely victimized by this metaphor: 'Language disguises the thought; so that from the external form of the clothes one cannot infer the form of the thought they clothe, because the external form of the clothes is constructed with quite another object than to let the form of the body be recognized.' Not quite.

innate significance.[1] It is conventional, but that is to say it expresses agreement. For the fundamental requirement of language is the name. A name is simple, but it has for its significance a concrete unity of diverse characterization.[2] It is not barely simple like the significance of the symbol, the onomatopoeic word, or the hieroglyph. The significance of the symbol is the abstract product which arises from analysis of a sensuous object, and it will require to be constantly changed because such analysis is largely contingent. But the meaning of the name is simple *qua* a unity of the diverse, *qua* a concrete universal. It grows as thought grows, so that every time a name is uttered or written it is different, although the sound or the visual sign is the same. Verbal language is the system of interconnecting names and a phase in the development of spirit.[3] But a mathematical symbol does not grow. It signifies a fixed abstract type. It can express only the most formal characteristics of a thought-content, and upon that fact its fixity rests. Such symbols adequately express mathematical thinking, and because mathematics *is* manipulation, their manipulation can help to solve mathematical problems. In formal logic the construction and manipulation of symbols may help to determine the formal characteristics of thought,[4] and so ultimately produce results remotely bearing on the nature of live, concrete thinking. But quasi-mathematical symbols cannot be so manipulated as directly to solve philosophical problems, because they are neither the medium through which philosophical

[1] Hegel is not directly concerned with the historical origin of language. He regards it, on the physiological level, as developing in terms of the various postures (*Gebärden*) of the speech organs.

[2] Cf. Bosanquet, *Logic*, ed. 2, Introduction, p. 12: 'A name then is a sign which rouses the mind to a set of activities having an identical element'; and p. 13: 'That which the name signifies *is*, for us at all events, an identical character exhibited by different contexts, or different contexts united by a common character.'

[3] 'Name' is a grammatical term and as such itself a product of abstractive analysis. What Hegel says of names is not intended to exclude the subsidiary linguistic elements, the other 'parts of speech', which explicate names. The linguistic whole is the sentence. Cf. Bosanquet, loc. cit., pp. 18–21.

[4] To determine, that is, the form of thought at its lowest, most abstract level.

thought struggles to become articulate nor the adequate vehicle of its expression in so far as it succeeds.[1]

7·31. The reasoning which underlies this error is clear. Language always retains an unanalysed residue of presentation, and the effort to purge it of emotion and imagery in order that it may adequately express thought is sound enough in so far as by 'thought' is intended thought in antithesis to sense, the abstract thought of the Understanding. You may trace this purging and thinning of the technical language used as you pass from biology through chemistry and physics to the symbols of mathematics, and you may trace it again in the historical progress of each special science as its subject-matter becomes more sharply abstracted from the confused fullness of everyday experience. But this purgation of language is in either case at once an aspect and a consequence of the gradual definition and appropriate expression of the more and more abstract thinking of a more and more abstract subject-matter. To suppose that it can lead towards an ideally adequate philosophical language such as the proposed *Characteristica Universalis* of Leibniz is literally preposterous. For philosophical thought is not mere antithesis of sense but, as logic, the synthesis of the thought which sustains sense-experience with the thought of the understanding, and, as philosophy of Nature and spirit, the development of this logic in concrete manifestation. We shall see, if we have not already seen, that human experience cannot fully realize this ideal, and that the language of philosophy is therefore never adequate. But the shortcomings of philosophy scarcely justify a complete reversal of direction.

[1] Cf. ch. xi, § 2·11, below. The mathematical symbol, Hegel remarks in ΦG, § 459, is in fact a hieroglyph, really a symbol and not a sign. He presumably held that it is a hieroglyph because mathematics is concerned with the sensible world, but that it has adequate fixity because mathematics deals with the sensible world in such abstract and formal characters that any instance of a mathematical entity is as good as any other. The modern view that mathematics is directly concerned not with the sensible world, nor even with quantity or number, but with order, no doubt entails important consequences for the logic of mathematics, but it does not imply the identity of all logic with mathematics. If mathematics is not immediately concerned with the sensible world, quantity, and number, it yet is more directly applicable to them than to the more concrete realities of experience.

7·32. Such an error is analogous to supposing that Esperanto, or any other simplified 'universal' language selected from living tongues to facilitate intercourse in a specialized commercial or tourist world where all the inhabitants have purposes of intercourse which are common without significant diversity, can become the one adequate and genuinely universal language of mankind. When logic is conceived as essentially symbolic the destruction of philosophy and the denial of reason are already in sight. It is not surprising that the most commonly vaunted achievement of those who manipulate logistical symbols is the reduction of other men's philosophical problems to nonsense. In effect their reduction demonstrates not the nonsensical nature of the problem but the inadequacy of the symbolic machine, make it and remake it as they will, for the task of criticism. It demonstrates that the manipulators have forgotten that verbal signs grow, and that the meanings of words which sound, or on paper look, barely identical depend upon contexts far too indefinitely variable to permit any hope of producing by logical analysis a universal symbolic language which will infallibly express and solve (or dissolve) philosophic problems.[1]

8. The problem of expounding the Hegelian categories is, of course, in the first instance Hegel's own problem and only secondarily his commentator's. At first sight he may seem to solve it over-easily. Early in LL he remarks that because dialectic is one with its content,

'the divisions and headings of the Books, Sections, and Chapters which are given in this work, and also to some extent the explanations which are attached to them, are made for the purpose of a preliminary survey. They have, properly speaking, a merely historical value. They do not belong to the content and body of the science. They are the compilations of external reflection, which has already run through the whole exposition, and hence foreknows and indicates the sequence of its moments as they introduce themselves in and through the subject itself.'[2]

Hegel is here contending that his Logic exhibits thought as a single self-developing and, therefore, self-explanatory activity

[1] It is refreshing to note a partial recognition of this fallacy in Mr. Stuart Hampshire's article, 'Logical Form', *Proceedings of the Aristotelian Society*, 1947–8, v.

[2] LL, i, p. 52.

which is revealed not to external reflection but only to the thinker who becomes identified with it because it becomes fully immanent in him. There is no suggestion that the linguistic expression of this thinking presents any special difficulty.

8·01. Sometimes, it is true, Hegel does talk as if to philosophize were to observe passively from without the self-development of the object.[1] But by the use of such expressions he only means that we cannot bring to philosophy any presupposed principles, any hard and fast assumptions or criteria themselves to be held immune from criticism in the actual course of our philosophical thinking.[2] The dialectic, in Hegel's view, is no more a movement displaying itself to a passive beholder than it is a technique externally applied to a subject-matter. If it be objected that Hegel himself merely assumes that reality is the one activity of spirit, his retort is that his argument 'assumes' this not as a fact ascertained or intuited by minds of which it is independent, but as what is indubitably given in, or rather as, the self-consciousness which must precede logically any dubitable detail of experience. This 'assumption' is the self-certainty without which even scepticism is impossible: the denial of it annihilates the denier. It is the truth both of the Cartesian *cogito ergo sum* and of Kant's 'original' unity of apperception. Moreover, just because it is activity which is 'assumed', all that, in the language of the Understanding, 'follows from it' through the course of the Logic is the self-development of the 'assumption'. In short, to Hegel any thinking seems to presuppose that thought is both 'originally' autonomous and also self-developing. Thought cannot, in order to furnish itself with a premiss, appeal to any 'fact' outside itself, and it can reach no conclusion which is not a manifestation of its own nature. But Hegel does not explicitly tell us how philosophical thinking manifests itself in words.

8·1. From the doctrine of language in ΦG we have already deduced a paradox if not a dilemma. On the one hand, language logically precedes thought, and thought sublates language. As this sublation progresses the sensuous element in language dwindles. The word ceases to be a mere symbol,

[1] LL, i, p. 72. [2] Cf. IH, ch. xii, § 1·01.

and the universal meaning differentiates itself freshly in every fresh context of thinking, unrestricted by the mere sign which by agreement attaches to it but does not vary in precise concomitance with it. On the other hand, the sublation cannot be complete in any phase of Concrete Spirit; not in the thinking of the Understanding, the *Denken* of Theoretical Mind, nor even in the philosophical thinking which consummates Absolute Spirit and has the logical categories and beyond them the forms of Nature and spirit for its content. In all thinking language survives to subserve thought as its indispensable expression. Without discourse thought cannot fulfil itself as thought. But this dependence of thought for the fulfilment of its own nature upon a lower, still sensuous phase of spirit precludes the perfecting of this fulfilment. Even philosophical thought is an incomplete synthesis of language with thought. It can never quite pass from meaning to truth, from reference to an object to utter self-identification with its object.

8·2. The bearing of these conclusions on Hegel's or any other philosophical system concerns us at present only in so far as they touch its verbal expression, but there they are important. Compared with the symbol the sign does not vary and does not restrict the development and differentiation of the meaning. But its fixity, it would now seem, is after all only relative, and the free development of the meaning does after all gradually demand variation in the signs it uses. It remains true that when a thinker, as we commonly say, pauses to choose his words, he is not selecting ready-made garments for his naked thoughts but struggling to develop his thoughts by expressing them; the words he uses are in effect already expressed thoughts which he re-thinks and modifies in developing his own thought. Yet as philosophic thought develops, philosophic terminology, even in the sense of a set of sensuous signs, does slowly alter. Words do not only change their meanings; they sometimes grow obsolete and perish. Sometimes, too, new words appear, because the survival in thought of a sensuous remnant is a survival of the arbitrary and contingent. To that small extent the convention upon which language rests has caprice in it. The wise philosopher will use his limited power of arbitrary choice as little as he can, because he knows that to do so tends to break the development of meaning in which philosophic thought essentially progresses; nevertheless, if meaning cannot pass completely into truth, and if this defect entails the use of a sensuous sign, then the sign must in a degree vary with the meaning, and the variation must in a degree be contingent.

8·3. It follows that a philosopher, when his soul discourses with herself, and even more so when he talks or writes for the benefit of others, must continually remodel, adjust, and expand his language, and that nevertheless he can never quite succeed in expressing all he means even to himself, because meaning falls always short of truth; because, that is, the world of meanings, even the world of philosophical meanings, is itself not fully real. Educated men, and most philosophers among them, move habitually and most comfortably at a pre-philosophical level of thinking and, therefore, of linguistic expression. So far as that is so the philosopher's task is to render flexible and to differentiate in fresh but not simply novel meanings the relatively rigid phrases in which the Understanding expresses its finite object, rejecting explicitly some of their customary associations and converting others—but not by force or fraud—to his own uses. If his system is detailed and complex he may very well find his material scanty, but only in dire need and then provisionally will he offer in place of a phrase self-explanatory in its context the stopgap of a technical term, an arbitrary definition, or a word constrained to bear a 'Pickwickian sense'. For he knows these to be dead patches in the living tissue of philosophical discourse, destined to swift decay.[1] There was a medieval thinker who prayed nightly to be delivered from the Devil and from metaphors. But the philosopher cannot shun contact with metaphors; he can only wrestle with them, hoping to tame them and not to become entangled in their grip. For the use of metaphor in philosophy consists in the analogical expression of the whole in terms of the part, and

[1] Cf. R. G. Collingwood, *Essay on Philosophical Method*, pp. 202–8. A great array of technical terms and words employed in senses which merely flout familiar usage makes A. N. Whitehead's *Process and Reality* an obscure work. Only a man with a natural genius for philosophy could have progressed so far despite his ignorance of the nature of philosophical expression.

that is an inescapable task of philosophic thinking and writing.

Thus when the philosopher starts at the level of the Understanding he will perpetully expand and elevate the tissue of workaday meanings which he appropriates. When he adopts and adapts the phraseology of other philosophers he will make sure that he has first established his own right of possession. In all his task he will work as a man who actively develops his own thinking by expressing it, not as one who clothes his *excogitata* in a ready-made dress, or decks them with external ornament; for such a dress can only shroud a corpse, and such ornamentation is nothing but a speedily forgotten monument. And yet he will never quite succeed in saying what he means.

8·4. Hegel, I have said, does not explicitly tell us how philosophic thinking expresses itself in words, but his practice as a writer conforms well enough to this pattern. His Logic, particularly LL, is a densely woven fabric. The expression is highly finished; nothing survives of vague suggestion and mere hint, nor of the ambiguity which springs from incompleteness. Every phrase, accordingly, receives and gives significance in so wide a context that the reader soon finds his attempt to comprehend and criticize piecemeal entirely baffled. But when he penetrates farther he finds that in a degree probably unparalleled by any other writer each phrase is at once familiar and newly created in its context. Hegel made his language very much his own, but he did not fabricate technical terms in the narrow sense,[1] preferring to develop the gleams of Reason which he believed he could detect in the thought, and therefore in the language, of the Understanding.

Yet the labour which it cost Hegel to utilize these gleams of Reason in re-creating the familiar is often obvious. Rather than coin the purely arbitrary technical term he will torture a metaphor with violence; seize and press the at least obsolescent etymological meaning of a word;[2] even, to the

[1] An Hegelian Lexicon can select specially important terms, but to explain them it cannot go far beyond the assembling of relevant citations. The lexicon appended to JE is compiled on that principle.

[2] Cf. § 5·5 on *Gedächtnis* above, and LL, i, pp. 120–1 on *Aufheben*. Cf. also Kant's similar views on this subject in KRV, B, pp. 368–9.

scandal of those who have not learnt how to read him, resort to a pun. The titles, as they stand at the heads of sections in the Logic and ΦG, not only, as he himself observes,[1] give a quite inadequate indication of the contents of the section but also, as a glance at the Tables will show, are sometimes actually repeated in different places.[2] Hegel's metaphors, his etymological twists, even his puns, do not deceive him—the faults in his dialectic do not spring from that source—and the reader who knows what philosophic discourse is will not suppose that they do. But they will remind that reader that the problem of expression is not in Hegel's philosophy completely solved, and that on Hegel's own theory of language pursued to its conclusion no complete solution is possible.

9. A philosophical colleague whom I told of my intention to write this book replied that I should have to translate Hegel into intelligible modern language. The only sense in which I could do that would be to write a book developing Hegel's system into a fresh philosophy. That, however, would be translation in a pretty Pickwickian sense, and were I competent to write it I doubt whether it would be written in what my colleague would recognize as intelligible modern language.

My aim, in fact, is less ambitious but not easy. I have remarked that the problem of expounding Hegel is primarily Hegel's and only secondarily his commentator's.[3] But completeness of expression achieves completeness of communication only between minds in sympathy and of equal calibre, and Hegel concedes little to human weakness. His expositor must try to bridge gaps which Hegel ignores. His problem is not to translate Hegel into ordinary language but to show more clearly than Hegel has thought worth while how Hegel has developed ordinary language. At the same time he is

[1] See § 8 above.

[2] 'Understanding', e.g., is used to denote both a phase of Consciousness and a phase of Mind. This loss of significance when the titles of dialectical phases are taken apart from the close context of the actual dialectic provides some answer to the taunt that Hegelians can never accurately remember the categories of the Logic. The reader will find in the logic of Essence constant examples of the difficulty Hegel has to develop an ordinary usage of words into a philosophical.

[3] See § 8 above.

faced with difficulties the same in kind as Hegel's own and in one sense more severe. He has not, at any rate till he turns from exposition to criticism, to think out a new philosophy, but whereas Hegel may pursue where the argument leads and care little who follows, his expositor at least can never ignore the warning of Aristotle that all learning and teaching must proceed from pre-existent knowledge.[1] He must begin then at the level of Understanding, and he must not leave it without taking his reader with him. He is bound to make, and cannot do much more than make, preliminary surveys and interim summaries, even if these are products of external reflection, and he cannot but be more embarrassed than Hegel by the poverty of language at this level.

9·1. In my *Introduction to Hegel* an attempt was made to characterize briefly the three main divisions of Hegel's Logic, viz. Being (*Sein*), Essence (*Wesen*), and Notion (*Begriff*),[2] and to indicate their respective relations to sense, Understanding, and Reason.[3] In the following chapter we must begin to elaborate this characterization, and the difficulty entailed by starting at the level of Understanding, where abstract thought partly transcends and partly still co-operates with sense, will soon be evident. The categories of the Understanding comprise the categories both of Being and of Essence, but we are not called upon in ordinary experience to distinguish the former from the latter, in which they are sublated. Hence (*a*) in discussing the categories of Being, which are presupposed and sublated in the categories of Essence, we nevertheless shall be unable to avoid much anticipatory use of the latter categories. We shall find ourselves speaking, for example, of the 'difference', or of the 'contradiction', between two categories of Being, although 'difference' and 'contradiction' are categories of Essence. And (*b*) when we discuss the Notion the converse difficulty will beset us. As of Being we shall have said too much, so of the Notion we shall be saying too little. As we shall have displayed mere Being too concretely, so we shall find ourselves displaying the concrete Notion too abstractly. Approaching Hegel's Logic, as we must, from a level of

[1] *Posterior Analytics*, opening sentence.

[2] IH, ch. xi, § 5·3.

[3] Ibid., footnote 1, p. 137.

everyday thinking, we are always feeling the need of some non-committal, undenominational category. But on Hegel's view, which we are in no position yet to criticize, there is no such thing. Since *ex hypothesi* any category has its meaning only within the Logic, it follows that we can only supply this need by borrowing in advance from the Logic categories which we shall have eventually to establish and justify in what Hegel regards as their proper place, and we can never guard ourselves securely against ambiguity.

9·2. Moreover, the factor of sense in our habitual level of experience entails a difficulty which pervades the whole exposition of the Logic. We cannot go far towards making one another understand what we mean without using illustration. But the use of illustrative instances implies that the 'deictic' attitude of sense-perception[1] is not wholly overpassed and, as we have seen, it cannot even at the level of philosophical thinking, *a fortiori* at the level of an exposition designed to assist the average philosophical student, be wholly overpassed. Hence we shall be speaking constantly as if categories were instances of categories. Probably the risk of confusion thereby entailed will be greatest when we discuss Essence. For it will sometimes be impossible to avoid talking as if categories of Essence, which are dualities, were themselves particular pairs of different or contradictory terms, or as if one category of Essence were different from or contradicted another. But as soon as we begin to discuss the categories of Being we shall be involved in this sort of difficulty. The reader, when he sees ahead, will be generous in discounting an inevitably clumsy terminology.[2]

[1] Cf. IH, ch. i, §§ 1·1 ff., and v, § 2·2.

[2] The further difficulty of commenting in English on German philosophy is, I think, sufficiently obvious from what I have said about language.

II

BEING: QUALITY

1. HEGEL's subdivision of Being into Quality, Quantity, and Measure has been shortly described in IH.[1] We shall perhaps do well to begin a fresh characterization of the categories of Being in their general nature by comparing them with Kant's 'mathematical' categories of Quantity and Quality.[2]

The Hegelian categories of Quality and Quantity are, in Kant's language, 'pure' and not 'schematized' categories.[3] They are in a sense, like Kant's mathematical categories, constitutive of the object of (primarily) a pure intuition. Among them Kant's mathematical categories—Unity, Plurality, Totality; Reality, Negation, Limitation—appear transformed but not unrecognizable. On the other hand, Hegel differs from Kant (*a*) in reversing the order of Quantity and Quality;[4] (*b*) in holding that Kant's schematized categories, when stripped of spatio-temporal specification, are phases of thought in which Kant's pure categories are further developed;[5] (*c*) in regarding thought as never devoid of intuition.

The full significance of the reversed order will appear when we examine the logic of Being in detail, but it follows from (*a*) and (*b*) that Number and Degree, which Kant makes the schemata of Quantity and Quality respectively, are included among Hegel's categories of Quantity; and from (*c*) that the Understanding, to which I have said that the categories of Being belong, excludes sense but includes intuition. The categories of Being are in fact thought at the level where it is almost bare intuition below discursion. That is why Hegel is prepared to call the first of them, viz. Pure Being, either empty intuition or empty thought.[6] It is empty because as yet it lacks any developed content, not of sense but of thought. Kant believed his objective deduction to

[1] Ch. xi, §§ 4–4·3. [2] Cf. ibid., p. 137, footnote 1.

[3] See IH, ch. ix, §§ 5·21 and 5·22.

[4] Not that Kant himself attaches any importance to this order.

[5] Cf. ibid., § 5·21. [6] See LL, i, p. 88.

show that the pure categories are presupposed in any experience wherein thought is discursive and co-operates with sense-intuition.[1] Thus the correlate of his pure categories is an *a priori* form (which is presumably also a pure content, a manifold) of not necessarily spatio-temporal intuition. If we conceive such an intuition as thought and not as sense I think it is pretty nearly what Hegel means by Pure Being. Yet equally, if we conceive this intuition as thought and not as sense, we can regard Pure Being as Kant's transcendental unity of apperception. It is the barest affirmation of that identity which will come to distinguish itself as subject and object; it is the undeveloped germ of all the categories.[2]

1·1. Nevertheless the categories of Being are those which operate *par excellence* when we perceive with our senses.[3]

We are not yet in a position to criticize directly Hegel's doctrine of the phenomenal embodiment of the categories, but already we are faced by the dilemma which began to emerge in § 4 of the opening chapter. We may say that sense-perception 'illustrates' the categories of Being, and that they are what sustains and animates it, gives it such truth as it possesses. 'Illustration' is thus in some sort the converse of philosophic interpretation, and at once it strikes a paradoxical note to speak of a content of sense-perception 'illustrating' categories which 'sustain' and 'animate' it and might therefore be thought rather to throw light on the sense-content than to receive illustration from it. A partial explanation of the paradox lies in the fact that the sense-content 'illustrates' the categories of Being only for the mind in a state of pupillage. 'Illustration', we may say, is an aid to the student in his effort towards philosophizing, towards a thinking which is ultimately to sublate this very conception of 'illustration' upon which to begin with he must rely. But we have already in our first chapter seen reason to suggest that this sublation can never be fully completed in Hegel's or any other philosophical thinking.

1·11. We must not, however, over-simplify Hegel's doc-

[1] See IH, ch. ix, § 5·22.

[2] As will appear in § 1·11 below.

[3] They operate in Consciousness implicitly. Thought only becomes explicit in Theoretical Mind, which begins with Intuition. That is why Hegel calls Pure Being 'intuition' (see § 1 above).

trine. Our sketch of a section of ΦG in Chapter I should have warned us not to suppose that the categories of Being are effectively 'illustrated' either by a process of sense-experience taken subjectively in abstraction from its object, or by a sense-object taken in abstraction from an experient. The titles which Hegel gives to the categories of Being may tend on the whole to suggest to common sense the latter alternative. But that is because common sense is barely self-conscious; because it is a realist attitude, a level at which the presence of the subject in its object is latent and not yet *for* the subject. The dialectical movement of spirit in and through the categories of Being *is*, on the other hand, *for* the interpreting philosopher: it *is* his interpretative thought. Therefore, although the distinction of subject and object is in these categories only implicit, yet for the philosopher spirit enters whole into each of them: each category of Being is a phase of the indivisible activity of spirit. In this sense Hegel remarks:[1]

> 'Die Kategorie, welche sonst [sc. in Kant especially] die Bedeutung hatte, Wesenheit des Seienden zu sein, unbestimmt des Seienden überhaupt oder des Seienden gegen das Bewusstsein, ist jetzt [sc. in Hegel's philosophy] Wesenheit oder einfache Einheit des Seienden nur als denkender Wirklichkeit; oder sie ist dies, dass Selbstbewusstsein und Sein dasselbe Wesen ist; dasselbe, nicht in der Vergleichung, sondern an und für sich. Nur der einseitige schlechte Idealismus lässt diese Einheit als Bewusstsein beider auf die eine Seite, und ihr gegenüber ein Ansich [sc. a reality *per se*, detached from consciousness] treten.'

In this passage *Sein*, *Wesen*, and *Wirklichkeit* are used in more or less general senses. Hegel's phraseology is affected by the fact that he is controverting Kant. He means not that self-consciousness and Being are names for two elements related under any *particular* category, but that the self of which self-consciousness is conscious is Being, and that the self-consciousness of spirit is spirit's being. The unity of self-consciousness and Being is 'original' because first and last there *is* only active spirit. The Pure Being with which Hegel's Logic begins, *die Kategorie* in its most abstract phase, is just this 'original' unity; it is Descartes's *Cogito* and Kant's unity of apperception in their true meaning. That is why

[1] *Phän.*, pp. 185–6.

Hegel is prepared to call Pure Being an empty intuiting or an empty thinking.[1]

The passage which follows shows how Hegel conceives this original unity of self-consciousness and Being as the spring and germ of spirit's activity expanding into and as the particular categories:

'Diese Kategorie oder einfache Einheit des Selbstbewusstseins und des Seins hat aber an sich [sc. implicit in the 'original', simple unity] den Unterschied; denn ihr Wesen ist eben dieses, im Anderssein oder im absoluten Unterschiede unmittelbar sich selbst gleich zu sein. Der Unterschied *ist* daher; aber vollkommen durchsichtig, und als Unterschied, der zugleich keiner ist.[2] Er erscheint als eine *Vielheit* von Kategorien.'

Thus, hard as this often is to express, the sense-experience which 'illustrates' the categories of Being is the total concrete activity of percipient and *perceptum*.

1·2. We cannot perceive without thinking, but so far as our experience is merely sense-perception we take things at their immediate face value. There is so far no distinction present to us between surface and inner core, between what things appear to be and what they really are; between the contingent and the necessary, the accidental and the essential; even between things and their properties. As soon as such distinctions do arise we are already thinking in the categories of Essence; we are explicitly thinking and not merely perceiving. Until the categories of Essence operate, the thinking, the rudimentary rationality in our experience, involves no genuine mediation of what is experienced.

1·3. In short, Being is the sphere of immediacy. Its dialectic is not at once easy to comprehend. Our first impression is likely to be that the movement from category to category is one of sheer substitution. Each category will present itself as just thus and thus characterized, and as having no sort of connexion with its predecessors. On second thoughts we shall most likely see the movement as sheer transformation. What *is* in one phase will appear to have simply turned into what *is* in the succeeding phase. But we shall next discover that it is barely possible to separate these two thoughts. In sensuous experience at so low a level that

[1] See § 1 above. [2] Cf. IH, ch. viii, § 3·11.

it approximates (as, for example, in some dreams) to a mere Heraclitean flux of presentation, have we to do with the sheer superseding of one image by another? Or do we watch the absolute, unreserved self-transformation of some one thing whereof we yet can say no more than that it persists as a bare identity in its successive shapes, as a bare formal unity of its determinations? We shall tend, maybe, to the second interpretation when we consider the theses of Being: each will seem to have arisen as a new positive form of Being which simply ignores its predecessors. On the other hand, in the transition to antithesis we shall perhaps seem to find mere substitution, cancellation, and not true mediation of the thesis. The synthesis will then seem to be not a real union of opposites but one in which, as it were, the terms are too fluid and indifferent either to resist or to accept union. But whether the phase we consider be thesis or antithesis, we shall oscillate between these two interpretations. Everywhere we shall seem to watch a portrait of Proteus in the making.

Yet the cause of this oscillation will not be our own mere infirmity. It will spring from the fact that in the categories of Being we shall indeed have before us the one unbroken activity of spirit, but we shall be witnessing this activity in an initial phase which might almost be called impotence; not a paralysis, but an incontinent, unstable self-transformation, which for the faintness of its continuity may well seem substitution; a movement which is an essential initial phase, but is at the same time a privation, or at most a dim prefiguration, of spirit's true activity.

2. Pure Being, Nothing or Not-being, Becoming (*Werden*)

We have now to amplify the brief account of Hegel's first logical triad[1] given in IH.[2]

The general character which in the present chapter I have attributed to the categories of Being is gradually sublated as the dialectic of Being develops. It belongs *par excellence* to the categories of Being in the narrower sense, viz. to the opening triad.

[1] Which he again entitles 'Being', in a narrower sense; see Table I.

[2] See IH, ch. ii, §§ 3 and 3·1.

When Hegel declared Pure Being, the minimal characterization of reality, to be the same as Nothing the shock to common sense was severe. The common objection, he says, has been based on an appeal to the principle *ex nihilo nihil fit*: an utter blankness can form no premiss for deducing a system. But this appeal to a principle is, on Hegel's view, an instance of the cardinal error of the Understanding when it mistakes itself for Reason. Thus to exempt a principle from criticism and presuppose it as a criterion by which to condemn a logical method is grossly and barbarously to beg the question. Moreover, though it is true enough that no concrete thing—i.e. no object of sensuous *Vorstellung*—comes to be save out of another such concrete thing, Pure Being is not a concrete thing. It is a moment of pure thought abstracted and reflected upon by itself solely for purposes of exposition, and only reflection, 'which has run through the whole exposition', can so abstract it. Nothing, or Not-being, is equally abstract. Neither of these initial opposites has any but a proleptic sense. 'Becoming', says Hegel, 'is the first concrete thought, and therefore the first Notion;[1] in contrast with it Being and Nothing are empty abstractions. . . . As the first concrete thought-determination, Becoming is the first *true* thought-determination.'[2]

Hegel means that Pure Being and Nothing are empty abstractions which do not accord with their notion save in Becoming: apart from Becoming they have *no* truth as *Denkbestimmungen*, but are *leere Gedankendinge*.[3]

2·1. Hegel's position becomes clearer if we here contrast it with the Aristotelian view of being and not-being.

Aristotle, except perhaps in his doctrine of privation,[4] seems to have been little influenced by Plato's *Sophist*.[5] He insists that his categories are the *summa genera*, and that being, τὸ ὄν, is not a supreme genus specified in the categories. Rather τὸ ὄν (and analogously not-being, τὸ μὴ ὄν) is like a grammatical stem declined through the cases of a noun substantive, and is without meaning except in those

[1] See IH, ch. xi, § 5·31.
[2] EL, § 88, *Zusatz*.
[3] Hegel may have in mind Kant's division of the concept of Nothing; see KRV, B, pp. 348–9.
[4] See IH, ch. ii, § 6.
[5] See IH, ch. x, §§ 2·3 ff.

cases.[1] Taken by itself, it is the vanishing-point of characterization in τὰ ὄντα, a *sheerly* logical *prius* of determinate character (as substance, quality, quantity, &c.) in whatever actually exists, a mere *Gedankending*.

Aristotle's doctrine of the categories is puzzling, and his only extant exposition of it[2] is very elementary in form, but he appears usually to conceive his categories more or less realistically. They are the highest *genera* of predicates as well as the highest *genera* of τὰ ὄντα,[3] but I think that we must on the whole say that in the latter aspect they characterize τὰ ὄντα conceived as indifferent to mind. For example, Aristotle instances νοῦς and God as substances falling under his first category; he does not treat his categories as an explication of the divine activity which is thought having itself as object. From this realist, or at any rate not idealist, position it follows that Aristotle's sheer being, taken by itself, *is* in Hegelian terminology, a mere *Gedankending* and not a *Denkbestimmung*.

But Hegel's Pure Being is not, like Aristotle's sheer ὄν, simply what remains if the reflective Understanding abstracts all determinate character from things which it presupposes to be 'detached' from itself. It is the 'original' unity of thought and being. So to call it is, no doubt, to speak proleptically. But we find this difficult only because coming to comprehend it *is* a passing from a 'detached' understanding to a truly active reasoning. Only when this transition is made shall we see that the triad is the *minimum rationale*.[4]

2·11. The triad is the *minimum rationale* because the unity of thought and being is 'original' and originative. This will perhaps become clearer if we pause to dwell again for a moment on Hegel's conception of activity, which in effect is here at stake.[5]

There is not activity where there is less than self-severance

[1] On Aristotle's categories see IH, ch. vi, § 4·1.

[2] In the *Categories*, the first book of Aristotle's *Organon*.

[3] As J. A. Smith used aptly to express it, Aristotle's categories classify τὰ ὄντα ᾗ λεγόμενα.

[4] See IH, ch. xi, § 3·2.

[5] Dr. Ewing's view that 'in talking of thought Hegel had less in mind the thinking than the content thought' (*Idealism*, p. 61) hopelessly misrepresents Hegel.

and self-reunion. Only that which has put and is putting itself forth from itself, and yet has remained and does remain one with itself, is active. There are not here three temporal stages, viz. the subject as yet inactive, the subject in self-diremption, the subject in self-reunion. Spirit not *has* but *is* activity. As Aristotle saw, activity is timeless.[1] In common life we tend to think of a man as preceding his activities, and so come to think of him in abstraction from them; though what he then is it would be hard to say. We ordinarily envisage human activities as processes of change in time, but their truth—what they genuinely are, and what we think them so far as we genuinely think them—is not temporal process. This was what Aristotle, who held pleasure to be a consummation supervening upon free activity, meant when he said that we can become pleased quickly, but we cannot *be* pleased quickly.[2] Hegel puts it thus: 'Das reine Sein und das reine Nichts ist also dasselbe. Was die Wahrheit ist, ist weder das Sein, noch das Nichts, sondern dass das Sein in Nichts, und das Nichts in Sein—nicht übergeht, —sondern übergegangen ist.'[3] The substitution of perfect for present tense is intended to signify that the reciprocal oscillation is not temporal.

2·12. One might add in passing that language is pervaded by tense, and that Hegel's constant effort to express the timeless—or better, perhaps, the supra-temporal—nature of activity is bound to lead him often into a prima facie self-contradiction. Sometimes, as here, he will amend and compensate a present with a perfect tense. It is to him significant that the word *Wesen*, Essence, recalls the past participle *gewesen*,[4] and his choice of the past rather than of the present as a symbol of eternity is reminiscent of the Greek philosophic imperfect which appears in Aristotle's formula for essence: *τὸ τί ἦν εἶναι*. It is also exemplified in Hegelian phrases such as *In-sich-zurückgekehrtsein*, 'returnedness-into-self', used to express the self-synthetic nature of activity. On the other hand, Hegel will sometimes correct the impression

[1] See IH, ch. vi, § 3·1. For the Neoplatonic conception of spiritual activity as return upon itself see Wallace's note on EL, § 17 in his *Logic of Hegel*, pp. 386–7.

[2] *Nicomachean Ethics* 1173ª 34.

[3] LL, i, pp. 88–9.

[4] Cf. ch. v, § 1·2 below.

of temporal process which formulae such as 'self-diremption and self-reunion' are apt to give, by emphasizing the abiding of spirit with itself in its negative, but *eo ipso* self-expressive, moment of self-diremption: 'bei sich selbst bleibt', he will say, 'in seinem Anderssein'. Sometimes, again, he will present the contradiction starkly, and say that spirit both issues from itself and does not issue from itself. The clue to this language is always his conception of activity, and the illustration most likely, in Hegel's view, to help the reader is his own self-consciousness.

2·2. Becoming, then, is the initial, the logically first, manifestation of the timeless activity which spirit is.

In Becoming, Pure Being and Nothing, or Not-being,[1] are not so much united as inseparable in their reciprocal transformation—'vanishing' or 'vanishedness', Hegel calls it—into one another. Neither is thinkable without the other, and to think them together is the thought of Becoming.

2·21. Becoming is the thought sustaining and animating our experience of the ceaseless cyclical coming to be and passing away of all perceptible things in the spatio-temporal world. But Becoming is not identical with change, nor with any type of change. For Becoming is a category, a first abstract self-formulation of Spirit's timeless activity; whereas the types of change are forms of Nature,[2] and presuppose Space and Time as logically prior forms of Nature. Matter-and-Motion, for example, is the synthesis of Space and Time, and it is with this triad that Hegel's Philosophy of Nature opens. On the other hand, the position of Becoming as the first synthesis of the Logic should serve to remind us that whatever we may take as a concrete 'illustration' of Becoming, or of any subsequent category, cannot be anything less than an instance of temporal process.

2·22. Hegel considers many of the positive categories of his Logic—i.e. the theses and syntheses—to be exemplified in the history of philosophy. He holds that Pure Being and Becoming are illustrated respectively in the philosophies of

[1] Hegel remarks in LL, i, p. 89 that 'Nothing' better expresses the *immediate* negation of Pure Being in its antithesis, whereas 'Not-being' better expresses the *relation* of these two opposites in their synthesis.

[2] Cf. IH, ch. ix, § 6·11.

Parmenides and Heraclitus. Parmenides, denying change, took Pure Being for the ultimate nature of the real; the flux doctrine of Heraclitus, who said, 'Being *is* no more than not-being', was in Hegel's eyes an attempt to make Becoming the ultimate definition of the Absolute.

This view of the pre-Socratics is anachronistic in so far as Hegel reads into them a conception of pure thought of which they were innocent. The One of Parmenides, which only *is*, was conceived by him as a solid corporeal plenum, and the not-being which he denied was a physical void. The fluent reality of Heraclitus was ordinary fire. These conceptions, that is, were largely in the medium of imagination. Yet the conclusions which these early philosophers reached by thinking out the implications of those physical characters of the world which they selected as ultimately real, may justifiably be regarded as the germ of Hegel's thought no less than of Aristotle's.[1] It is absurd to criticize Hegel's interpretation of the pre-Socratics without considering how their doctrines are developed in mature Greek speculation.[2] To Plato, who derived his doctrine of sense-perception from Heraclitus, the perceptible object is between Being and nothing; to Aristotle it is that which both is and is not. It is the developed Greek doctrine of *γένεσις* which inspires Hegel's first triad, and when Aristotle observes that coming-to-be cannot itself come to be or pass away,[3] he is half-way to the conception of Becoming as a category.

2·3. To the external reflection of the Understanding Hegel's first triad will, on his own account of it, always remain unintelligible, and since in approaching Hegel's Logic the language of the Understanding cannot be avoided, it is worth while remarking on a difficulty which that occasions in the exposition of any triad.

We first think of the synthesis as combining two elements, thesis and antithesis, which are such that each can be to some extent truly characterized apart from their synthesis. Then we discover that on Hegel's view they have no truth apart from synthesis. But the fact that thesis and antithesis are true in synthesis and untrue apart from synthesis must

[1] See IH, preface, §§ iii and iv. [2] See IH, preface, footnote p. xiv.

[3] See, for example, *Physics* 225^{b} 33 ff.

signify the presence of spirit *whole* both in thesis and antithesis. And that is very difficult to express. We shall perhaps attempt to express it by saying that the antithesis preserves as well as cancels the thesis, and we can scarcely fail to add that positive and negative moments are *both* present even in the thesis—not otherwise is Pure Being the original unity of thought and being. But that, though we must often talk as if it were so, is in effect to say that thesis and antithesis are already synthesis. And that will doubtless seem absurd.

It is in fact, on Hegel's own showing, utterly impossible to express dialectical movement in terms of the Understanding without distortion and contradiction. The triad is the *minimum rationale*, and the movement is timeless. To the reader who finds this incomprehensible Hegel would reply that the only way of enlightenment lies through discovering gradually (*a*) that the Understanding eventually reaches contradiction in the consideration of any object upon which it reflects; (*b*) that this contradiction is the Understanding's self-contradiction; (*c*) that this self-contradiction is the working in Understanding of Reason as the spring of the Understanding's self-sublation into Reason. It follows that until the reader has become an actor in the dialectic, and with the passage of Essence into Notion transformed his own way of thinking, this will remain obscure. The effort to 'understand' a triad, or a section of triads, can bring no profit beyond the conviction that dialectic cannot be 'understood'. That this conviction is hardly won, Hegel is well aware. His observations upon the stubbornness of common sense are frequent and emphatic. They recall Plato's belief that it requires conversion and a divine chance to bring a man to philosophy.

2·31. It may be further remarked that to allow that the Hegelian triad is even a *minimum rationale* is a concession to the exigencies of exposition. Within the dialectical movement there is, strictly speaking, no distinction between the synthesis of one triad and the thesis of the next: there is no movement from the one to the other. The difference of title (which in EL Hegel often omits) is only obtained by expounding the synthesis as something less than it truly is.

Triplicity is the mere external aspect of dialectic. The antithesis is a first negation, and the synthesis is negation of negation and so return to immediacy. In discussing the Absolute Idea as method[1] Hegel remarks:

'If we are simply to count, then in the whole course of the movement this second immediate [sc. the synthesis] is the third term, following the first immediate term and the mediated term. But it is also a third term following the first (or formal) negative and the absolute negativity or second negative. Now since the first negative is already a second term [sc. because it follows the affirmative thesis], this third term may also be counted as fourth, and the abstract form may be taken as quadruplicity instead of triplicity. In this latter way of looking at it, the negative, the differentiation, is reckoned as a duality. The third (or fourth) term is just the unity of the first and second moments, of the immediate and the mediated. The apprehension of this as a unity, and of the method as a whole as a triplicity, is no more than the superficial, external side of the cognitive mode' [i.e. of the Understanding's reflection].[2]

In short the dialectic, in Hegel's eyes, is a form which nothing but its own actual content can truly explicate.

2·4. Yet this defence of Hegel's first logical triad may fail to satisfy the reader. He may have felt that a certain objection lies against even the merely general account of Hegel's dialectic which I offered in IH, ch. x, an objection which will perhaps have come to a head in his reading of my attempt in this chapter to expound Becoming. I can conceive him to formulate it after this manner. 'You state in § 2', he may say, 'that Hegel's Pure Being is the minimal characterization of reality. This you at once proceed to qualify by saying that Pure Being and Nothing are, if taken in abstraction by themselves, mere *Gedankendinge*; that they are terms which only signify proleptically; that the triad is the *minimum rationale*, and that Becoming is the first genuine category. Now one might perhaps accept this qualification and allow that in two intelligibly distinguished senses Hegel begins his Logic with (*a*) Pure Being and (*b*) Becoming. One might even add that there is an intermediate sense in which his Logic may be said to begin with Being-and-Nothing as coupled opposites between which, as Hegel himself says, the

[1] See below, ch. xviii. [2] LL, ii, pp. 343–4.

distinction is "*nur gemeint*".[1] All this we might allow, but does not Hegel in fact prove too much? On his account, does not Becoming, too, if taken apart from the ensuing triads, have a merely proleptic meaning? It may be true that every phase and transition in the Logic has its own unique significance which is not precisely determinable save in the light of the whole Logic, yet is it not clear that, if we pursue Hegel's line of argument, we shall be unable to fix the true beginning of the Logic anywhere? Will it not flee before us, like our own shadows, until we reach what to begin with we confidently called the *final* category?

'It would seem', the objector might continue, 'that Hegel makes Pure Being (or, in another sense, Becoming) the real *primum* of the Logic on the ground that any more concrete thought would be a borrowed hypothesis which could not be justified, could not prove itself, within the Logic. On this view (and also judging from your account of activity in § 2·11) the *primum* of a dialectical logic can be nothing but the germ of its concluding phase. But in that case Pure Being (or Becoming) is not an absolute beginning, for Absolute Idea—and, indeed, every intervening category, too —is *presupposed* by Pure Being (or Becoming). In fact the Logic is, as Hegel himself often calls it, a circle; and every phase of the circle is either prior or posterior to any other according to which way you look at it from the outside. Hence there can be no true *primum* in a philosophical logic, no πρῶτον φύσει, but only a πρῶτον πρὸς ἡμᾶς, a beginning external and wholly contingent, determined by nothing but the historical chance of a man's happening to start philosophizing at this or that level of general education.

'Moreover,' he might add, 'this objection can be extended to the whole Hegelian dialectic. Its corollary is that the pretence of necessary and irreversible order by which in the *Encylopaedia* the *Logic* is followed by the *Philosophy of Nature*, and the *Philosophy of Nature* by the *Philosophy of Spirit*, is no more than a sham.'

2·5. The difficulty raised by this objector is the converse of the difficulty which we raised in Chapter I. There the

[1] 'Merely intended', 'merely meant and not a fully possessed thought'; cf. LL, i, p. 101 and EL, § 87, *Zusatz*.

need of thought, including philosophic thought, to express itself in speech seemed to indicate a defect in the whole dialectic whereby its progress was conditional upon the imperfect sublation of each succeeded phase. Here we are faced with the problem that if sublation is complete the dialectic becomes a circle and not a real movement with a real beginning, middle, and end.

2·51. I believe that both these objections have weight, and we shall have again to consider them towards the end of this *Study*. I shall attempt no more now than to suggest the lines on which Hegel would have replied to the second, and I shall confine the discussion to logic. I freely confess that I have more hope of eventually drawing a fruitful conclusion from the two objections together than of producing a fully convincing answer to the second.

2·52. Logic has, I suppose, no concern with what is sometimes called the 'psychical setting' of this or that singular individual's thinking, nor with the temporal occasions of its beginnings and endings, nor with its, in some sense, concomitant emotional moods. It is a differentia of judgement that it involves a claim on the individual thinker's part to be asserting truth which does not, in order to be true, depend upon his judging, nor upon the judging of any other singular individual thinker. No truth is created *ex nihilo* by his act of thought, nor dies when it ceases to fill his mind. Truth, even if it be truth 'about' temporal happenings, is in some sense timeless. Yet, save on some such view as Husserl's, the logician cannot regard as irrelevant to his study the fact that where judgement is, there a finite thinker judges. This does not, however, mean that the logician's proper study is a psychical process generalized after abstracting from the emotional and historical idiosyncrasies of this and that singular individual thinker. For the logician studies finite thinking only by seizing upon that in it by virtue of which it is thinking, not that which constitutes its 'vice' of finitude. Moreover, even this suggestion of a separating of the wheat from the husk is a delusive metaphor. For the 'wheat' is not a dead, subjectless content. It is not a timeless truth, enduring lifeless, which by good luck any singular thinker may catch on to and assert, or by ill fortune may merely miss. And the 'husk' is not what is left of finite subjects when they fail to grasp truths. For finite *thinking* is the constituting of the finite thinker by an activity which therein also, not *ex gratia* but by the free necessity of its own nature, constitutes itself. There remains in fact no 'rejected husk' at all, for in that from which the logician abstracts there is no subject. The conception of finite experient subjects for the moment out of touch with truths is pure and baseless myth: so long as a man can say 'I' he is thinking, and what cannot say 'I' is not a man.

2·53. Hence thought as the philosophical logician studies it is (*a*) the self-transcendence of the finite thinker; but it is the reconstitution, not the discarding, of his finitude. And it is also (*b*) the self-constitutive activity of absolute spirit. But (*a*) and (*b*) do not indicate two complementary parts of the logician's subject-matter, two claims which his exposition must successively satisfy, or two tasks to which he may attend alternately. His subject-matter is one, the claim he must meet is single, and his task is always the same. For the process of learning, the self-reconstituting of the finite thinker, presupposes no 'husk' consisting of mind in a state of sheer finitude, and it has neither spring nor movement save the activity of spirit in him. Conversely the self-constituting of spirit is essentially and only manifest in finite activity. But this is no level and equal reciprocation; for the activity of spirit is the truth, the real nature, of finite thinking, and not vice versa. Hence the logician's single task is to set forth that activity. There is no logic of finite thinking save *qua* a moment within the activity of absolute spirit.

2·54. Nevertheless the logician must set forth the activity of spirit as at once *in esse* and *in fieri*. His business is not to display it as an *aeternitas* within which the moment of finitude is merged without trace. Such an *aeternitas* would not be the self-manifesting of spirit through, and return upon itself from, finitude. Hence the dialectic which he must exhibit is as little some mystic act of vision indifferent to time as it is a temporal process of learning. It is throughout and essentially the sublating of temporal process, and to contrast it by stark opposition with temporal process makes equal nonsense of both terms of the contrast.[1] Hegel's Logic is a circle wherein any one phase is both prior and posterior to any other, but by the virtue in it of the temporal process which it sublates—by the virtue of that temporal process *qua* preserved as well as cancelled—it has two inseparable characteristics. (i) It has irreversible direction, and (ii) its most abstract phase, the original, indubitable unity of thought and being, the assurance of Reason that it is all the world, is in a special sense its real beginning. This beginning is not contingent, although it is determined as a beginning by the fact that the activity of spirit *is* the sublating of finitude and contingency, *is* a knowing within which learning is an ideal moment.

Pure Being (or Becoming) *is* thus a πρῶτον φύσει within the Logic of Hegel, but not because it is either the highest or the lowest stage in some eternally static hierarchy of the real divorced from time and mind; nor because it is 'primitive' within some timeless truth-structure of mind-independent propositions; nor because it is a primal or a supreme pulse in the eternal thinking of some utterly transcendent God. Indeed there could not in any sense at all of the words be a 'before and after' in *such* a real hierarchy, in *such* a truth-structure, or in *such* a divine thinking. Pure Being (or Becoming) is also in a sense a πρῶτον πρὸς ἡμᾶς; but not because it is contingent, not because it is the start of a finite thinker's sheerly external approach to a hierarchy of the real or a structure of independently subsistent propositions, nor because it marks the beginning of his simply otiose attempt to walk in the ways of an eternally self-complete and alien God. It is a πρῶτον πρός ἡμᾶς only if 'we' be interpreted not as those quite chimerical beings, *sheerly* finite thinkers, but as the ideal moment of finitude within the activity of spirit.

2·55. Yet when all is said by Hegel or on Hegel's behalf, there remains a problem in one sense insoluble. Spirit in its issue into finitude reserves no residue, yet the logician, however firmly he conceives finitude within and not without the activity of spirit, cannot display in finite thinking the whole movement of spirit's issue and return upon itself.

[1] 'Temporal process' in this context refers to finite thinking, but in the last resort the same is true of temporal process in any form.

His task is essentially single, but he cannot, strive as he will, perform it wholly and unreservedly *as* a single task.[1] For all his perseverance in grasping the way of learning as a moment in spirit's activity, he cannot wholly escape lapse to a lower level where it *appears* as a finite thinking, the exposition of which has to be *complemented* with an equally abstract exposition of spirit as absolute thought merely innocent of finitude. He can never quite master the weakness which leads, if indulged, to a Kantian restriction of knowledge to phenomena, and in the end to the confusions of Locke: the attempt to assign fixed limits to the powers of the human mind, the substitution of temporal process for thinking and of a 'plain historical method' for logic, even the occasional failure to distinguish mind from brain.

2·56. I have tried to meet an objection raised against the first triad of Hegel's Logic and touching the whole character of his dialectic. The defence may be held to fail, but the problem cannot, I think, in the nature of human experience be finally solved. The solution which I have offered as Hegel's at least seems adequately to criticize the ground upon some form of which, as I see it, the objection must rest. For I do not think it can lie unless the objector assumes either (*a*) a sheerly timeless structure of reality or truth which ready-made finite subjects come contingently to know, or (*b*) a divine activity totally indifferent to finitude.

3. Transition from Becoming to There-being (*Dasein*)

The exposition in LL of *Dasein*, the main antithesis of quality, is too complicated to epitomize. In EL it is simplified, but sometimes rather bewilderingly telescoped. I shall on the whole follow EL with slight modifications, taking as the three main phases of *Dasein* Somewhat (*Etwas*), Limit (*Grenze*), and the True Infinite. What follows expresses, I think, the general nature of a difficult dialectic.

The transition from Becoming to *Dasein* is this. The term 'Becoming' is more or less an abbreviation for 'coming to be and passing away'. 'More or less', because within Becoming, Pure Being and Nothing *are* each the other; or

[1] In branches of philosophy other than logic this impotence is even more obvious.

rather nothing less than what-is-and-is-not-and-therein-becomes is spirit. That is to say that though *qua* different 'directions' (coming to be and passing away) these opposites 'penetrate and paralyse each other', yet they do not *externally* cancel one another.[1] Hence *mere* oscillating unrest of opposites is not the full nature of Becoming: Becoming is spirit in a mode of Being, and oscillation is, further, equilibrium. In the phenomenal world the things of sense arise and perish, but because they once were not and do not abide, it does not follow that this alternating show is illusion.

Hegel calls this equilibrium *eine ruhige Einheit*,[1] and despite his previous metaphor of paralysis he evidently means by *ruhig* not 'static' but 'poised', or 'steady'.[2] Moreover, it is to be remembered that the equivalence of Pure Being and Not-being does not cancel the priority of Being to Not-being: if it did, the activity of spirit would lack direction and not be activity at all. The equilibrium is positive: if we think Becoming, we think what *is* rather than what is not. Hence Becoming, as a positive equipoise, has *eo ipso* passed into There-being, or *Dasein*.

4. *Dasein* as Somewhat

Dasein, *qua* a category of Quality, is *quale* from which its quality cannot be distinguished. It is a mode of Being immediately one with Being; as Quantity, for example, is not. For Quantity is a mode of Being external and indifferent to Being. Quantity, as we shall see, logically presupposes Quality: *quantum* is as such quantified *quale*, *quale* further determined as *quantum*. But this further determination is indifferent to qualitative determination. An alteration in quantity does not, as such, affect the quality of what is altered, whereas an alteration in quality is *eo ipso* a transformation of the *quale*.[3]

4·1. But *Dasein* is only the antithesis phase of Quality. As against the opening triad of the Logic, *Dasein* contains its negation, its determinateness, within itself; yet in no stage is *Dasein* in full possession of its own determinateness. In any phase of it spirit fails to be *for itself* what it is. The

[1] See LL, i, pp. 118–19. [2] *Bewegtheit*, not *Bewegung*.
[3] Cf. IH, ch. xi, §§ 4–4·1.

opposition rather than the unity of positive and negative is the theme of the dialectic of *Dasein*.

4·2. Somewhat, the first subcategory of *Dasein*, is at first rather difficult to grasp. The word misleadingly suggests a concrete thing among other concrete things. To make Hegel's meaning plain we must for a moment anticipate the general nature of the categories to which Somewhat leads up. Somewhat is only the thesis of *Dasein*: it is the thought embodied in the object of Sensuous Consciousness,[1] and so prior to, the germ only of, that opposition which sense-perception is dimly conscious of when it distinguishes 'this' from 'that'. Yet if we, as perhaps we may, assume that 'that' implies mediation whereas 'this' does not, we may say that Somewhat is what we think so far as we experience the object-world of Consciousness Proper[2] as mere 'this', not yet 'this and that and that, &c.', and as not yet distinct from the percipient 'I'. That is to say, Somewhat is the bare universal character which we go on to specify when we differentiate 'this' from 'that'; but if the object of Sensuous Consciousness, which is immediate, may be called 'this' rather than 'that', then the thesis of *Dasein* may be called Somewhat even before *Dasein* has developed into the opposition of Somewhat and Other, as in the categories of Limit it will develop. We must not, however, forget (1) that the triad is the *minimum rationale*, and that to call the immediate object of sense-perception 'this' is to name it proleptically, nor (2) that this first bare universal immediacy of sense-perception is immediate subject as well as immediate object: it could not be called any sort of universal if the Ego were not implicit in it.[3]

5. *Dasein* AS (QUALITATIVE) LIMIT (*Grenze*)

In Limit the opposition latent in Somewhat grows explicit. Somewhat as positive thesis is called by Hegel *an sich*, a phrase which means (*a*) 'in itself', in the sense of merely *per se*, and also (*b*) 'merely potentially', as when Aristotle contrasts being δυνάμει with being ἐνεργείᾳ.[4] But so soon as Somewhat positively affirms itself as *an sich*, it *eo ipso* negates itself and expresses its Being as *Sein-für-anderes*,

1 See ch. i, §§ 3–3·2 above.

2 See Table II.

3 Cf. § 8 below.

4 Cf. IH, ch. i, § 2·61.

Being-for-another. So the mere 'this' of Sensuous Consciousness becomes a focus of attention,[1] a 'this' against 'that and that and that . . .'.

5·1. Hegel's conception of Limit will not be fully intelligible until the categories of Quantity have been considered in some detail. The two points of preliminary importance are these. (A) Within Quantity categories of Limit are thoughts which sustain spatio-temporal experience, but they are not *Vorstellungen*. The boundary of an area, for example, is not an adequate 'illustration' of what Hegel means by quantitative limit, because Space is not a category but a phase of Nature. Limit is always a *Denkbestimmung*, a certain intelligible determinateness which spirit manifests at some levels. (B) Limit is not confined to Quantity, and here it is qualitative Limit with which we are concerned.

5·2. Nevertheless a comparison with Quantitative Limit will serve best to explain the nature of Qualitative Limit. We may take as a concrete phenomenal illustration a piece of land three acres large. The quantitative limit of this land is not its mere boundary line but its precise area, the determinateness it possesses by virtue of being just three acres in extent.[2] The land is also, let us say, meadow-land and not woodland, bog, or moor.[3] But this quality of the land makes no difference to its quantitative limit. On the other hand, the fact that it is meadow is its qualitative limit, the limit which stops it from being any other sort of land. And this qualitative limit, in contrast to its quantitative limit, is immediately one with it and constitutes it what it is. So a man may sometimes feel himself limited by his own character.

5·3. Qualitative Limit, then, is a case of Quality not distinct from *Quale*, and this explains the form which Limit assumes as antithesis to Somewhat. Doubtless *qua* limited, Somewhat is negated, and in being negated is opposed by an Other. But this Other is not external to Somewhat, as it would be if Somewhat were quantitatively determined: the

[1] According to ΦG attention emerges only with Intuition (cf. ch. i, § 3·1, above), but Hegel's doctrine was modified in the interval between *Phän.* and ΦG, § 418.

[2] So the quantitative limit of a solid body would be not its surface but its volume.

[3] Or the solid body is also golden, silver, or leaden.

Other is Somewhat's very self. For Somewhat is as much Other as the Other is, and the Other is as much Somewhat as Somewhat is. In fact, as the opposition becomes explicit, *Etwas* develops itself not merely as *Sein-für-anderes* but also as *Anderssein*: it not only *is* only for an Other, but equally is itself Other. Hegel finds apt illustration of this in the Latin idiom *aliud aliud*.

Sensuous experience 'illustrates' this thought. Thus (*a*), subjectively, as the focus of sense-perception shifts, what was 'this' becomes 'that other', and what was 'that other' becomes 'this'; and (*b*), objectively, 'this now' becomes 'that which was', as the sense-object suffers what we doubt whether to call transformation or supersession. 'The highest level of maturity', says Hegel, 'which any Somewhat can attain is that at which it begins to perish.'[1]

6. The Subcategories of (Qualitative) Limit

It is here specially important to bear in mind that we have not yet reached the thought of quantity. Limit as thesis is

The Finite (*das Endliche*)

To be at once Somewhat and Other is, on Hegel's view, precisely the nature of the Finite; of that, that is, which does not contain its own whole nature—is not *für sich*—but is determined by what is 'beyond', or 'outside', it. We must, however, beware of introducing here from Essence any opposition between real and apparent nature. The 'beyond' implied by the Finite is a context strictly homogeneous with it.

The antithesis phase of limit is

6·1. Alterability (*Veränderlichkeit*)

For what the Finite is implicitly (*an sich*) becomes explicit as its *alter*ability, its 'othering'. Its Being-for-other (and so its own Being-other) now opposes its *Ansichsein*, its mere potential Being-in-or-by-itself.

The synthesis Hegel calls

6·2. The Spurious Infinite (*Die Schlechte*, *Abstrakte*, or *Einseitige Unendlichkeït*)

This may be called 'indefinite regress', but although we

[1] LL, ii, p. 50.

are approaching the categories of Quantity, it is not a quantitative category. It is the synthesis of Finite with Alterability, because Somewhat, though 'othered', is yet repeated, or reinstated, in its Other. Finite becomes its Other: the Other which opposes it is just as much Somewhat as Somewhat is Other. And because in this begetting of, or becoming, an Other which is merely the repetition or reinstatement of itself, Somewhat fails still to contain its own nature, this synthesis is an endless regress of Somewhat and Other.

6·3. The whole triad of Limit might be summed up as 'the endlessly self-othering, yet self-reinstating, Finite'. Hegel in fact in LL labels this triad Finitude, making Limit its antithesis and naming the synthesis once again Finitude. This difference in terminology between LL and EL is not important. The finite is that which of its own nature passes beyond itself to *find* and possess its own nature in a *Sollen*, an 'ought-to-be'. *Qua* Limit (*Grenze*) the Finite is also Barrier (*Schranke*): its finitude is a determinateness, but also a restraining limitation which of its own nature it breaks through and contradicts in further determining itself. Whether this is better expressed by calling the whole triad Finitude and exhibiting the movement as development of the thought of Limit, or by calling the triad Limit and taking the movement as development of the thought of the Finite, is a mere question of how best to employ the associations conveyed by these terms in current usage.

6·4. The movement of this triad begins to manifest itself phenomenally when the reflective analysis of any finite thing yields a diversity of empirical characters, each of which links it to a context of other things by relations which determine its nature as it determines theirs; or again when empirical diversity is experienced as the changing phases of a finite thing.[1] In the recognition that this analysis is inexhaustible we reach the Spurious Infinite. As against the True Infinite,

[1] Hegel does not explicitly distinguish. The two analyses are hardly separable, but the former is logically prior to the latter.

The reader must here remember that 'thing', 'character', 'relation' are phrases inevitably proleptic. The *Etwas* is only a *quale* one with its quality, but one cannot explain the thought embodied in sense without recourse to the terminology of the Understanding.

which is the self-determining,[1] the Spurious Infinite is the mere endless determination *ab extra* in which results the effort to explain any finite in finite terms, the effort to interpret without sublating. Kant's phenomenal world bears this character, though only as a moment sublated in categories of Essence, in particular in the category of Cause and Effect. The 'terms' of Hegel's Spurious Infinite, on the other hand, are not necessarily, as opposed to accidentally, connected.

6·5. The Spurious Infinite is of course a phase of spirit's movement. Hence it dimly prefigures an individually centred activity, the activity of a subject. Consequently its 'terms' are not absolutely indifferent to one another, as if they were, so to say, the result of a pre-established disharmony falling simply outside spirit.[2] But they constitute not so much an order as a centrifugal dispersion. The Spurious Infinite is no more than a low qualitative analogue of quantitative plurality. There is before us, on Hegel's view, the thought underlying, or 'animating', the 'this and that and that . . .' of sense-perception, a multiplicity or miscellany such that it is a matter of indifference what succession of terms we select as 'that and that and that . . .', and even such that any term indifferently may be selected as the initial 'this'.

7. The True, or Affirmative, Infinite

This is the synthesis of Somewhat with Limit, i.e. with the endless 'othering' of Somewhat which endlessly reinstates it. In the thesis Somewhat rested stably poised and merely *an sich*. In the negating antithesis it was the Finite turning endlessly into an Other. But just because Somewhat is, contradictorily, reinstated in its Other—just because the endless Others are the Somewhat's very self—therefore Somewhat and itself-as-endless-othering synthesize in the True Infinite. The true Infinite is the inevitable self-completion of Somewhat.

[1] See following section.

[2] This is, indeed, always to be remembered in respect of any category which is a multiplicity recalling the Spurious Infinite; e.g. Repulsion, for which see § 9·1 below.

7·1. It is of paramount importance to observe that Hegel's True Infinite is neither a final term in the indefinite regress, nor again the opposite of the Finite, but the synthesis of the Finite with the spurious infinity of its own self-othering; i.e. with its own endlessly unachieved effort to complete itself in another *finite* term of the multiplicity. If the True Infinite were either a final term or the opposite of the Finite, then Finite and True Infinite would be merely particular elements juxtaposed within a universe which was not one active spirit; they would limit one another, and the Infinite would *eo ipso* itself become finite. The True Infinite is the truth of the Finite, sublating it and not juxtaposed to it. It is again vital to remember that less than the triad is not rationally intelligible. To take the Finite or the Spurious Infinite by themselves—or even to take them together but apart from the True Infinite—as genuine characterizations of reality, is the mere futile effort of the Understanding to philosophize without self-transcendence. The *minimum rationale* here is the total movement of active spirit putting forth itself (Somewhat) as endlessly self-othering Finite, and sublating these phases of itself in the self-union of the True Infinite. And—to repeat—in sense-perception this activity of spirit is manifest as movement from (i) the object-world as mere 'this-for-me' prior to any 'that', to (ii) the endlessly regressive perception of 'this and that and that . . .' and to (iii) an awareness of totality as immanent in but also transcending, and so neither a final term nor the unreachable 'sum' of, this endless qualitative regress.

7·2. The True Infinite is called by Hegel the fundamental notion (*Grundbegriff*) of philosophy, and the reader may be surprised to find it included among the categories of Being, and even placed before the categories of Quantity. But Quantity is to Hegel the significant negation of Quality, and if we bear in mind that every synthesis of the Logic from Becoming onwards displays nothing but the activity of spirit, we shall find nothing strange in the early emergence of the Infinite.

In an important passage Hegel points out that the True Infinite is not a static unity of Finite with Spurious Infinite, but 'essentially is only as Becoming, but Becoming now further characterized in its moments. Its characterizations are at first Being and Nothing; as Alterability its moments are determinates (*Daseiende*), Something and Other; as Infinite it has Finite and Infinite [sc. Spurious Infinite], which are themselves Becoming (*Werdende*).'[1] Hegel is here attacking any dualist philosophy which severs the finite from an infinite which is held to be an unknowable, or a mere 'ought-to-be', an unattainable ideal of will. In particular he remarks that the ethic of Kant and Fichte never gets beyond this dualism.[2] And Hegel is attacking this dualism at its not always quite obvious empiricist foundation, endeavouring to show that even the most rudimentary sense-perception has nothing to reveal but the activity of spirit dimly prefigured.

Throughout the rest of the Logic, even in the categories of the Idea, Hegel often uses the term 'finite' in a general sense to describe the incompleteness of an antithetical category.

8. Being-for-self

The general character of Being-for-self is the explicit self-relation which is reached in the True Infinite. Spirit is now the explicit negation of its negative, other self, and is therefore *for* itself. It has, that is, some measure of self-possession as against the impotent, unstable self-othering and self-reinstating of *Dasein*; although this self-relation, or self-possession, is still immediate as all the categories of Being are immediate.

In EL, § 96, *Zusatz* the 'I' is given as the readiest instance of Being-for-self. Although we know ourselves as *Daseiende* distinct from, but also related to, other *Daseiende*, yet we also know this whole expanse (*Breite*) of *Dasein*, 'contracted to a point, as it were, in the simple form of Being-for-self. When we say "I", we express the relation to self which is infinite and at the same time negative.'

Hegel illustrates from self-consciousness because the self-conscious subject is 'for itself'. Self-consciousness in its bare minimal nature is a movement of the mind from itself to an Other which is yet itself, a movement which may therefore be called a return upon itself. The Other to which mind

[1] LL, i, p. 173. [2] Cf. EL, § 94, *Zusatz*.

moves, finding itself therein, is thus not the next 'term' of a spurious infinite. It includes all the 'multiplicity' of that lower level, and it is that whole sublated content, that whole 'expanse', which the self-conscious subject takes as at once its Other and itself. The self-conscious subject, that is, recognizes as the *prius* of all its experience a rudimentarily universal self which constitutes it one with other selves as well as distinct from them. It is, says Hegel, this knowing of himself as 'I' which distinguishes man from the brutes and from Nature generally. Natural things have no free Being-for-self, always and only Being-for-other.[1] Being-for-self is illustrated from human self-consciousness more properly than is Somewhat. 'Das Negative des Negativen', says Hegel, 'ist als Etwas nur der Anfang des Subjects.'[2]

8·1. 'In Being-for-self', Hegel remarks, 'enters the category of Ideality.'[3] He has previously applied the contrasting term 'Reality' to *Dasein*. I have hitherto ignored this use of the word 'real' in Hegel, because in the language of British idealism, which I have so far largely retained, 'real' and 'reality' have a much fuller significance.[4] By 'real' in this context Hegel means that which is not explicitly self-transcendent. 'The notion of ideality', he says, 'consists expressly in its being the truth of reality; i.e. when reality is explicitly posited as what it implicitly is, it is seen to be ideality.'[5] The True Infinite, which is Being-for-self, is the ideality of the Finite, and 'this ideality of the Finite is the chief maxim of philosophy; and for that reason every genuine philosophy is idealism'.[1] Thus the 'real' to which the 'ideal' is here opposed is the *merely* actual,[6] and what Hegel wishes to emphasize is that in this opposition the 'ideal' is not a mere fanciful ideal contrasted with 'hard fact', nor a mere

[1] Cf. IH, ch. viii, § 4·3. Hegel is illustrating Being-for-self from the minimal nature of self-consciousness, but he does not mean that this consciousness of oneself among other selves is something apart from one's consciousness of natural things which are not selves. Recognition of oneself as subject among other subjects necessarily involves recognition of a community of content in the experience of oneself and other subjects. For Hegel's account of self-consciousness see ΦG, §§ 424–37, and p. 5 footnote 1, above.

[2] LL, i, p. 130.

[3] EL, § 95.

[4] See, however, IH, ch. xi, § 5·01.

[5] EL, § 96, *Zusatz*.

[6] Not actual in the sense of *wirklich*; see ch. vi, § 1·3 and ch. viii below.

'ought-to-be' which cannot, alas, be realized—as, if we mistake the Spurious for the True Infinite, we must hold it to be—but the true nature of the Finite in contrast with its *merely* real or actual nature.

8·2. To translate this into the phraseology of idealism such as Bradley's would require a change-round of terms. Ideality, we should have to say, is Reality *qua* the Reality of its Appearance. But that would be to give to Ideality a sense in which Bradley does not commonly use it. Bradley's doctrine of judgement as the expansion of the immediately given in ideal content derives no doubt from Hegel's conception of *Idealität*, but to Bradley the end of truth is to be and to possess Reality in an ideal form. But to Bradley truth is the whole universe realizing itself in one aspect *only*, and Reality to him is more than truth[1]; whereas to Hegel truth is the supreme, all-sublating, form of the universe. Hence, while Bradley is sometimes not quite certain that he desires the title of idealist, Hegel proclaims all true philosophy to be idealism, and might well have retorted upon Bradley that just because his idealism is still subjective and not the whole of his philosophy, by a dialectical nemesis Bradley's more than ideal Absolute turns out to be after all a *mere* ideal.

8·3. Having asserted idealism to be the chief maxim of philosophy, Hegel adds that the next point to consider in respect of any particular philosophy is how far this principle is carried out.[2]

This distinction between implicit and explicit idealism removes an apparent contradiction in Hegel's statements which may puzzle the unwary reader. In saying that all genuine philosophy is idealist, he means *implicitly* idealist. If there be any two thinkers from whom Hegel learnt not to take the finite at its face value, they are Plato and Spinoza. Yet he can find fault with Plato's *Republic* for not being ideal enough, and he links the Substance of Spinoza with the Eleatic Being, saying that Spinoza's Substance is 'only the abstract negation of all determination; no ideality is posited in the negation itself'.[3] With Spinoza 'Infinity is only the absolute affirmation of a thing, and thus immobile oneness;

[1] Cf. IH, ch. xiii, § 4·5.
[2] LL, i, pp. 181 and 188.
[3] Ibid., p. 188.

Substance thus does not even reach the determination of Being-for-self, much less that of Subject or Spirit.'[1] To Leibniz, on the other hand, Hegel attributes the merely abstract notion of idealism, because the self-related (and therefore essentially ideal) activity of the monads depends upon the harmonizing activity of the *Monas monadum*, which remains external to them.[2]

9. *The Subcategories of* BEING-FOR-SELF[3]

Being-for-self is completed Quality, and the difficulty of comprehending its dialectic lies in the fact that we are on the very verge of Quantity. We are approaching a transition which is not, Hegel remarks, found in our ordinary consciousness; for that takes Quality and Quantity as a pair of categories each existing independently beside the other, and asks no further question as to their derivation and mutual relation.[4]

The thesis of Being-for-self is

The One

In considering the One it is vital to remember (1) that we are not yet in Quantity; (2) that the One is, therefore, not one among many: its being as One is no more, or scarcely more, the singularity conferred by membership of a plurality than is the being of Somewhat as thesis of *Dasein*.[5] It is One *qua* immediately self-related, or self-possessing; it is the immediate qualitative negation of negation. This infinite self-relation of spirit as the One of Quality is, however, a phase of activity. Spirit as the qualitative One must put itself forth as new self-determination. It cannot do so by any qualitative self-othering—that would be merely the self-othering of finite Somewhat over again. The One is infinite, and therefore not such as to lose its nature in self-othering. Hence its other self must be utterly external and indifferent to it, a self which it repels as not sharing qualitative character with it, since Quality is already completed in the One. We are thus on the verge of quantitative distinction which is indifferent to

[1] Ibid., p. 188.
[2] Ibid., pp. 189–90.
[3] I follow here the simplified dialectic of EL.
[4] Cf. EL, § 89, *Zusatz* (2).
[5] Cf. § 4·2 above.

quality, and we have reached the antithesis of the One, namely,

9·1. The Many, *or* Repulsion

The One repels itself, putting itself forth as endless multiplicity of Ones. This 'multiplicity' is more than the Spurious Infinite, but not yet Quantity. Indeed quantitative multiplicity, or plurality, is not even the first and simplest category of Quantity. Multiplicity in any sense of the term presupposes and develops dialectically out of unity in the corresponding sense,[1] as was foreshadowed in the dialectic of *Dasein*.

But the multiple Ones, though entirely external to and other than one another, are just as much entirely the same with one another. 'Consideration of Repulsion shows that as a negative attitude of many Ones to one another, it is just as much a relation of them to each other.'[2] Hence the One and the Many, in and through which the One puts itself forth as endlessly self-repellent, synthesize in what Hegel calls

9·2. Repulsion and Attraction[3]

In this synthesis of a still just qualitative One and Many we have at length reached the most simple and abstract self-expression of spirit as Quantity, of that determinateness, that is, which distinguishes without affecting the qualitative nature of the distincts.

[1] Cf. EL, § 97, *Zusatz*, an important passage. [2] EL, § 98.

[3] Repulsion and Attraction are terms borrowed from physics and used figuratively.

III

BEING: QUANTITY

1. The general nature of spirit as Quantity has already been indicated in the discussion of Qualitative Limit.[1]

'Quantity', says Hegel, 'is pure Being where the determinateness is no longer taken as one with the being itself, but explicitly posited as sublated or indifferent.'[2] He means, I think, that the sublation of Quality in Quantity is that phase of the dialectic in which sublation approaches most nearly to sheer cancellation without preservation. But our immediate concern is rather with the (minimal) moment of preservation. The three main divisions of Quantity given in EL are Pure Quantity, Quantum, and Degree, and these recall respectively Being, *Dasein*, and Being-for-self. It is natural in illustrating from empirical experience to speak of quantity as an abstraction from quality—as, for example, when we measure water, wine, and whisky with a common pint measure external and indifferent to their qualitative characters. But such an illustration misses something essential in the self-development of spirit as Quantity. Quantity is external to Quality only because it is *self*-externality, externality of spirit to itself. Quantity is best illustrated in space. To be spatial is to be constituted of homogeneous *partes extra partes*. Space is the opening thesis of Hegel's *Philosophy of Nature*, and this self-externality is distinctive of Nature as such.[3] Thus in the antithesis phase of Quantity the self-negation, or self-othering, of spirit will always be a self-repulsion. The sharp precision of quantitative distinction supersedes the impotent self-othering of Somewhat. Nevertheless this self-externalizing, self-repelling movement presupposes in Quantity the preservation of Quality as well as its cancellation. Quantity has a positive moment which is the further development of infinite Being-for-self. Accordingly the dialectic of Quantity will throughout reproduce that of Quality in a developed form.

[1] And in IH, ch. xi, § 4·1.

[2] EL, § 99.

[3] Cf. IH, ch. viii, §§ 4·2 ff.

1·1. It may be remarked that there is a special difficulty in the relation of the categories of Quantity to their illustration (*a*) in empirical experience, and (*b*) in mathematics. It is not so hard to distinguish the thought of Quality from red, sour, or malodorous things, but it is hard to distinguish the thought of Quantity from its sensuous embodiment. In trying to do so we find ourselves first imagining spatial figures without sensible qualities (differentiations of a Kantian pure manifold of spatial intuition), and then these geometrical entities stripped of extension and reduced to mere numerical units. But the question at once arises whether we are really here imagining or thinking. The puzzling midway position of the objects of mathematics soon struck the Greeks. Aristotle attributes to Plato the doctrine that the 'mathematicals' are multiple like sensible things, but invisible and eternal like intelligible entities (the Forms), and Plato does at any rate distinguish between Number-Forms and the *μοναδικὸς ἄριθμος* which the arithmetician manipulates. However the *mathematical* thought of quantity is to be distinguished from its embodiment in sensible things—whatever, that is, the objects of mathematics are—it must be borne in mind that the objects of mathematical thinking are themselves merely illustrations of Hegel's categories of Quantity. For in Hegel's view, as in Kant's, geometry assumes space as a constitutive principle, and arithmetic at any rate presupposes time.[1]

[1] In his youthful dissertation, *De Orbitis Planetarum*, Hegel sees the relation of time to arithmetic as precisely analogous to the relation of space to geometry: 'Matheseos parte geometrica a tempore, arithmetica autem a spatio abstrahente, illa totam geometricam solius spatii, hac totam arithmeticam solius temporis principio constituente . . .'; JE, i, p. 4. But he realized later that the connexion of time with arithmetic is not so simple as that: 'Geometry is the science of space, but there is no corresponding science of time. Temporal distinctions lack that indifference of self-externality in which the immediate determinateness of space consists. Hence they do not admit of configuration, as space does. The time principle only admits configuration through paralysis; i.e. when its negativity is reduced by the Understanding to the One. This dead One, the supreme externality of thought, admits of external combination, and the combinations thus formed, the "figures" of arithmetic, admit a further determination by the Understanding: they can be identified and differentiated in terms of equality and inequality.' NΦ, § 259; JE, ix, pp. 83–4.

2. The positive and negative moments of Quantity are respectively continuity and discreteness. The continuous and the discrete constitute, as it were, a twin thread running through Quantity. Spirit now 'discerns' and now reasserts its own continuity with a movement already prefigured in the triads of Quality as these ascend from Pure Being, Nothing, and Becoming to the One, Repulsion, and Attraction of Being-for-self. Hegel in fact even speaks of the distinction between the continuous and the discrete as qualitative: the continuous is the qualitative moment preserved in Quantity, without which Quantity would not be the express cancelling of Quality, and thereby self-externality. It is, Hegel thinks, ignoration of the precise mode in which Quantity sublates Quality which creates all the difficulty in the philosophical theory of mathematics and some of the difficulties in mathematics itself.

The Subcategories of PURE QUANTITY

3. The very curt account of Quantity in EL requires expansion from LL, but the subcategories of Pure Quantity which I give are, I think, those implied in EL.

The thesis of Pure Quantity is once again labelled

Pure Quantity

Here the continuous and the discrete are not explicitly distinct, but Pure Quantity is rather to be called continuity than discreteness, just as the thesis of *Dasein* was called Somewhat even prior to the opposition of Somewhat and Other in Limit,[1] and as the One preceded the Many of Repulsion.[2] For Pure Quantity is the first emergence of Quantity from Being-for-self as Attraction.

The antithesis is

3·1. Continuous and Discrete Magnitude

Here the opposition becomes explicit, but the title is nevertheless misleading. Quantity is here not yet Quantum, because it is not yet limited. Quantity will exhibit Limit when continuity and discreteness synthesize, but we have so far only reached the antithesis which precedes that synthesis.

[1] Cf. ch. i, § 4·2 above. [2] Cf. ibid., § 9.

Hegel asserts emphatically that there are not two species of magnitude, continuous magnitude and discrete magnitude. The clue to his whole conception of Quantity is that continuity and discreteness are inseparable. Quantity in all its phases is continuous only because it is also discrete: its continuity is that which runs through and unites *discreta*. Again, it is discrete only because it is also continuous: its discreteness consists solely in the discerning of the continuum. If, Hegel implies, it be said that arithmetic deals with discrete quantity, and geometry with continuous quantity, this specific distinction is to be taken as no more than the external specification which mathematics, like the natural sciences, is bound to use because it is an operation of the reflective Understanding. And even in mathematics this abstract separation is largely overridden. Geometry (sc. synthetic geometry) does not measure; it compares. But there is no definite spatial magnitude without number, and once space is developed beyond a mere geometrical point, it is discrete as well as continuous: it is of the essence of a line to be divisible at points. Again, numerical magnitude does not lack the moment of continuity. If it did, units would not constitute a sum, and there would be no order of integers.

3·11. In Hegel's view Aristotle showed his grasp of this truth when he solved Zeno's puzzles with his conception of a line as *potentially* divisible *ad indefinitum*.[1] Aristotle, that is to say, recognized that discreteness in the form of divisibility at points is, in Hegel's terminology, an essential moment of line but not its whole concrete nature. This moment by itself is abstract, and the other constitutive moment of line is its continuity. In the actual concrete line the two moments are inseparably synthesized, and only as this triad is the nature of line intelligible.

A careful reading of *Physics* VI, in which Aristotle discusses Zeno's paradoxes, undoubtedly confirms Hegel's interpretation of him. In Aristotelian terminology line is a πεπερασμένον, a concrete (συνόλον) of form (which is here πέρας, limit) with matter (which is here τὸ ἄπειρον, mere continuity).[2] It is worthy of note that the most recent editor of the *Physics* is dissatisfied with the solutions of Zeno's problems offered

[1] See LL, i, pp. 237–8.

[2] See § 5·62 below.

by modern mathematicians, but has no philosophical solution to offer on the basis of his own realist position.[1]

3·12. Hegel also acutely criticizes Kant's Antinomies on the same lines.[2] In the first place, he says, the completeness of the four cosmological Antinomies is illusory—merely borrowed from the Kantian scheme of categories.[3] 'A deeper insight', he continues, 'into the antinomous or, more truly, dialectical nature of Reason shows every Notion[4] without qualification (*überhaupt*) as a unity of opposed moments, which can therefore be offered as antinomous assertions.'[5]

Hegel is here making the general criticism that Kant, despite his immortal discovery of *a priori* synthesis, failed to make good its implications, and confined cognitive thought to the categories of the Understanding, which, as we shall later see more clearly, express antithesis never truly sublated in synthesis. Kant recognizes that Reason cannot avoid these antinomies, but he misconceives the dialectical character of Reason. He sees in its activity a mere subjective oscillation between contradictories which cannot be resolved, and draws the moral that Reason must not try to soar into the unsupporting void above sense-perception, but take the phenomenal world as it is. 'The true solution can only be this: that the two determinations (*Bestimmungen*), being contradictory and yet necessary to the same Notion, cannot be valid each for itself in its own one-sidedness, but that they have their truth only in their sublatedness, that is, in the unity of their Notion.'[6]

3·13. Hegel then applies this criticism to Kant's Second Antinomy.[7] The dilemma, he says, depends solely upon the dogmatic assumption of sheer discreteness in the proof of the thesis ('Every composite consists of simple parts'), and of sheer continuity in the proof of the antithesis ('No composite thing consists of simple parts'). Once this is seen, the cumbrous apogogic arguments in parallel columns turn out to be

[1] See Sir D. Ross, *Aristotle's Physics*, pp. 75–85.

[2] See LL, i, pp. 227 ff.

[3] i.e. from Kant's schematized categories. Hegel's point (see the following section) is that Kant's introduction of space, time, and matter obscures a purely logical problem.

[4] 'Notion' means here any category which is a synthesis.

[5] LL, i, p. 227. [6] Ibid., p. 228. [7] Ibid., pp. 228 ff.

mere tautologies. If discreteness alone is essential to substance, then continuity is not essential to substance, and vice versa. But 'substance' here means no more than 'sensuous material thing'. It plays no operative part in the antinomy, and Kant might just as well have substituted 'space' or 'time'. All it does is to conceal Kant's fallacious severance of the two moments which are inseparable in the *Denkbestimmung* of Quantity, by reducing the whole matter in dispute to the level of *Vorstellung*. Thus Kant's proof of the antithesis might be fairly summarized as follows: 'Our whole sensuous experience shows us only what is composite; the best microscopes and the keenest knives have never yet allowed us to hit upon anything simple.' Moreover, Hegel points out, Kant in this proof states that everything real occupying a space contains a manifold of mutually external parts, and is therefore composite. Yet in the Transcendental Aesthetic Kant had shown his grasp of the truth that the continuity of space is not compositeness. Space, he had said, is one, and its parts are limitations of it, not antecedent elements of which it is composed.

3·131. We might perhaps sum up Hegel's general criticism of Kant in this passage as the contention that contradiction exists in thought, and that we can properly call phenomenal objects 'contradictory' only with reference to the thought which they manifest. When Hegel strips Kant's Antinomies of space, time, and matter, and points to the logical category of Quantity as the essence of the contradiction, it might perhaps be objected that in Hegel's *Philosophy of Nature* Space, Time, and Matter appear as stages in the dialectic. Hegel's reply would presumably be (*a*) that they are quite irrelevant to Kant's Antinomies, since Kant is there professing to speak as a logician, and (*b*) that in his own *Philosophy of Nature* they appear as forms of Nature, not as sensuous *Vorstellungen*.[1]

3·2. In Continuous and Discrete Magnitude, as against Pure Quantity, the emphasis is on Discreteness. But Discreteness can only be emphasized by discerning a continuity

[1] I do not, however, wish to suggest that Hegel solves the problem of the phenomenal manifestation of the categories in Nature with complete success; cf. IH, ch. ix, § 6·3.

from a continuity beyond it, and the synthesis of Continuous and Discrete Magnitude may therefore be called

Limitation of Quantity;

for the notion of Quantitative limit is precisely the discerning of the Continuous.

4. Quantum

With the notion of Quantitative Limit Pure Quantity becomes Magnitude in the true sense, viz. Quantum.

The subcategories of Quantum[1] are Quantum, *Einheit* and *Anzahl*, and Number. Quantum—'Limited Quantity' or 'Quantitative Limit': it does not matter which we call it—exhibits in antithesis the opposed moments of continuity and discreteness further developed. *Einheit* is the German both for unity and unit, and is not here perfectly easy to translate. Hegel appears to mean by it 'the general determinable character of being constituted by units'. It is the moment of continuity analogous to the finite Being-in-self within Alterability.[2] For 'Quantum is the *Dasein* of Quantity',[3] and the phases of quantitative limit are therefore closely analogous to those of Qualitative Limit. The corresponding moment of discreteness, the determinant, is *Anzahl*, 'Sum' or 'Amount', or, as Wallace effectively translates it, 'Annumeration'. The synthesis of *Einheit* with *Anzahl* is Number, the number illustrated in arithmetical number. It is thus the first analogue in Quantity of the qualitative Spurious Infinite.[4] A fuller analogue is to be found in Degree.[5]

4·1. Hegel is emphatic that the only rational, or notional, moments which operate in arithmetic are *Einheit* and *Anzahl*.[6] These are the qualitative moments, and the only logical moments, upon the sublation of which the self-externality of Quantum depends.[7] Only to that extent does arithmetic embody the logical category. The diversity of arithmetical

[1] I follow EL, expanding its curt exposition from LL where necessary.

[2] Cf. ch. ii, § 6·1.

[3] EL, § 101, *Zusatz*.

[4] See ibid., § 104.

[5] See §§ 5·1 ff. below.

[6] On this section see LL, i, pp. 246 ff. 'Notional' here means only 'logical', or 'categoreal'.

[7] Perhaps they might be called '*quasi*-qualitative' moments; see § 2 above.

numbers as quanta derives from another source: it consists in equality and inequality, the external identity and difference which belongs to the reflective comparison of the Understanding. But this diversity is not a logical determination of Number.

Hegel might seem to be excluding this external diversity in arithmetical numbers and geometrical figures[1] on the ground that Diversity is a category of Essence.[2] But he is not. He holds quite definitely that the necessity in mathematical thinking does not express the operation of any categories beyond those of Quantity.[3] The categories of Essence all express an active mediation of Being, but the relations between arithmetical numbers and between geometrical figures are purely quantitative, and have the general immediacy of the categories of Being. In mathematics the moment of contingency appears only as the incommensurability symptomatic of the return of Quality within Quantity, and there is a strictness in mathematical reasoning to which natural science can never attain. But this necessity in mathematical connexion is only a little developed beyond immediacy: the distinction between essential and accidental has not yet arisen. Mathematical thinking barely rises above intuition to discursion. That is why some mathematical propositions sometimes seem to possess isolated self-evidence and sometimes to be tautologous. Hence the equality and inequality of numbers and figures is purely quantitative 'identity and difference', and is not a category of Essence.

4·2. So arithmetical operations produce numbers quite contingently. In counting we colligate units external to one another, which are inevitably imagined under a sense image. We can only *point* to an instance of four or five, and where we break off from counting is quite arbitrary, not, that is, dictated by anything in the nature of Number. We do not, Hegel means, in counting approach any whole which determines its elements to special difference. Each added unit is precisely identical with, and precisely different from, the last; for that just is the self-externality in which Quantity consists. In addition proper—strictly the first species of

[1] See § 3·1 above. [2] See ch. vi, § 5·2 below.

[3] See ch. xvii, § 3·3 below.

arithmetical operation—we go on to number these arbitrarily produced numbers. The relative magnitude, the equality or inequality, of the numbers added is contingent, and Kant was quite wrong in regarding '$7+5 = 12$' as a synthetic proposition. It is a 'notionless[1] connexion' (*begrifflose Verbindung*), and only synthesis in the literal sense of mere aggregation. The corresponding negative process of subtraction does not differ in principle from addition.

4·3. Multiplication and division, between which again there is no difference in principle, constitute the second species of arithmetical operation. In multiplication we add a sum of units, each of which is already a sum. The numbers here numbered are equal not as numbers but inasmuch as either indifferently can be taken as *Einheit* or *Anzahl*: 4 (*Anzahl*) times 3 (*Einheit*) is the same as 3 times 4. Similarly in division, if the problem is put as the question how many times (*Anzahl*) a given number (*Einheit*) is contained in another number, then the divisor is *Einheit*, the quotient *Anzahl*. But if we are asked to divide a number into equal parts and to state the magnitude of the part, then the divisor is taken as *Anzahl* and the quotient as *Einheit*.

4·4. In the third species, involution, the numbers related as *Einheit* and *Anzahl* are still *qua* numbers contingently related in respect of equality and inequality—*überhaupt ungleich*, Hegel calls them. But *qua Einheit* and *Anzahl* they are now expressly equal, at any rate in the square and the square root. In fact a squared number is genuinely self-related, and when it is raised to a higher power than the square the continuation is merely formal. With the odd powers it brings a recurrence of inequality, but this is not a notional differentiation, and that is the reason why higher equations have to be solved by reduction to quadratic equations, just as in geometry the other figures require reduction to the right-angled triangle for their complete determination.

These three species of arithmetical calculation do not represent any fresh development of the Notion; they merely follow from the notional moments, *Einheit* and *Anzahl*. They have not been philosophically deduced. They can even be

[1] = non-logical, or non-categoreal.

embodied in a calculating machine, and calculating is not thinking.

5. With the equality of *Einheit* and *Anzahl* the nature of Quantum is complete, and we pass to the main antithesis of Quantity which, in the terminology of EL, is

Degree

The subcategories of Degree may be taken as Degree (or Intensive Magnitude), Quantitative Infinite Progression, and Quantitative Ratio.

The dialectic of EL is obscure here from its terseness, that of LL from its extreme elaboration. Though on Hegel's view the categories of Quantity operate in mathematics but are only to a slight extent criticized in mathematics, yet to follow the detail of the exposition in LL requires more mathematical knowledge than I possess. I can offer only a compromise between the two expositions, hoping that its faults may be those of omission rather than of distortion.

5·1. The transition from Number to Degree as small-scale thesis—that is, to the merely general, *an sich*, nature of Degree—appears to be as follows. (A) The units of Number are utterly external to one another, but (B) Number *qua* Limit is *Anzahl* ('Annumeration' or perhaps 'Annumeratedness'), and therefore the mutual externality of the units is solely relevant to, is nothing but the complementary moment of, their *Anzahl*; it does not depend on anything outside this. Accordingly Limit (which in Number is *Anzahl*) is called by Hegel 'identical with the whole Quantum'.[1] To put this in other words: Number as such, the whole Quantum, that is, as synthesis of *Einheit* and *Anzahl*, is *extensive* Quantum. For (A) its units lie outside one another; and (B) they only do so because Number is the synthesis of *Einheit* and *Anzahl*. Thus (A) the limiting unit of 10, in which the moment of *Anzahl*, or Annumeration, is expressed, is related externally to the other nine units; but (B) this externality depends entirely on the fact that the tenth unit of 10 does express the moment of *Anzahl*. Number, therefore, is extensive Quantum.

5·11. But this thought of Number as *Anzahl* discerning

[1] EL, § 103.

continuous *Einheit* has emerged as the final stage of Quantum, which is antithesis to Pure Quantity. It was an emphasis on discreteness opposing the undifferentiated continuity of Pure Quantity. The synthesis of this opposition comes when—to speak as if we were spectators of the movement—we see that the mutual externality of units, though essential to the notion of Number, equally betokens their identity. *Einheit* was after all the moment, though a latent moment, of continuity in Number. Hence the limiting term of Quantum must after all contain the other terms within itself and cannot remain external to them. But such a limiting term is no longer mere Number, for it no longer expresses mere *Anzahl* in relation to *Einheit* of mutually external units. It is in fact *intensive* Quantum, or Degree. In Number, Limit *qua Anzahl* of units is multiple (*vielfach*) in itself, for the summed units are mutually external. But Limit *qua* Degree is in itself simple (*einfach*); for the tenth degree, unlike the tenth unit, sums up *within itself* ten degrees. For example, the intensity of heat signified by 100° Centigrade is not a mere numerical sum of 100 units of heat; the 100 degrees are terms which have, as it were, collapsed together in simple immediacy in the hundredth term.

'Degree', says Hegel, 'is determinate Magnitude, or Quantum, but it is not also a multitude (*Menge*) or a "more and more" (*Mehreres*) within itself [sc. as Number is]; it is only a "moreness" (*Mehrheit*). And the "moreness" is the "more and more" taken together in simple determinateness—*Dasein* returned into Being-for-self.'[1]

5·2. *Degree in antithesis:* Quantitative Infinite Progression

When Quantum passes from Number to Degree, the units cease to be mutually external; they coalesce in the limiting unit, which thereby becomes a degree and not a mere unit. But Quantity as such is self-external. The self-externality of Number was the mutual externality of its units, and so was contained solely within Number itself.[2] But as soon as the mutually external terms coalesce, we see that Degree is relation of Degree to further degrees beyond it.

[1] LL, i, p. 264.
[2] *Qua Anzahl*; see § 5·1 above.

The self-externality of Degree lies not within it, as does that of Number, but without it. Degree implies, and now becomes explicit as, infinite progress, or regress, of degrees. Thus 'the ascent or descent in a scale of degrees becomes a steady progress, a flow of uninterrupted, indivisible altering (*Veränderung*)'.[1]

It must, of course, be remembered that Degree here is not degree of a sensible *quale*, but the pure thought which such a *quale* 'illustrates'. Hence Hegel can regard Degree in antithesis as the Spurious Infinite in the sphere of Quantity. He seems to hold that it is the category involved in all non-convergent mathematical series.

5·3. Hegel takes occasion in this context to remark that though Degree is Intensive Quantum, yet it does not thereby lose the character of being Extensive Quantum as well. Neither is reducible to the other, but they are no more two different species than are discrete and continuous magnitude. They do not exist separate in the phenomenal world, nor do they there, as has sometimes been supposed, vary in inverse proportion. A given degree of temperature, for example, has a perfectly simple sensation corresponding to it, i.e. a sensation which is not a sum of units of sensation. But it has also corresponding to it a certain expansion of mercury in the tube of the thermometer; and that is an extensive magnitude which varies directly with it. It is the same in the world of Concrete Spirit: a more intensive character has a wider range in its effects than a less intensive.[2] When in EL, § 80, *Zusatz* Hegel approves Goethe's saying that the man who would do something great must learn to limit himself, he adds that the man who would do everything really would do nothing, and fails. He means, I think, that self-limitation does not necessarily entail narrowness, because the alternative to it is a futile indeterminateness. Only by self-limitation can a man develop his whole capacity, and the fact that he does so shows that the apparently rejected alternative lines of self-development were not real possibilities.[3]

[1] LL, i, p. 265.

[2] Cf. EL, § 103 and *Zusatz*.

[3] Cf. ch. viii, § 7 below.

5·4. *Degree in synthesis:* Quantitative Ratio

Degree and the Infinite Progression of degrees synthesize when we observe that the degrees are after all linked by identity. The dialectical movement is here analogous to the self-othering of the finite Somewhat, the endless reinstating of Somewhat in its Other, and the synthesis of Somewhat with the Spurious Infinite in the True Infinity of Quality. In Quantitative Ratio Quantum is related only to itself; it is infinite in the true sense, a self-determining negation of negation.

5·5. Hegel's explanation is worth following in some detail, for it contains his philosophical theory of the true mathematical infinite, the clue to which he finds in ratio. A ratio gives the relation of two quanta as a third single quantum. It thus expresses the negative moment, the distinctness of the quantum from its other, which is already given in the Infinite Progression. But it also expresses their identity. For example, $\frac{10}{5} = 2$. Here 10 and 5 as such are quanta external to one another; but in 2, the exponent of the ratio, they are linked, and the negation is negated. Thus Quantum as the exponent of a ratio is self-related; for the related quanta can vary indefinitely (20 and 10, 30 and 15, &c.), but the exponent remains constant. On the left-hand side of the equation the two quanta are still pure quanta, but the exponent is in infinite self-relation.

This is to say—and it is the vital point to grasp—that a ratio is a qualitative and not purely quantitative relation between quanta. Quality was negated by Quantity, and the characteristic of being at once self-external and external to Quality is the differentia of Quantity. But spirit in developing itself through the phases of Quantity is again *qualifying* itself.[1] This re-emergence of Quality will only become explicit in Measure, but it has necessarily begun with the beginning of dialectical movement in Quantity. In Quantum as Ratio it becomes important, and, Hegel believes, to the mathematician who cares to think at all what he is doing, disturbing.

5·6. We can now see how the convergent infinite series of

[1] See EL, § 106, *Zusatz*.

mathematics occur, and what is the thought which they embody. If we substitute for $\frac{10}{5}$ a fraction the exponent of which is not an integer, the only further expression which we can give to this fraction is that of an infinite series. For example,

$$\frac{2}{7} = 0{\cdot}285714\ldots, \quad \text{or} \quad \frac{1}{1-a} = 1+a+a^2+a^3+\ldots$$

The fraction is then commonly called the finite expression of the infinite series. But the fraction is here a far truer expression of True Infinity than the series. The latter in its form expresses only the Spurious Infinite, and is superior to the non-convergent infinite progression only by virtue of signifying the fraction. Its content, however many the terms to which it is extended, is posited as finite; i.e., as something which it ought not to be. It is a self-contradictory effort to represent a qualitative determination of infinite self-relation in terms of mere Quantum.

5·61. Hegel is here criticizing only the mathematician's representation of his own procedure; his habit, for example, of calling 'irrational' what is precisely the hint of Reason which mathematics exhibits. He is not condemning the manipulation of infinite series in mathematics as a futile proceeding. True mathematical infinity presupposes Degree and the Spurious Infinite of Progression: those are the moments which synthesize in the True Infinite of Quantity, and are therefore essential to the thought of it.

Hegel's criticism of Spinoza and Kant makes quite clear that this is his attitude. Spinoza, he says,[1] recognized the difference between spurious and true infinity when he distinguished the *infinitum actu* from the infinite of imagination, although he failed to conceive the *infinitum actu*, the absolute affirmation of the existence of any nature, as negation of negation. Spinoza's substance, that is to say, is not subject, and is therefore not self-mediating; its infinity is not the sublation of self-othering finitude. On the other hand, Kant's conception of the 'true transcendental infinite' does not rise above the spurious infinite: Kant defines infinity as consisting in the fact that the successive synthesis of a unit in measuring a quantum can never be completed.[2]

[1] See LL, i, pp. 306 ff. [2] Ibid., i, p. 298.

5·62. One might add that Aristotle's ἄπειρον—'that, some part of which is always beyond'[1]—is Hegel's Spurious Infinite, whereas his 'finite', τὸ πεπερασμένον, is something whole and τέλειον, containing its τέλος (its end or consummation; in Hegel's terminology its notion) in itself, and is therefore closer akin to Hegel's True Infinite than to Hegel's Finitude. But τὸ πεπερασμένον still falls short of Hegel's True Infinite, because Aristotle still thinks of it as coming short of a 'beyond', though not of a 'beyond' which is a part of itself: he does not, like Hegel, make perfection a function of comprehensiveness. That is why on Hegel's view Aristotle's God remains finite in the sense of limited by the world, and the Aristotelian world, correspondingly, a spurious infinite, an endless cyclical repetition of coming to be and passing away.

5·7. Hegel pursues the expression in mathematics of the True Infinite through the functions of variables, the calculus, and the relations of incommensurables in (synthetic) geometry.[2] For example, a formula such as $y/x = p$ expresses a qualitative self-relation more clearly than does a fraction, and it is obvious that the infinitesimals of the calculus are not pure quanta: in dx/dy the terms signify only as moments of the relation. Quantum from being posited as in a ratio has become itself a ratio.

5·8. *The Subcategories of* Quantitative Ratio

These, only given in LL, are Direct Ratio, Inverse Ratio, Ratio of Powers. They are the dialectical phases which Hegel finds illustrated in the mathematical treatment mentioned in the last section. Any attempt to examine Hegel's interpretation in detail would be equally beyond the scope of this *Study* and the competence of its author. The general character of the movement may be expressed by saying that the exponent of the ratio becomes throughout it more obviously qualitative. In Direct Ratio the exponent does express the self-relation of Quantum, its return from sheer self-externality, but it expresses it only as the fixity of an amount of units: *qua* mere numbers numerator and denominator can vary indefinitely, and their mutual relation

[1] See *Physics* 206^{b}33 ff. [2] See LL, i, pp. 293–389.

within the ratio is not the whole of what they are. In Inverse Ratio the Quantum is in explicit negative relation to itself: the two terms of the relation are still variable, but their mutual relation within the ratio touches more of their nature. In Ratio of Powers the variability of the terms becomes irrelevant, and Quantum is now in full self-relation as negation of negation. For the two terms of the ratio are at once different and, because of this difference, identical: the opposition of *Einheit* and *Anzahl* is reconciled, and the exponent is wholly qualitative.[1]

5·9. How far Hegel's logic of Quantity is affected by modern views which tend to divorce mathematics yet more sharply from space and time, and even to base it on order rather than on quantity, I am incompetent to judge. Hegel seems to imply that, as natural science supplies the raw material for the philosophy of Nature, so mathematics supplies the raw material for the logic of Quantity. If so, advance and change in mathematical conceptions must in principle modify the dialectic of logical categories alleged to be 'illustrated' in mathematics. Yet mathematics on any view of its nature still has closer reference to quantity, and even to space and time, than to more concrete realities, and the prominence of order in modern mathematics does not necessarily quite invalidate, even if it does necessarily modify, Hegel's logic of Quantity. Moreover, although in the logic of Number Hegel does not explicitly treat of the fact that the integers manifest properties which depend on their position in the series, yet he certainly assumes it, and in the logic of Measure he states plainly that the nodal line of degrees which is punctuated by abrupt qualitative changes[2] has been already prefigured in the integer series.[3]

[1] For Hegel's account of the logic of mathematical method see ch. xvii, §§ 3·3 ff. below.
[2] As, for example, in any scale of musical tones.
[3] See ch. iv, § 3·1 below.

IV
BEING: MEASURE

1. 'Quantity is a stage of the Idea, and as such it must have its due, first as a logical category, and then in the world of objects (*in der gegenständlichen Welt*), natural as well as spiritual.'[1] But the category has very different importance at different stages of Nature and Concrete Spirit, a fact which is liable to escape the reflective Understanding. 'If Quantity is not mediated through thought [sc. not grasped dialectically as a phase of spirit sublating Quality and itself destined to sublation], but taken uncritically (*unmittelbar*) from sensuous imagination (*Vorstellung*), we are liable to exaggerate the range of its validity, or even to raise it to the height of being the absolute category.'[1] In Nature Quantity is of great importance, because in Nature the form of spirit is *first* self-negation: spirit is divided from itself. Yet because spirit still abides and persists in its divided, or 'extruded', natural self, that natural self is distinctively characterized by self-externality,[2] and self-externality is precisely Quantity. But in the categories which distinctively characterize Concrete Spirit Quantity, though not merely cancelled, has been again and again sublated. Yet this is easy to forget. In all the spheres of spiritual experience the language of Quantity comes readily to our lips. We call a man's emotions intense, his deeds great, and his thoughts profound. We pluralize these expressions of his unitary nature in language which suggests that they are no more than mutually external classes of mutually external singulars, and we singularize the man himself among other men as if he were no more than one unit of a sum. Sometimes we are aware that we are using the abstract to symbolize the concrete, and sometimes a practical interest limits the context in which we speak, but largely we say such things because we are not very apt to think, but very apt to suppose we do. If only those sciences the objects of which submit to mathematical calculation are allowed the title of 'exact', then, Hegel thinks, our ethical knowledge would be reduced to a mere *Vorstellung*, and all detail in the sphere of conduct would become a matter of individual

[1] EL, § 99, *Zusatz*.

[2] Cf. IH, ch. viii, § 4·2.

caprice. Yet 'it is at once clear that when we speak of God as a Trinity, the number 3 has a far more subordinate significance than when, for example, we consider the three dimensions of space or the three sides of a triangle'.[1] The same is, of course, true when Hegel's dialectic is called 'triadic', or his philosophy 'monistic'.

1·1. The fact that self-externality distinctively characterizes Nature is no excuse for neglecting mathematics; it necessitates the pursuit of mathematical studies.[1] But that is so because self-externality is distinctive of Nature, but not of the highest to which Nature attains; it is not the notion of Nature (*that* is spirit), but the distinctive character of Nature as antithesis to spirit. The phases of Nature manifest from the outset the return of spirit from self-alienation: otherwise spirit could not be said to abide with itself in its other. Hence the category of Quantity itself, as we have seen, resolves into phases wherein Quality is preserved and develops—whatever account mathematicians may give of their procedure—and Quantity does not exhaust the categories manifested in Nature. Nature even manifests categories of the Notion, but the categories most conspicuous in Nature are, after Quantity, those of Measure.

2. The general character of Measure as synthesis of Quality and Quantity has been indicated in IH, ch. xi, § 4·2. Measure at its lowest and most abstract is illustrated, we may say, in the fact that we necessarily experience any sensible thing as having a quality of its own and a quantity of its own, neither of which can alter without altering the other. But if we use this illustration, we must recognize that 'thing' here means a mere somewhat immediately one with its quality and, further, quantified; not a thing with properties from which it is distinguishable. 'Thing and Properties' is a category of Essence,[2] but here we have only a qualified magnitude, a 'this' which includes determinate quantity. Nothing we experience, at least at a level not below sense-perception, can fail to have Measure in this lowest phase of that category. 'Alles was da ist hat ein Mass.'[3]

[1] EL, § 99, *Zusatz*.

[2] See ch. vi, §§ 8 and ff. below.

[3] LL, i, p. 413. *Gestalt* psychology seems to be based on a rediscovery of this fact.

2·1. The category of Measure is prominent throughout Nature, and it is well to remember that although mensuration, in which Plato found the beginning of transition from the sensible to the intelligible, proceeds by abstraction from Quality, yet it has always an eye to the quality of what is measured. Hegel observes[1] that in statistics the figures are only of importance in relation to the qualitative results which they condition. At a low level of Nature, Measure which, as we saw, began to emerge in Quantitative Ratio, is exemplified in the formula S/T to express velocity. In this formula space and time are qualified quanta in a ratio, and so moments of motion in so far as motion exemplifies Measure. Measure, in Hegel's view, is the essential structure of the solar system, but in the microcosmic study of inorganic nature we constantly find Quantity and Quality indifferent to one another: the quality of a rock or a river is not linked with a definite magnitude. On the other hand, in chemical analysis Measure becomes again an important category: a quantitative proportion governs qualitative character. Again, the quality and pitch of a note depend upon the number of vibrations. In organic Nature Measure appears in the essential connexion between size and constitution, although in some lower forms both of plant and animal life it is relatively vague and indeterminate.

2·2. As in the phases of Concrete Spirit Quantity becomes more and more subordinate, so in a less degree does Measure. Yet there Measure still plays its part; for the phases of Concrete Spirit are phases in spirit's 'conquest' of the natural,[2] and the categories which sustain and animate sense-experience are not fully sublated save in philosophy.[3] Measure is evident in the essential relation of political constitution to size of population and territory, and its presence in all forms of aesthetic experience is too obvious to need exemplification.

2·3. Measure is the Greek notion of ἐμμετρία. In Greek religion 'nemesis' represents it, and the precept μηδὲν ἄγαν embodied for the Greeks its significance in ethical life. In short, wherever Quantity is still present in Concrete Spirit, there a deeper insight reveals also Measure. Plato states

[1] EL, § 106, *Zusatz*.

[2] Cf. IH, ch. viii, § 5·3.

[3] If even there: cf. ch. i, above.

very clearly the relation of Measure to Quantity in *Politicus* 283 D–285 C. The Stranger divides the art of measuring into two parts, one to measure mere relative quantity, the other to measure excess and defect in relation to a mean. He emphasizes the importance of the latter for dialectical division. Aristotle develops this doctrine when he defines virtue of ἦθος (that is, of character taken in abstraction from moral intelligence) as a mean, and he has often been criticized for conceiving moral virtue in purely quantitative terms. But quite apart from the fact that he defines as a mean only goodness of ἦθος and not complete moral virtue, the definition is in terms not of mere Quantity but of Measure. The criticism is typical of that incourageous habit of mind which seeks truth along the line of least resistance, and sees everywhere nothing but the lower category.

3. In LL there are fifteen categories of Measure. In working them out Hegel labours to elicit the logical elements in mathematical physics and chemistry. The dialectic, as he himself admits, is not easy. It is often also unconvincing. In EL three categories are rather obscurely indicated: (1) Rule or Standard, the general character of Measure; (2) the Measureless; (3) the True Infinite of Measure. I shall try to follow EL with some assistance from LL.

3·1. RULE *or* STANDARD

Measure in this first phase is, as we have seen in the previous section, mere Somewhat developed to *quale* which is, further, quantified. Here Measure takes the form of a scale of degrees, on which qualitative change occurs at certain points only. Quality and Quantity are still only implicitly related. Increase or diminution on the scale of degrees proceeds by arithmetical progression, and is only limited by apparently abrupt transitions of qualitative character. So solids liquefy and become gaseous at certain temperatures between which no change occurs, and so musical notes are determined in pitch and quality according to a harmonic progression, the terms of which are certain velocities of vibration between which vibration increases its velocity in arithmetical progression until a sudden revulsion

(*Umschlag*) to quality occurs. We may think of this scale under the figure of a nodal line.

Hegel calls this transition of Measure to and fro between Quantity and Quality an antinomy,[1] and remarks upon its familiarity to the Greeks. Puzzles such as the problem when a horse's tail becomes bald as hair after hair is plucked out of it really turn, he thinks, on just this relation of Quantity to Quality in the opening phase of Measure.[2] Hegel finds quantitative analogues of this nodal line in the integer series, e.g. the irregular incidence of square numbers.[3]

3·2. THE MEASURELESS

In Rule, or Standard, Quantity does limit itself qualitatively, but only at certain points on a quantitative scale. Hence the scale contradicts the very nature of Measure. For there is nothing to limit the extension of the nodal line, and there arises inevitably the thought of an indefinite regress of degrees, and of an indefinite regress of new qualities occurring at intervals upon it. The Spurious Infinite thus returns in a new shape as a Spurious Infinite of Measures.

3·3. THE TRUE INFINITE OF MEASURE

This synthesis is analogous to the emergence of the True Infinite both in Quality and Quantity. It comes with the thought that the endless Measures are after all identical; that Measure as Rule is in this endless regress related only to itself, since what appeared in the Measureless as stretches of mere Quantum are limited by, and signify only in reference to, the nodes of Quality. There is now not a conflict of quantum and quale which oscillate endlessly into one another: Quality and Quantity are now entirely equivalent (*gleichgültig*) to one another. There is no longer any difference between them. For in Measure only Quantity can differentiate Quality, and this quantitative differentiation is now complete. There is not thinkable any further out-

[1] In LL it appears as a small-scale antithesis to the bare, abstract nature of Measure, which is there called Specific Quantum.

[2] Cf. Aristotle, *Physics* 253b23–6.

[3] See LL, i, p. 458.

break of Quantity against Quality which could negate and so further develop Measure.

In the True Infinite of Measure all the 'otherings' of Being are sublated and absorbed, and Spirit expresses its Being-for-self as a proportioned 'whole' in which Quality and Quantity are one.

V

TRANSITION TO ESSENCE

1. We see that and how a proportioned whole is what it is, but we do not understand why. The union of Quality and Quantity which we reach in the True Infinite of Measure is the final category of thought in which intuition still dominates discursion, and we should still naturally call the sense-experience which illustrates it perception rather than thought. The equivalence, or indifference, of Quality and Quantity is the final phase of that absence, or rather privation, of true differentiation in which the immediacy of Being in all its transitions consists. 'Das Sein', says Hegel, 'ist die abstrakte Gleichgültigkeit.'[1] The activity of spirit, as we saw in Chapter II,[2] is here a kind of impotence. Each phase seems to cancel what went before; or, alternatively, spirit in its negativity seems in Being to lose its whole character and transform itself unstably from opposite to opposite. And in this equivalence of Quality and Quantity in which Measure culminates, the activity of spirit is still 'indifferent', not truly self-differentiating. The union of Quality and Quantity, despite all the 'otherings' which have been sublated in the last phase of Measure, is only an immediate unity. So far, Hegel means, as we can abstract from higher categories, renouncing 'any interest unborrowed from the eye', and naïvely seeing a landscape, for example, or a picture as a unity of quality and quantity, we do not distinguish these moments; we see them as immediately one. This experience is perhaps even better illustrated in the tasting of a good wine.

1·1. In Being, then—in the transformations of Quality, in the self-external negations of Quantity, and in the movement of Measure, which still finds its only spring in the outbreak of external quantitative determination—spirit may seem hardly at all to abide with itself in its other. Yet spirit is activity, and, to use a metaphor which must not be taken

[1] LL, i, p. 466. [2] § 1·3.

to imply anything static,[1] spirit must after all be permanent throughout the transformations. The fabric of the vision cannot be really baseless; and this base,[2] this inner permanence of spirit which now reveals itself in contrast and opposition to the naïve unmediated shifting of phases in which Being consists, betokens the development of spirit to Essence (*Wesen*).

1·2. We noticed in Ch. II, § 2·11, Hegel's use of the past tense to indicate metaphorically the timeless. He sees a significant connexion between *Wesen* and *gewesen*, the past participle of *sein*. Each phase of Being vanishes, and spirit *is* only in its now vanishing phase. But spirit *was* in all its vanished phases, and to grasp this is to see that spirit's being is more truly to-have-been-and-to-be than merely to be: 'Das Wesen ist das vergangene, aber zeitlos vergangene Sein.'[3] In the immediately preceding passage Hegel has said that knowing (*das Wissen*) first finds Essence when it '*erinnert*' *sich*, 'inwardizes' itself, out of Being. He is here deliberately recalling *Erinnerung*, Recollection, and he clearly implies that the transition from Intuition to Recollection[4] is closely analogous to the transition from Being to Essence.

1·3. Essence, then, is the truth of Being, and with Essence the emphasis passes from intuition to discursion, and so from thought which sense-perception illustrates to thought which finds its illustration in empirical thinking. As Locke discovered, substance (which we shall find to be one form which Essence takes) cannot with any plausibility be treated as a sensuous idea (*Vorstellung*), and in a strictly empiricist philosophy it can only survive scandalously as the idea of an unknown. But in interpreting Hegel's Essence there is another danger to be avoided. We cannot say that the *Wesen*, the 'has-beenness', which is the truth of *Sein*, consists simply in the base, or inner permanent, taken by itself. Such an

[1] I fancy that Being and Essence reflect the distinction which Kant draws between 'mathematical' and 'dynamic' categories and principles; see ch. ii, § 1 above.

[2] Or perhaps *punctum saliens*, a phrase used metaphorically to describe the Notion in EL, § 166, *Zusatz*.

[3] LL, i, p. 481.

[4] Cf. IH, ch. v, § 2, and ch. i, §§ 5·1 and 5·5 above.

Essence would be, says Hegel, 'a bare name, a mere *caput mortuum* of the abstracting Understanding'.[1] It would not be a form of spirit carrying further the determinateness which has taken place in Being, but a non-entity as little known as Locke's substance; not a phase of antithesis into which spirit issues whole in fresh self-determination, but a mere sham opposite to Being, an explanation which merely explained away the *explicandum*. So in EL, § 112, Hegel remarks:

'When the Absolute is defined as Essence, the negativity (which this implies) is often taken to mean only the withdrawal from all determinate predicates. This negative action of withdrawal or abstraction thus falls outside the Essence, which is thus left as a result apart from its premisses, the *caput mortuum* of abstraction. But this negativity is not external to Being, but Being's own dialectic; hence the truth of Being, viz. Essence, is Being retired within itself.'

1·31. Indeed, the mere common notion of Essence should enable us to avoid this danger; for Essence is obviously unthinkable save as a relative term. It is nonsense to say that the essential character of x is so-and-so, and at the same time to deny the implication that x has also a non-essential, an apparent or an accidental, character. When spirit reveals the latent truth of its Being as a base or inner permanent, then this base is only manifest *qua* the base of a superstructure, or the inner of an outer. It is only as having-been-*and-being* that spirit is more truly itself in Essence than in Being. In common life we begin to think as soon as we suspect that things may not be what they seem to be. The distinction which we then begin to make expresses itself in many ways, which the categories of Essence will explicate. We distinguish between real and apparent, fact and fancy, necessary connexion and its outer show of mere juxtaposition and mere succession, knowledge which is true and opinion which may be false. But though in seeking true knowledge of the real necessitated fact we are denying and, as it were, turning from and eschewing the contingent show, yet we are not and could not be simply superseding it. The reality we hold to is the reality of an appearance, not the correlate of an absolute illusion; an absolute illusion could have no real correlate,

[1] EL, § 112, *Zusatz*.

could not be at all. Our fact is what our fancy became; our true knowledge contains developed what alone gave our opinion any content. In so far as we had not thought, our experience was innocent of these distinctions; but when we began to think the two terms of the distinction emerged together. In passing from sense to Understanding we do not pass from experience of the purely apparent to experience of the purely real. In Understanding sense is sublated; yet when we understand we also still perceive. Conversely, any stability, any solidity and actuality, which the object of sense-perception has for us, it has only so far as sense is sublated in Understanding. Being is presupposed by Essence, but Essence is the truth of Being.

1·4. Admittedly there is paradox and contradiction in this relation of sense and Understanding. Essence is to be all that counts; yet Essence apart from the unessential (or the apparent, or the contingent), which is not to count, is simply nothing. This seeming 'insolvency to sense' under which Understanding labours inclined Kant to the view that sense co-operates with Understanding on equal terms and not by virtue of sublation in Understanding. Kant's merit is to have seized precisely what the Understanding is for itself; what it must *qua* Understanding appear to itself to be. But he failed to see that his achievement is the mere prelude to philosophic interpretation of the Understanding. He had felt that there must be some significance in the duality of each dynamical category,[1] but he did not grasp that for philosophic insight categories such as substance and accident, cause and effect, *develop out of* categories which are illustrated by sense-perception. Hegel, on the other hand, recognizes this paradox and contradiction in the relation of sense and Understanding, but he sees that the problem is reflected in two different spheres, which Kant, holding thought to be purely discursive, had failed to demarcate clearly when he distinguished between a subjective and an objective deduction of the categories.[2] The co-operation of sensuous and intellectual faculties—or, as Hegel sees it, the sublation of subservient sense by intellectual faculties—is a matter which concerns the Philosophy of Spirit;[3] whereas

[1] See KRV, B, p. 110. [2] Cf. IH, ch. ix, § 5·22. [3] Cf. ibid., ch. viii.

for logic the contradiction does not occur between sense and thought, but emerges as thought sublates its own immediate, intuitional level. The Understanding, so soon as it becomes explicitly discursive, must *think* the essential and the unessential as inseparably related yet in mutual contradiction.

Hence to Hegel every category of Essence is a contradiction of inseparably coupled moments. In Essence Being and Nothing have at length emerged respectively as essential and unessential, but these two moments are now together in each phase of every triad: Essence is only Essence as the Essence of Being. 'Die Wahrheit des Seins ist das Wesen.'

2. There is a further point which the reader must on pain of utter bewilderment bear constantly in mind throughout the following chapters.

In every coupled category of Essence spirit is just as much indivisibly whole in each of the coupled moments as it is in any category of Being, although one of the moments will always be more or less 'unessential'.[1] That each pair of moments is a contradiction means that spirit is self-contradictory in each of them as well as in the couple taken as a couple. It is impossible to be perpetually showing this in a brief exposition, and Hegel's attempt in LL to do so produces a sort of flickering effect which is apt at first to baffle and discourage the reader. The point to be grasped is that not one of these coupled moments can be thought without *eo ipso* thinking more than that moment; and this 'more' is not an external addition, but the truth of the 'first' moment, which was only 'first' because it was to be followed. This is precisely the nature of dialectical movement, but it is easy in Essence to forget it. In the next chapter, § 3, on positing and presupposing, and §§ 5·4 ff., on contradiction, will, I hope, make this clearer. It follows, moreover, from the nature of activity.

3. Hegel expounds his conception of Essence in other and complementary ways. Being is the sphere of immediacy, Essence that of mediation. The base, or substratum, which comes to light as the dialectic of Measure closes, mediates the vanishing phases of Being, and the further movement of

[1] Yet integral to the category. The term 'unessential' is privative, not merely negative.

spirit makes explicit this mediation; i.e. in Essence spirit truly differentiates itself because it now persists explicitly identical through its phases, whereas it has suffered in Being impotent transformation in which its self-sameness was so utterly latent that transformation was hardly a truer name than substitution. Nevertheless Essence is mediation without explicit re-immediation. As explicitly each category of Being was thesis only, so explicitly each category of Essence will be antithesis wherein thesis is preserved in contradiction as well as cancelled. For the differentiation of spirit in Essence is in open contradiction with its identity: spirit, though no longer transformed into its opposite, does not in Essence return fully reconciled to itself from its negative moment of self-expression. When we remember that this negative moment of Essence is the more or less—more to begin with, less as we proceed—'unessential' moment of Being-within-Essence, it is clear that this must be so.

3·1. To express the relation of Being and Essence within Essence Hegel adapts the terminology of Being, and calls Being *Ansichsein* and Essence *An- und Fürsichsein*. Marcuse makes effective use of spatial metaphor by calling Being the first, Essence the second dimension of spirit's activity.[1] The point is that two-dimensional space cancels sheer linearity, and yet, also preserving it, gives it its significance and only so gains its own significance. The metaphor also warns us that Essence is a mere 'Flatland' if we contrast it with the Notion.

4. The coupling of essential and unessential in each category of Essence leads Hegel to call Essence the sphere of 'reflection'. The term is borrowed in the first instance from the sensuous *Vorstellung* of a ray of light which strikes a mirror and is thrown back. Hegel observes[2] that we have here a double fact: first an immediate which merely *is* (sc. the light as so far simply self-luminous), and secondly the same thing as derived or mediated (sc. the light reflected in the mirror). So the movement of the Understanding is reflective: we aim at knowing the object not in its prima-facie immediacy but as mediated, as the derived reflection of what it truly is.

[1] *Hegel's Ontologie*, Frankfort, 1932. [2] Cf. EL, § 112, *Zusatz*.

4·01. At first sight this recalls Plato's common metaphor for expressing the relation of particulars to Forms, especially his simile in *Republic* vii of the prisoners released from the cave who study the sun in its reflections before they can look directly at it. But Hegel's analogy is not quite the same as Plato's. Hegel means, I think, that the (in fact) *derived* phase of the object is at first for us, as it were, something simply self-luminous. Our reflective thought in subsequently recognizing it for a derived phase of an original essential nature is then analogous to the light's reflecting itself in the mirror. Hegel, that is to say, conceives the light as original only in its origination of its own reflection. As merely self-luminous, it symbolizes mere Being; as soon as (but no sooner than) it reflects itself, it is at once original illuminant and reflection, and this symbolizes Essence mediating Being. Plato, on the other hand, sometimes tends to suggest indifference of the Form to its particulars[1] and the possibility of contemplating the Good (symbolized by the sun) apart from its 'reflections'. But Essence wholly apart from Being is to Hegel an unthinkable *caput mortuum*.

4·1. This metaphor of light and mirror must not be allowed to obscure the fact that the reflective movement is revealed to the understanding subject only as his own activity. Hegel's dialectic of Essence, on the other hand, attempts to display this movement as it is for philosophic interpretation, i.e. as the activity of spirit. Whereas the understanding subject himself in his empirical thinking conceives his reflection from immediacy to mediating Essence as a purely subjective movement over and above the real and independent thing about which he is reflecting, Hegel offers his dialectic of Essence as a criticism and reconstruction of this detached attitude as well as of the various forms of Essence, the various essential entities, which the Understanding supposes itself to have established as subsisting both independent of mind and indifferent to one another. Hegel is endeavouring to show that all these severances belong to the Understanding merely as it is for itself, not as it truly is; they do not belong to Understanding *qua* sublated in self-conscious Reason. On the other hand, the

[1] Cf., for example, *Rpc*. 596.

dialectic has to show this sublation in process and not merely in result. Hence the reflective movement of the categories of Essence is at once subjective and objective. 'Reflection' comprises both the conception of an immediate which mediates itself into original-and-reflection, and the conception of an understanding subject which moves without true self-consciousness from an immediately presented object to the mediate form of that object as original-and-reflection. To this understanding subject the original, the Essence, appears as *causa essendi* of its own reflection, while the immediately presented object appears to him as his subjective *causa cognoscendi*. But to the philosopher this distinction appears as the interplay of conflicting moments in the self-development of spirit; for him it is spirit which moves both in what for the Understanding is an independent movement of an immediate to mediation (of a force, for example, to its expression in phenomena), and in what for the Understanding is its own subjective reflecting movement from immediacy to mediation.

4·11. It was not easy for Hegel to express this in the titles of his categories. He has to wrench rather than naturally develop the common meanings of words stamped on them by that very sort of thinking which he is in process of criticizing. A glance at the categories of Essence shows titles such as Matter and Form, Thing and Properties, Substance and Accident, Cause and Effect, all of which suggest to common sense something 'objective', i.e. mind-independent; titles such as Show, Appearance, Likeness and Unlikeness, which sound at first merely 'subjective'; finally several categories of Ground which seem to leave it ambiguous whether *causa essendi* or *causa cognoscendi* is intended. In fact both the seeming alternatives are intended by Hegel in every case, and the alternation implies only a shifting of emphasis as the dialectic progresses; only the interplay of subjective and objective moments, which despite their contradiction are inseparable in thought.

4·2. 'Reflection', then, is a single movement of spirit. But even when we grasp this, Hegel's expression of it remains difficult. Essence, as I have laboured to explain, is the movement of spirit from immediacy to a mediated phase of original-and-reflection, a phase of Essence coupled with a relatively 'unessential' self-expression. Yet this very relativity entails that spirit is only Essence by contrast with this 'unessential'; the 'unessential' reflection is nothing whatever but expression of its original. But for this reason the reflection is the same as its original; i.e. spirit in its very issue into the expression which reflects it is being reflected back into itself. Within the coupled category as a whole the two movements of (*a*) reflection into Other and (*b*) reflection into self, or intro-reflection, reciprocally imply one another. That, indeed, is a mere corollary of the doctrine, now sufficiently familiar to us, that negation is *significant* otherness, always an alter *ego*. But it has further to be remembered that since the reflection or expression, although it is the 'unessential' moment, is yet the same as the essential moment, it follows that both reflection into Other and intro-reflection characterize (within the whole coupled category) the 'unessential' moment as well as the essential. The transition of one category of Essence into the next has therefore in principle to be described from the point of view of each of the two moments, and at the same time to be displayed as a single movement of spirit. This is what gives the dialectic of Essence in LL its peculiar difficulty.

5. Certain further preliminary problems in Hegel's exposition of Essence remain to be discussed.

The first of these is the question of 'illustration'. The categories of Being could, we saw, be effectively illustrated only by the total activity of percipient and perceptum, and in all illustrative appeal to 'this' or 'that', or again to the percipient 'I', there was an inevitable risk of evoking a one-sided response on the part of the reader. In attempting to 'illustrate' the categories of Essence this risk is doubled. Only the total movement of the Understanding, as it reflects upon the content of its sense-perception, truly 'illustrates' a category of Essence. Neither a physical process realistically imagined, such as the reflection of light, nor a subjective process of mind conceived as moving over an object indifferent to mind, is at all adequate. And it is easier to grasp that there is no 'this' or 'that' without a percipient and vice versa, than that a physical process is not independent of mind but is a content of mind, and that mind is nothing without its content.[1]

5·1. Hence the account of Reflection given in § 4·1 was inevitably a simplification of the facts. I have there spoken somewhat as if for the Understanding the immediately presented thing from which its reflection starts, and the mediating Essence which it seeks, were both simply independent of it. I have, that is, tended to assume the Understanding at the level of its first movement of abstraction from sense, as it is described in EL, § 80, *Zusatz*:

'The activity of the Understanding consists in general (*überhaupt*) of imparting the form of universality to its content. The universal posited by the Understanding is an abstract universal: that is to say its opposition to the particular is so rigorously maintained that it is itself at the same time also reduced to the character of a particular again.'[2]

But in fact the Understanding does not remain in naïve acceptance of its datum and its goal, the immediate presentation and the hidden essence, as mind-independent. It very soon begins to philosophize, though without self-transcendence.[3] It then discovers that, by its very denial that what it finds is in fact as it is found, it is involved at once in the kind of difficulty about appearance which Locke tried to solve by a distinction between primary and secondary qualities. The problem of what status is to be accorded to the universal, the Essence, when it is revealed, arises with the first rudimentary effort of the Understanding to interpret itself. It takes shape in such questions as Are universals *in re*, or are they mere *entia rationis*? Do things cause other things to change, or is causality merely our subjective and dubiously justifiable connecting? Is a Law of Nature an immutable principle governing a world of things independent of mind, or a statistical computation which justifies only probable prediction? Or, again, does mind-independent Nature herself behave merely probably? These controversies

[1] This is difficult to grasp because the distinctive characteristic of the Understanding *is* its detachment, its insistence that its object is a thing independent of mind.

[2] As it is by all philosophers who assume that there is a plurality of universals.

[3] Cf. IH, ch. viii, § 5·7.

all crudely assume a stark either/or for their premiss, but the mere fact that they arise shows the germ of Reason in Understanding. It is Hegel's purpose in the dialectic of Essence to criticize and reconstitute the whole industry of the Understanding from its initial movement of abstraction from sense to the metaphysical theories of his predecessors, which he treats one and all as being, in contrast with his own idealism, philosophies of the Understanding.

6. I have stressed the inseparability of subjective and objective moments in the dialectic of Essence. In the Introduction to LL Hegel divides the Logic into two parts, viz. Objective Logic comprising the categories of Being and Essence, and Subjective Logic which contains the categories of the Notion.[1]

The reader may well be puzzled. It was at best misleading to apply to the Logic itself a distinction which it is the business of the Logic to examine. Hegel's ostensible purpose in so doing is to mark the Logic of Being and Essence as together constituting his criticism and reconstruction of 'the former metaphysics, which was a scientific structure superimposed upon the world, and supposed to be constituted of thoughts alone'.[2] Presumably this 'former metaphysics' covers the whole history of philosophy from Parmenides and Heraclitus to Spinoza and Leibniz.[3] Hegel, I think, calls the Logic of Being and Essence 'objective' because he regards all pre-Kantian philosophy as being (*qua* philosophy and therefore so far idealist) subjective idealism, a thought structure which is *a priori* in a pre-Kantian sense and offers merely the truth about the world instead of revealing the world as truth. He is thus asserting against his predecessors the 'objectivity' of philosophic thought, insisting that thought is constitutive of its object. This seems to be confirmed in the passage which follows:

'If we consider the final form into which this science [sc. the 'former metaphysics'] developed, we find that in the first instance it is Ontology which Objective Logic supersedes, i.e. that part of this metaphysic which was to investigate the nature of *Ens* without qualification [*überhaupt*].

[1] See LL, i, pp. 64–6.

[2] Ibid., p. 64.

[3] Although Hegel is clearly thinking of his more recent predecessors, and he can scarcely mean to include Plato and Aristotle.

Ens comprehends both Being and Essence, a distinction for which the German language has happily preserved different terms.'[1]

Hegel then proceeds to characterize Subjective Logic as the logic of the Notion, which is Essence when it has become the free self-subsistent Subjective, determining itself in itself. He thus implies that Subjective Logic displays thought not merely as constitutive of its object but as also therein constituting itself; as an explicitly self-conscious activity, subjective in a concrete sense. Yet such a view would surely demand that Objective Logic be preceded by, instead of itself contain, the logic of thought in which the distinction of subjective and objective has not arisen; one would, that is, expect the term 'objective' in this connexion to be confined to the Logic of Essence.

6·1. The fact seems to be that Hegel is for the moment absorbed in a polemical attitude towards recent philosophy. Wishing to stigmatize this as subjective idealism, he is led to disturb the articulation of his own Logic. This solution becomes almost certain when Hegel, having drawn this distinction, immediately warns his reader not to attach any special importance to it, and when we find that in EL it has totally disappeared.

7. I will end this perhaps rather forbidding chapter with a further remark on the special difficulty of nomenclature in the logic of Essence. In LL language is strained and stretched to yield titles for the subcategories of a complicated dialectic. In the greatly simplified version of EL not only does the articulation of the movement seem sometimes to be different, but often where it is clearly the same as in LL the titles of the categories are nevertheless altered. Nowhere so much as in the Logic of Essence has the reader need to remember that these titles, however indispensable for exposition, are mere 'compilations of external reflection'.[2] It is easy to lose one's way in Essence, and since my hope is to offer a clue rather than an epitome, I shall dwell chiefly on

[1] For the Ontology to which Hegel refers see Paton, *Kant's Metaphysic of Experience*, i, p. 257. Hegel regards Kant's Transcendental Logic as a reconstruction of this Ontology, which his own Objective Logic now purges of all mere subjectivity and further develops—perhaps even finally completes.

[2] See ch. i, §§ 8 and 8·5 above.

the large-scale forms of the dialectic, and I shall select from both Logics those titles which seem most likely to carry the right suggestion to a modern reader. My general policy will be to eke out the rather sparse EL version from LL. We may have to note a few discrepancies between the two versions, but to discuss them in detail would take us beyond the scope of this *Study*.

8. Hegel calls Essence the hardest branch of logic, and I fear that I may have but too easily persuaded the reader to agree with him. Yet in the Logic of Essence Hegel marvellously revitalizes categories grown stiff and dead in the everyday thinking of common sense. The effort to look the familiar in the face and think again is worth making: 'Nun aber ist das Geschäft der Logik eben nur dies, die bloss vorgestellten und als solche unbegriffenen und unbewiesenen Gedanken, als Stufen des sich selbst bestimmenden Denkens aufzuzeigen, womit dieselben dann zugleich begriffen und bewiesen werden.'[1]

[1] EL, § 121, *Zusatz*, JE viii, p. 283.

VI

INTRO-REFLECTION[1]

1. I SHALL call the three main phases of Essence Intro-reflection (so LL: EL has 'Essence as Ground of Existence'), Appearance, and Actuality (*Wirklichkeit*).

The general character of movement in Essence is perhaps to begin with most easily observed if we watch only the gradual increase of significance in the moment of Being which is subordinated and preserved in Essence. This is at first (A) a mere unessential Show (*Schein*). This Show is *not* mere fugitive, baseless Being; it is *not* a mere proportioned whole of Measure which, because it is all on the surface, is strictly neither surface nor interior. For it is the reflection of Essence; the Show is the present being (*Gegenwärtigkeit*) of that 'having been' which Essence is. Yet the reference of Show to the Essence reflected in it is only implicit. The subject has but a faint inkling that the Show is a showing of anything other than itself. Next (B), the sublated moment of Being becomes Appearance, wherein reference to Essence and distinction of the moment of Being from the moment of Essence are obvious. Lastly (C), the sublated moment of Being reveals the whole nature of its Essence. It is no more a mere reflection, a representative outward symbol. It is spirit as actual (*wirklich*), no longer differing from and contradicting Essence, but manifesting it without reserve and itself become fully essential.

1·1. We may now complement this abstract description by watching the dialectical movement from the point of view, so to say, of the essential moment.

(A) It must not be supposed that as the moment of Being increases in significance, so the moment of Essence decreases in significance and becomes in inverse proportion 'unessential'. Essence is Essence *and* Being. Despite the contradiction of the moments, spirit is one in each moment *and* one in their duality. Essence shows not merely *in* but *as* Show, and we can come at Essence only through its Show.

[1] See ch. v, § 4·2 above.

To imagine Show as a veil thinly hiding a bright light involves precisely the wrong metaphor. The moment of Being in which Essence shows is within Essence—as, indeed, the moment of Being as Appearance will also be; but in the latter case contradiction will be explicit, whereas in Show it is not. Hence Essence in its Show is intro-reflected into or on to itself, and the instability of Show is a token of the initial instability of Essence: the dimness proclaims that the source of light is itself still feeble.

1·11. It is only if we remember that Essence in its Show is not merely reflected but intro-reflected that we can understand Hegel's meaning when he speaks of Essence just emerged from Being as Being returned into itself:

Das Wesen als die volkommene Rückkehr des Seins in sich ist so zunächst das unbestimmte Wesen; die Bestimmtheiten des Seins sind in ihm aufgehoben; es enthält sie an sich, aber nicht wie sie an ihm gesetzt sind. Das absolute Wesen in dieser Einfachheit mit sich hat kein Dasein [sc. has not yet the differentiation which is the analogue in Essence of Dasein in Being].[1]

1·2. (B) In Appearance the contradiction between Essence as the Essential moment and Being as the 'unessential' moment becomes explicit. But the Appearance gains the relative solidity with which it confronts and contradicts Essence only inasmuch as it more fully expresses Essence, *is* more fully Essence: the contradiction only serves to mark the sameness of the moments.

1·3. (C) In Actuality Essence finds full expression in the moment of Being, so that Being is at length fully sublated in Essence. Essence is now one with its Appearance just because between *complete* expression and that which completely expresses itself there can be neither severance nor contradiction: the two moments are in complete synthesis. This complete self-expression of spirit in Actuality is called by Hegel, in contrast with Show and Appearance, 'Manifestation' (*Offenbarung*). *Wirklichkeit* is a most important category in the sphere of Objective Spirit,[2] and it is well to emphasize that the word *wirklich* never in Hegel means an actual which might have been or ought to be something else, but always that as which the possible, because it was really

[1] LL, i, p. 483. [2] See IH, ch. viii.

possible, has been necessarily actualized. It is a central tenet of Hegel's idealism, as against Leibniz's teaching, that there is no merely possible wider than the actual. We shall discover later that the actual which might have been otherwise (i.e. not *das Wirkliche* but *das Zufällige*, the contingent), and the merely or barely possible, are inseparable correlates. They are respectively the moments of Being and Essence, which together constitute one category of Essence, and they can only be thought together.[1]

1·4. The clue to Essence, then, is the progressively changing relation between the coupled moments of the successive categories, between what is expressed and its expression. Yet this progress has a second aspect, which Hegel does not stress so much, because he takes for granted that it is bound up with the first. But unless we properly appreciate it, the transition from Essence to the Notion, from substance to subject, will remain obscure. We must note that throughout the categories of Essence that which is expressed takes on more and more the nature of an objective and unified world. Essence more and more *is*, and what it is becomes more and more clearly revealed as a single systematic totality. In the categories of Intro-reflection we shall seem to watch the mind reflecting subjectively in terms of principles so general that any sort of an object must needs conform to them. In Appearance there will appear as object an explicitly unitary world, although the essential and the apparent moments will be unstably balanced, and the objectivity of the world not securely fixed. In Actuality this objectivity of the world (for the Understanding, be it remembered) will be gradually determined through its progressively systematized unity; Essence will come at last to *be*, and to *be* as one coherent actual world.[2]

2. We may follow EL in taking the three main divisions of Intro-reflection (for which, as I have said, is there substituted the title of 'Essence as Ground of Existence') as 'The Pure Categories of Reflection', 'Existence', and 'Thing'. In LL the first of these is preceded by a triad called

[1] Cf. ch. viii, §§ 5 and ff. below.

[2] I.e. the Understanding universalizes (cf. ch. v, § 5·1, above), and the universal passes from abstract to concrete.

'Show' (*Schein*), and both Existence and Thing fall outside Intro-reflection into Appearance. The chief significance of this discrepancy seems to be that in LL the general nature of Intro-reflection as mere *Schein* which is not yet *Erscheinung* is more marked; but in LL both Matter and Form and Content and Form precede Existence, whereas in EL they follow it. Here EL gives the more easily intelligible order. It may be that Hegel is deliberately using the terms Matter, Form, and Content in slightly different senses in the two Logics, but I think it much more probable that he introduced this change into EL as an improvement.

The three Pure Categories of Reflection are Identity, Difference, and Ground; and of these Difference subdivides again. In LL these Pure Categories of Reflection are called *Wesenheiten* (Essentialities?) *der Reflexion*, but the main difference of treatment in LL lies in the insertion before Identity of the triad of Show, which is somewhat difficult but so important that I must endeavour to give the gist of it.

3. Show

(A) Essence 'posits' (*setzt*) its sublated moment of Being; i.e. constitutes it an unessential show of itself, a Show which apart from Essence is nothing, a sheer negation. But (B) Essence arose out of Being, and therefore *presupposes* (*voraussetzt*) qualified, quantified, and measured Being as that which preceded it, and which it *finds*. Essence, that is to say, does not simply 'posit' Being as the mere utterly dependent and unessential consequent of itself; for, after all, the sheer negation of Essence, the utterly unessential, could not be any sort of significant 'other' of Essence. But now the relation of dependence seems to have become reversed. Essence in its first movement is a movement of external reflection which starts from an immediate presupposed datum which it has found: it is merely reflection into Other proceeding away from, and failing to determine, the nature of the datum. But (C) this presupposed Being was a *posited* moment of Essence: it is within Essence, not external to it. *Only* qua *starting-point of reflection can it be called presupposition*. In fact, we may say, the moment of Being is *posited* as *presupposed*. In other words, the relation of dependence between the two moments is not merely reversed: it turns out to be reciprocal. Hence reflection is not now merely external; i.e. it is not now merely (*a*) a movement away from a datum which it cannot determine, and correspondingly (*b*) a movement subjective in the sense of an arbitrary passing over from one term to the other which is not immanent in the terms, a transition in which the terms are what they are only *für uns*.[1] Instead, reflection is now a determining reflection which does also posit what it presupposes, and is therefore still intro-reflection.[2]

3·1. Hegel has in mind here primarily the distinction which Kant draws in the *Critique of Judgement* between reflective and determinant judgement.[3] But he is implying generally that, although the Understanding may regard itself as a 'detached' subject looking on at an object-world which exhibits some utterly external relations, yet *any* movement of thought constitutes an implicit denial of this detachment and this externality; a denial which to philosophic interpretation becomes explicit.

The 'positing' of something as a consequent, and the presupposing of something as an antecedent, imply a necessary relation between the terms. It is, however, to be remembered that we are far as yet from having reached explicit necessity: in the whole dialectic of Identity, Difference, and Ground, which will occupy the rest of this chapter, the self-differentiation of spirit is Show rather than Appearance.

4. (Self-)Identity

This Determining Reflection, the first phase of spirit as genuinely reflected into itself through the Being which it sublates, is the immediacy of Essence—immediate Intro-

[1] See LL, i, pp. 498–9. It is essential to bear in mind that the movement of Essence is properly 'illustrated' only by taking together what common sense splits into (*a*) a relation *in re*, and (*b*) a movement of a 'detached' mind; cf. ch. v, § 5 above.

[2] The reader will see that the dialectic of Show, indeed the dialectic of Essence generally, is well illustrated in the paradox of language which we discussed in ch. i. Thinking posits language as its reflection and expression, but language is logically prior to thinking, and is therefore posited as presupposed.

[3] See LL, i, pp. 499–500; also ch. xii, §§ 9·21 ff. below.

reflection—as opposed to the immediacy of Being. It is in fact Identity, which appears in EL as the first category of Essence. For Identity, if it has any other meaning than self-identity, can only be a synonym for Pure Being.

4·1. Hegel throws light upon the self-reflecting character of Identity by a discussion of the law of identity and its negative form, the law of contradiction.[1]

I have already in IH, ch. xii, given the gist of his teaching and indicated its importance as a defence of his idealism against the criticisms of a logic of the Understanding. This so-called law of thought, taken by itself abstractly as the Understanding ordinarily takes it, is sheer tautology. '*A* = *A*' denies the very form of the proposition; for the propositional form implies that the predicate is different from as well as identical with the subject; otherwise nothing whatever has been asserted. There can be no sheerly analytic judgement. But the truth is that the law of identity has a significance which escapes the logic of the Understanding. This is obvious to us just so soon as it occurs to us to ask why thought should have a law of identity only, and not also laws of Being, Quality, Quantity, &c. For it is surely not less significant to say that everything is a *quale*, or a quantum, than it is to say that everything is identical with itself. But the special promotion of identity to the status of a law is really due to the implicit recognition that in the thought of identity there is self-relation, as there is not in any category of Being: Identity can only be thought as self-identity.

This implicit recognition is even more obvious in the alternative form, the so-called law of contradiction. For the formula '*A* cannot be both *A* and not-*A*' expresses identity as negation of negation: it states in effect that *A* is *A* by virtue of not being not-*A*. In this formula the truth that self-identity signifies only proleptically and contains the germ of self-difference can already be detected.

5. Difference (*Unterschied*) *and its Subcategories*

(Self-)Identity is the whole immediate self- or intro-reflection of Essence; the antithesis is Difference, which has

[1] See EL, § 115, and LL, i, pp. 510–15.

the corresponding meaning of self-difference. But for this very reason Difference apart from Identity is as meaningless as was Identity apart from Difference. As there can be no self-relation except through difference, so self-difference is unthinkable save through self-identity.

Here if anywhere in the Logic it is clear that the triad is the *minimum rationale*. The opposition of Difference as antithesis to Identity as thesis signifies only within their synthesis, and the difficulty which Hegel has in expounding this serially is obvious in his account of it:

'Difference in itself is self-relating Difference: it is thus its own negativity [sc. *movement* of self-negation]. It is Difference, i.e., not from an Other, but from its own self: it is not itself but its Other. But that which is different from Difference is Identity. Difference is therefore both itself and Identity. The two together constitute Difference: Difference is the whole and its moment' [sc. spirit in its moment of Difference is at once self-identical and different; it abides *explicitly* with itself in its other, as in Being it did not]. . . . 'Difference is the whole and its own moment, just as self-identity is the whole and its moment' [sc. spirit in its moment of Identity is only self-identical *qua* the starting-point of its self-diremption into Difference. Identity 'posits' Difference, but is presupposed by Difference; yet Identity is presupposition only *qua* starting-point of differentiation]. 'This is to be considered the essential nature of Reflection and *the precise original basis of all activity and self-movement*.'[1]

5·01. This inseparability of Identity and Difference, which the Understanding finds it so hard to accept as the truth of its own operation, is put more clearly in EL, § 116, *Zusatz*:

'To ask how Identity comes to Difference, presupposes that Identity as mere abstract Identity is something of itself, and Difference also something else equally independent. This presupposition makes an answer to the question impossible. If identity is viewed as diverse (*verschieden*) from Difference, all that we in fact have in this way (*hiermit*) is but Difference; and hence we cannot demonstrate the advance to Difference, because the person who asks for the How of the advance thereby implies that for him the starting-point is non-existent. The question, then, when looked at more closely, has obviously no meaning, and its proposer may be met with the other question, What does he mean by Identity? Whereupon it would soon

[1] LL, i, pp. 516–17.

appear that he does not think when he says the word, and that Identity is for him an empty name.'

Alternatively, perhaps, we might ask the man who tells us that Identity and Difference are diverse, by what sort of diversity is Identity diverse from Difference? If he reply, 'Are they, then, identical?' his retort is scarcely crushing. For he is assuming that one or other of these answers must be true—as must, indeed, be the case, if it be assumed that to be diverse is to be not identical. But in holding Identity and Difference to be inseparable, Hegel denies that assumption; for he holds them inseparable as moments which are phases of one activity of thought.

5·02. The doctrine of identity in difference has been prominent in British idealism, and has caused endless bewilderment to logicians of the Understanding. The controversy, owing perhaps to errors on both sides, has become sadly confused.[1] The doctrine depends on the *active* nature of the real. It is a purely idealist doctrine, and one utterly untenable on a realist assumption of mind-independent things.[2] From such a realist position identity and difference prove an insoluble contradiction if their significance is honestly pressed. A *modus vivendi* can only be achieved by the short-term policy of relying on the immediacy of sense, and taking things to be simply identical in some respects with other things, simply different from them in others. This is to assume in each thing a miraculous power of retaining its self-identity and resisting logical dissolution. That the miracle cannot be explained is supposed not to matter because it is matter of fact.

When, as commonly by J. S. Mill, resemblance is made into an unanalysable relation linking singular things *per se* in independence of mind, the confusion seems to grow worse. But in fact this shows what really is going on. The solution by diverse respects is really a transplantation of the contradiction out of the 'detached' things into the 'detachedly' comparing mind. Such a solution is no help to realism, but it does indicate that this bewilderment of the Understanding before the doctrine of identity in difference is due to the Understanding's retention of sense incompletely

[1] Cf. IH, ch. xiii, § 5·2. [2] Cf. ibid., §§ 6–6·3.

sublated in thought. Mill, when he speaks of 'unanalysable resemblance', is imagining rather than thinking; just as when he talks about 'conceiving' he believes he is talking about thinking, but scarcely ever succeeds in distinguishing it in his own mind from imagining.

The categories of Being escape contradiction because they are below it; because each of them is for the subject of sense-experience either a sheer substitution for its predecessor, or a sheer transformation of it. But because the inseparable but self-contradictory coupling of intuition and discursion is the very nature of the Understanding, these solutions by diversity of respects and unanalysable resemblance will, as we shall see, be reflected in the dialectic of Difference.

5·03. To Kant identity and diversity (*Einerleiheit* and *Verschiedenheit*) are not categories but concepts of reflection. They are subjective, and not determinant of objects.[1]

5·1. *The Subcategories of* Difference

Without Identity there is no Difference, but since Difference is the antithesis which negates Identity, the subcategories of Difference will show the moment of Identity as first merely implicit and subordinate to Difference, then finally explicit and on a level with Difference. The termini of this movement, however, are not exactly the same in the two Logics. In LL the first subcategory is Absolute (in the sense of sheer or abstract) Difference. This synthesizes with Diversity (*Verschiedenheit*) in Opposition (*Gegensatz*), and Contradiction (*Widerspruch*) falls outside Difference to constitute the larger-scale synthesis of Identity with Difference. In EL, on the other hand, Difference is not very clearly articulated. The thesis is Diversity, the antithesis is Positive and Negative (or, alternatively, Opposition), and the synthesis appears to be Contradiction, but Hegel is not very explicit. Both in LL and EL Likeness and Unlikeness is made a transition stage between Diversity and Opposition, and though it is not given a dialectical label, I think it is vital to the movement. Possibly the EL version would be helped by taking it as the antithesis. The discrepancy and laxity of form are chiefly due to linguistic difficulty.

[1] See KRV, B, pp. 316 ff.

5·2. Diversity (*Verschiedenheit*)

Difference is self-difference; it is simple negation of *itself* as Other, not of an Other external to it.[1] Hence itself and its negation are two moments, each self-identical. *Diversa* are therefore indifferent (*gleichgültig*) to one another in their difference: only by virtue of the identity which they possess *qua* each self-identical are they different.

Since the relation of Diversity in which they stand is indifferent to the *diversa*, this relation falls outside them into an externally reflecting and comparing subject, a *Vergleichender*;[2] and as their identity this relation is Likeness (*Gleichheit*), as their non-identity it is Unlikeness (*Ungleichheit*). The likeness of the compared terms is an identity not in and for itself, and their unlikeness is external difference, not in and for itself the difference of the unlike terms. That is, *qua* like and unlike the terms are not intro-reflected, but related to intro-reflection (the comparing subject which stands over against them) as mutually external. The compared terms are for the subject identical in some respects, diverse in others.[3]

But though this solution of contradiction by diverse respects is no solution which can save realism from ruin, yet the comparing subject, on Hegel's view, is not indulging in the entirely arbitrary assertion of relations which do not hold objectively. External Reflection, as we saw in §§ 3 and 3·1, has its place in the dialectic; it is the first movement of spirit as Essence presupposing Being. The comparison is not arbitrary, for Likeness and Unlikeness cannot be thought apart from one another. It is because each compared term is *both* like *and* unlike the other that (1) the terms can be called *either* like *or* unlike one another, and that (2) if either term be called like, it must be confessed also to be unlike. Thus the moment of Identity becomes explicit, and diversity of respects is now seen in fact to have implied a completely reciprocal relation of two moments within each compared term. That is, so far as the terms do really enter into the

[1] In LL this is Absolute Difference, the antithesis of (self-)Identity and the first thesis of Difference.

[2] See § 5·02 above and ch. v, §§ 4·1 and 4·11.

[3] Cf. § 5·02 above.

relation of comparison,[1] their whole nature is exhausted in their mutual Likeness and Unlikeness taken together, and they fully determine one another. Diversity, in other words, now turns out to be essential, strictly determinate Difference, in which each term is confronted not by *any* other but by its *own* other. And that is

5·3. OPPOSITION (*Gegensatz*), CONTRARIETY, *or* POSITIVE AND NEGATIVE

In Opposition (Contrariety) one moment is intro-reflected self-likeness containing relation to unlikeness, and that is the Positive; the other moment is Unlikeness in its relation to Likeness, and that is the Negative. The two moments are thus reciprocal. Each is at once intro-reflected and reflected into the other, and they constitute together one phase of spirit. Yet we have still not reached Contradiction. Despite the reciprocity of the moments in contrary Opposition, one moment is still, as it were, the logical descendant of Identity, Essence *qua* essential moment, and Likeness; whereas the other is the descendant of Absolute Difference, Show, and Unlikeness. The Positive is still the Positive in itself, and the Negative is still the Negative in itself. Thus, to take an illustration which Hegel considers peculiarly apt, positive and negative electricity are in a completely reciprocal relation, but this polarity does not simply annul their difference *in se*. Or again in arithmetic + and − signify only with reference to one another; but if neither sign is attached to a symbol, it is assumed that the symbol is to be taken positively, and though $-a \times +a = -a^2$, yet it is not true that $+a \times -a = +a^2$. There is a qualitative difference implied, and $-a \times -a = +a^2$, because the negation of negation is the Positive. In both these cases the opposition is between terms of which, despite their reciprocity, one stands to the other in a relation of what might loosely be called dominance.

5·4. (SELF-)CONTRADICTION (*Widerspruch*)

Contrary Opposition is now succeeded by Contradiction, and I think that to follow what seems to be the dialectical

[1] As, for example, in Mill's four Inductive Methods they must be assumed to do before the methods can be applied.

order of EL and take Contradiction as the synthesis of Diversity and Opposition probably represents Hegel's mature view better than to make Contradiction the synthesis of Identity and Difference as the LL version does. In fact even the account in LL, i, pp. 535–7 seems to suggest that the former order is what Hegel really intends. It runs roughly as follows: Difference in general and without qualification (*überhaupt*) contains its two sides as moments. In Diversity they fall apart mutually indifferent. In Opposition they are Positive and Negative, and (*a*) mutually determinant. But in Opposition they are also (*b*) each determinate in itself: they are mutually indifferent and mutually exclusive, and so each self-dependent. And this is Contradiction; for each owes its indifferent, exclusive self-dependence precisely to its relation to the other. Each is indifferent to the other only because it is different from it; each excludes the other in precisely the respect in which it includes it (or each is *self*-exclusive); each is independent solely inasmuch as it is dependent.

From this I think it may fairly be inferred that Contradiction should emerge rather as synthesis of the utter indifference, or self-difference, of Diversity with the exhaustive reciprocation of contrary Opposition—in short as the consummation of Difference as such—than as synthesis of Identity and Difference. It will, I think, be clear from the next section that Identity and Difference synthesize more naturally in Ground than in Contradiction.

5·41. In Contradiction Positive and Negative are *posited* contradiction, because each posits itself (i.e. determines its own nature independently of any Other; is, so to say, its own consequent), and at the same time cancels its own nature by positing the other as its consequent. But, Hegel observes, 'Difference in general is already implicitly (*an sich*) Contradiction; for Difference is the unity of terms which only *are* inasmuch as they are not one, and the separation of terms which are only separate by virtue of this very same relation of unity.'[1]

In short, Hegel's view is that contradiction is everywhere experienced. It is the self-diremptive moment of spirit's activity, and the spring and impulse of all movement and activity; for all movement and activity are the activity of spirit.[2]

[1] LL, i, p. 535.

[2] Cf. § 5 above.

5·42. Thus to those who complain that Hegel denies the law of contradiction his reply in effect is that the law of contradiction is the law of his whole system. His treatment of Contradiction as that category of Essence in which difference is fully realized as Contradiction of Essence and Being shows precisely and importantly the clash between his logic and logics of the Understanding, which attempt to interpret the thinking of the Understanding without rising above the level of that thinking. In common sense and special science, and therefore also in any logic of the Understanding, contradiction, Hegel points out, is a bugbear to be avoided at all costs. As far as possible it is maintained or implied by the ordinary logician, using some such device as solution by diverse respects, that no actual existent thing is contradictory. He accordingly transfers contradiction into the process of subjective reflection, which he imagines as in play over against real things.[1] 'But even in this reflection it is said', remarks Hegel, 'not properly to be present, for the contradictory cannot be imagined or thought.'[2] Hegel means that this transference to subjective reflection wholly fails to explain what self-contradictory reflection is. It is only plausible partly because realism never takes the reality of thought seriously, and partly because it takes contradiction as an accident, a sort of abnormality or paroxysm of sickness which will pass away and cease to infringe the abstract laws of thought.[3]

5·43. The point at issue between Hegel and ordinary logic perhaps becomes clearer if we suppose an ordinary logician to retort that Hegel's view of contradiction lays on him the onus of supplying an alternative theory of error.

To this Hegel's answer would be that philosophical error consists not simply in self-contradiction but in *persistence* in self-contradiction. Truth is not the avoidance of self-contradiction, but the passage through it to self-reconciliation, to accordance with the Notion; error is the arrest of this activity. The Understanding, when it struggles without self-transcendence to philosophize, implicitly denies that of its own nature it is that which Reason sublates; it discounts and explains away the touches of Reason in itself. Hence for the Understanding Contradiction is necessarily a deadlock

[1] See § 5·02 above. [2] LL, i, p. 546. [3] See ibid.

to be escaped at any cost. Even Kant saw only a warning in the Antinomies. If we assume with Kant that the effort after self-transcendence is merely a congenital disease of human thought, and that the categories signify in isolation and not dialectically, then when self-contradiction looms ahead we can only do our best to avoid it in speculation as we avoid it in common sense. Any attempt to erect a dialectical philosophy—or indeed any sort of coherence theory of truth[1]—on a realist basis would be the stupidest *persistence* in contradiction.

Hegel has of course no intention of maintaining that for the Understanding a self-contradictory statement can be true—or, rather, correct. But the context in which '*A* is *B*' is correct, and '*A* is not *B*' necessarily incorrect because contradicting it, is just the context of arrested movement, of 'detached' inactive 'real' things, which forms the proper object-world of the Understanding so far as it is *not* Reason. The question at issue, however, touches the status of the Understanding itself. And that is a philosophical context where truth and not correctness is concerned. It must not be naïvely assumed that, because in a limited context, where the finitude of things is *ex hypothesi* fixed, self-contradiction betokens incorrectness, therefore contradiction is, philosophically speaking, a mere disease: the Understanding is not simply the collection or the class of its singular finite acts. When Hegel says that every finite thing is a contradiction, he is considering finite things in relation to Infinity; he is not suggesting that Big Ben can now read both 9 p.m. and not 9 p.m. To assert contradiction in the nature of Time is not to say that there is no precise answer to the question, What is the time?

5·5. Contradiction, then, already prefigured in the antitheses of Being, becomes explicit as the full significance of Difference. We shall easily detect it in all the remaining antitheses of Essence, but it now loses immediate prominence—*zu Grunde geht*, as Hegel puts it with a pun of no particular significance—in the synthesis of Identity and Difference as Ground or, as it might better be named, the self-grounded.

[1] See IH, ch. xiii, §§ 6–6·2, and ch. xiv, § 4.

6. GROUND

In Contradiction Positive and Negative are in an equilibrium which, abstracted from the movement of spirit, must appear as a deadlock.[1] But though in Contradiction Positive has lost its 'dominance' over Negative—i.e. although Negative is now no longer an unessential posited Show but on a par with Essence *qua* Positive, and just as much posits the Positive as it is posited by it—yet Essence is the Negative as much as it is the Positive. Essence is the totality of the equilibrium, for the whole mutual attitude of Positive and Negative displays nothing but the one activity of spirit as Essence. Hence spirit, entering into Difference and persisting through Difference until this equilibrium of Positive and Negative is reached, is not in Contradiction abruptly paralysed, but through Contradiction recovers its 'dominance' of the Negative. Difference was all the while spirit's own self-differentiation, and, to express it formally, Identity and Difference synthesize in Ground. Spirit is now Essence as at once its own consequent and the ground of that consequent: it is self-grounded. 'Ground is Essence posited as totality';[2] i.e. *qua* consequent Essence is its own consequent, or, as Hegel also puts it, 'Ground *qua* sublated determinateness is not indeterminate Essence: it is Essence determined through itself, but determined as undetermined, or as sublated, positedness.'[3]

6·1. In EL the dialectic of Ground is curt to obscurity. Hence it must be filled in from LL, which offers three triads of Ground. The first of these triads introduces the relations of Form to Matter and to Content. These relations in EL are placed later, Matter and Form as the third category of Thing, Content and Form as the antithesis phase of Appearance. These relations seem to fall more naturally into place in EL, yet it is difficult to explain Ground without making use of some such distinctions as they express. When we remember the wide scope of matter and form in Aristotle's

[1] Just as the notion of physical movement, which is 'der *daseiende* Widerspruch' (LL, i, p. 547), must escape the Understanding. [2] EL, § 121.

[3] i.e. 'undetermined', *unbestimmt*, means only that the determinateness of being a 'posited', a consequent upon another, is sublated. LL, i, p. 555.

system, and the difficulty which Hegel has in finding an adequate variety of titles for categories, we need not be surprised at this double appearance of Matter and Form and Content and Form. In the circumstances I shall give a brief account of Ground as it appears in LL; but I shall postpone the more detailed consideration of Matter, Content, and Form until we reach Existence, and I shall simply assume these categories if they seem required in order to speak of Ground.

6·2. Ground (*LL version*)

The LL central triad of Ground is Formal Ground, Real Ground, Complete Ground.[1] It is important throughout to remember that Essence as self-grounded is far less than *causa sui*; it is not even spirit as Thing.

(A) Ground in its first bare and formal meaning is best illustrated by an abstract law, which is offered in explanation of a multiplicity of phenomena but does no more than restate the phenomenon. If, for example, the ground of planetary motion round the sun is given as the attractive force because of which the planets revolve round the sun, then there is no difference in content between the alleged ground and the consequent of it. Gravitation is here offered simply as an utterly immanent law by which certain things do what they do. The proffered explanation is a tautology which merely indicates by its form the unfulfilled demand for some *difference* of content between ground and grounded. That some difference of content is required is even more obvious when we see that this Formal Ground is also inadequate because it is incommensurate with its consequent. Gravitation is a law operative in all movement of bodies; it cannot *adequately* ground any special consequent such as planetary revolution.

6·3. Hence (B) Real Ground must be *different* in content from its consequent. But the Formal Ground was the essence of, the essential element in, its consequent, and by contrast all other determinations of content in the consequent—the *special* nature of the consequent—must be unessential. Therefore the Real Ground can after all be only an unessential moment in the consequent, and therefore external

[1] See Table I.

to it. Moreover, within that for which a real ground is to be found there is no principle upon which we can decide which of the unessential determinations is to be selected as real ground. Hence Real Ground turns out to be no more than the bare general nature of a 'reason', a 'because'. In practical debate Ground is the bare generic nature of all pros and cons. The 'because' of an action may be given as desire for pleasure, economic pressure, revenge, duty, &c.; each of these alleged grounds is equally a ground, but each is unessential because it is inadequate. If it were adequate it would be not ground at all but necessitating cause.

6·4. Thus (C) Complete Ground is both essential and unessential, and each moment of this contradiction is self-contradictory, since Ground, *qua* essential and immanent, is merely formal and tautological, and is real only *qua* unessential and external.

6·5. With this contradictory category of Complete Ground we reach the thought of Condition and Conditioned, wherein Condition is the *sine qua non* of its consequent, the Conditioned, but is still impotent to produce it. This thought is the thesis of the third triad of Ground in LL, and it is still self-contradictory. Only as Condition develops itself through the third triad into Totality of Conditions[1] is this contradiction reconciled; a reconciliation which comes when we see that with the conception of Ground as a totality of conditions we have at once the thought of self-grounded Fact (*Sache*). For from the *totality* of its conditions the conditioned itself cannot be excluded. The totality of conditions is in fact just the same totality which the conditioned is.

6·51. The reader must remember that the contradiction of the coupled moments in the categories of Essence is always self-contradiction: the moments of Ground and Grounded or consequent, and again of Condition and Conditioned, are identical in and through their contradictory difference.

We may illustrate the passage from Real Ground to Totality of Conditions as the transition from one among several conditions of, for example, an explosion to the collec-

[1] See 'The Issue of Fact (*Sache*) into Existence', LL, i, p. 592. The dialectic of Ground is excessively difficult, and I am more than usually uncertain of my interpretation.

tive and therefore successful operation of all the conditions. But we must note that if there is anything whatever in the explosion for which there is no correlate among the conditions, then we have so far failed to assign all the conditions. We are apt, influenced by Hume's statement of the causal problem, to forget that the only hope of explaining the linkage of effect with cause, or of conditioned with conditions, is to try to show them as two phases of the same thing, into each of which that thing enters whole. This must be borne in mind through the rest of the dialectic of Essence. Perhaps the best illustration of the movement here is to think of the universe as at once grounded and at the same time dependent upon a condition which yet cannot essentially determine it. So far the universe *is*, and is essentially determinate; but—to anticipate an analogous later category of Essence—its being is so far merely possible. Then follows the thought that this contradiction of essential and unessential compels the conclusion that what has been inadequately thought in this contradiction is the issue of the universe as totality of conditions into existent fact. More simply, we may think the universe first as a totality of facts such that any one of them is the inadequate but indispensable ground and condition of any other, and then go on to think it as a totality of existent fact which is self-conditioned. In the second thought existent fact and the totality of conditions are clearly identical.

7. EXISTENCE (*Existenz*)

In Existence Ground and Grounded are *immediately* one. Existence, or existent fact, proceeds from Ground, but not as a consequent posited by Ground. If you have the totality of conditions, you have *eo ipso* the existent fact and not a Show reflecting an Essence over against it or hidden within it. In EL, § 123, *Zusatz* Hegel's meaning is made plain:

'Having issued from Ground, Existence contains Ground in it. Ground does not remain behind Existence, but is precisely the sublating and translating of itself into Existence. This is illustrated even in our ordinary consciousness. When we consider the ground of something, we take this not as an abstract inward but as itself again another existent. We take, e.g., the lightning flash which has set a house on fire as the ground of the conflagration; or the manners of a nation and the condition of its life would be regarded as the ground of its constitution. Such indeed is the ordinary aspect in which the existent world originally appears to reflection, viz. as an indeterminate multiplicity of existents which, being simultaneously reflected upon themselves and upon one another, are related reciprocally as ground and grounded.'

Thus Existence recalls Self-identity and the immediacy of Being; but its immediacy is the immediate unity of intro-reflection and reflection into Other. For this reason (*a*) Existence is the antithesis to the Pure Categories of Reflection in which spirit expressed itself in Difference developing to Contradiction;[1] but (*b*) this immediacy is gravid with new self-differentiation of spirit, just because it contains reflection into Other. The existent world is the world of the Thing, or Thinghood.

8. THING[2]

Thing has in EL three subcategories: Thing and Properties (*Eigenschaften*), Thing and Matters, Matter and Form.

Thing and Properties

Thing in its first emergence, *Ding an sich*, is below the distinction of number: it is the analogue of Somewhat,[3] and is no more and no less a thing than it is things.[4] But as Reflection into Other it shows itself in endless diversity of one thing from other things, and so does possess number, although there is so far nothing in the nature of Thing to determine what is to be taken as one thing—the whole tree or the branch of the tree, the book or the page of the book, &c. Nevertheless each thing sustains itself in its relations to all things; these relations are its differentiations in virtue of which it is an identical totality, the totality of its peculiar properties.[5] Moreover, these properties are, in relation to

[1] At any rate in EL. In LL Existence is treated as already Appearance.

[2] See Reyburn, *Hegel's Ethical Theory*, pp. 19–21, for an excellent treatment of this category.

[3] Cf. ch. ii, § 4·2 above.

[4] Hence in LL Thing and Properties is further subdivided.

[5] To grasp this sameness of property and relation it is necessary to transcend the attitude of external reflection which takes things as a 'real' plurality and seeks solution of the problems which then arise by talking of diversity of respects and assuming a quota of sheerly external relations; cf. § 5·02 above, and also IH, ch. xii, §§ 3 and 3·1.

one another, merely diverse. Their self-identity, or intro-reflection, is not mediated for each through the others, but for all through the thing. A lump of sugar, for example, is white, sparkling, cubical, has a certain weight, &c., but there is no essential mutual connexion of these properties. To the question why are they together it can only be answered that there is a thing which 'has' them.

8·1. Hegel contrasts this relation of 'having' with the immediate union of Being and Quality. The relation of 'having' has no place in the sphere of Being. Somewhat, if it loses its quality, ceases to be, but Thing persists in its changing properties. Hegel also sees significance in the association of *haben* (like that of *Wesen*) with the past tense. He says in EL, § 125, that the past is sublated Being, subsisting only in the mind,[1] though he adds (perhaps for fear this should sound like subjective idealism) that the mind also distinguishes this sublated Being from itself.

8·2. Thus Thing as 'haver' of its properties does not truly link them. For Thing abstracted from its properties is mere *Ding an sich*, i.e. not initial *Ding an sich*—that was the analogue of Somewhat and the potentiality of Thing-and-properties—but the abstracted moment of intro-reflection bare of all determinateness, which, in Hegel's view, Kant erected to a position of dignity in his philosophy but was compelled to confess unknowable. Thing is thus a mere *kraftlose Verbindung* of its properties. It cannot sustain and explain them. Rather they may seem to subsist independently of their 'haver'.

But there are no properties floating loose from things, nor can properties revert to mere *qualia* as if we were still in Being. Hence we reach here open opposition, and pass to the antithesis of Thinghood, namely, Thing and Matters (Materials).

9. Thing and Matters

Here the essential moment is no longer the Thing, but its properties *qua* its constituents. This category is the thought that the truth, the true nature, of a thing is simply a product of analysis; that the thing is just its component

[1] Cf. Aristotle, *Prior Analytics* 67a39 ff.

elements, and on its part only their nominal or formal unity wherein they are in merely quantitative relation to one another. There is no need to expatiate on the familiarity of this thought in ordinary experience.

But the category is an open contradiction. For (*a*) the properties in becoming constituents have, as it were, thrown off attachment to the Thing and become independent Things: they are now each a real Thing. But (*b*) they are only quasi-independent Things; for in ceasing to be the peculiar properties distinguishing *this* thing, and becoming instead *this* thing's constituents, they *ipso facto* continue themselves into *other* things which they also assist to constitute.

9·1. Hegel regards this category as properly referring to the sphere of inorganic Nature, though commonly applied there in a somewhat confused way. LL, i, p. 613, makes his meaning plain:

'The transition of property into a matter, or independent stuff, is the well-known transition which chemistry operates upon sensible matter when it seeks to represent the properties of colour, smell, taste, &c., as material of light (*Lichtstoff*), colour, smell, sour or bitter material, &c., while it merely assumes others like that of heat (*Wärmestoff*) or electrical and magnetic matter, convinced that it is now handling properties in their very truth. The expression that things 'consist' (*bestehen*) of diverse materials or stuffs is equally current. Care is taken not to call these matters or materials 'things', although it would be admitted that, e.g., a pigment is a 'thing'; but I do not know whether, for example, the materials of light, heat, electricity, &c., are called 'things'. Things and their constituents (*Bestandteile*) are distinguished, but it is not stated exactly whether or to what degree the latter are things, or perhaps only half-things. Certainly they come under the general head of existents.'

In LL, i, §§ 618–22, Hegel expands this point, and argues the futility of extending this category to Concrete Spirit. In EL, § 128, *Zusatz*, he urges that it cannot even apply to organic Nature.

In modern natural science this form of analysis may be less favoured, but the controversy whether light is undulatory or corpuscular seems to illustrate just this contradictory phase of thought.

10. This unstable opposition now passes to synthesis in

Matter and Form

The constituents or Matters of the antithesis, like the Properties of the thesis, have no mutual relation beyond Diversity. They do not, *qua* independent *diversa*, differ significantly from one another. Hence they coalesce into one undifferentiated Matter; for if they are simply different, they are *eo ipso* simply identical. They are now seen after all to have possessed their *significant* difference not in themselves but in the Things they constituted. The Thing becomes the essential moment as the Form of the Matter, the bearer of all significant negation, all determinateness.

Yet spirit is whole in each of its moments, and Matter and Form are each equally the totality of Thinghood. Each is thus self-dependently for itself.

'But', says Hegel, 'Matter, which is meant to be the positive and determinate Existence, contains *qua* Existence reflection into Other just as much as it contains Being-in-self. Accordingly as uniting these determinations it is itself the totality of Form. Form, on the other hand, being a totality of determinations, *ipso facto* contains Intro-reflection; in other words, *qua* self-relating Form it has the characteristic which was meant to constitute Matter. Both are implicitly the same. Posit this their unity, and you have the relation of Matter and Form, which are also no less distinct.'[1]

10·01. This is close to Aristotle's conception of form and primary matter in the natural world. In IH I have discussed the emphasis Aristotle lays on the essentiality of form as against matter,[2] and his hesitation as to what contribution matter makes to reality.[3] Aristotle's conception of proximate matter will emerge when we discuss Content and Form in the next chapter.

At the same time Hegel is offering the category of Matter and Form as his philosophic interpretation of what contemporary natural science meant by matter. It is therefore a specialized shape of the Aristotelian conception.[4]

The effort to comprehend the correlation of Matter and Form is an excellent lesson in dialectic, because in making it we discover that, hard as it is to rise above the *Vorstellung*

[1] EL, § 129.
[2] See IH, ch. i, §§ 2·6 and 2·61.
[3] Ibid., ch. iv, §§ 4 ff.
[4] Cf. § 6·1 above.

of matter as a separate positive constituent of the thing, yet matter so separated from form is not a possible object of experience in any mode. Matter cannot be *thought* at all save as a moment of the coupled category Matter-and-Form, as Aristotle grasped when he denied that either form in general or matter in general undergo change.[1] Moreover, the *Vorstellung* of a separate matter is nothing but an already informed matter, as Aristotle knew, and as Berkeley in effect brilliantly demonstrated when he destroyed the empiricist conception of matter. Kant, too, confessed it when he called sense-intuition blind without concept, but Kant never quite succeeded in thinking matter-and-form. Although in the KRV he constantly envisages his problem as one of matter and form, yet his official view of matter and form is that it is a mere concept of reflection.[2]

The reader may be helped by concentrating on the category of Matter and Form, and using it as a first clue to all the categories of Essence.

10·1. With Matter and Form the presence of Essence in and as Being, which began with Existence, becomes explicit, and we pass to the level of spirit as Appearance.

In LL this transition to Appearance occurs in the transition from Ground to Existence, which in LL embraces the categories of Thing.[3] It is not very clear why in EL Hegel postpones Appearance, for in both versions the important transition is the passage from Essence which remains behind or within its Show, to Essence which is on a level with its Show. That is the passage from Show to Appearance, and it seems to occur quite explicitly in the transition from Ground to Existence. In EL, however, the first category of Appearance is the World of Appearance, and it may be that Hegel came to regard the categories of Thinghood as not evincing a sufficiently explicit totality to justify their inclusion in Appearance.[4] Moreover, in LL the main antithesis of Appearance is again called Appearance, and it has in effect the same detail which fills the thesis and antithesis of Appearance in the EL version, viz. World of Appearance and

[1] See IH, ch. i, § 2·4.

[2] See § 5·03 above.

[3] See Table I.

[4] See § 1 of the following chapter.

Content and Form. The question is mainly one of terminology, but most readers will, I think, feel that the significant transition really occurs between Ground and Substance, and that the LL version is the clearer. I have taken EL as a basis, however, because the reader unfamiliar with Hegel is likely to start with EL rather than with LL.

VII

APPEARANCE

1. The general character which contrasts Essence as Appearance with Essence as Intro-reflection is the emergence of the essential moment from the background to a position of relative equivalence with the unessential moment, which has so far been more or less mere Show. Yet though thought now moves between two equally apparent moments of Essence, contradiction for that very reason becomes all the more acute. It is precisely this opposition of the two moments at the same level which marks Appearance as the main antithesis of Essence, and persists through it until we reach the unreserved manifestation of Essence in Actuality.

But Essence, when it 'appears' and no longer merely 'shows', necessarily does so as a totality, a world.[1] In EL the three main divisions of Appearance are (1) The World as Appearance, (2) Content and Form, (3) Correlation (*Verhältnis*); and The World as Appearance is nothing but the explicit characterization of Matter and Form as a totality, or as at least a *quasi*-whole.

2. The World as Appearance

If we examine again what has been said of Matter and Form, it becomes clear that they are in effect such a totality. Matter and Form were each the totality of the Thing. Matter was the Thing as positive but indeterminate existent. Yet Matter exists, and has therefore not only self-identity, or intro-reflection, but also reflection into other: i.e. Form is that which reflects and reveals what Matter is. Hence Matter is implicitly Form. Conversely Form is not merely reflected into and revealed by Matter: it is the totality of the Thing's essential characteristics, and so *exists* intro-reflected. Form, that is to say, possesses that self-subsistence which in the first contrast of Matter and Form seemed to belong to Matter and not to Form. Thus the category of Matter and Form is in effect an oscillating contradiction of self-

[1] See ch. vi, § 1·4 above.

subsistence and dependence. But this is just the thought of a *world* of phenomena, each of which claims a self-subsistence that nevertheless at once shows itself to be dependence on a multiplicity of other phenomena with which its Form connects it. Inasmuch as the essential moment is not hidden but apparent, spirit here clearly determines itself as some sort of system or world. The contradiction between the essential and unessential moments, both apparent, will now break out in a fresh antithesis, but their first immediate linkage as a *quasi*-whole is what Hegel means by the World as Appearance.

3. CONTENT AND FORM

The best way to grasp the transition to this antithesis is to begin by contrasting Content (*Inhalt*) and Form with Matter and Form. Matter is the positive but totally indeterminate which remains when one has thought the whole significance of the totality into Form, thus opposing sheer Matter to sheer Form. But Content contrasted with Form is not purely indeterminate, and we approach more nearly to Hegel's conception of Content through Aristotle's proximate matter, the already informed matter of a special form.[1] But proximate matter is less, I think, than Content, because it does not include the final information—the marble is the already informed proximate matter of the statue, but as such excludes the shape of the statue; or again the proximate logical matter of the *infima species* excludes the final differentia.[2] But Content includes the final information as well, and conversely Form includes the whole determining information. For to Hegel Content and Form are each the whole totality:

'While a formless Content can be as little found as a formless Matter, the two (Content and Matter) are distinguished by the fact that Matter, though implicitly not without Form, still in its *Dasein* manifests an indifference to Form, whereas the Content as such is what it is only because it contains in itself the matured (*ausgebildete*) Form. . . . True works of art are those only whose content and form exhibit a thorough identity.'[3]

[1] See IH, ch. i, § 2·61.
[2] See ibid., ch. iv, § 1·2.
[3] EL, § 133, *Zusatz*.

3·1. This conception of Content and Form becomes clearer if we recall the previous category. In the World as Appearance the essential moment, the Ground, was Form endlessly mediating the self-subsistent phenomena, and so contradicting their self-subsistence. But this essential Ground is just as phenomenal as the phenomena which it mediates: it is not hidden behind them. Form, as we saw, possesses the self-subsistence of Matter—that indeed is why the World as Appearance is some sort of a totality, a *quasi*-whole. Hence Form *is* Content. That is to say, the dialectical movement from Matter and Form through the World as Appearance to Content and Form is the passing of Matter, which was only implicitly Form, into Content which *is* Form. Whereas the essential moment was Form as against Matter, it is now Content as against Form; but this essential Content is, as Matter to begin with was not, almost as much Form as it is opposed to Form. I say 'almost', because the identity of Content with Form (wherein Content contrasts with Matter) is not yet complete; it is only completed in the synthesis of Appearance, viz. Correlation.

3·2. In EL, § 133, Hegel remarks that the developed expression of Form as the essential Content of the phenomenal world is the Law of Appearance. He does not there pursue the point, but his conception of Law at this stage is important, and we must endeavour to elicit his meaning from the rather different dialectic of LL. From LL we learn that Law as the positive essential world, the World as Appearance, is a realm (*Reich*) of laws which constitute '*das ruhige Abbild*, the stable image, of the existent or appearing world'.[1]

Abbild means not a secondary, derivative copy but the essential structure apparent in the existent world. As against this essential content the existent world is unessential Things with their properties and matters restlessly shifting into one another by virtue of their Form, their moment of negativity or significant difference. But it must not be forgotten that each of these moments is implicitly the whole, or *quasi*-whole, World of Appearance:

'The realm of laws is the *stable* content of Appearance; Appearance is this same content, but presenting itself in restless interchange and as

[1] LL, i, p. 628.

reflection into other. Appearance is Law as negative and unreservedly (*schlechthin*) self-changing existence, the moment of transition into an opposite, of self-sublation and return into unity. Law does not contain this side of *restless* Form or negativity; Appearance therefore, as against Law, is the totality, for it contains Law, but also more, viz. the moment of *self-moving* Form.'[1]

3·21. Law, or the Realm of Laws, is thus not, like Formal Ground, mere tautologous repetition of sets of phenomena, and it is present in and as, not latent within or beyond, phenomena. But it is defective as an explanation of the World as Appearance. As against Law, the unessential moment, viz. the existent world of things, is a multiplicity of closer, i.e. more particular, determinations which belong to the 'this' or the concrete, and are not contained in Law but are determined by something else.[2] This existent world thus appears possessed of a further content beyond and against the content of the Realm of Laws, and so as a *prius* externally connected with Law, although this further content is unessential and *is* the regress (*das Zurückgehen*) into the content of Law.[3] Correspondingly the content of the realm of laws is a diversity of laws indifferent to one another, and the two sides of any particular law, though posited as essentially linked, are not yet in explicitly necessary connexion. The law of gravitation, for example, professes to lay down the essential connexion of spatial and temporal magnitude: spaces passed through vary as the squares of the times elapsed. But this connexion is merely immediate; the essential *unity* of the two terms has not yet emerged. For the notion of space traversed by a falling body does not itself contain correspondence to time-lapse squared, and the law is so far only empirical, lacking the mediation of proof. Hence the realm of laws is not a genuinely self-subsistent system, but only a *quasi*-whole whose defect can be seen

[1] Ibid., p. 629; italics ('*restless*' and '*self-moving*') mine.

[2] Cf. ch. vi, § 6·3, on Real Ground.

[3] LL, i, p. 629. Hegel means that the realm of laws can never as such absorb and stabilize the endless fluidity of empirical differentiation, although—as will become explicit in the transition to Correlation—the whole flux of empirical differentiation is nothing whatever but the presupposition of Law, that which is to be absorbed in the realm of laws.

equally (*a*) by looking at the endless diversity of the empirical world, as that still stands out against it with a rich, though unessential, unabsorbed content of its own; or (*b*) by noting its internal incoherence and diversity.

3·22. Hegel here acutely seizes a phase never wholly superseded in the industry of any special science.

Though Hegel's Realm of Laws still falls short of causal principle, yet he is clearly writing with special reference to Kant. In Kant's phenomenal world particular laws—presumably, indeed, all further empirical differentiation as well—are particularizations of the schematized categories. But they cannot be deduced *a priori*, and Kant must rely on the 'influence' of things-in-themselves through sensibility to account for all differentiation in phenomena beyond that which the schematized categories supply. Hegel's Law of Appearance precisely grasps a phase of this self-contradictory thought. It is vital to note that Hegel is not trying to reduce all empirical diversity to categories of pure thought—to substitute the logic of Essence for the laws of special science, and ultimately to deduce Krug's pen—but to express the truth that the very contradiction between empirical diversity and law which is designed to absorb it, but cannot wholly do so, is itself a category, a necessary phase of thought. Hegel's position here entails no criticism of special science in its own sphere, and none of Kant save so far as Kant confines knowledge to objects of the phenomenal world, forgetting that our knowledge of that world's phenomenality is a knowledge of more than a phenomenal object.

4. CORRELATION (*Verhältnis*)[1]

In the opposition between an empirically existent world and a realm of laws Appearance is in effect split into two worlds: (*a*) 'this' empirically existent world, and (*b*) a suprasensible world claiming to exist in itself *qua* the truth of

[1] In translating Hegel into English one commonly renders both *Verhältnis* and *Beziehung* as 'relation'. But throughout Hegel's Logic it is vitally important to remember that he thinks of a relation much more as a unity of two terms than as a coupling between two terms. *Verhältnis* is always connected in his mind with *verhalten*: it implies an active attitude towards something. *Beziehung* usually denotes a looser unity of terms than *Verhältnis*.

'this' world. Thus the two moments subsist external to one another, and the aspiration of special science to exhaustive reduction of empirical difference to a realm of laws is doomed to disappointment. Nevertheless the two moments owe their subsistence precisely to this mutual externality: each is posited in its external subsistence by virtue of its essential relation to the other. They are in fact correlates, and each correlate is the totality of the relation.

The subcategories of Correlation are Whole and Parts, Force and its Expression, Outer and Inner. The dialectical movement through them reveals the gradual collapse of the externality between the moments under the stress of their now explicit mutual equivalence, the collapse which heralds Actuality.

5. Whole and Parts

Whole and Parts is the thought of an aggregate. The two moments of Essence are now explicitly equivalent. The Whole is just the 'sum' of its Parts, and as the Parts are mutually indifferent, so the Whole is indifferent to them. To call something 'a whole which is more than the sum of its parts' is in effect to deny that this category is adequate to it. In this immediate thesis of Correlation 'the Content', says Hegel,

> 'is the Whole, and consists of the Parts (the Form), its counterpart. The Parts are diverse from one another. They are the self-subsistent element. But they are Parts only in their identical relation to one another; or in so far as, taken together, they make up the Whole. But this "together" is the counterpart and negation of the Part.'[1]

In LL, i, pp. 646–8, Hegel explains Kant's Second Antinomy (simple and composite substance) as the endless oscillation between the moments of this category: (A) If the simple part be taken as fundamental and the whole, or composite, as contingent, the part is not properly a part at all. But it can then only be itself a whole and consist of parts, and so *ad indefinitum*. Alternatively (B), if composition, or wholeness, be made fundamental and simple parts are denied, then the whole becomes not properly a whole at all, since it has no

[1] EL, § 135.

parts. Hence it can only be itself a part. Any effort to consider one moment in abstraction is defeated by the re-emergence in it of the other moment.

6. Force (*Kraft*) and its Expression (*Aüsserung*)

This category may not seem a very obvious antithesis to Whole and Parts. Hegel is interpreting its use in current physics and empirical psychology, and he also has Herder in mind.[1] He stigmatizes Whole and Parts as essentially a dead mechanical Correlation, the immediate revulsion (*Umschlag*) of self-identity into diversity. As against it Force *issues* in its Expression. In Whole and Parts the Parts are the more truly subsistent and essential moment, although the two moments are explicitly equivalent. But in Force and its Expression this emphasis is reversed. There is no electric or magnetic force save *in* electric or magnetic phenomena, and these phenomena *are* only as the exertion of force—it is absurd to maintain that only the expression of force and not force itself can be known—yet Force is the (immanent) Ground and the essential moment. Nevertheless Force is not free self-determining activity. For (*a*) Force exists embodied in a Thing the other properties of which remain independent: for example, the colour, weight, relation to acids, &c., of iron are independent of its magnetic property. And (*b*) one force for its exertion presupposes another force to solicit or stimulate it, and vice versa: the Expression of Force consists in reciprocal interplay of forces. Hence Force is not a teleological category, but is simply reflected back into itself from its Expression. It is not a synthesis of itself with its Expression; the two moments still merely oscillate into one another. This category, like every category of Essence—more particularly every antithesis in Essence—has itself the form of antithesis, of coupled opposition, and not of the whole triad.[2]

[1] Cf. EL, § 136, and the notes to Wallace's translation of it. Possibly the modern physical concept of energy conforms fairly well to the category of Force and its Expression. Kant excludes force from categoreal status, but regards it as one of the pure but derivative concepts of the Understanding which a complete system of transcendental philosophy would be bound to include in order to present the complete genealogical tree of the pure Understanding; KRV, B, pp. 107–8.

[2] Cf. ch. v, § 3 above.

6·1. Whether or not Force and its Expression is the dialectically inevitable antithesis to Whole and Parts, no category brings out more clearly the general distinction which Hegel means to convey between (i) the impotent unstable flux of spirit in Being, which experience 'illustrates' so far as it is sensuous; (ii) the mechanically determined movement in terms of which the Understanding interprets its world, a movement—we may hesitate whether to call it 'occurrence' or 'behaviour'—which readily shows itself to be reciprocal and to express some sort of a whole, but can never reveal itself as truly subsistent, that is to say as a freely self-determining whole; (iii) the explicitly active expression of spirit in the categories of the Notion, each of which will be itself inherently triadic.

7. INNER AND OUTER

Whereas Whole was only the immediately external equivalent of Parts, Force was the immanent Ground of its Expression. In the former category Parts were the essential moment, in the latter Force. In synthesis these emphases cancel, and the distinction between the two moments becomes purely formal. EL, §§ 138–9, put very clearly the meaning attached by Hegel to a category which is to him of great importance:

'The Inner is the Ground when it stands as the mere Form of the one side of the Appearance, the Correlation—the empty Form of intro-reflection. As counterpart to it stands the Outer—Existence, as correspondingly the Form of the other side of the Correlation, with the empty characteristic of Reflection into other.[1] Their identity [sc. their real identity beneath this merely formal distinction] is identity brought to fullness in the Content, that unity of Intro-reflection with Reflection into other which was posited [Wallace: "forced to appear"] in the movement of Force. Both are the same one totality, and this unity makes them the Content.

'In the first place, therefore, the Outer is the same Content as the Inner. The Appearance shows nothing which is not in the Essence, and in the Essence there is nothing which is not manifested.'

[1] The reader must remember that to Hegel the external is always the self-external, never a merely subjective aspect, never merely what a spectator sees when he cannot see inside.

7·1. The importance of this category is that it marks the close of Appearance and the transition to Actuality. Hegel finds fault with the abstract separation anywhere of Inner from Outer. Nature, for example, is external *überhaupt*, not merely external to Concrete Spirit but also and for that very reason self-external; and to seek for an Inner within Nature as such is absurd.[1] But this means not that Nature is an absolute Outer uncorrelated with any Inner—there is no such thing —but that spirit as Idea, which is the common Content of Concrete Spirit and Nature, is in Nature as mere Outer, and for just that reason equally as mere Inner. Similarly Hegel takes it as the essential doctrine of Christianity as against Judaism that all which God is, his Creation reveals. There remains no unissuing residue in the activity of spirit.

7·2. It is perhaps in the practical sphere that Hegel most impressively insists upon the inseparability of Outer and Inner. His whole conception of the will is here entailed, although the will expresses *par excellence* categories of the Notion. It is therefore worth while to dwell on some of his illustrations.

A child is, *qua* a human being, a rational creature, and it might seem plausible to say that his rationality is merely inward—his natural ability and vocation. But this potential rationality has its outward side in strict correlation with it, namely, the environment in which it develops. The will of his parents, the mature attainments of his teachers, and the whole surrounding world of Reason are for the child at first a mere outward. The course of his education is at once (*a*) the externalizing of his inner potential nature as he grows actually rational, and (*b*) the internalizing, the recognition and taking possession of, this outward rational environment as his own.[2] So again the criminal—the man who perverts his real nature by retaining intellect and will in bondage to the natural man—experiences punishment as an external act of violence, whereas in fact it expresses nothing but his own criminal will. In the same vein Hegel pours scorn upon the man who pleads his good intentions and sentiments in order to excuse his bad deeds; the man who asks to be judged not by his feeble poems and paintings but by his high ideals; the

[1] Cf. IH, ch. viii, § 4·2.

[2] Cf. ibid., ch. ii, § 5·1.

pragmatic historian who, armed with a pseudo-psychology, fancies himself able to trace secret and selfish motives behind the historical actions of great men. 'If the heroes of history', he says, 'had been actuated by subjective and formal [sc. private and capricious] interests alone, they would never have accomplished what they have. If we have due regard to the unity of Inner and Outer, we must own that great men willed what they did, and did what they willed.'[1]

[1] EL, § 140, *Zusatz*, from which I have drawn most of these illustrations. But this insistence on the absurdity of separating Inner and Outer permeates ΦR and ΦH, and large parts of *Phän*. It is a direct consequence of Hegel's conception of activity. For Kant inner and outer is a concept of reflection; see ch. vi, § 5·03 above.

VIII

ACTUALITY: THE ABSOLUTE AND ACTUALITY PROPER

1. 'ACTUALITY (*Wirklichkeit*)', says Hegel, 'is the unity of Essence and Existence; in it shapeless Essence and unstable Appearance,[1] or indeterminate persistence and non-persistent (*bestandlose*) multiplicity, have their truth.'[2]

When the distinction between Outer and Inner collapses and spirit is manifested as one system instead of a contradictory duality of two worlds, it might seem as if no further dialectical advance were possible. In fact, however, the categories of the Notion are still to come, and Actuality itself subdivides into categories. With the transition to the Notion we shall be later concerned, but it may be here observed that though in Actuality spirit becomes one with that other self in which and as which it puts itself forth, yet this is in Actuality the merely *immediate* result of the self-diremptive phase of spirit's activity. Actuality is the final synthesis of this antithesis, the close of the movement of spirit from itself. It is not the self-identification of Spirit as explicitly *subject* with the world in which it has revealed itself. Actuality is (*a*) the failure of the unessential moment of Being, which has survived sublated in Essence as apparent Existence, any longer to maintain itself as subsistent against Essence; and (*b*) the transfiguration of this apparent moment into a revealing moment which *is* Essence. But though Actuality is this open manifestation of the universe as spirit, it is not the detailed explication of the universe as a spiritual system in the form of thought. That is what the categories of the Notion are. On the other hand, Actuality is a *Denkbestimmung* which is not in the Notion superseded as one category of Being is superseded by another, nor at once and contradictorily superseded and preserved as is each category in the dialectic of Essence. Actuality is sublated in the Notion in

[1] *Haltlose Erscheinung*: sc. Appearance which cannot retain the Form in which it differentiates Essence, because it is Being sublated and so a moment of transiency.

[2] LL, i, p. 662.

the sense of being developed. The categories of the Notion as they first emerge will give no impression of introducing fresh content; they will seem at first rather puzzlingly to repeat the categories of Essence. In point of fact they will not, in Hegel's view, repeat them, but rather restate them in their undisguised truth as phases in the activity of spirit *qua* Subject and not mere Substance. In the Notion, as it were, spirit enjoys and administers the conquered territory, the 'objective' system, which *qua wirklich* only proclaims its submission and nativeness to spirit.

1·1. The subcategories of Actuality differ considerably in the two versions. In LL the main triad is The Absolute, Actuality Proper (*Die eigentliche Wirklichkeit*), and Absolute Correlation. In EL the content of the two latter is given in a simplified form, while the first is altogether omitted. In both Logics the dialectic explicates the single actual system into which Inner and Outer have collapsed, and explicates it as still 'objective', i.e. as still falling short of the Notion.[1] For the unity into which Inner and Outer collapse is only the synthesis of Appearance; it clearly requires further explication within Essence. Though we have now explicitly one actual world, as in the previous categories of Essence we had not, nevertheless we have not yet before us the constitution of this world as the reconstitution of all that content which has been exhibited in Intro-reflection and Appearance, the main thesis and the main antithesis of Essence. The difficulty lies in the discrepancy between the two versions. In EL Hegel passes straight from Inner and Outer to Possible and Actual, taking the Actual in its first abstract phase to be so much of reality as is possessed by that of which it can be said that at least it is possible. In LL he prefers to dwell first on Actuality as the character of being explicitly one system, implying that that is the minimal meaning of the term 'the Absolute'. The category of The Absolute is inspired by Spinoza, and reconstructs critically his conception of spirit. It also owes something to Leibniz and possibly Schelling. In the Introduction to LL Hegel makes clear that one of the tasks he sets before himself in the Logic of Being and Essence is to interpret the metaphysic

[1] See above, ch. v, § 6.

of his predecessors.[1] I confess I can find no good reason for the large omissions in the EL version, and I shall try to offer the reader a simplified account of the more complete dialectic of LL.

2. The Absolute

In LL the Absolute subdivides—with obvious reference to Spinoza—into (1) Exposition (*Auslegung*) of the Absolute, (2) Absolute Attribute, (3) Mode of the Absolute.

Exposition of the Absolute

The Absolute is first just the bare self-identity of spirit as the identity of the two self-subsistent total moments which as Inner and Outer collapsed into one. It is absolute Form as against this 'collapsed' totality of diverse multiplicity. But it is at the same time absolute Content, because only by virtue of the Absolute as its immanent Ground is this diverse multiplicity *one* actual world. From this it becomes clear that the Absolute is the purely affirmative or positive. Determinateness is here nothing but simple negation, as Spinoza held, not concrete negation of negation. The Absolute is the Ground of all the manifold determinateness which the categories of Being and Essence have so far revealed; but it also cancels and swallows them up, leaving them the status of mere Show, or even mere illusion, and not of Appearance. It is at once their *Grund* and their *Abgrund*, as Hegel puts it, and he may be referring to Schelling's Absolute, which he elsewhere ridicules as 'the night in which all cows are black'.[2] The 'Show' of the Absolute is a medium which is absorbed by that which shows through it.

That is to say that we have here a category of External Reflection. Thought moves from the diversified Show, which it simply finds given, to an Absolute Ground in which that Show is simply dissolved. Thought thus remains external to the Absolute system and merely expounds it.

3. Absolute Attribute

But this thought *is* after all the activity of the Absolute itself. The Absolute, when it is thought as a mere goal of

[1] See ch. v, § 6.

[2] *Phän.*, JE, ii, p. 22.

external reflection which started from the merely discovered datum of diversified Show, is quite inadequately thought. It is not, as Hegel puts it, the absolute Absolute. But this mere Absolute of external reflection readily passes to antithesis. For it is just as much (merely) Inner as it is (merely) Outer. Hence it is after all not abstract self-identity but Attribute; i.e. it is the Absolute as a Form-determination which is, though only formally, the whole Content of the Actual world. Absolute Attribute differs from the paired total moments of the sphere of Appearance—Whole and Parts, Force and Expression, Inner and Outer—because those pairs, though equivalent, had persistence against each other; whereas Absolute Attribute is posited as the sole true persistence of the Absolute.[1]

3·1. But this determining of the Absolute as Attribute is not a genuine determining. The Absolute has not issued from itself into a genuinely external Other and returned in concrete self-synthesis. Instead of the true activity of spirit we have had only (1) the movement of External Reflection from the given manifold Show back to a Ground which dissolves it utterly, and (2), as the other side, the antithesis of this movement, a mere inner (purely formal) issue and Intro-reflection of the Absolute, a return to itself from no true self-diremption. Spinoza elaborates two parallel attributes, thought and extension, and he indicates that an indefinite plurality of others is required in order to exhaust the Absolute. He thus admits that he can show no true differentiation of his eternal substance into its attributes. In effect the attributes cannot persist in this empty intro-reflection of the Absolute any more than could the diversified Show. They are just as much merely negative as was that Show; they too must perish by the edict *determinatio est negatio*.

3·2. Thus each of these categories, Exposition of the Absolute and Absolute Attribute, is a true category of Essence. Each is a coupled pair of moments in antithesis, a putting forth of spirit which returns, as it were, baffled and unsatisfied from its untrue self-diremption, an oscillation rather than a new concrete self-integration. The

[1] Hegel has in mind Spinoza's attributes, thought and extension, as against his modes.

Exposition of the Absolute was a movement of External Reflection from a *de facto* given Show to its sheer cancellation in the engulfing Absolute; the Absolute Attribute is a converse internal issue of the Absolute as essential Attribute which is to be the Absolute's sole true persistence, but it suffers the same dissolution as was suffered by the Show of finite diversity from which External Reflection started. The Attribute turns out to be just as much an external Show, or mere way and manner of being, as was the external diversity which served External Reflection for datum. Both, in Spinoza's terminology, are mode. The Absolute which failed to ground its own expression fails equally to posit it.

4. The Mode of the Absolute

But this contradiction of reciprocating moments has now become explicit; i.e. it has become clear (*a*) that the diversified Show was starting-point for External Reflection only so far as the Absolute was presupposed, and (*b*) that the Absolute equally presupposes the Attributes in which it issues. The external Show and the Attributes have in fact turned out to be one and the same expression of the Absolute: they are its Mode, in which it manifests itself neither as mere external Show nor as mere internal Show but, subject to the limitation of the sphere of Essence, as concrete negation of negation.

Hegel puts the transition from Attribute to Mode thus:

'The *distinctive* characteristic of the Attribute taken as the *Inner* of the Absolute is to posit itself as Mode. Mode so far is the externality of the Absolute, its losing of itself in the instability and contingency of Being: Mode is the Absolute's accomplished transition (*übergegangensein*) into the opposite *without return* to self. . .[1] But Mode, the externality of the Absolute, is not this alone. It is also externality *posited* as externality; a mere *way and manner*, and hence Show as Show, or *the Intro-reflection of Form.* Consequently it is *that self-identity which the Absolute is.* Therefore in effect it is *only* in Mode that the Absolute is posited as absolute identity; the Absolute is what it is, namely self-identity, only as self-relating negativity, as showing which is posited as showing.'[2]

[1] This to Hegel represents Spinoza's inadequate conception of mode.
[2] LL, i, p. 670.

That is why it is the first phase of Actuality; but the next triad will show more clearly what this first phase of Actuality has been.

4·1. Hegel's criticism of Spinoza[1] is important because it shows precisely how he intends these categories as a reconstruction of Spinoza's thought.

In Hegel's view, Spinoza's defect was that he grasped negation only as 'first negation', movement from thesis to antithesis. His exposition of the Absolute is complete in that it moves through Attribute to Mode, but it exhibits no necessity in the issue of the Absolute in unessentiality. Spinoza's attributes, as his confession of their indefinite plurality betrays, are no active dialectical self-differentiation of the Absolute. Spinoza's mode, the affection of substance which is in an other and apprehended through that other, is not the necessary explication of that otherness which the attribute implicitly contains, but a mere immediately given mode not recognized as intro-reflection.

4·2. Thus in Spinoza the progress of the Absolute resembles the oriental conception of emanation, which is only a progressive loss; not a progressive self-manifestation, but a gradual obscuring, of the Absolute. Spinoza defines his attribute as a manner in which the intellect (*intellectus*)[2] comprehends the essence of the Absolute. But thereby the intellect, which to Spinoza is a mode and so posterior to the attributes, inevitably becomes something upon which the attribute is dependent: although absolute substance is God, yet intellect emerges externally over against it. In short, Spinoza fails to make his substance active spirit. Thought, both as attribute of substance and as intellect and mode, is of course included in Spinoza's Absolute; but it is included only as a cancelled insubsistent differentiation, which for that very reason becomes merely external over against a dead inactive Absolute.

4·3. In Hegel's eyes this oriental conception of the

[1] See LL, i, pp. 672–5, and ii, pp. 9–12. In EL it appears under Substance; see EL, § 151, *Zusatz*.

[2] In LL, i, p. 673, Hegel translates *intellectus* as *Verstand*. But if *Verstand* here bears its usual meaning in Hegel's philosophy, he is anticipating the conclusion of his argument against Spinoza. Hence I think it does not.

Absolute is the essential *prius* of all further philosophic development. To Hegel, Spinoza is an idealist and a philosopher—they are synonymous terms—because he does not take finitude at its face value, and because he knows only spirit to be real. Spinoza fails not because he treats spirit in terms of absolute substance, but only because he fails also and further to treat it as absolute subject. Hence Hegel's reconstruction of Spinoza is (*a*) the demonstration of spirit as the Notion, and (*b*) the exhibition of Spinoza's substance, attribute, and mode as a dialectical triad prefiguring the Notion within Essence.[1]

4·4. Hegel finds the complementary one-sidedness in Spinoza's contemporary, Leibniz. As against the dead impersonal Absolute of Spinoza, the Leibnizian monad is an intro-reflected totality of the Universe. Though it is finite, it is active concrete negation, an essentially individual entelechy, whose proper business is self-manifestation. This new conception of individuality was in Hegel's view a vitally important step, because it expressed individuality as a totality or system of active intro-reflection. On the other hand, each Leibnizian monad has a peculiar content and a peculiar way and manner of manifestation determined against the peculiar content and manner of manifestation in each of the other monads. This mutual and complementary determination, however, is not expressed in the active self-manifestation of each monad: it belongs to their inherent nature, their *Ansichsein*, but they never possess it *für sich*. Leibniz is forced to pre-establish their harmony as a mere dogmatic assumption.[2]

5. Actuality Proper

In the categories of Actuality Hegel writes largely with Kant's modal categories in mind.[3] The topic of possibility and probability is common in contemporary philosophy, and

[1] On the relation of Spinoza's attributes and modes to Aristotle see IH, ch. vi, § 3·11, and for a parallelism between them in respect to the emergence of *intellectus* over against absolute substance see ibid., § 5.

[2] See LL, i, pp. 675–7.

[3] These were discussed in IH, ch. ix, § 4·311, and I there commented on the difficulties which beset any realist doctrine of possibility and probability. See also ch. xii, §§ 9·1 and 9·11, below.

no part of Hegel's Logic better exhibits the relation of his idealism to philosophies of the Understanding than that which we now approach.

The clue to the general advance of the dialectic from this point to the end of Essence is the movement of spirit to necessity, and thence to the free activity of overt self-manifestation. There is no essential difference between the treatment of Actuality Proper in the two Logics. We may perhaps modify the rather cumbrous nomenclature of LL, and take as sub-titles (1) Formal Possibility and Contingency (*Zufälligkeit*), (2) Real Possibility and Real Actuality, (3) Absolute Necessity.

6. Formal Possibility and Contingency

The Actual in the full sense of the term is that which is rationally necessitated; i.e. that which can be *thought* as necessary. It is this sense of rationally necessitated which the term bears in Hegel's famous and seldom understood remark that the rational is actual and the actual is rational.[1]

But the Actual in its full nature we have not yet reached, and the minimal characterization of the Actual is that it is at any rate Possible. In the foregoing categories of the Absolute we reached only the *formal* self-identity of the Absolute in its modes. The diversified Show turned out in the end to be not indeed mere illusion, but self-manifestation; yet this was not explicitly necessary self-manifestation. The Absolute in its modes is, in short, no more than the bare possibility or potentiality, the quite indeterminate Ground, of its own actual expression as system. Accordingly the Outer to this Inner, the actual moment of this possibility (which is no more than the Absolute's formal self-identity, its bare absence of self-contradiction in modal expression), can only be contingency, the casual fact which might be otherwise than as it is.

6·1. It is here vital to remember that Formal Possibility and Contingency are two moments of a category, and are not only (i) for that reason inseparable thoughts, but also (ii) equivalent totalities such that in each of them and in both together spirit is whole. They cannot be thought apart, and

[1] Cf., for example, ΦR, JE, vii, Preface, p. 33, and EL, § 6.

they must be thought as each the totality of an Absolute which is yet only total in each of them because they cannot be thought apart. The mere contingent matter of fact, the 'actual' of common sense, only is 'actual' as the outer of an inner possibility. If we cut away this grounding possibility from matter of fact we lapse back at once to the categories of Being: we have not any sort of matter of actual fact, but a mere *daseiendes Etwas*.

6·2. This equivalence of bare Formal Possibility and Contingency effectively illustrates Hegel's reconstructive attitude not only to Kant but also to Aristotle and Leibniz.

Aristotle had defined the possible (τὸ δυνατόν) as the non-self-contradictory,[1] and he had also formulated the law of contradiction ontologically as an attribute of Being *qua* Being.[2] The contingent (τὸ ἐνδεχόμενον καὶ ἄλλως ἔχειν) he sometimes treats as if it were an element in the real simply juxtaposed to the necessary (τὸ μὴ ἐνδεχόμενον καὶ ἄλλως ἔχειν), and the result in his logical doctrine is that one judgement differs modally from another only because it categorically asserts a different type of predicate. Yet at other times Aristotle regards the contingent as merely the defective appearance of the necessary, and chance as a cloak for ignorance.

Thus his teaching remains ambiguous. He appears to regard the merely non-self-contradictory possible, τὸ δυνατόν, as either equivalent to, or at any rate commensurate with, the contingent. But if non-self-contradictory possibility is an attribute of all Being as such, whereas the contingent is a part of Being merely juxtaposed to the necessary, then τὸ δυνατόν and τὸ ἐνδεχόμενον καὶ ἄλλως ἔχειν cannot be either equivalent or commensurate.

This contradiction occurs because Aristotle is not sure whether contingency is or is not a character of some things in independence of their being objects of mind, and it will be helpful, though Hegel does not do so, to formulate Hegel's solution of the problem with direct reference to Aristotle.

Mere absence of self-contradiction—mere 'logical' possibility—is, taken by itself, just the negative formulation of the

[1] See *Metaphysics* Δ 1019^{b}27 ff. [2] See ibid. Γ, ch. 3.

category of (Self-)Identity.[1] Formal non-self-contradictory Possibility (which in effect is what Aristotle meant by τὸ δυνατόν) and contingency (Aristotle's τὸ ἐνδεχόμενον καὶ ἄλλως ἔχειν) are not equivalent synonyms but a commensurate couple unthinkable apart. The former is that which issues in the latter, and together they constitute a category developed far beyond bare (Self-)Identity. Nevertheless *this* (formal) possibility is a minimally characterized possibility: Formal Possibility is the Inner of the Contingent. But—as we shall see in § 7—there is a Real Possibility which is the Inner of Necessity. Hence possibility in a merely formal sense may be called an attribute of Being as such, provided that it be not equated with a 'real' contingency independent both of the necessary and of mind.

We may add that Aristotle himself was far from unaware of real possibility. Proximate matter for Aristotle is also the positive potency of realization in the form to which it is proximate.[2]

6·3. The commensurate coupling of Formal Possibility and Contingency is also an answer to Leibniz. The Leibnizian actual world is the product of divine selection from within a wider *a priori* possibility, and by selecting not the best possible world for actualization God would not have violated the law of contradiction. But this unrealized residue of possibility, together with God's selective act and his establishment of harmony between the monads of the selected world, remains a mere assumption external to Leibniz's system.

6·4. The possibility expressed in Kant's first modal category is not the mere logical possibility of the problematic judgement-form. It is not something wider than the actual; it is a real possibility coextensive with the actual and the necessary, having no significance apart from its reference to a passive intuition. On the other hand, Kant offers what turns out to be a mere psychological and realist interpretation of modality.[3]

We shall discuss Hegel's attitude to Kant's modal doctrine in Chapter XII,[4] and it perhaps comes out most clearly

[1] See ch. vi, § 4·1 above.
[2] See IH, ch. ii, § 6·1.
[3] See ibid., ch. ix, § 4·311.
[4] §§ 9·1 and 9·11.

in his criticism of Kant's attack on the ontological argument.[1] But it is necessary meanwhile to emphasize the important point of contrast here between Hegel on the one hand and on the other both Leibniz and Kant. Neither Leibniz nor Kant fully grasped the truth that if a fact is experienced as contingent, as such that it might be otherwise than as it is, then the alternative possibilities which happen not to have been realized form a genuinely constitutive moment in our thought of that fact as contingent: that is the way the Understanding thinks and characterizes its object. The unrealized possibilities do not belong to a reservoir of possibility upon which God chose not to draw, nor are they a multitude of contents which we miraculously entertain without judging. Formal Possibility and Contingency are the inseparably coupled moments of one constitutive thought of the Understanding.

7. Real (*reale*) Possibility and Real Actuality

Since the Contingent is that in which the formally Possible has actually issued, it must be after all in a rudimentary formal sense necessary. We cannot rest in the thought of an entirely contingent fact. 'The Contingent', says Hegel, 'has no ground, because it is contingent; and equally because it is contingent it has a ground.'[2] That is to say, a mass of unactualized possibilities may seem to us just as *a priori* likely as what has actually occurred, yet Possibility is the inseparable ground of the Contingent. It is only the indolent mind which either accepts the bare present fact as finally true, or indulges in the imagining of possibilities which might have been or yet may be. A man, we might say in illustration of Hegel, may wonder idly what he would have been had his father begotten him on some other night or upon some other woman, or he may speculate upon the consequence of a thousand turns which life may take tomorrow. He may view as contingent any point in his own or the world's history, weaving within an Absolute of Formal Possibility an indefinite regress of future histories and alternative past histories in endless permutation and combination,

[1] See ch. xiv, § 4·1 below. [2] LL, i, p. 684.

and he will neither violate the law of contradiction nor ever lack some ground for his conclusion. His day-dreaming, moreover, may serve to teach him the fatuity of taking bare fact *wie es geht und steht* for absolute truth, for he may eventually see that so long as he does so, no fact favours any one line of prediction more than any other, nor save by its brute presence is any more real than what might have been. Nevertheless the merest brute fact is somehow other than what might have been: it is actual. In *any* fact experienced there is a presumption of necessity both backwards and forwards in time. The ordinary rational man discriminates in the past between a might-have-been which came near to being and one which did not, and he does not predict without a ground of probability. He presumes, though he cannot fully establish, a necessitating system of which Formal Possibility and Contingency are the abstract minimal determination.

7·1. Hence the category of Formal Possibility and Contingency begets its own antithesis. The fact which appeared sheerly contingent must be formally necessary, since it has occurred; and this form is found to have its content in the circumstances, the environing conditions of the fact's occurrence. 'In so far as the characteristics (*Bestimmungen*), circumstances, and conditions of a fact (*Sache*) are explored in order to deduce its possibility, Formal Possibility is left behind, and what is now under consideration is its Real Possibility.'[1] The bare fact now emerges as that which flows from a circle of conditioning facts; what seemed mere external circumstances for no obvious reason determining the issue of a mere contingent become facts which necessarily determine a really actual fact. Moreover, the relation between these really actual facts is reciprocal. Each is condition as well as conditioned. Thus the Real Possibility of each really actual fact is the other facts as really actual. We have here the Absolute as a totality of conditions which is *eo ipso* a total actuality. In the issue of Real Possibility in Real Actuality a real necessity operates.

7·2. It is well here to take our bearings, and observe what precisely this real necessity is. Hegel speaks of fact (*Sache*)

[1] Ibid., p. 686.

and conditions, but he is careful to point out that we have passed far beyond that transition of Ground into Existence which his terminology seems to recall.[1] The issue of conditions in fact is here the *production* of one determinate actual by another.

'At this point Real Actuality as such is the Thing of many Properties, the existing world; but it is not the Existence which dissolves itself in Appearance. Just because it is Actuality it is also implicit Being (*Ansichsein*) and Intro-reflection; it *preserves* itself in the multiplicity of pure Existence [italics mine]; its externality is only an inner attitude to itself. What is actual can act (*wirken*), and whatever manifests Actuality does so through what it produces (*hervorbringt*). Its Correlation (*Verhältnis*) with Other [sc. what Hegel called its "externality" in the last sentence but one] is the manifestation of *itself*; it is neither a transition (*Übergehen*)—the way in which the Somewhat of Being relates itself (*bezieht sich*) to Other—nor an Appearing—the way in which the Thing is merely correlated with other Things and, though self-subsistent, has its Intro-reflection, its determinate essentiality, in another self-subsistent.'[2]

That is to say, Real Possibility is not a mere non-self-contradicting δυνατόν but a positive δύναμις, a potency and not a mere potentiality. And for that very reason it is a Real Actual: that which has in it any measure of positive development so far *is* actually, though so far as it is not fully developed it *is* only potentially.[3] Hegel is here very close to Aristotle. There is no clearer clue to his thought throughout the categories of *Wirklichkeit* than the Aristotelian doctrine of δύναμις and ἐνέργεια considered as the more concrete characterization of matter and form.[4] Particularly illuminating is the progressive transition in the meaning of ἐνέργεια from actuality to activity.[5]

7·3. Thus Real Actuality is self-manifestation in effective production, self-realization—if we may borrow from the sphere of will, which of course involves also teleological categories—in and as work done.[6]

[1] Cf. ch. vi, § 7 above.

[2] LL, i, p. 686. Cf. also EL, § 146, *Zusatz*: 'Thus there comes into being quite another shape of things; and yet it is not another, for the first Actuality is only posited as what in essence it was.'

[3] See IH, ch. i, § 2·61.

[4] See ibid., § 2·5.

[5] See ibid., ch. ii, § 6·1.

[6] Cf. Aristotle, *Nicomachean Ethics*, ix, ch. 7, on benefactors.

But we must not advance too quickly. The Real Actual in its working is a condition which is itself actual, and so is more than, for example, Force; but it is not yet even causality,[1] and we have now to observe the defect of this category and the sharp contradiction which marks it as antithesis. It is true that the issue of Real Possibility into Real Actuality is a real, not a mere formal, necessity; for the two moments, (*a*) the circle of conditions which are actual, and (*b*) the really actual fact which they produce and are therein reproduced, are one in content. But, on the other hand, this content is only a restricted content, *irgendeine beschränkte Wirklichkeit*.[2] The movement of thought to Real Possibility and Actuality began from any contingent brute fact: it was any bare fact which was to be interpreted in terms of the necessity which we had to presume.[3] Hence the really actual fact and the circle of its conditions remain in each case a restricted content inadequate to the necessity which binds them. Therefore this Real Necessity, too, retains the moment of Contingency.

7·4. An illustration may be helpful. If we analyse the circle of conditions necessitating a given explosion, we shall readily discover that they and the explosion are one in content. For in the explosion the explosive material passes to a fresh state of itself, and so does anything we take as a condition not physically contained in the explosive; the temperature, for example, and the humidity of the surrounding atmosphere, the local situation and rigidity of other parts of the physical environment, &c.

But here arises a dilemma. There is nothing in principle to limit the circle of conditions short of the whole environing universe,[4] and consequently nothing in principle to limit the really actual event which they produce, issuing therein. But if we thus expand the Inner and Outer of this one content, we reach nothing more definite than the thought of a total

[1] It is important to observe that Hegel solves the notorious difficulty of distinguishing logically between condition and cause by assigning them to different levels of thought.

[2] LL, i, p. 690.

[3] See § 7 above.

[4] Which is for the Understanding a mere *quasi*-Whole, indefinitely regressive.

state of the universe at one instant producing, and reproducing itself in, a fresh total state of the universe at the next instant. And we may also multiply the first state backwards through the past *ad indefinitum*.

We are thus back again at the level of Formal Possibility and Contingency, a level at which the content is indeterminate. We presumed necessity in the bare fact, and by analysis of conditions we have explicated this necessity in the shape of an identity of content between these relevant conditions and this really actual fact. But this procedure has entailed a restriction which we cannot justify in principle. Form and content are in contradiction, and the two sides of the restricted content are not after all strictly commensurate.

This is clearly shown when any really actual fact again becomes condition, i.e. real possibility of further really actual fact, and so on. Whatever we take as the actual real fact fails on examination to be the complete issue of the real possibility 'behind' it, and itself issues afresh. Thus the necessary issue of conditions into fact turns out to be also contingent. As Hegel puts it, 'Necessity has not yet determined itself as Contingency *out of itself*.'[1] That is to say, in any empirical case of really actual fact, or in the Absolute as a totality of such cases, necessity is still an external compulsive necessity, not a fully intelligible free activity of self-manifestation.

It is to be constantly remembered that for Hegel (1) free activity is everywhere the criterion which orders the categories; (2) any falling off from activity entails contingency; (3) to exert and to suffer compulsion are both unfree, and therefore (4) both entail contingency.

7·5. The category of Real Possibility and Real Actuality is that which operates *par excellence* in our experience of probability, a subject which Hegel does not discuss *eo nomine* in the Logic.[2]

We may illustrate by contrasting prediction with knowledge after the event. We think it probable, for example, that war will break out within a certain period between two countries; i.e. we infer from a real possibility to its issue in really actual fact, but, the conditions as we know them being

[1] LL, i, p. 690. [2] But see *Phän.* JE, ii, pp. 198–9.

inadequate, we admit that war may not occur within the period. We seem thus to contradict ourselves; to be asserting that war is really possible, and yet at the same time admitting that if it does not occur its non-occurrence will show that it was *not* really possible. Moreover, if war does occur we seem able in principle to determine as absolutely necessary the series of events which led up to and issued in it. Yet that seems equally to falsify our assertion that war was probable: if it has occurred it surely was certain to occur.[1] But if we look more closely at the supposed absolutely necessary train of events issuing in the actually occurrent war, it turns out to exhibit only a blind compulsive necessity, which is still also contingent. For to explicate this supposed absolute necessity fully would require the expansion of the train of events into the whole universe; but that would take us back once more to mere Formal Possibility and Contingency. Thus alike every successful and every unsuccessful prediction shows the assertion of probability to have been self-contradictory; but the important point is that the real actuality (the war which occurred at the predicted date or the actual peaceful state of affairs at that date) reveals itself by the contingency that is in it as the inseparable other moment of Real Possibility, or probability. Only if we mistake the 'really' actual for the self-subsistently real in the fullest sense of reality—which does not belong at all to the categories of Essence—need we fall back into the difficulties in which most modern theories of probability are entangled.

8. Absolute Necessity

'When anything is said to be necessary, the first question we ask is, Why? Thus we assume that anything necessary should come before us as something posited, as a mediated consequent. Yet if we go no farther than mere mediation [sc. by derivation from an antecedent], we have not gained a full comprehension of what necessity means. What is merely mediated is what it is, not through itself but through something else; and then it, too, is itself merely contingent. What is necessary, on the other hand, we would have be what it is through itself; and then, although mediate, it must still contain that which

[1] Aristotle in *De Interpretatione* 9 puts this contrast very aptly, though his conception of contingency wavers and he does not hold the two moments together.

mediates it sublated within itself. Hence we say of the necessary, "It is". We thus hold it to be simple self-relation in which all dependence (*Bedingtsein*) upon something else is removed.'[1]

8·1. The demand for self-necessitating actual fact is satisfied in what LL calls Absolute Necessity, but the transition to this synthesis is not very clearly indicated in either Logic. EL gives the clearer statement.

'The necessary *qua* mediated through an other is not in and for itself, but something merely posited. But this mediation is *eo ipso* immediately the sublation of itself; the Ground and contingent Condition is translated into immediacy, whereby the former positedness is sublated to Actuality, and the fact has closed with itself ("die Sache mit sich selbst zusammengegangen ist"). In this return to itself the necessary simply (*schlechthin*) *is*, as unconditioned Actuality. The necessary is so, *mediated* through a circle of circumstances; it is so because the circumstances are so. And at the same time it is so *un*mediated, so because it *is*.'[2]

Hegel calls this Absolute Necessity 'blind', i.e. still a compulsive *a tergo* necessitation in which no end, no final cause, is explicit.[1] Absolute Necessity, moreover, will pass next into Substance and Accident, to which Hegel applies the terms *Macht* and *Aktuosität*. Hence I think we may infer that the synthesis which gives Absolute Necessity occurs with the thought that if the really actual fact is compulsively necessitated then the really possible conditions—since they compel—must necessitate freely. But condition and fact are one in content; so that the relation of the moments is reciprocal, and the conditions are just as much posited as the fact—or in other words the necessitation is free because it is *self*-compulsion. Hence the moment of free necessitation and the moment of compulsion coalesce in what lies between mere external compulsion and genuine activity—something which may be called *Macht*, Power. This Power is a Possibility which is its own Actuality,[3] but it is still blind. The moment in Essence of Being, which has passed through the phases of Show and Appearance and is now Contingency,

[1] EL, § 147, *Zusatz*.

[2] EL, § 149.

[3] Cf. Kant, KRV, B, p. 111: 'Necessity is nothing but existence which is given through the possibility itself.'

is still not quite completely mastered. This is because the moments of the category, though explicitly equivalent, are still each a distinct Actual, as we shall see clearly when Substance and Accident is sublated by Cause and Effect.

8·2. Thus—if I have not misunderstood Hegel—Formal-Possibility-and-Contingency (wherein Form is identical) synthesizes with Real-Possibility-and-Real-Actuality (wherein Form and Content are in contradiction) in Absolute Necessity, or the Absolutely Actual; and this synthesis is an immediacy of two moments which are (*a*) Power and (*b*) what might perhaps be called submission to control.

This immediacy of Absolute Necessity is Substance and Accident.

IX

ACTUALITY: ABSOLUTE CORRELATION

1. The subcategories of Absolute Correlation are Substance and Accident, Cause and Effect, and Reciprocity (*Wechselwirkung*), titles which show clearly enough that Hegel has the Kantian categories very much in mind.

The movement through Absolute Correlation will show the final sublation in the Notion of Categories which have consisted of two moments coupled in contradiction. So far in every phase of Essence spirit has failed to reveal itself completely in its Other. Failing to be a full and complete return upon itself, the thwarted activity of spirit has taken shape in every antithesis as an incontinent outward movement analogous to the Spurious Infinite of Being. Essence, that is to say, has shown us the impotent instability of Being on the way to becoming, but not yet become, the steady self-production of a genuine and free activity; the syntheses of Essence are never a complete negation of negation. At the point we have reached, the coupled moments of the category are in contradiction because, though they are equivalent totalities, yet *each* is an Absolute Actuality. The sublated moment of Being expressive of Essence, which has hitherto been subordinate, has now developed to relatively complete manifestation of Essence; but this very completeness of its development as expression opposes it to that which it expresses. Both the moments are now absolutely Actual,[1] and with the solution of this contradiction we shall pass beyond Essence.

2. Substance and Accident

'Absolute Necessity is Absolute Correlation because it is not Being as such, but Being which is because it is, Being as absolute self-mediation.'[2]

This Absolute Correlation of Essence as Actual revealing itself as Actual is in the first instance the merely immediate

[1] We might say that the expressive moment now presents itself as at once plenipotentiary and potentate.

[2] LL, i, p. 697.

correlation of Substance and Accident. 'Because of this immediate identity and presence of Substance in the Accidents, there is as yet no real distinction. In this first determination Substance is not yet manifested according to its full Notion.'[1] Substance abides immanent in its Accidents, and they in abstraction from it are mere *diversa*. They succeed one another, neither simply coming to be and passing away nor so that one of them grounds and necessitates another; their only unity is the Substance which they manifest. But Substance in its Accidents is not the *kraftlose Verbindung* of Thing in its Properties.[2] The alternation of Accidents expresses 'die Aktuosität der Substanz als ruhiges Hervorgehen ihrer selbst'. In Accident all previous determinations are sublated to substantiality, and that is precisely to say that Substance in its Accidents is immanent productive power.

2·1. But since Substance produces *itself* in each Accident, and does so exhaustively and without reserve, it follows that each Accident is Actual Substance. So contradiction becomes explicit, and we pass from Substance and Accident to its antithesis, Cause and Effect. Or this transition to Cause and Effect may be equally well expressed by saying that it occurs when the self-relation, the return to itself, of Substance through its Accidents becomes explicit.

2·2. The substance of Kant's seventh (schematized) category is the *a priori* moment of permanence without which the alternating phases of phenomenal change would dissolve in sheer disconnexion; without which objective temporal experience would be impossible. Though it is permanent, it is yet that alone which changes, for the accident is nothing but the mode in which the existence of substance is determined. Kant expressly states in the First Analogy that he makes substance and accident a category of *Verhältnis* because it is the condition of the correlation we inevitably make between that which in the existence of a substance is subject to change and that which is properly permanent and radical.[3] Hegel's nearness here to Kant is even greater if Kant, as I think he does, conceives causality as a power of production and not merely as a law of necessary succession in time.[4]

[1] Ibid., p. 700. [2] See ch. vi, § 8·2, above. [3] KRV, B, p. 230.

[4] See Professor Paton, *Kant's Metaphysic of Experience*, i, p. 308.

2·21. It may be observed that Hegel's category of Substance and Accident is not the conception with which Aristotle works in formulating the logic of natural science. The Aristotelian distinction between substantial and accidental characters is not here preserved by Hegel, who conceives Substance as completely exhausted in its Accidents.[1] So also does Kant.

3. Cause and Effect (*Ursache und Wirkung*)

If we consider the correlation of Substance and Accident with reference to the Accident, we see that when the substantiality of each Accident becomes explicit, then the Accidents are no longer an alternation of *diversa* but a series of terms each one of which is equally a cause producing an effect and an effect produced by a cause: the Power of Substance has now descended upon the Accident. Or if we consider the same category with reference to Substance, we might say that Substance now, *qua* dominant, originative moment (*Ur*sache), opposes Accident, but does so *only qua* Cause; and yet Cause is only veritably actual, truly dominant and originative, in its Effect. 'The originativeness (*Ursprünglichkeit*) of the Cause is sublated in the Effect, in which the Cause has made itself a positedness (*Gesetztsein*).'[2]

3·1. In LL Cause and Effect passes in subcategories through Formal and Determinate Causality to Action and Reaction (*Wirkung und Gegenwirkung*). The dialectic is briefly this. (A) There is nothing in Effect which is not in Cause, and causality is at first a mere immediate tautology of external reflection. There is only one Fact, one identical content, displaying itself first as persisting original and then as determination in Other. We must not here be deceived by phenomenal 'illustration'. If we imagine Cause and Effect as two separate existents, *A* and *B*, such that *A* is the cause of *B*, it will appear to us as if *A* has much further content besides that characteristic which makes it the cause of *B*. But this further content is irrelevant to the *thought* of causal connexion, and even in common life when we say, for

[1] Cf. IH, ch. iv, § 3. Yet Aristotle's theory of the demonstrative syllogism directly provokes the comment that the substantial infima species can only be really complete in and through its essential accidents.

[2] EL, § 153.

example, that rain moistens, we recognize that it is the same water which is the rain and the wetness which the rain causes. Or again, we recognize that if one body propels another the same quantum of motion is present before and after the movement. Nor can we escape this tautology by tracing back the effect to a plurality of causes. We might attribute a man's success in his profession to the bullet which killed his father in battle and caused him to cultivate his talent young, or again to a knack inherited from his grandmother. But quite clearly such a plurality of causes can only *together* constitute *the* cause of his success, just as only the circle or totality of real possibilities can be actualized. Traced back only to one such 'cause', the 'effect' remains something merely contingent.

3·2. On the other hand, (B) our habit in common life of tracing back an effect through a series of ever remoter causes does truly 'illustrate' the category. For Cause and Effect is a correlation of Content as well as of Form, and the two moments do fail to coincide, and do therefore turn out to be an oscillation in indefinite regress. The effect which a cause has, and the effect which that cause is (in relation to a preceding cause), are different in content; and the cause which an effect has, and the cause which that effect is (in relation to a further effect), are different in content. This is because Substance-*qua*-Cause, in becoming absolutely actual in its Effect, *again becomes Cause*; and conversely Effect does not merely vanish in its Cause, but in this vanishing again becomes Effect. Thus the absolute commensurateness demanded by Formal Causality develops in antithesis into Determinate Causality; but it does so, as Kant recognized, only as an indefinite regress of terms. The contradiction exhibited here by Power or *Aktuosität*, by that Necessity which lies between impotent instability and genuine activity, consists in the fact that the Effect is (*a*) mechanically necessitated and so far passive, but is (*b*) necessitated to necessitate, i.e. to become itself active in the restricted sense of itself exerting Power.

3·3. But (C) it now becomes obvious, if we are not deceived by phenomenal illustration into locating Cause and Effect in two separate existents, that Effect is not simply passive to its Cause and active towards its own further Effect: it reacts upon its Cause. That is to say, (*a*) the formal identity of Cause with Effect, and (*b*) their endless difference of content, synthesize in the thought of Action and Reaction. In fact, even if we do start with a *Vorstellung* of separate existents, we are forced on to recognize this. A blow with an axe, for example, causes a dent in a solid thing; but the nature of the dent is partly conditioned by the degree of solidity in the thing. The effect is thus not merely passive: in suffering the cause to act it modifies the power of the cause. Moreover, if the thing struck be a sufficiently hard rock, and the axe be not hard enough, then the dent will occur in the axe and not in the rock. Thus the full and complete notion of Substance turns out to be the absolute reciprocity of Cause and Effect.

4. RECIPROCITY (*Wechselwirkung*)

When Cause and Effect turn out to be reciprocal, we have reached more than a reciprocity of these two moments: we have reached *a reciprocity of Substances*. So long as we think in terms of Cause and Effect, i.e. of finite causality, the reaction is not the full equivalent of the action; the reciprocation of the two terms is not so absolute as to exclude relation to a third term and so on. But with Reciprocity the second moment is on the same level as the first, and we have passed beyond the thought of an endless series of causes and effects. The linear series is, as it were, bent back upon itself in a circle, and Substance is at length in genuine self-relation. Substance is now self-expressive as Substance, absolutely actual in its self-differentiation. Reciprocity, in short, is infinite causality as against the finite causality of Cause and Effect, which can only take form as a spurious infinite.

5. It is worth while here to compare Hegel's doctrine of causality, so far as it has yet appeared, with the Aristotelian teaching.

In IH I tried to show how Aristotle's analysis of the world first as matter and form, then as potentiality and actuality, is completed in his conception of fourfold cause.[1] We have observed how Hegel makes this dialectic explicit: how he

[1] See IH, ch. ii.

incorporates matter and form *eo nomine*; how proximate matter and form become in Hegel content and form; how Hegel's treatment of Possible and Actual closely follows Aristotle's analysis in terms of potential and actual, contingent and necessary. It has become clear that Hegel's 'Objective Logic' is no less—perhaps more—a criticism and reconstruction of Aristotle than it is of the metaphysic of Descartes, Spinoza, Leibniz, or Kant. Though Aristotle's *Organon* contributes little to Hegel's Logic, yet there is no structural principle of the Aristotelian system which is not developed by Hegel. It is natural, then, to look for Aristotelian inspiration in Hegel's treatment of Cause and Effect.

5·1. In the first place it hardly needs to be pointed out that the Hegelian category of Cause and Effect is, like the Kantian, not teleological. It is not the thought of final cause, but of necessitation *a tergo*. That is why Hegel calls it finite causality, and holds it a category quite inadequate to express the correlations of spiritual life, and even of what he calls physico-organic life.[1] It is inadmissible to seek the cause of Homer's poems in the Ionic climate, of the downfall of the Roman Republic in the ambition of Caesar. Purely physical causation is not adequate even to mere natural life: 'It is not permissible to say that food is the cause of blood, or certain dishes, or cold or damp, the cause of fever.'[2] Even the living body, *a fortiori* spirit, transmutes that which acts upon it.[3]

Nor is Reciprocity a category adequate to these spheres. It stands only at the threshold of the Notion. It is 'still only an empty way and manner'.[4] It is the complete development of causality, but even in the study of Nature we have made only slight progress when we apply Reciprocity in place of a one-way causal relation.[5]

5·2. Thus it is not the full fourfold causal analysis of Aristotle which re-emerges in the Hegelian category of Cause and Effect, but only the Aristotelian efficient cause. Or perhaps it would be truer to say that it is Aristotle's material and efficient causes together; for the moment of Contingency in Cause and Effect is precisely the Aristotelian material cause in its aspect as cause of not-being. Further,

[1] See LL, i, pp. 707 ff. [2] Ibid., p. 707. [3] Cf. IH, ch. iii, §§ 5 ff.
[4] LL, i, p. 718. [5] See EL, § 156, *Zusatz*.

the transition in the significance of the term ἐνέργεια from actuality to activity is reflected in a half-way stage by Hegel's Cause and Effect. It was already paralleled, as I pointed out in ch. viii, § 7·2, in the Hegelian category of Real Possibility and Real Actuality. On the other hand, Aristotle allows nowhere the operation of sheerly efficient causality. Even in the compulsive necessitation of 'unnatural' physical movement there is something analogous to the operation of final cause,[1] and this is foreshadowed in Hegel's dialectic when Cause and Effect pass into Reciprocity. But Hegel's reconstruction of the Aristotelian final and formal causes in their full nature, and of Aristotle's ἐνέργεια in its full significance, comes only with the categories of the Notion.

[1] See IH, ch. ii, § 5·3.

X

TRANSITION TO SUBJECTIVE NOTION

1. HEGEL calls the Logic of the Notion (*Begriff*) 'Subjective Logic', and we have already discussed the meaning of this title.[1] The transition from Essence to the Notion is the passage from necessity to free self-conscious activity, from substance to subject. At the same time Hegel's Notion is a reinterpretation of the term *Begriff* in the Kantian (somewhat elastic) sense of 'universal concept'. Hegel, that is, identifies subject and universal. In IH I have tried to show the source of this doctrine in Aristotle's account of sense and thought,[2] and I have made many other anticipatory references to it, especially in connexion with Kant's transcendental unity of apperception.[3] Hegel sees in this original unity of subject and object the true meaning of the Kantian *a priori* synthesis, although Kant, as he thinks, lapsed often into regarding synthesis as a mere linking of elements in and for themselves separate, and into asserting that the *Begriff* is always conditioned by a manifold of passive intuition.[4] Indeed, Hegel's Notion, as it first emerges in the Logic, is the precise equivalent of Kant's transcendental unity of apperception.

1·1. Nevertheless it may be well here first to display the transition from Essence as the passage to free subjective activity, and then to show how precisely in LL Hegel comes to identify subject with universal. For both these purposes I shall draw mainly on LL, ii, pp. 5–23. The task is not easy. Hegel himself observes: 'The passage from necessity to freedom, or from Actuality into the Notion, is the very hardest, because self-subsistent Actuality has got to be thought of as not losing its substantiality in the transition and in its identity with the self-subsistent actuality confronting it.'[5]

1·11. In the categories of Actuality the immanent necessity of Substance and Accident was developed through Cause

[1] See ch. v, §§ 6 and 6·1 above.
[2] See IH, ch. v, §§ 2·2–4·1.
[3] See especially ch. ii, § 1·1 above.
[4] See LL, ii, p. 22.
[5] EL, § 159.

and Effect to its complete expression in Reciprocity. In Reciprocity the coupled moments distinctive of Essence became fully substantial, or completely actual, equivalent totalities. But that is to say the contradiction between the two moments, which is also distinctive of Essence, became reconciled. They are now no longer moments correlated by necessity; they have become phases of free activity. The truth of necessity is seen to be freedom, and we have passed from Essence to the Notion.

Here it may aid us to recall the general nature of dialectical movement in Essence. The unessential moment of Essence was first Show and then Appearance; it has now become the unreserved revelation of Essence. The reflection is no longer secondary and derivative, but as fully actual as the source which it reveals. When the contradictory correlation of essential with unessential moment is sublated, spirit no longer puts itself forth as a product, in some measure external, which it compulsively, and therefore in some measure contingently, necessitates; what it 'necessitates' is now purely itself. Spirit is now active in no merely proleptic sense, but fully self-conscious and free.

1·2. That spirit in its freedom as subject is the universal, Hegel argues in a hard passage:

'Being-in-and-for-self is immediately as positedness, and therefore the Notion in its simple self-relation is absolute determinateness; which, however, equally as self-relating is immediately simple identity. But this self-relation of determinateness as its own self-coincidence is equally the negation of determinateness, and as this self-equality the Notion is the universal.'[1]

To understand this passage I think we must assume Hegel to imply that any determinateness (*Bestimmtheit*) other than that of the Notion is determinateness in the Spinozistic sense of limitation. Moreover, it is clear that Hegel is here speaking of the universal in provisional abstraction from the particular (or specific) and the individual.[2] His meaning then appears to be this: If we retain the terminology of Being and Essence, out of which we are passing, we may say that in the first emergence of the Notion spirit posits itself as in and for itself; not, that is, as a particular product which is

[1] LL, ii, p. 12. [2] See ch. xi, § 4·2 below.

determinate in the Spinozistic sense of limited over against (and therefore reciprocally limiting) what posits it. But that is to say the terminology of Being and Essence is no longer appropriate. For spirit is now simply and immediately self-coincident; and in this self-coincidence it is determinate *per se* and not through limitation. It is in fact the very negation of Spinozistic determinateness. But spirit thus in possession of its own determinateness is precisely the universal, though it is the universal as so far only the germ of its own particularization.

1·21. This conception of the universal becomes clearer if we contrast it with the universal conceived as a common character elicited by abstraction from its particularization.[1] According to this latter formal conception, enshrined in Porphyry's Tree and still prevalent in Kant, the universal loses in intension as it gains in extension. It is universal just in so far as it is indeterminate; just in so far as it approximates not to Hegel's Notion but to his first category of Pure Being. It is not concrete and potentially self-particularizing; it is abstract, and awaits particularization by externally added differentiae. Moreover, the universal thus conceived to attain concreteness by external specification is the mere plurality of universals which belongs to the thought of the mere Understanding. It is the universal shattered into a multiplicity of empirical concepts which are in varying degree sensuous, and are only universal inasmuch as indefinite repetition in instances cannot exhaust them. Beyond these pseudo-concepts there is nothing save that aggregate which is all that the Understanding, when it philosophizes, can make of its principles, even of those principles which it proclaims to be the laws of its thought.[2] To this fragmentation of the mind's content corresponds a dispersion of the subject into subjects whose thinking is an intermittent series of acts. The Understanding begins and breaks off its

[1] Cf. EL, § 163, *Zusatz* (1).

[2] Cf. IH, ch. xii, §§ 1 and 1·02. It is this pulverizing of the universal which Aristotle notes in criticizing what was perhaps an early stage of the Platonic theory of Forms: 'The Forms are practically equal to or not less in number than the things in trying to explain which the Platonists proceeded from them to the Forms.' *Metaphysics* 990^{b}4–6.

thought contingently, and the more so the nearer its thinking is to sense.[1] In IH I endeavoured to approach the Hegelian category through these imperfect forms of the universal. What was there said of the category in comparison with them is yet truer of the Notion, which is what most truly the category is.[2] Moreover, it is precisely these imperfect forms of the universal which the dialectic of Essence has sublated.

1·22. We may next recall what was said of the movement of Essence in ch. vi, § 1·4. Throughout Essence spirit has expressed itself more and more fully as a single coherent world. The categories of Intro-reflection have seemed merely subjective. Position and Presupposing, Identity, Difference, and Ground, seem hardly to be more than the subjective movement of the reflecting mind. The object was whatever *is*, with the minimal distinction in it between what it is and that it is. It was in a bare sense universal, but it was the universal as the merely all-pervasive; it was at most an indeterminate expanse of singular individual things, differentiated but not self-differentiating. But in Appearance the object was articulated, however vaguely, as a totality; and the final category of Actuality revealed not a totality of mere things but a *universe* of substances in complete reciprocal action and reaction. This, for the Understanding, represents the limit of concrete articulation in the universal; it is the fullest objectivity which the Understanding can find in its 'detached' world. But what for the Understanding is in part its own principles of subjective reflection, and in part the characterization of its detached object, is for Reason transformed as a dialectic of spirit's *self*-expression. For the Understanding the subject must remain over against its object, but Reason now finds itself in its object. The world, grown concretely articulate in Reciprocity, is a world of Substance grown truly individual and unitary. It is universal because it is substantial and does not merely comprise any and every thing; and because it is substantial, whole, and individual it is universal no longer as substance only but as subject.

[1] Cf. IH, ch. x, § 4·3.

[2] Cf. ch. ii, § 1·1, above. On the relation of Hegel's universal to Kant's see also ch. xi, § 8, below.

1·23. We may express the identity of spirit as free subject with the universal by contrast with the lower level of finite subjects and universals as a multiplicity of abstract common characters. At the lower level a singular subject, thinking in terms of abstract universals, knows its object as an indefinitely extensible aggregate, and takes itself as extensible *pari passu*. Subject and object cannot, therefore, at this level be identical. But in the Notion the object is a concrete individual universe with which the subject *is* identical.

1·3. The further implication of the transition from Essence to Notion is made clear in Hegel's conception of the Notion as norm. I have tried in IH to explain Hegel's conception of truth as that which accords with its notion.[1] The notion of anything *is* its truth; i.e. its good which makes it what it is, or, in Aristotelian terminology, its form which is at once its final cause and also its formal cause in terms of which alone it can be defined.[2] In other words, the logical Notion, phenomenally embodied, appears as the notion of this or that particular thing. In the light of this it is easy to see that the logical Notion must be the self-accordant or self-coincident, and that nothing save the freely active subject is this. We only repeat this if we say that for Hegel self-consciousness and consciousness of value, or goodness, are one.

The Notion thus sums up and comprises the conceptions of (*a*) subject in activity; (*b*) the universal; (*c*) the good, or intrinsic value, and so truth.

1·4. A reference to Kant will perhaps make clearer still this doctrine of the good which Plato first formulated and Hegel in the Subjective Logic elaborates.

For Hegel genuine knowledge begins precisely where for Kant knowledge ceases and regulative, non-constitutive thinking begins. Kant finds knowledge exemplified *par excellence* in natural science, in which on Hegel's view only the categories of Essence operate. Knowledge is to Kant a detached consciousness of an object in which the subject finds not itself but an independent alien thing; a thing which behaves according to necessary and universal, but yet merely mechanical laws. In this object is no intrinsic value, no goodness; causation in the world of human knowledge is efficient,

[1] IH, ch. xiv. [2] See ibid., ch. ii, §§ 2 and 3.

not final and formal. Correspondingly, the subject is self-conscious only inasmuch as it possesses a formal consciousness of its own spontaneity in synthesis.[1]

Although the critical philosopher is aware that the object of human knowledge is phenomenal, and that the most universal laws of its behaviour are *eo ipso* active functions of the experiencing subject, yet this awareness must on Kant's showing be faith rather than knowledge.[2] Man's moral consciousness is seen, no doubt, by Kant as a kind of knowledge of what he ought to do, but it is not knowledge of what the good will is:[3] moral man must think, but cannot know, himself free. Again, man's aesthetic experience, in Kant's view, neither is nor carries with it *knowledge* of the beautiful, nor is his religion based on knowledge of God. If man's speculative Reason claims genuine knowledge—i.e. knowledge of an object—it lies. Its dialectic is mere sophistry, inherent in its nature but inevitably aborting in paralogism and irresoluble antinomy. Its pretensions must be curbed and criticized in the interest of morality, which is therefore a higher experience than speculation. But this criticism provides morality and religion with no foundation but faith.

To Hegel, morality, aesthetic experience, and religion are at least nearer to true knowledge than is positive science; and to him philosophy is neither a mere faith nor an empty regulative and purely critical thinking. It is, in its notion if not in the philosophical systems of particular thinkers, the concrete self-conscious dialectic of spirit. This dialectic alone is fully genuine knowledge, and its categories are *par excellence* the categories of the Notion.

[1] Our knowledge of our empirical selves is just as much knowledge of phenomenon as is our knowledge of external things.

[2] See IH, ch. ix, § 5·12.

[3] See further ch. xii, § 9·221, below.

XI
NOTION AS SUCH

1. Hegel displays the development of the Notion into a concrete, self-subsistent system of pure thought in three stages: Subjective Notion, Objective Notion, and Idea.

This main triadic division will be hardly intelligible unless we first consider the general nature of dialectical movement in the sphere of the Notion, and then follow the dialectic of Subjective Notion. I shall therefore attempt no preliminary characterization of the main triad.

1·1. It was observed when we discussed Actuality[1] that the categories of the Notion, as they first emerge, will give no impression of introducing fresh content; that they may even seem to do no more than repeat the categories of Essence. The reason for this prima facie impression is that the dialectic of the Notion is explicit development.[2] In the Notion the emphasis is not upon cancellation, as it was in Being; nor, as it was in Essence, upon equilibrium in contradiction; but upon preservation. For in the Notion, Hegel maintains, sublation manifests its complete nature. Hence the Actuality in which Essence resulted is never in the Notion cancelled or contradicted: every phase of the Notion is actual.[3] The Notion is spirit explicitly self-determining, and 'self-subsistent Actuality has got to be thought of as not losing its substantiality in the transition'.[4] In completed Actuality[5] begins activity, and we may say, adapting Aristotle's terminology, that *Wirklichkeit* does *not* relate to further stages of spirit's self-development as δύναμις to ἐνέργεια.[6] On the contrary, these further stages, the categories of the Notion, are all phases of ἐνέργεια, into each of which spirit enters explicitly whole. Each is τέλειον, consummate, inasmuch as the end is fully immanent in it. In the Notion 'the elements distinguished are without more ado

[1] See ch. viii above. [2] See EL, § 161.
[3] Cf. ibid., § 163: 'Individual and actual are the same thing.'
[4] Cf. ch. x, § 1 above.
[5] i.e. in Actuality as the final phase of Essence.
[6] Nor as apparent to real.

at the same time declared to be identical with one another and with the whole, and the determinate character of each is a free being of the whole Notion'.[1] In the *Zusatz* to the same section it is even said that 'the movement of the Notion is as it were to be looked upon as a mere play (*Spiel*): the Other which it posits is in fact not an Other'.[2]

Thus when Hegel says that nothing is true of the Actual except what is true of it by virtue of the categories of the Notion,[3] he means that Actuality is not cancelled or contradicted when the Notion sublates it, but preserved. The movement of the Notion is the *development* of the Actual, because into every phase of the Notion Spirit enters explicitly whole.[4]

1·11. Even the most everyday conception of temporal development requires that somehow all that is there at the end be there potentially at the beginning of the process; which is to say that somehow what develops is present as a whole at every stage of the process. In some types of temporal process this is more obviously true than it is in others, but in every type it presents itself as a not fully resolved contradiction.[5] In thinking temporal process we have to think in terms of the coupled and self-contradictory conception of potential-and-actual, which belongs to the sphere of Essence. For Hegel the logical movement of the Notion is illustrated *par excellence* in human self-consciousness; in that self-identity, that complicity of the whole person in all phases of a subject's activity, upon which depend equally, for example, a man's coherent thinking and his moral conduct. How far this doctrine of complete sublation is tenable we shall have to consider towards the end of this *Study*.

2. We can now consider generally the dialectic of Subjective Notion.

Its main subdivisions are Notion as such, Judgement, and

[1] EL, § 161.

[2] *Spiel* has, I think, the sense of utterly unhindered activity.

[3] EL, § 162, last paragraph.

[4] This is of the utmost importance for the understanding of Hegel's ethics, politics, and philosophy of history.

[5] Cf. EL, § 161, *Zusatz*. I have tried to develop this problem in an article on *Change* published in *Philosophy*, July and October 1934.

Syllogism. The first main phase of the Notion thus corresponds closely with the subject-matter of traditional formal logic. In the light of Hegel's repeated attacks upon formal logic this may seem puzzling; but it will not, if we remember that for Hegel error consists in the claim of a truth which is partial and conditional to be the whole truth.[1] Hegel's general attitude is expressed in LL, ii, p. 3: 'The logic of the Notion finds ready a perfectly finished and compact or, so to say, ossified material, and the task is to render it fluid, and to rekindle the living Notion in this dead matter.'

Hegel regards the traditional logic as a naturalistic description of formal functions, obtained by observing the empirical phenomena of thought. He ascribes infinite merit to Aristotle for undertaking this description.[2] 'It is esteemed', he says, 'no mean thing to have discovered sixty species of parrot, a hundred and seven species of veronica, and so forth. Far less should it be held a trifling matter to have discovered the forms of Reason. Is not a figure of syllogism an infinitely higher thing than a species of parrot or veronica?'[3] Formal logic, since it concerns the formation of subjective thinking, is also, on Hegel's view, of special importance in education.[4]

Traditional formal logic, then, is not a futile product of misplaced ingenuity. It is an indispensable industry, although the Understanding produces it in the effort to interpret its own thinking without transcending the level of that thinking, and it is therefore not philosophic but descriptive.

2·1. We may perhaps thus restate Hegel's attitude. For the formal logician there are countless concepts, empirical thought-contents in varying degree sensuous,[5] which provide the matter for countless judgements and countless syllogistic arguments. These concepts are taken as simple atoms, and a limited number of propositional or judgement forms are regarded as providing a sufficient diversity of form for these contents in so far as the latter actually work in the process of finite thinking. Thus these logical forms, although

[1] Cf. ch. vi, § 5·45 above.
[2] See LL, ii, p. 31.
[3] Ibid., p. 143. See also JE, xviii, ΦH, ii, p. 402.
[4] LL, ii, p. 143.
[5] Cf. IH, ch. ix, § 2·2.

they must in the last resort be the forms of their endlessly variable contents, are to the formal logician the forms of the subjective processes of thought; and he proceeds to classify these forms, which to philosophic insight are phases of activity, as if they were natural genera and species.

2·11. It is worth observing further that no logic can wholly evade the truth that form is form of content. Traditional formal logic in offering a method of logical division by dichotomy confesses at least to a minimal objective reference.[1] A logic professing to make an absolute divorce of validity from material truth, and to concern itself with sheer form and nothing else, professes sheer nonsense. Such a logic arises from the quite legitimate attempt to pass from the natural history to the mathematics of finite thinking, but it does not and could not succeed in conforming its practice to its profession. Unless some sort of unity and multiplicity are true of the world—and to know that they are is to know material truth—no logical or logistical form of thinking is even valid. In LL, ii, pp. 56–9 Hegel criticizes symbolic logic in a passage which is as significant to-day as when he wrote it. He concludes by pointing out that the Notion alone gives meaning to the abstract, usually quantitative determinations which are employed as symbols. Hence such symbols are only intelligible in the light of what they are made to symbolize. No manipulation of the former can yield any insight into the latter. 'Man', he observes, 'has language as the means of designation peculiar to Reason. Hence it is an idle fancy to engage in a weary search for a less perfect means of presentation (*Darstellungsweise*).'[2]

2·2. Inasmuch as it explicitly takes thought for its subject-matter, formal logic has in Hegel's eyes a claim to rank in aim at least as the highest product of the Understanding. We have seen that Hegel tries in the logic of Essence to reconstruct dialectically the industry of the Understanding from its first movement of abstraction from sense and its activity in common sense and special science, to the 'ontology' of his comparatively recent predecessors.[3] The logic of Sub-

[1] It is instructive to ask oneself whether the ideal genus of formal logic is subjective or objective. [2] LL, ii, p. 59. Cf. above, ch. i, §§ 7·2 ff.

[3] Cf. ch. v above, esp. §§ 4·1 and 5·1–6.

jective Notion is an analogous reconstruction of formal logic; not an alternative to it but a sublation of it. The subjective thought-forms remain for formal logic a class system which is little more than an aggregate.[1] They are described in partial abstraction from the empirical matter which gives them content; for although no logic can abstract entirely from content, yet it is the implication of any formal logic that *not* all the determinateness in things is *Denkbestimmung*. *Per contra* the categories of Subjective Notion are not abstractions from empirical content. They have arisen as the further self-development of all the determinateness which there is in empirical content, and in them the categories of Being and Essence have been sublated; for to Hegel all determinateness *is Denkbestimmung*.

2·3. But although the categories of Subjective Notion revitalize the dead forms of traditional logic as phases of activity, yet they remain subjective and formal. As they develop they give no impression of presenting fresh content; or rather they develop a purely subjective and formal content, and only with the transition to Objective Notion will Spirit attain concreteness—*not* through reunion with empirical content, but by developing its own objective content.[2] Subjective Notion is formal because it is implicit, not because it is an ossified abstraction from content. Moreover, because they are subjective, the earlier phases of the Notion are not explicit categories of intrinsic value, or goodness. Spirit knows as good only that in which it recognizes spirit,[3] and Subjective Notion does not at first attain this self-consciousness. That which in Subjective Notion is in course of sublation is thought as still a process of Understanding, though of Understanding at its highest, at the level where it begins to reflect critically upon its own nature. It is in this portion of the Logic that Hegel prepares the way for his doctrine of Cognition Proper,[4] and does justice to that moment

[1] For a detailed criticism of this empirical procedure see LL, ii, pp. 52 ff. Hegel justly observes that logic thereby affords a very poor example of following its own precepts, since it neglects its own rule that concepts (*Begriffe*) must be derived and scientific propositions demonstrated.

[2] Cf. IH, ch. x, § 4·11.

[3] Cf. ch. x, § 1·3 above.

[4] See ch. xvii below.

of thought as mere 'finding', which some thinkers mistake for the whole nature of thought.[1]

3. These general remarks may serve to introduce the account of Subjective Notion which Hegel gives in LL, ii, pp. 32–3. Using, as he so often does and must, the terminology of earlier categories to introduce a new dialectical phase, he observes that

'the Notion is at first the truth only implicitly (*an sich*). Because it is only an Inner, it is just as much only an Outer. At first it is simply (*überhaupt*) an immediate, and in this phase its moments have the form of immediate and fixed determinations. It appears as the determinate concept (*Begriff*), the sphere of mere Understanding.'

In this account of the initial appearance of the Notion as fixed concepts (the word used in both contexts is *Begriff*) Hegel, as we have seen,[2] has in mind formal logic.

Hegel continues:

'This form of immediacy is a There-being (*Dasein*) as yet inadequate to its nature, since the Notion is that free entity which relates itself to itself alone. It is therefore an external form in which the Notion is valid as something posited, or as something subjective, not as Being-in-and-for-self.

'The phase of the immediate Notion constitutes that standpoint from which the Notion is a subjective thinking, a reflection external to the object [sc. the standpoint of formal logic]. This stage accordingly constitutes subjectivity or the formal Notion. Its externality appears in the fixed being of its determinations, by virtue of which each emerges on its own (*für sich*) as something isolated, or qualitative, which is merely in external relation to its other. But the identity of the Notion, which is their inner or subjective essence, sets them in dialectical movement [sc. in Hegel's as opposed to formal logic], by means of which their individual isolation (*Vereinzelung*) . . . transcends itself.'

4. Notion as such

Notion as such has three subphases: (1) *Allgemeinheit*, Universality. (2) *Besonderheit*, Particularity in the sense of the word preserved in formal logic, not in the sense in which many English philosophers have used the term 'particular', viz. as equivalent to 'singular'. 'Specificness', or 'Speciality' might serve as well for a translation. (3) *Einzelheit*, Indivi-

[1] Cf. IH, ch. xiii, § 6·1. [2] Cf. also EL, § 162.

duality, which only means singularity when the context concerns mere quantity.

4·1. For purposes of exposition these three moments can be treated under separate heads. But the Notion develops in free self-mediation as *totum in toto et totum in qualibet parte*. The Universal cannot be thought save as Particular and Individual: 'Only mere Presentation (*Vorstellung*), for which abstraction has isolated them, can steadfastly keep apart Universal, Particular, and Individual.'[1] 'Each moment of the Notion can only be apprehended immediately out of and with the rest.'[2]

So Hegel reconstitutes the 'simple concept' of formal logic, and the reader will observe that the seeming fixity of notional determinations of which Hegel speaks[3] refers not to the moments of Notion as such but to the forms of Judgement and Syllogism, which we have yet to consider.

Hegel's exposition of Notion as such in LL consists largely in contrasting this transparent 'play' of the Notion with the dialectical movement at various levels of Being and Essence. In Being one category merely passes into the next. In Essence thesis and antithesis, and also the coupled moments of each category, are inseparable, but in neither case can the second term be said to constitute the full exposition of the full self-identity of the first: it is always the show, the posited consequent, the reflection, the appearance, &c., of the first, never its wholly free self-determining. That is why no category of Essence is the Universal truly self-particularizing or self-specifying. Hence synthesis in Essence always reveals a fresh contradiction. But the Universal, truly self-particularizing, is *eo ipso* Individual; not a singular thing but a *subject* concrete, though formally, in and for itself.

5. THE UNIVERSAL

The Universal in this provisional and merely imaginable abstraction from Particular and Individual has already in Chapter X been characterized and contrasted with the universals of formal logic.[4] If we hold it thus provisionally

[1] LL, ii, p. 62.
[2] EL, § 164, para. 1.
[3] See § 3 above.
[4] §§ 1·2 and 1·21.

apart by itself, we must not think of it as the *mere* potentiality of all determination, which would be Pure Being; nor as *together with* its undeveloped particularity, which would be the mere self-identity of Essence. Rather we are compelled by the fact that the Notion is fully actual and has transcended the contradiction of potential and actual, paradoxically to call the Universal the *explicit* germ of its own particularization.

6. THE PARTICULAR

The Notion, self-particularized, remains Universal as a man retains his personality in a specific activity. Conversely the Universal, as in its antithesis opposed to its own particularization, is *eo ipso* particular. What negates it is overtly and transparently itself, because its negative moment is nothing but its own activity.

6·1. The relation of natural genus to species illustrates this. The species differ from one another, but they do not differ from the genus,[1] for a genus *is* its species, and the species are universal. The differentia which constitutes a species is nothing external: it is simply the 'difference' between Universal and Particular.[2]

But a natural genus, the object of a natural science, has an indefinite number of species, and the difference between these is more or less indeterminate, mere variety. The wholeness of Universal in Particular appears there only in the fact that the species are assumed to exhaust the genus,[3] for the natural genus falls short of its notion. Hence if the natural genus is to illustrate the Universal, it must be conceived as particularizing itself in only two species, whose difference is not mere variety but immanent opposition (*Gegensatz*); i.e. it must be conceived as conforming to the genus dichotomously articulated in logical division.[4]

Yet even Opposition is only a category of Reflection, and even in the later categories of Essence the difference which lies in the correlations of coupled moments has not yet the form of being one determinateness.[5] That is to say, the antithesis in Essence never is the completely particularized thesis. The self-conscious activity of man, and even mere

[1] LL, ii, p. 43.
[2] Ibid., p. 45. Cf. also IH, ch. iv, § 1·2.
[3] LL, ii, p. 43.
[4] See below, ch. xii, §§ 7·2 ff.
[5] LL, p. 45.

natural life, more nearly illustrate the self-particularizing Universal than does the ideal genus.

7. THE INDIVIDUAL

If the particularization or specification of the Universal is one determinateness into which the Universal enters whole, then the Universal is *eo ipso* Individual. Even in a natural genus, if it were to conform to the ideal of dichotomous logical division, there would no longer remain below the *infimae species* an indefinite residue of sensible singulars with properties which cannot be taken up as specific differentiae. The species would constitute not a mere *de facto* totality provisionally assumed to exhaust the genus, but the final actualization of the genus as a single, not a singular, whole. This Aristotle was on the way to recognizing when he made the *infima species* substance.[1]

7·1. It is instructive to contrast the Individual of the Notion with the finite singular individual of sense, natural or artificial. This dog, or this table, is a determinate individual by virtue of negation, i.e. by significant relation to an other. But its determinate individuality, such as it is, is given it only by relation to an external other, indeed by relation to endless external others. Consequently the universal, or *quasi*-universal, which it implies, is that mere abstract and general concept which the Notion is emphatically not. It is 'dogness' or 'tableness', the abstract common character of all dogs or all tables, powerless to specify the number and nature of its singulars, which it classifies as their mere mark. *Per contra* the Notion as Individual is subject: it contains within itself, and itself sets forth, the negation which determines it. Inasmuch as its significant negation is its own activity, nothing outside it determines it. And that is to say that it is the Universal—the Universal determining itself as Individual. So man as self-conscious individual is essentially not singular individual. He is finite singular individual only so far as he is in part natural.

8. Here most clearly Hegel sets his own interpretation on the original unity of thought and being adumbrated in Kant's transcendental unity of apperception. Here in its

[1] Cf. IH, ch. iv, § 4·3.

simplest and most striking form is Hegel's declaration of war on Kant's teaching that the moment in knowledge of individual reality is given through a passive sense-intuition by an alien thing-in-itself. Here, too, originates the doctrine of the concrete universal which has inspired British nineteenth-century idealism and found perhaps its most consistent expression in Bosanquet's Gifford Lectures.[1]

[1] See IH, ch. xiii, § 8.

XII

JUDGEMENT

1. In identifying subject and Universal, Hegel, as we saw in the last chapter, gives its first explicit shape in the Logic to the 'original' unity of subject and object, which Kant had indicated in his doctrine of the transcendental unity of apperception. He accepts the etymological significance of the German word *Urteil* as accurately expressing the 'original partition' which must arise as antithesis to Notion as such.[1]

1·1. The transition from Individual to Judgement is as follows. Individual is the self-subsistent totality of the Notion in which Universal and Particular are merged immediately in one. Yet Individual contains Universal and Particular. Since, then, the Notion develops in phases into each of which it enters whole, it follows that if Individual is self-subsistent totality, so also are Particular and Universal. Thus the immediacy of Individual so mediates itself that Universal, Particular, and Individual emerge as three judged, or sundered, totalities of the Notion. Thus judgement is not, as ordinary logic sees it, the external linkage of two atomic concepts, but the self-mediation of the simple concept. Similarly the Hegelian Judgement transcends Kant's distinction between analytic and synthetic judgements:[2] for Hegel, as after him for Bradley, all judgement is both analytic and synthetic.

1·2. But the emergence of the three moments of the Notion as sundered totalities requires all the categories of Judgement to complete it, and when it is complete Judgement will pass over into Syllogism, the middle term of which will, in its first phase, be the Particular explicitly uniting Individual and Universal as the extreme terms. Meanwhile, the formula of Judgement is 'The Individual is the Universal', and the triplicity of the Notion is expressed in the less developed form subject-copula-predicate. In Judgement, that is to say, the unity of Universal and Individual is as yet no true middle term, but the mere 'is' of predication. The copula 'springs

[1] See EL, § 166, and cf. IH, ch. vii, §§ 6 ff. on Fichte.
[2] See IH, ch. ix, § 4·32.

from the nature of the Notion, to be self-identical even in parting from its own (*in seiner Entäusserung*)';[1] but it is at first present in Judgement only 'as the still indeterminate relation of Being in general',[2] and when it becomes the fully developed unity of Universal and Individual it is no longer copula but middle term of inference.[3]

1·3. As the copula is at first a quite abstract unity, a mere link, so in the subject the distinction between Individual and Particular is at first latent and merely implicit, although the formula of Judgement is 'The Individual is the Universal': 'At first subject may be taken against predicate as Individual against Universal, or again as Particular, inasmuch as they are opposed to each other just simply (*überhaupt*) as the more determinate to the more universal.'[4]

This of course implies that, correspondingly, the predicate is not yet strictly Universal as opposed to Particular.

1·4. In short, so long as the unity of the Notion is only the copula the three moments of the Notion are imperfectly articulated. Thus: (A) The subject, *qua* the rudimentary Individual moment, is the immediate concrete, the self-subsistent substratum, in which the predicate inheres dependently. But (B) the subject—as the copula, the 'is', expresses—is identical with the predicate. The predicate is what the subject really is, and without it the subject is a mere name.[5] Hence (A) 'Since the subject is in general and immediately concrete, the determinate content of the predicate is only one of the subject's many characters. Thus the subject is ampler and wider than the predicate.' But (B) 'Conversely the predicate *qua* universal is self-subsistent, and indifferent whether this subject is or is not. The predicate outflanks the subject, subsuming it under itself, and hence on its side is wider than the subject. Only the *determinate* content of the predicate constitutes the identity of the two.'[6]

[1] EL, § 166.

[2] LL, ii, p. 74.

[3] For this 'ontological' doctrine of the copula compare IH, ch. xii, § 2. Compare also Bosanquet's treatment of the copula in *Essentials of Logic*, pp. 99–100.

[4] LL, ii, p. 66.

[5] Cf. Bradley's doctrine of the 'what' and the 'that', and also IH, ch. xiii, §§ 4·6 and 4·61.

[6] EL, § 170. E.g. in the judgement 'this rose is red', 'this rose' is only identical with 'this' determinate redness; cf. § 5·1 below.

Hence the dialectic of Judgement-forms will show the gradual development in subject and predicate of what might be called concrete notional identity, and finally the transition to Syllogism, in which the copula becomes the explicit middle term unifying the extremes.

2. It may be helpful now to collect and amplify what has been said by noting four points of contrast between Hegel's theory of Judgement and formal logic.

(1) A sentence with a grammatical subject and predicate may express no more than a singular action or state with no reference to universality.[1] In that case it does not illustrate Judgement.

'"Aristotle died aged seventy-two in the fourth year of the 115th Olympiad" would contain an element of Judgement only if one of the circumstances—the date of the philosopher's death or his age—had been questioned, and the numbers stated were being nevertheless upheld on some ground. For if this were the case, it would mean that these dates were being taken as something universal: as time having some other filling and persisting even apart from that determinate content of Aristotle's death, or even as empty time.'[2]

In other words, a judgement is not the proposition of formal logic, which is an abstraction from it, but a verdict, and it has always an implicit universal ground, in a broad sense of the term 'ground'.

2·01. In this connexion it may be well to observe in passing that when Hegel follows the custom of other logicians in using phenomenal examples to illustrate all the categories of Judgement, it is wholly irrelevant whether these examples are actually correct statements of fact. Their purpose is merely to illustrate the degree of truth in each category, the degree to which each category of Judgement is a form adequate to express the agreement of a thing with its notion.[3] A statement asserting the failure of something to conform with its notion—e.g. the assertion that a man is sick or has committed a crime—may be correct in fact, but it is untrue as Judgement.[4] It may even be advisable to select trivial examples, so that the reader's attention may not be distracted from the logical form to the phenomenal content, from truth

[1] Cf. EL, § 167 and LL, ii, pp. 69–70.
[2] LL, ii, pp. 69–70.
[3] Cf. IH, ch. xiv, §§ 1–2·2.
[4] See EL, § 172, *Zusatz*.

to correctness.[1] On the other hand, Judgement can only be phenomenally illustrated at all because the example has a context and an implied ground. The abstract text-book example of Judgement must always be taken as carrying with it an abstract context and implication, a fact which logistic has ignored with the oddest results. Hence the presence in an example of a sensible singular such as 'this rose' does not mean that the sheer singular can be a logical subject of judgement.[2]

2·1. (2) Judgement is not a purely subjective act which combines two independent entities. It does not, as it appears to *Vorstellung* to do, link a self-subsistent thing with a universal predicate existing in the finite subject's head, nor, as the traditional formal logician supposes, one simple concept with another. The Notion is one, and the copula expresses the identity within the Notion of subject and predicate: the subject not merely *has* but *is* the predicate.[3]

2·2. It follows (3) that the copula expresses not only the identity of subject and predicate but also the objectivity of the two terms in their connexion. To suppose that by some fantastic miracle of language the verb 'to be' has come to be used equivocally in most European languages in existential and predicative senses which have nothing to do with one another is, in Hegel's view, the utterest nonsense.[4] All things are a judgement, a universal individualized.[5] The Notion in Judgement is subjective in the sense that it has not yet developed its own objective content,[6] but the categories of Judgement are none the less objective in the sense that they are integral phases in the self-definitory development of spirit.

2·3. (4) In Judgement the triplicity of the Notion becomes only gradually articulate. Hence in concrete illustration

[1] See LL, ii, pp. 77–8.

[2] The early chapters of Bradley's *Logic* make this point admirably.

[3] See EL, § 166, and cf. Bradley's polemic against the view that judgement combines two ideas (*Principles of Logic*, ed. 2, ch. i, § 16), and his consequential rejection of floating ideas; see IH, ch. xiii, § 4·3.

[4] Although to abstract the predicative sense of 'to be' and base on it a classification of propositions may be a legitimate procedure in formal logic. For a fuller discussion see IH, ch. xii, § 2.

[5] See EL, § 167.

[6] Cf. ch. xi, § 2·3 above.

Hegel is compelled to select successively different types of thing to represent the subject, and successively different types of character to represent the predicate. There must, for example, eventually emerge a phase of Judgement which can only be illustrated by a predicate of intrinsic value or goodness. In EL, § 171, *Zusatz*, it is pointed out that even common sense, looking upon judgement as a faculty, recognizes this difference of level:

'We should not hesitate to ascribe a very slight faculty of judgement to a person who habitually formed only judgements such as "This wall is green", "This stove is hot". We should only credit with a genuine capacity of judgement a man whose criticisms concerned such questions as whether a certain work of art was beautiful, whether a certain action was good, and so on. In judgements of the first-mentioned kind the content forms only an abstract quality, the presence of which can be detected by immediate perception. To pronounce a work of art beautiful, or an action good, entails on the contrary a comparison of the objects with what they ought to be, i.e. with their notion.'

Thus the Judgement-forms are not, as in formal logic, indifferent to their content. Moreover, the copula, though its verbal form remains constant, will cease, as the dialectic advances, to express mere indeterminate Being: it will signify a variously graded unity of subject and predicate. In fact it will, *in itself* and not as the mere link between subject and predicate, gradually come to manifest the whole Notion. This is Hegel's meaning when he speaks of 'that continuous determining by which Judgement, through a copula charged with content, comes to be Syllogism'.[1] The copula is a relation (*Beziehung*) between subject and predicate, but it is a notional 'relation': it is the unity of subject and predicate, and it is itself, although implicitly, the whole Notion as Particular. Judgement is always, at least implicitly, a *triplicity* of moments into each of which the Notion enters whole.

3. The main phases of Judgement are not three but four,[2] although each of them subdivides into three. They are (A) Qualitative Judgement, or Judgement of *Dasein*, or Judgement of Inherence; (B) Judgement of Reflection, or

[1] EL, § 171.

[2] See § 5·4 below.

Judgement of Subsumption; (C) Judgement of Necessity; (D) Judgement of the Notion.

In EL, § 171, Hegel says:

'In respect of the two preceding spheres of Being and Essence the determinate Notions as Judgements [sc. the categories of Judgement] are reproductions of those spheres, but posited in the simplicity of relation peculiar to the Notion.'

The *Zusatz* to the same section amplifies this:

'We found the inner ground for the systematization of Judgements in the fact that the Notion is the ideal unity of Being and Essence, and when it unfolds, as it does in Judgement, it must begin by reproducing these two stages in a transformation (*Umbildung*) proper to the Notion. The Notion itself is seen, after that, determining itself as the genuine Judgement.'

3·1. The first three main phases of Judgement, then, both 'reproduce' and 'transform' the categories of Being and Essence. Hegel's meaning is, I think, as follows. (A) The Notion has its own principle: it is Universal-Particular-Individual. Although in Judgement it is Subjective Notion, yet it has developed dialectically through sublation of Being and Essence, and it is not subjective in the sense that Judgement is an external activity directed contingently upon an indifferent, 'realistic' world. The Notion therefore does not reproduce the categories of Being and Essence one by one, so that for every such category there emerges a category of Judgement. But (B) in the first place the transparent 'play' of notional development is sublation which preserves; and secondly the Notion in Judgement *is*, though in a different sense, subjective. Hence the categories of Being and Essence remain openly and explicitly present in the Judgement-forms. The relation of *ideell* to *reell*[1] in this phase of the Logic is not what it was in the pre-notional dialectic. As ideal moments within the content of the Judgement-forms, the lower categories are not dissolved as they were in Being, nor contradicted in the same way as they were in Essence.

3·2. Thus Judgement appears at first sight as a sort of *double* sublation of the lower categories, at once direct and indirect. (A) It has developed directly out of them, but (B)

[1] See IH, ch. xi, § 5·01.

it, as it were, recapitulates or reviews them transparently, so that they are clearly detectable in it, and in the progress of Judgement no fresh content seems to emerge. But (A) and (B) are inseparable within that sublation of Being and Essence which Judgement is: (B) is the further development of (A).

3·21. This seeming duplication, I might remark, is conspicuously illustrated in ordinary experience. Our present experience develops out of our past experience, but in memory, an integral moment of *present* experience, we review the past, remembering it *as* past. Again, in all thinking which is below the level of complete self-consciousness we are conscious (or upon the least reflection become conscious) not only of our object as something 'detached' and independent of our thinking, but also of the 'principles', or 'categories', or 'concepts' (as we then choose to name them) of our thinking as entities in varying degree separate from ourselves *qua* thinking subjects, which we somehow use as instruments to think with. And so far as in or together with such thinking we also perceive, we tend on a first reflection to take a like instrumental view: our senses seem to us faculties which at will we employ or suffer to rust, and the content of our perceptive act appears to us a representative image, or a 'sensum' whereof we find it hard to say whether it is 'mental' or 'physical'. Thus we are in two minds. If we can think and perceive truly, these 'principles', 'categories', 'concepts', and 'images' must be integral to the nature of the real object we experience. But they appear to us to be duplicated; to have a sort of second being as modes and even instruments of our experiencing. All philosophic, or rather pseudo-philosophic, dualisms spring from hardening this duplication—one might almost say duplicity—which distinctively characterizes certain pre-philosophic levels of experience.

3·3. It follows from this doubleness of notional sublation that there is no one–one correspondence of Judgement-forms with categories of Being and Essence: that would mean 'reproduction' without 'transformation'. It is the main lower levels (in each of which, of course, all yet lower levels are sublated) which are most clearly detectable within the

Judgement-forms as these emerge in the Logic. Hegel would presumably hold that a more precise determination of one particular category of Being or Essence other than these main levels is only possible and relevant in reference to a particular context of phenomenal experience.

3·31. This is to be borne in mind when Hegel illustrates Judgement with examples. 'This rose is red', for example, illustrates Judgement because it asserts in a rudimentary way that Individual is Universal. The lower category involved is most naturally taken to be, in general, Being as Quality, and so Hegel takes it when he uses it to illustrate Qualitative Judgement.[1] But it might in a particular context involve the category of Thing and Properties. Logicians of all sorts in using (as they must) examples of judgements are too apt to forget (*a*) that their sentence in inverted commas, which seems to impart a wholesome touch of reality to an abstract discussion, is itself an abstraction from a living context of judgement, and must, if it is to illustrate judgement at all, carry with it a typical context;[2] and (*b*) that this context can be no more than *merely* typical. It must remain partially indeterminate, since its further context in experience cannot be fully specified.

3·4. There is a further aspect of this double sublation which the reader must not miss. We have seen that Hegel's logic of the Subjective Notion is a sublation, a dialectical or speculative reconstruction, of formal logic.[3] It follows (*a*) that the subjectivity of Subjective Notion in all its phases is an advance upon the pre-subjective categories of Being and Essence, because it expresses the first phase of that emergence of spirit as free, active subjectivity which characterizes the *whole* logic of the Notion and led Hegel in LL to call the logic of the Notion, rather misleadingly, Subjective Logic;[4] but also (*b*) that in the subjectivity of Subjective Notion there is transparently reflected that subjectivity in the sense of contingency and arbitrary caprice which belongs to finite thinking and is fixed and enshrined by formal logic, the forms of which are the forms of the subjective processes of thought.[5] Within the progress of the Notion through

[1] See § 5 below. [2] Cf. § 2·01 above. [3] See ch. xi, § 2·2 above.
[4] See ch. v, §§ 6 and 6·1 above. [5] See ch. xi, § 2·1 above.

Notion as such, Judgement, and Syllogism towards its own objectivity, we shall be watching, openly reflected, the gradual lessening of that mere arbitrary and contingent subjectivity, which (*a*) we seem to observe occurring in ordinary experience as we pass from 'entertaining' a concept to judging and thence to inferring, and which (*b*) duly stamps itself upon and dictates the procedure of formal logic.

3·5. The type of error which springs from misinterpreting the apparent duplication which Judgement involves has been indicated generally in § 3·21. Certain further consequences are worth mention. If we fail to understand the open presence of the lower categories in the Judgement-forms, we shall readily tend to treat all categories as co-ordinate. We shall take the lower categories as explicitly universal, whereas they are only implicitly universal. We shall fail to remember, for example, that although Cause and Effect is a principle of universal connexion, it is—as Kant saw[1]—only universal by virtue of its operation in judgement. We shall forget, that is, that when we predicate Being or Essence of a finite thing, it makes a difference to the thing so characterized to be judged, to be held in the mind and become the content of explicit thought. It is of that which Hegel reminds us when he says, 'All things are a Judgement.' If we pursue this false scent farther, we may even come to talk as if there were a plurality of singular universals.

4. We may now sum up in three complementary ways the special nature of dialectical progress through Hegel's categories of Judgement.

(1) The development of Judgement is measured by the lessening of discrepancy between the lower category and the higher.

(2) Judgement progresses through the growing congruence of subject and predicate, as they both come more explicitly to express the total Notion; and through a corresponding, though verbally inexpressible, expansion of the copula from the level at which it is, subjectively considered, a mere relation (*Beziehung*) and, objectively considered, a sign of no more than Being in general, to the level at which it becomes the totality of the Notion as Particular.

[1] Cf. IH, ch. ix, § 4·2.

(1) and (2) may be expressed together if we adapt the terminology of Essence and say that the content of Judgement becomes gradually adequate to its notional form.

(3) Judgement has always a universal ground. When this becomes fully explicit, Judgement passes into Syllogism.

5. (A) Qualitative Judgement (Inherence)

'In the subjective judgement', says Hegel, meaning in the Judgement of the Notion, the fourth and highest phase of Judgement,[1] 'one tries to see one and the same object twofold: first in its individual actuality, secondly in its essential self-identity, or in its Notion. That is, one tries to see it as the Individual raised to its universality or—the same thing—as the Universal individualized into its actuality. In this manner Judgement is truth: the agreement of the Notion and the reality. But at first Judgement is not so constituted; for at first it is unmediated, since no Reflection and movement of determinations has come to light in it.'[2]

Judgement at this level below mediation is Judgement of *Dasein*, or of Quality in a sense of the term which includes abstract immediate universality. It may, *qua* immediate, also be called Judgement of Inherence: the subject is the immediate, therefore essential and logically prior, element upon which the formally dependent predicate is founded.

The subdivisions of Qualitative Judgement are (1) Positive (i.e. affirmative) Judgement; (2) Negative Judgement; (3) Infinite Judgement.

5·1. Positive Judgement

'The rose [i.e. this singular individual rose] is red' will serve to illustrate Positive Judgement. Here truth as opposed to correctness is hardly present at all. Spirit affirms itself as no more than immediately qualitative. Individual is here Universal, but equally and indifferently Universal is Individual. For subject and predicate outflank each other, and touch, as it were, only at one point, while the copula, accordingly, expresses their unity only as a relation, not explicitly grounded, of terms which merely 'are there', are mere *qualia*.[3]

Hence arises the antithesis

[1] See § 8 below. [2] LL, ii, p. 75. [3] Cf. §§ 1·2 and 1·3 above.

5·2. Negative Judgement

For now clearly it is equally true that the Individual is here *not* Universal, and the Universal *not* Individual. Considering the process subjectively, we may say that we have failed by mere affirmative judgement to express the truth which we mean, the truth that Individual is Universal. We are faced after all by the incompatibility of subject and predicate outside their point of contact: this singular cannot as such *be* the Universal. Hence we are forced to supplement positive by negative judgement and to assert that 'This rose is not yellow'.[1]

But this negation is not sheer negation. For if 'This rose is not yellow' is significant judgement, it is made with reference to an excluding universe of discourse: it implies that this rose is at any rate coloured. The logical truth-form we are now using is, 'The Individual is the Universal, but one particular determination of the Universal.' We have denied one qualification of the subject, and so taken the first rudimentary step towards significant negation, which in the sphere of the Notion is particularization.

This appears equally in predicate and copula. The Negative Judgement may be expressed either as '*A* is not-*B*' or as '*A* is-not *B*'. 'This rose is not yellow' has a positive side or moment. It contains and openly develops the truth of 'This rose is red', for it implies that the rose is not merely coloured otherwise than yellow, but that it has a particular colour.

5·201. The reader will not here make the mistake of objecting that the positive judgement 'This rose is red' already expresses more than the fact that this rose has some particular colour. In 'This rose is red', as an illustration of Positive Judgement, the predicate is to be taken as meaning not red-as-a-species-of-the-genus-colour, but a purely affirmative, therefore *undifferentiated*, red-colour. Bradley's examples of judgements which contain no explicit subject and predicate[2]

[1] Hegel in both Logics illustrates Negative Judgement with 'The rose is not red', because he is only concerned with Judgement as a truth-form, a category. But it is perhaps less confusing to assume for the purpose of illustration a series of judgements made by the same finite subject in the same situation.

[2] See Bradley, *Logic*, i, ed. 2, pp. 56–7.

would perhaps illustrate Positive Judgement less misleadingly.

5·21. Negative Judgement, though an advance upon Positive, nevertheless clearly shows its failure in form. We have asserted in effect that Individual is Particular, and by implication that Universal is Particular. But Particular within the Negative Judgement is only *a* particular. The point of contact between Individual and Universal has been expanded, but Individual and Universal have not become commensurate. The particularity of the rose is self-contradictory: it is at once (*a*) the colour it actually is, and (*b*) any-colour-bar-yellow. And as particularization of the Universal this particularity is equally self-contradictory. The Universal is here determinate in *a* particular; i.e. it does not enter whole into this determinateness, and is therefore not truly Particular.

We thus appear to have succeeded only in reaching a form of Judgement in which we assert that the Individual is the Individual, and the Universal is the Universal. Yet there remains this definite result: through their failure to coincide, through their mutual repudiation, Individual and Universal are for the first time intro-reflected and so posited in their respective natures, as in Positive Judgement they were not.

This result gives us the synthesis of Qualitative Judgement,

5·3. Infinite Judgement

This in effect is a duality of two inseparable forms, viz. Identical Judgement and Infinite Judgement. Identical Judgement is bare tautology in the form, 'The singular individual is the singular individual' ('This rose is this rose'). Infinite Judgement predicates the complementary and equally empty negation, 'The singular individual is not another singular individual' ('This rose is not some other singular thing'). In this duality bare Identity and bare Difference are the lower categories *par excellence* sublated into Notional form. The subject is not qualified at all, but the form of the Judgement is an advance, as we have already seen, in that Individual and Universal are now intro-reflected, and are no longer in the immediate togetherness of

Being. The copula, one might add, takes here the dual form of is-and-is-not: it begins to assert its claim to mediate by particularizing.

5·31. Hegel offers crime as a phenomenal illustration of the Infinite Judgement: the thief, for example, by his action denies altogether right to property. A civil suit, on the other hand, illustrates Negative Judgement only, because it only denies a particular right. Death, again, is an infinite judgement, disease merely a negative one.[1] In short, Infinite Judgement totally splits subject from predicate, and leaves the subject unqualified. That is why it differs only formally from Identical Judgement.

Hegel's treatment of Identical and Infinite Judgement—or, as he also calls them, Positive Infinite Judgement and Negative Infinite Judgement—is, however, somewhat ambiguous. In LL[2] he calls Infinite Judgement an absurd (*widersinniges*) Judgement, and says that examples of it such as 'The Understanding is not a table' are not judgements at all. Elsewhere he calls the assertion that a man is sick or has committed a crime untrue as Judgement.[3] Yet in LL[4] he calls an evil deed a more real (*reelleres*) example of Infinite Judgement than statements like 'The Understanding is not a table', and, because the duality of Infinite Judgement does express the intro-reflection of Individual and Universal, he has no hesitation in treating it as a definite phase in the dialectic of Judgement. The real reason why absurd statements such as 'The Understanding is not a table' do not exemplify Judgement is that they do not imply any context or ground;[5] or as Hegel puts it in EL, § 173, 'They can only occur in subjective thinking [sc. in the thought, e.g., of a writer of text-books on formal logic], which can hold fast even an untrue abstraction.' But Hegel should not, I think, in EL, § 172, *Zusatz* have suggested that crime and disease, because they assert the failure of a man to conform to his notion, have no truth at all as Judgement.[6]

[1] EL, § 173, *Zusatz*.

[2] LL, ii, pp. 89–90.

[3] EL, § 172, *Zusatz*; cf. § 2·01 above.

[4] LL, ii, p. 90.

[5] Cf. § 2 above.

[6] The *Zusätze* were competently compiled from notes taken at Hegel's lectures and are fairly reliable.

5·4. The emergence of bare Identity and Difference as the lower categories *par excellence* involved in Infinite Judgement betokens a transition from Judgement-forms which sublate Being to Judgement-forms which sublate Essence. The latter occupy two main phases of Judgement, viz. Judgement of Reflection and Judgement of Necessity. Hence there are, formally, four main phases of Judgement. But really Judgement of Reflection and Judgement of Necessity go together to constitute the main antithesis of Judgement. The fundamental differentiation of Judgement is still triadic, and the phase of antithesis is double because it corresponds to Essence, which is the stage *par excellence* of Difference. This statement, which seems to be Hegel's only comment on the apparent failure in dialectical symmetry, occurs in EL, § 171, *Zusatz*. His point is, I think, that what at the higher level of Judgement corresponds to the 'coupled' nature of every category of Essence is just this partition of the main antithesis into two phases. The Notion, sublating the categories of the Understanding, is still, as it were, broken-backed in its movement, not fully mediated.

6. (B) JUDGEMENT OF REFLECTION (SUBSUMPTION)

Judgement of Reflection subdivides into Singular, Particular, and Universal Judgement. Particular and Universal Judgement might perhaps be better entitled respectively Judgement of Someness and Judgement of Allness, since these categories reflect markedly the distinctions of quantity in judgement as these appear in a formal logic which construes its terms in extension. But in Judgement of Reflection we have to do with something more than Being as Quantity, just as in Qualitative Judgement we had to do with more than mere Quality: Judgement is the Notion, and every category of Judgement is therefore Universal.

The lower categories which Judgement of Reflection conspicuously sublates are those of Essence as Intro-reflection. We have seen that the Individual determined through Qualitative Judgement is intro-reflected. It has failed to be fully particularized Universal, but through this very failure it is reflected back upon itself: it is Individual as neither the Somewhat nor the Unit of Number can claim to be. Hence the 'some' of Particular Judgement is not a mere plurality, and the 'all' of Universal Judgement is not a mere aggregate *de facto* complete. As in Essence both as Intro-reflection and as Appearance the explicit necessity of Essence as Actuality was foreshadowed, so here the notional necessity, which will emerge in Judgement of the Notion, is already present in germ. The copula, correspondingly, begins here to express connexion instead of mere relation. This is amply verified in ordinary experience: judgement never lacks at least the implication of a ground in a broad sense of the term.

In Judgement of Reflection the nature of the subject develops directly, that of the predicate indirectly. The procedure of Qualitative Judgement is thus reversed, and this change of emphasis accords with the transition from immediacy to mediation. It is for this reason that Hegel contrasts Judgement of Reflection with Qualitative Judgement as Judgement of Subsumption with Judgement of Inherence.

6·1. Singular Judgement

Since Individual and Universal are now each intro-reflected and so presuppose each other, their mediation has begun. The formula for Singular Judgement may be expressed as 'This is essentially something universal', but 'This', the subject, is not a mere one among many. It is best illustrated by a proper name expressing one individual possessed of essential content; for example, 'Gaius is ——.' Accordingly the predicate must be no longer a mere quality, but an essential property of the subject, though not expressive of its notion; for example, 'Gaius is a Roman.' Here the copula expresses essential relation of the subject to the predicate and to other individual subjects; of Gaius to his Roman nationality and to other Romans.

But 'This' is *not* essentially universal: to be Gaius and to be Roman are not commensurate. That 'This' has an essential character implies that some other individuals, some other 'this'es, have it too; implies, that is, that 'This' does not possess it *qua* 'This'.

Thus in antithesis Singular Judgement develops into

6·2. Particular Judgement (Someness)

Here the subject must change its nature; for we cannot say 'Some intro-reflected individuals have the essential character *x*', for example, 'Some Gaii are Romans.' 'Some' implies a determination of content, and in order to illustrate Particular Judgement we must put as subject a term signifying a genus; we must say, for example, 'Some *men* are Romans', or 'Some *plants* are wholesome'. For 'someness' contains universality.

Thus Particular Judgement asserts that the Particular is the Universal.

But the relation of content in subject and predicate is not adequate to this form. The Particular Judgement is as much negative as positive: if some men are Romans and some plants wholesome, then also some men and some plants must lack these properties. 'Some' fails fully to particularize the Universal, and on the other side the universality which 'some' contains is still separated from the individuals. Formally the Particular Judgement asserts the broadening of the 'This' into particularity. 'But this universalization is not congruent (*angemessen*) with the "This": "This" [sc. the intro-reflected singular individual] is completely determinate, but "some this" is indeterminate.'[1]

The synthesis which reconciles this contradiction is

6·3. Universal Judgement (Allness)

The subject now becomes expressly Universal, and so expressly identical with the predicate. This is the form of Judgement most commonly illustrated in ordinary reflection, viz. the predication of a common character. When we assert that all men are mortal we suggest a necessary connexion, and we accept any empirical generalization only on the tacit agreement that unless and until an exception occurs we are to take a subjective 'all' (all known cases) as equivalent to an objective 'all'.[2]

6·31. This *quasi*-quantitative character of the Judgement of Reflection is now transcended. The proper expression of the subject, if we illustrate, is not, for example, 'all men' but

[1] LL, ii, p. 96. [2] Ibid., p. 98.

'man as such'. The Universal has now emerged as the genus, and 'the genus is not a predicate inhering in a subject, nor is it one property—nor a property at all—of the subject: it contains every individual determinateness resolved in its substantial solidity'.[1]

In this concrete, objective (in the sense of necessary) universality of the genus we may say that the relation of subject and predicate is inverted, for the genus is essentially subject. But it is not a subject subsumed under a predicate, and it is truer to say that with the coincidence of subject and predicate, and the emergence of explicit necessity, Judgement develops a new character. The distinction of subject, predicate, and copula now becomes unimportant. In becoming identical as genus, subject and predicate have, as Hegel puts it, 'coalesced into the copula'.[2] Judgement has become objective in the sense of necessary. In the Judgement-forms of Necessity the genus, in and for itself, will develop its own inner distinctions, for which the formula '*S* is *P*' is no longer fully adequate.

7. (C) Judgement of Necessity

The phases of the Judgement of Necessity are Categorical, Hypothetical, and Disjunctive Judgement. The lower categories which they most transparently reveal are those of Absolute Correlation, the final triad of Actuality.

Categorical Judgement

In this, the immediate Judgement of Necessity, wherein Judgement of Allness has become explicitly Universal as genus, the conspicuous lower category is Substance and Accident. But the genus has its distinctions immanent in it, whereas Substance has its distinctions only in its Accidents.

Categorical Judgement asserts that Particular is Universal. If we retain the terminology of subject and predicate and illustrate, we must exemplify the subject by a species and the predicate by its genus; for example, 'Gold is a metal.' The predicate is universal, but it contains negative determination immanent in it, so that the connexion of subject

[1] Ibid., p. 99. [2] Ibid., p. 100.

with predicate, of gold with the genus metal, is necessary: subject and predicate are identical in content.

But subject and predicate are not yet an identity of form. If we think only the identity of species with genus, we have determined the genus as a subgenus of higher genera, without succeeding in determining it as proximate genus of the species. Metal is neither *summum genus* of gold, nor does it at once differentiate gold as an *infima species* of itself. Particular now shows itself as after all *not* fully identical in content with Universal, as failing to particularize fully. Gold and metal do not exhaust each other's natures: metal has other species besides gold.

Thus it turns out that the truth we succeed in asserting is not categorical, but at once less and more than categorical. We thus pass to

7·1. Hypothetical Judgement

For we find that we are only entitled to assert the necessity of connexion between subject and predicate. Their contents have proved incommensurate, and only the formal necessity of relation can be explicitly asserted: 'If gold, then metal.' The categorical moment is preserved in this transition, but as a not fully determinate implication: hypothetical judgements, as Bradley taught, merely *imply* a categorical basis.

The lower category here conspicuous is Cause and Effect; although through Cause and Effect also Ground and Consequent, Condition and Fact, &c., are clearly sublated in Hypothetical Judgement. Like Cause and Effect, the two sides of the Hypothetical Judgement are identical and also reciprocal: if Effect then Cause, if genus then any given species of it. But as Effect not merely reciprocates with Cause but is also itself Cause to a further Effect, so the genus has further species beyond the given species. The difference between the two categories is that Correlation is not immanent distinction, whereas genus *specifies* itself in further species, and does not, like Cause in its series of Effects which are also each in turn again Cause, merely *repeat* itself in them.

The synthesis of Categorical with Hypothetical Judgement is

7·2. Disjunctive Judgement

The category of Essence perspicuously sublated is Reciprocity. The categorical nature of Judgement is restored at a higher level through synthesis with the formal necessity into which it developed, when the genus becomes explicitly whole in the totality of its species. The species are mutually exclusive: the genus is *either* this species *or* that. But the genus is the unity of the species: it is this species *as well as* that. Thus only do universal, particular, and individual moments of the genus become commensurate and coalesce; or rather, perhaps, only in the concretely specified genus do Universal, Particular, and Individual coalesce in a strictly necessary Judgement-form.

7·21. It is again of very great importance to observe that the genus which emerges in Judgement of Necessity is logical and not natural genus.[1] Traditional formal logic sets forth a method of division by dichotomy of a genus, and it is this genus of formal logic which Hegel began to reconstitute in Notion as such, and is now further developing in Disjunctive Judgement. The genus of Nature which illustrates the logical genus is in large measure contingent. It is not such as to dictate the number of its species. These remain more or less co-ordinate and merely various, and each of them is accordingly manifested in an indefinite multiplicity of singular individuals. If the natural genus is to illustrate Disjunctive Judgement at all adequately it must be conceived with two contrary species only.[1] But even this illustration would fall short. In Nature Number and Quantity generally are conspicuous; but in the Notion Number is a long-transcended category, and the *plurality* of species is irrelevant to logic save that Number is a category sublated in Judgement. Only in the mutual exclusiveness of the species within the unity of their genus is logical disjunction illustrated. Itself it consists solely in the duality of the Universal *qua* whole both as the positive and as the negative—more precisely, as the generic and as the specific—totality of its self-particularization. These two moments alone, in the union of which the genus is Individual, are the members of logical disjunction.

[1] See ch. xi, § 6·1, above.

7·22. Hegel expounds this doctrine in LL, pp. 107–10. His illustration from colour is specially to be noted. He evidently regards logical disjunction as more adequately expressed in the blending opposites which constitute an Aristotelian *quasi*-genus, an essential accident,[1] than in Aristotle's conception of a true genus of substantial species: 'If colour is conceived (*begriffen*) as the concrete unity of light and dark, then this genus has in it the determinateness which constitutes the principle of its particularization into species.'[2] This suggests a comment of some interest upon Aristotle's sharp distinction between substance and accident. Hegel would have held, I think, that Aristotle in his conception of a *quasi*-genus—colour and sound are Aristotle's favourite examples—had grasped the real nature of the genus, but that the rigid final reality which he came to accord to the substantial species had forced him to take, so to say, an official view of the true genus as a whole of merely co-ordinate species which do not differ in degree. Aristotle consequently came to relegate the truer conception of genus to the mere inhering accident, which exhibits its specific, or *quasi*-specific, variation on a scale of degrees between contrary poles because it is a manifestation of change.[3]

Thus if the direct question be asked whether Aristotle admits categorical, hypothetical, and disjunctive as genuinely distinct types of judgement, it can only be replied that on his official view all judgement is categorical.[4] Yet it is clear that in constructing his ideal basic syllogism of demonstration he stumbles upon the hypothetical judgement. For the major premiss of that syllogism—the nexus of essential accident with one constitutive element in the substantial *infima species*[5]—is obviously an hypothetical and not a categorical judgement. Moreover, the ideal type of *proprium* which the major term of the basic syllogism reflects is disjunctive, since it is a capacity of change (in mathematics of variation) between contrary poles within a *quasi*-genus.[6] Once we deny the ultimate metaphysical truth which Aristotle's doctrine of atomic individual substances (whether specific or singular)

[1] See IH, ch. iv, §§ 3 and 4·51.
[2] LL, p. 109.
[3] Cf. IH, ch. iv, § 4·51.
[4] Cf. ch. viii, § 6·2 above.
[5] See IH, ch. iv, § 3·1.
[6] See my *Aristotle*, p. 199 footnote.

officially claims, the conflict in his philosophy between true genus and *quasi*-genus can be resolved, and the real distinction between categorical, hypothetical, and disjunctive judgement can be made explicit.

7·23. In the background behind the Aristotelian conception of genus, species, and property lies the Platonic genus as we find it especially in the *Sophist*, *Politicus*, and *Philebus*. It divides by dichotomy and is the direct origin of traditional logical division, although Plato makes it the object of dialectic.[1] It is innocent of the Aristotelian distinction between substantial character and accidental property. One might, I think, say that Hegel is not merely reconstituting the genus of traditional logical division, but also resynthesizing the opposed conceptions of genus and *quasi*-genus into which Aristotle differentiated the naïve breadth of the Platonic genus.

7·24. The doctrine of Bradley and Bosanquet that logical disjunction is the union of hypotheticals on a categorical basis, and consummates the distinction between affirmative and negative judgement, is clearly inspired throughout by Hegel. They differ from Hegel in working at a more empirical level, and are on the whole content to conceive the disjunctive totality, which appears to them to be the ideal of thought, as not essentially a duality. Bradley, at any rate, appears to think of a disjunctive system as one in which the 'either/or' merely relates each member of the system in turn to the rest taken together in a lump.[2]

8. (D) Judgement of the Notion

The clue to comprehension of Judgement in its final phase is the explicit emergence of intrinsic value, or goodness.

In the Disjunctive Judgement the Universal is explicitly necessary. It is transparently identical with its total self-particularization. In subject-predicate terminology this means that the subject no longer has an imperfectly commensurate predicate, but is Individual as fully particularized Universal. In fact now first emerges the true Individual; that for which it is one and the same thing to be and to

[1] See my *Aristotle*, pp. 57–8.

[2] See Bradley, *Logic*, ed. 2, vol. i, pp. 137–8.

possess that Universal nature which it does possess; that, in scholastic language, whose essence and existence coincide. And with this coincidence the copula ceases to be at once and contradictorily (*a*) a relation and (*b*) a mode of being, and becomes the whole Judgement. But the Individual in this unreserved possession of its own intrinsic nature is not merely necessary, or self-necessitating; it is good. Its individuality, we may say, is nothing else but intrinsic value; but we can only loosely speak as if it possessed individuality as a character, for it transcends the distinction which the grammatical difference between substantive and adjective expresses.

8·1. The Notion as intrinsic value is, moreover, *eo ipso*, judging subject in self-conscious activity,[1] and ordinary experience amply illustrates this. When we judge a picture beautiful or an action good,[2] we claim to possess the faculty of judgement in a degree we should not pretend to be exercising if we merely judged the picture to be dusty or the action to have occurred to-day. In 'value-judgements' we profess to assert an objective nature, the conformity of something to its notion, which it requires some little intelligence to discriminate. But although we mean to assert an objective nature and not a contingent caprice of subjective taste—although, that is, we assert the conformity of something to *its* notion—yet we do further mean that, in the beauty or moral goodness which we assert, we recognize that in which our own nature is realized; that which, as we might put it, not only conforms to *its* notion, but also therein realizes *our* ideal. The objectivity is not that which belongs to the 'detached' object-world of natural science, which justly denies any intrinsic value in its object; it is objectivity in a world wherewith we implicitly identify ourselves, not as so many singular experients having each his private tastes, but as universal judging subject. We implicitly assume our judgements of intrinsic value to evince an activity of self-consciousness, unless we have sophisticated ourselves with a 'scientific' outlook into mistaking the subjectivity of value-

[1] See ch. x, § 1·3 above.

[2] Or, since in finite judgement the finite is judged, a picture ugly and an action bad.

judgements for caprice engendered by a forever inexplicable stimulus of private emotion.[1]

8·11. This coincidence of the true Individual, or concrete Universal, with (*a*) intrinsic value or goodness and (*b*) subjectivity, can be interestingly paralleled by reference to Aristotle's conception of what I have called a '*quasi*-genus', the species of which are formed by blendings of contrary opposites.[2] In a *quasi*-genus, an essential accident such as colour or pitch, the species exhibit difference of degree on a scale, but no one species of an essential accident belonging to the sphere of the natural or mathematical sciences can be called in any sense better or worse. But Aristotle appears to regard the moral virtues as essential accidents of man's sensory and appetitive soul, and so as *quasi*-genera. These virtues are, on his view, habits of susceptibility in a certain degree, and reaction in a certain manner, to innate feelings which, before the habit is developed by training, are linked pairs of contrary emotional tendencies, the one of which is the more positive, the other the more negative (privative). Courage, for example, is an habitual blending of confidence and shrinking in a certain definite proportion, and an accordant habit of reaction. A moral virtue thus exhibits what Aristotle calls a 'mean',[3] in the sense of an equipoise of contraries; and it is, moreover, the one precisely right blend (with accordant reaction) of these contraries. Blends on either side of it—in the case of courage those which contain either too much or too little confidence—are not species of virtue but vices respectively of excess and defect; whereas from among the blends of white and black, or of high and low, no colour or sound can be singled out as the one good specification of the genus. Thus (A) in a moral virtue the opposites constituting the generic nature are at once and in one particularized and individualized; there is here no plurality of species whereof the genus is a more or less mere *de facto* totality. In its own sphere a moral virtue is a concrete universal.

[1] Of course value-judgements may be subjective in the sense of capricious. But that is merely to say that they are finite judgements, which in varying degrees fail to illustrate Judgement.

[2] Cf. §§ 7·21 and 7·22 above.

[3] Cf. ch. iv, § 2·3 above.

Moreover (B), on Aristotle's view this equipoise of contrary opposites in a unique mean is determined in accordance with the 'ratio' of the agent's own nature to that of a normal, i.e. ideal, agent. In order to become courageous my habit of action in my circumstances as given from time to time must embody a degree of feeling and reaction proportionate to that degree of feeling and reaction which the ideal hero would embody in ideal circumstances. And this reference to a relatively external norm must continue until I myself come to embody that norm by developing the rational virtue of practical wisdom in which moral virtue, the virtue of the sensory and appetitive soul, is consummated or, as Hegel would say, sublated. Hence this uniquely excellent mean, which moral virtue is, has its place only where there is subjectivity; only in the self-expressive activity of spirit and not in Nature. One may add, I think, that as for Hegel Nature is not the non-spiritual but the pre-spiritual,[1] so for Aristotle in the *quasi*-genera of colour and sound the emergence of the uniquely good is foreshadowed in the fact that the precise blends of white and black, high and low, which constitute species of colour and sound, are determined by the nature of the percipient's discriminative capacity as well as by quantitative differences which, at any rate in principle, are exactly measurable.

8·2. Thus from the coincidence in notional Judgement of the true Individual, or concrete Universal, with intrinsic value and subjectivity follow two important consequences. (1) In order to illustrate Judgement of the Notion the judgement selected must have a predicate expressing value. But (2) notional Judgement is not Judgement of Necessity with a mere change in the type of predicate asserted: it is Judgement openly expressing self-consciousness. Hence the judgement selected is effective as an illustration not merely because it has a value-predicate, but by virtue of the attitude of the judging subject which it implies; by virtue, that is, of his claim to be a judge,[2] and of his implied consent thereby to pass judgement on himself. If I judge that this rose is red,

[1] See IH, ch. viii, § 4·2.

[2] Cf. LL, ii, p. 110: 'Solches Urteil enthält daher erst eine wahrhafte Beurteilung.'

that Gaius is a Roman, and that gold is a metal, I claim perhaps observation and even a rudimentary scientific insight; but I am primarily concerned to state the nature of something which I take as 'detached' and independent of consciousness. On the other hand, in my moral, aesthetic, and philosophical judgements, although I assert them as objective, yet I at the same time tell the world what it is in which I find my satisfaction. I deliberately reveal my own nature.

But, as we shall see, this subjectivity, which distinctively characterizes notional Judgement, first emerges as a merely contingent subjectivity. Judgement of the Notion is at first contingent, whether we consider (*a*) the activity of the judging subject, or (*b*) the relation of subject and predicate in the content. For the mere unmediated assertion that this picture is beautiful or this action good expresses an as yet unjustified faith, which may be a mere caprice just because it offers no ground. It is not an accident that value-judgements are far more commonly disputed than judgements of fact. In the course of notional Judgement this assertion of immediate faith must be developed until it is justified in a content which demonstrates itself as intrinsically good.

8·3. The notional Judgement develops through three phases: Assertoric, Problematic, and Apodeictic Judgement.

Since in Disjunctive Judgement what I have called the 'review' of the categories of Being and Essence is completed, Judgement of the Notion will not openly display any of those lower categories sublated in it in the precise manner in which this has occurred in the three earlier phases of Judgement. On the other hand, there is an important analogy between Judgement of the Notion and the proportioned whole of Measure; and there is between the Judgement-forms of Necessity and the categories of notional Judgement, which *directly* sublate them, a prima-facie closeness of resemblance which has deceived many thinkers.[1]

8·4. Assertoric Judgement

The true individual has emerged from Disjunctive Judgement as immediately one with Universal and Particular. But this unmediated unity is so far subjective in the sense of

[1] See § 10 below.

contingent. It is illustrated by a judgement in which the predicate expresses value but the subject is a singular: for example, 'This house is good'. But 'This house', *qua* singular, cannot be *necessarily* good:[1] the assertion may with equal right, or want of right, be denied and the house judged not good.[2] Hence, by a transition which is the analogue in terms of value to the transition from Categorical to Hypothetical Judgement, we pass to

8·5. Problematic Judgement

For the truth which it thus turns out that we can assert is that the house may or may not be a good house, may or may not conform to its notion. The difference between Problematic and Hypothetical Judgement is that in Problematic Judgement the predicate, being a 'value-predicate' expressing an 'ought', has for its explicit content the relation of the subject to the Notion. Thus the contingent subjectivity of the assertion 'may-or-may-not', the mere possibility which it expresses, is actually present in the Judgement-form, as in Hypothetical Judgement it is not.

But Assertoric and Problematic Judgement pass to synthesis in

8·6. Apodeictic Judgement

For, if we remember that truth and not correctness is in point, we can see that if in fact 'this house' *is* good, then the 'is' is not the mere immediacy judged assertorically, which equally may not be: 'this house', if good, not *is* but *must be* good by virtue of its actual constitution. Goodness, or intrinsic value, cannot, *ex vi termini* and as common experience amply testifies, be demonstrated as the consequent of any alien ground: it must be self-demonstrating. If it is not self-demonstrating, it can only be either the inexplicable pronouncement of emotional caprice, or the content of a purely miraculous isolated intuition. Moreover, this self-

[1] Lacks, that is, not the necessity of Judgement of Necessity but, so to say, notional necessity, explicit conformity to the Notion. 'Good' may, I suppose, mean here practically adequate, or beautiful, or both.

[2] The reader need scarcely be reminded that not the correctness of the judgement but only its truth-form is in point. This proves inadequate to its content.

demonstration must consist in the sublation of categories which, so far as they are *reell*, do not express value. If it does not, intrinsic value, be it emotional fancy or mystic intuition, is not integral to the world but a veneer upon its surface. Such is the essence equally of Hegel's theory of truth and of the Platonic doctrine of the Good.

8·61. In Apodeictic Judgement Individual, through total self-particularization, coincides with Universal. The copula becomes the Particular as middle term: '*A* is *C*' is replaced by '*A qua B* is *C*'. Judgement passes into inference in syllogistic form.

9. With this transition I shall attempt to deal in the next chapter. Meanwhile it is worth while here to pause and take our bearings with regard to Kant.[1]

Kant's first nine categories are at once and in one (*a*) structural principles which inform and articulate the phenomenal object-world of our knowledge, and (*b*) functions of judgement; modes, that is, of the Understanding's activity into which the transcendental unity of apperception is articulated. (*a*) In the first of these aspects these Kantian categories contribute, as we have from time to time observed, to Hegel's Logic of Being and Essence. Kant's categories of Quantity and Quality appear, greatly recast and augmented, in Hegel's categories of Being, and Kant's categories of Relation re-emerge with comparatively little modification in the final triad of Essence.[2] It is, however, to be remembered that already in Essence Hegel is offering a quite un-Kantian criticism of the whole attitude of the Understanding.[3]

(*b*) If from Kant's first nine categories in their second aspect as functions of judgement we abstract the bare forms of judgement which underlie them, we arrive at that which, subject to considerable reconstruction, constitutes Hegel's first three triads of Judgement. Kant's categories, *qua* functions of judgement, are modes in which any finite mind must

[1] What follows largely repeats what was said in IH, ch. ix, esp. §§ 4·2 and 4·3–4·311. I have again ignored the difference in Kant between pure and schematized categories; see ibid., §§ 5·21 and 5·22.

[2] There is, I think, an analogous correspondence between the transcendental unity of apperception in its objective aspect and Hegel's category of Identity, which in EL is the opening category of Essence; cf. ch. vi, § 2 above.

[3] See ch. v, § 4·1 above.

judge in its synthetic activity of constituting an object with the co-operation of sensuous intuition. But he holds that these functions of judgement can be considered apart from this concrete synthetic activity, and that so considered they are the types of formal relation which unify concepts in judgement whatever their content may be. This abstraction, Kant thinks, has been actually long ago made by formal logic, and is the basis of the traditional distinction between validity and material truth. Thus, although it is Kant's view that analysis necessarily presupposes synthesis, and that all thinking is both analytic and synthetic, yet he believes that if this abstraction from concrete synthetic function is made, there remain certain formal types of judgement, certain differentiations which judgement exhibits whatever its content may be. In short, his doctrine is that, if you abstract and consider by itself the aspect of the first nine categories as mere forms of judgement—i.e. if you abstract them from their concrete synthetic function of constituting with the help of sense an objective world—you then have before you nothing but the judgement-forms of formal logic.[1] And these are forms of judgement, but they are not categories: they constitute no object, and are so far subjective.[2]

Hegel's view is very different. His forms of Judgement are not empty forms of thinking but categories constitutive of reality at a level higher than that of Kant's phenomenal world. Kant's judgement-forms are *less* than his categories; they are mere formal abstractions from the latter. Hegel's forms of Judgement are categories more concrete than Kant's categories. For Kant the transition from Understanding to Reason is the transition from constitutive categories to non-constitutive Ideas which are merely regulative. For Hegel it is the re-emergence of free subjectivity; a subjectivity which, although it is at first (in Subjective Notion) unpossessed of its own true objective content, is yet an integral phase in the elevation of the objective world of the Understanding which the categories of Essence have defined.

9·1. Thus there seems to be a fairly clear correspondence between Kant's first nine categories, (*a*) *qua* structural prin-

[1] See IH, ch. ix, § 4·32.

[2] They are only objective in that they are the same for every finite mind.

ciples with Hegel's categories of Being and Essence, and (*b*) *qua* forms of judgement with the first three triads of Hegel's Judgement.[1]

But the reconstruction in Hegel's Logic of Kant's doctrine of modality is far harder to state.[2] In Kant the categories of modality have nothing to do with intrinsic value, which is never to Kant an object of theoretical knowledge. They are said by him to express variations of subjective attitude towards the same unvarying content. This must surely mean that they are only modes of judging, and not also three fresh structural principles of the phenomenal object-world.[3] From this it should follow that the categories of modality constitute no advance on the modal judgement-forms of formal logic. That is to say, their synthetic activity in cognition of an objective world, which is supposed to render them categories and so more than mere forms of judgement, is little short of a sham. Yet Kant does not regard them as mere formal types of judgement,[4] and the view which he does take reveals an ambiguity which was really latent in his conception of the first nine categories. He has conceived those categories as at once modes of the mind's activity and structural characters of the object. This should imply that 'subject' and 'object' have no meaning save as correlated terms which emerge within an experience not in the last resort merely finite-centred. This position is idealist, even if Kant failed fully to realize it. It supersedes the realist assumption that the problem of knowledge is adequately stated as the problem how singular finite minds can make contact with a 'detached' real world.

But side by side with this latent idealism we find in Kant the reiterated assertion that the categories are forms of 'possible experience', and the force of this assertion seems clearly to be that the categories must apply to any object which any individual mind may actually experience.[5] Kant, anchored by his view that sense and thought are separate

[1] Considered only as the unity of the subject, Kant's transcendental unity of apperception (and so the 'simple concept' of formal logic) reappears transformed in Hegel's Notion as such.

[2] See IH, ch. ix, § 4·311.

[3] See LL, i, pp. 405–6.

[4] Cf. KRV, B, p. 219.

[5] Ibid., pp. 272–3.

sources of experience, would appear to be thinking of 'possible experience' as a field which radiates out from the actually present experience of a singular individual mind, lying open for that mind to explore and so to actualize, and further—whatever this may mean—to necessitate. In fact when Kant equates the phenomenal world with 'possible experience', he seems to be merely generalizing a finite thinker's view of himself and his world. But this is barely concealed realism, and when Kant approaches the problem of modality it ceases to be concealed at all. The view that the difference between '*A* may be *B*', '*A* is *B*', and '*A* must be *B*' is merely the difference between degrees of subjective certainty is open realism. Accordingly Kant becomes in effect committed to the doctrine of 'floating ideas', the doctrine that we can entertain a content in our mind without judging.[1] Although Kant does not explain how a sheerly arbitrary imagination is possible, yet he is quite clear that it makes no difference to the content of a *Vorstellung* whether it is merely imagined, or is a really possible, or an actual, or a necessary constituent of objective experience. This doctrine, on which he bases his peculiarly shallow criticism of the ontological argument,[2] exposes Kant to all the difficulties which spring from the view that truth is correctness.[3]

9·11. If we turn to Hegel's Logic for a reconstruction of this confused teaching, we must say that Hegel absorbs the objective aspect of Kant's modal categories (the possibility, actuality, and necessity which Kant has in effect reduced to mere degrees of subjective certainty) into the logic of Essence, where they appear as categories prefiguring Substance and Accident, Cause and Effect, and Reciprocity. On the other hand, Kant's modal categories *qua* functions of judgement are recast by Hegel as the phases of notional Judgement. But he places Assertoric before Problematic Judgement, reversing the Kantian order, which was a merely psychological and not a logical order.[4] Moreover, in accordance with his treatment of the Judgement-forms as logically more concrete,

[1] See IH, ch. xiii, § 4·3.

[2] See below, ch. xiv, §§ 4 ff.

[3] See IH, ch. xiv, § 3.

[4] As Prof. Kemp Smith notes; see *Commentary to Kant's Critique of Pure Reason*, p. 194. See also IH, ch. ix, § 4·311.

i.e. as higher *Denkbestimmungen* than the Kantian categories in their objective aspect, Hegel reinterprets the subjectivity of modal judgement, which in Kant is ultimately subjective only in the sense of non-constitutive, as the re-emergence of free, self-conscious subjectivity in the judgement of value.

9·2. But to present the Kantian root of Hegel's Judgement of the Notion as no more than Kant's modal categories would be to conceal the real debt which Hegel, I believe, owes to the father of German philosophy. For Hegel evidently reconstructed Kant's modal categories largely with the aid of Kant's *Critique of Judgement*. Hegel's notional Judgement is a *Denkbestimmung* of goodness without distinction of one form of goodness from another. In notional Judgement what is judged is the realizing of an 'ought' in general, the individuality which consists in conformity with the Notion. Yet Hegel's inclusion both in LL and EL of 'beautiful' among the possible predicates of notional judgements suggests strongly that he is here transforming and applying to the *thought* of goodness *überhaupt* Kant's non-logical judgement of aesthetic taste.

9·21. In the *Critique of Judgement* Kant tries to mediate the chasm left between Understanding and Reason in the first *Critique*. He treats Judgement as a third *a priori* faculty between them, and he lays a new emphasis on the distinction between judgement which is determinant and judgement which is reflective.[1] Determinant judgement subsumes the particular under a given universal concept, although it also supplies the *a priori* conditions of that subsumption, viz. the pure concepts, the categories. Judgement is merely reflective when a particular object alone is given and the universal has to be found for it.[2]

If these two types of judgement be developed into inference, clearly the distinction between them becomes that between deduction and induction. Clearly, too, the germ of reflective judgement lies in that analytic factor which Kant,

[1] See ch. vi, §§ 3·1 and 5·01 above; cf. also IH, ch. ix, § 4·11.

[2] Introd., § iv. Kant's reflective judgement is of course not Hegel's Judgement of Reflection, which in fact Hegel also calls Judgement of Subsumption. To Hegel all judgement is determinant in Kant's sense of the word.

as we saw, assigns to all judgement yielding knowledge of an object; in that analysis whereby concepts are elicited by reflective comparison of intuitions.[1]

The distinction of Understanding, Judgement, and Reason as the three *a priori* faculties of the mind appears already in the *Critique of Pure Reason*, but Kant there maintains—without, I think, more than perhaps a verbal inconsistency—that judgement is the distinctive function of the Understanding, and that it is cognitive and determinant. In the third *Critique* Kant still upholds the determinant cognitive judgement, but to merely reflective judgement he now assigns new roles in aesthetic and teleological fields. It is always an *a priori* faculty, but it operates here with principles which are merely regulative Ideas of some form of purpose, and not constitutive of the object. Both in determinant and in reflective judgement, imagination and Understanding co-operate. For our Understanding can only constitute an object by working through imagination, because its cognitive function depends on the given in sense. But in reflective judgement the function of imagination is far the more important of the two.

9·22. Kant's position is—inevitably, I think—far from clear. If all cognitive judgement is both analytic and synthetic, it is hard to see how the analytic and reflective factor in it can develop into an exercise of judgement which is expressly stated to be non-cognitive. And conversely, the minor role which is still assigned by Kant to Understanding is somewhat mysterious. Two main considerations seem to lead Kant into this ambiguity. (*a*) He perceives the very real difficulty that empirical concepts and particular laws can only be ascertained *a posteriori*: although the categories are particularized in particular laws, yet the latter cannot be deduced from the categories, and although empirical concepts must conform to space, time, and the categories, and apply only to objects which the categories constitute, yet their special natures cannot be derived from the *a priori* forms of sense-intuition and Understanding. (*b*) The categories, on Kant's view, supply the phenomenal world only with principles of mechanical determination *ab extra*. In that world

[1] See IH, ch. ix, § 4·32.

there is no freedom. Hence no purposiveness of any sort can be an empirical concept or a particular law, and it cannot be a category.[1] It must therefore be some sort of regulative Idea, analogous to the speculative Ideas of Reason but operating in the exercise of either the imagination or the will.

9·221. In the third *Critique* Kant is concerned only with aesthetic judgement and the teleological judgement of purpose in Nature. In both these types of judgement there is an essential reference to purpose, but there is no recognition of a purpose as actually willed. Kant's official view of the moral good, the good will, appears to be that it operates in determining desire through practical Ideas of Reason. Its rationality is not then a knowing of an object, and it is also different in kind from the regulative thinking which operates through the speculative Ideas of Reason: it is a sure and certain practical faith. Yet in the *Critique of Judgement*[2] Kant does state that 'judgements of the good . . . have logical . . . universality, for they are valid of the object as knowledge of it'. This looks exceedingly like the admission of a noumenal object of knowledge, but we are here primarily concerned only with Kant's aesthetic judgement.

9·23. According to Kant the judgement of beauty, being purely reflective and not determinant of any object, is also pure of any interest in the existence of an object. That is to say, in judging a thing beautiful I neither judge its existence as gratifying desire nor judge that it ought to exist. The judgement of beauty is, further, essentially a singular judgement: its form is 'this is beautiful'. The judgement that things of a certain sort are beautiful is not an aesthetic judgement at all, but a cognitive, or logical, judgement reached by comparison of singular aesthetic judgements; it is not any expression of the nature of beauty. For beauty is not a discursive concept which in co-operation with sensuous intuition constitutes a phenomenal object. When I exercise aesthetic judgement of taste I must be cognizing a phenomenal object, but to judge aesthetically I must abstract from this cognition. I do habitually express my aesthetic judgement by ascribing beauty to this object as its property; but

[1] See IH, ch. ix, § 4·11.

[2] p. 25.

in fact beauty is not a property of phenomenal objects, and I am mis-stating the real nature of my judgement.

The judgement of beauty, then, is not founded on a concept; it is singular and not objectively universal. On the other hand, it *is* subjectively universal. It does not express a private feeling of pleasure in something, an idiosyncrasy of taste such that my claim that I feel thus and thus carries with it no claim whatever that other men must or should feel so too. My singular judgement of beauty does carry with it a claim to the agreement of all men, no less than does a cognitive judgement. In judging this object beautiful I am not—though I may misconstrue what I do—ascribing any character to the object, but I *am* imputing universally to all men a certain delight which I enjoy. This delight is felt in the harmonious and free play of my faculties of Understanding and imagination as I exercise them in the judgement of aesthetic taste. These faculties operate together in all men in all judgement, cognitive as well as aesthetic, determinant as well as reflective, and that is why I can impute the delight I feel to all men. But my delight is felt in the exercise of these faculties not in my cognitive judgement of the object but in my aesthetic judgement of what I erroneously call *its* beauty. For the beautiful is not empirically real.

9·24. This difficult theory culminates in the doctrine that 'beauty is the form of the purposiveness of an object in so far as this is perceived in it without any presentation of a particular purpose'.[1] A purpose (*Zweck*) is, according to Kant, an ideally conceived end, a final cause wherethrough an object is brought into existence. It is thus the essential nature of the object produced, its *forma finalis*.[2] Beauty is not the nature of an object *qua* produced by a final cause; not the purposiveness (*Zweckmässigkeit*) of an object as a means to an end, nor its internal purposiveness as an end in itself, i.e. as completely in itself realizing purpose. For if it were either of these the judgement of beauty would be a cognitive judgement asserting an object to be practically useful or good, affirming it to be that in which a particular purpose of the

[1] See *Critique of Judgement*, p. 61.

[2] Ibid., p. 32; cf. also IH, ch. ii, § 5·2.

will is realized. Beauty is purposiveness, but it is subjective purposiveness. Speaking as the ordinary man speaks, we may say that in the judgement of beauty we refer a purposiveness in the object to will, but to no particular purpose of will. Kant's favourite examples of the beautiful are an arabesque without objective meaning and a piece of music which is not an accompaniment to words. In these we find a purely formal purposiveness which is not the expression of a particular purpose, but is what we commonly call the beauty of the arabesque or the music, speaking as if they were phenomenal objects. But in fact this purposiveness lies in a harmonious and free exercise of our Understanding and imagination. It is our own purposefulness, although we are not exercising our will any more than we are knowing; and when we judge aesthetically what we do is to delight in our free activity and impute this delight to all men.

9·25. It is hard to be sure of Kant's meaning. In calling aesthetic judgement subjective he does not intend, as some passages might seem to suggest, to deny that beauty is a content experienced as well as a delightful experiencing. Yet what the status of this content is remains doubtful. Kant seems to fear that if he makes it anything which the subject distinguishes from himself it will turn into either an empirical object or some other sort of reality of which it would be difficult to deny that we have knowledge. Hence he tends to fall back upon simply identifying beauty and subjective delight. The beautiful, as a content experienced, then hangs uneasily between the mind and its empirical object. It seems in the end to differ little in status from the famous imaginary hundred dollars with which Kant attacked the ontological argument.[1] It seems to be a mere floating idea.[2]

Yet it is important to consider how Kant did think of the beautiful as a content experienced. When he speaks of the play of the faculties in aesthetic judgement as free, he no doubt means that their purposeful activity is not bound down to the given as it is in their cognitive exercise. But when he also calls it harmonious, it is tempting to suggest this contrast: In cognitive judgement the thought of the Understanding, the discursive conceptual factor, does not perfectly

[1] See below, ch. xiv, § 4·1. [2] See § 9·1 above.

harmonize with the given intuition synthesized by the imagination: there is, as Bradley puts it, a 'what' outrunning a 'that'. But in aesthetic judgement they do coalesce, and the beautiful is therefore the truly individual. It is the universal fully particularized to single, not singular, individuality, although for Kant our awareness of it cannot be cognitive. What corresponds in aesthetic judgement to the conceptual element of cognitive judgement is an aesthetic Idea which is an intuition and, like the Ideas of speculative Reason, not constitutive.

'An aesthetic Idea cannot become a cognition, because it is an intuition (of the imagination) for which an adequate cognition can never be found. A rational Idea can never become a cognition, because it involves a concept (of the supersensible) corresponding to which an intuition can never be given.'[1]

9·26. Kant's judgement of beauty remains ambiguous. In admitting an intuition of the imagination which is not the passive intuition of sense co-operant with Understanding to yield knowledge, Kant advances from his position in the first *Critique*. But the gulf between Understanding and Reason is not adequately bridged. Between two levels of thought nothing but thought can mediate, and though in aesthetic judgement the Understanding is somehow in play,[2] Kant continues firmly to deny any intuitive moment to thought.

Yet two elements in Kant's theory of the aesthetic judgement have been, I think, the main inspiration of Hegel's Judgement of the Notion. Kant had perceived (*a*) that what we judge beautiful is individual in the sense of self-complete, and (*b*) that the judgement of beauty is subjective in the sense that it is not cognition of a detached object through subsumption of an intuition under a discursive concept. But he had interpreted this subjectivity as the free enjoyment of a content which, because it is not an object of knowledge, tends to float ambiguously. Hegel accords a moment of intuition to thought, and thereby synthesizes these two elements which Kant cannot reconcile. That the content experienced in aesthetic judgement is truly individual means

[1] *Critique of Judgement*, p. 240.

[2] Does Kant mean that the transcendental unity of apperception is operative in it, but not the categories?

to Hegel that in it the subject recognizes itself: the free play of the subject's activity and the 'mere play' of the developing movement of the Notion as content[1] are one and the same. Beauty is the Idea, the synthesis of Subjective and Objective Notion, in sensuous embodiment; but when within the aesthetic judgement abstraction is made from sensuous embodiment, there remains a *Denkbestimmung* which is the *thought* in *any* value-judgement, viz. the Judgement of the Notion, of the Universal self-particularized as Individual. This Judgement is subjective, but not as expressing a scarcely intelligible purposive-purposeless play of faculties. It is subjective because Judgement belongs to Subjective Notion; and although the Notion is the *return* of subjectivity, which was latent in Essence,[2] yet in Subjective Notion thought has not yet developed its own proper object. Even in Judgement of the Notion—the value-judgement in which this subjectivity culminates and foreshadows Objective Notion[3]—Judgement remains still 'a reflection external to the object':[4] the notional Judgement concerns the conformity of an object to *its* notion.

The difference between Hegel and Kant, here as everywhere, is this. Hegel affirms that thought is itself intuitive, and that all thinking, so far as it really is thinking, is knowing. Kant, regarding as quite problematic the unity of sense and thought as sources of knowledge, is driven towards treating mind as singular minds capable on occasion of exercising their cognitive faculties so far *in vacuo* and out of contact with the objectively real that this exercise ceases to be cognitive—almost, one might say, as mills may turn whether they have corn to grind or no, or as a ship's propeller races when heavy seas lift her stern clear of the water. Kant is then forced to look for the significance of this isolated subjective exercise in the mind's internal workings, in the harmonious revolution of its machinery. Yet Kant's real position is not so crude as this, because it is ambiguous; and this ambiguity is a hugely pregnant re-formulation of the problem. I doubt whether without Kant's brilliant flash of insight into the nature of aesthetic experience Hegel could

[1] See ch. xi, § 1·1 above.
[2] Cf. ch. x, §§ 1–1·2 above.
[3] See ch. xi, § 2·3 above.
[4] Ibid., § 3.

have reached his conception of the Notion as concrete Universal.

10. The treatment of modality in the logic of Bradley and Bosanquet is not easy to follow. They both appear to waver between accepting the Kantian view that modality does not touch content, and regarding the problematic and apodeictic forms as varieties respectively of hypothetical and disjunctive judgement. It is significant of some confusion, I think, that in their respective Logics Bradley treats of probability and chance under the head of modality, while Bosanquet deals with them in his chapter on disjunction. Although their doctrine of the affiliation of judgement-forms is so largely borrowed from Hegel, yet neither Bradley nor Bosanquet was prepared to countenance the overt treatment in logic of judgement as a category. Hence, when they discuss possibility or necessity, one is never sure whether they are treating it as Hegel treats it in Essence, or as he treats it in the Notion. Neither makes any reference to the connexion which Hegel sees between modality and intrinsic value. Bradley conceives that logic must move on a level near to common sense,[1] but he seems to forget that the man in the street quite commonly makes judgements of value.

11. We have seen that notional Judgement is the Judgement of intrinsic value *überhaupt*. There remain two points which may perhaps cause the reader difficulty.

(1) Among predicates of notional judgements Hegel includes *richtig* (correct) and *passend* (convenient or suitable).[2] These, or at any rate the latter, may suggest to some readers a value which is not intrinsic but characterizes something only good as a means. But, as we shall see when we examine Hegel's doctrine of teleology,[3] it is not his view that anything can be good merely as a means and possess no goodness in itself. A good instrument still conforms to its *own* notion in subserving well the ultimate purpose of its user.

(2) The difference between one value and another is irrelevant to Judgement of the Notion, but Hegel does not treat it as wholly irrelevant to logic. In Chapter XVII we

[1] See IH, ch. xiii, § 5·3. For Bosanquet's view of intrinsic value see ibid., § 8.

[2] See LL, ii, p. 113.

[3] See ch. xv below.

shall see that the difference between (*a*) the theoretical truth of the Understanding and (*b*) the good will is reflected in the categories of the Idea. On the other hand, the values experienced in aesthetic and religious experience are only differentiations of Concrete Spirit. They appear in the Philosophy of Spirit, but they contribute no special categories to the Logic. It may well be questioned whether this is consistent with the view that philosophy is *par excellence* logic.[1] But adequate discussion of this difficulty would require a detailed account of the final triad of Concrete Spirit, and that does not fall within the scope of this book.

[1] See also ch. xviii, § 2·11 below.

XIII
SYLLOGISM

1. THE categories of Essence have defined spirit as an actual (*wirklich*) world devoid of value. The categories of Judgement, openly sublating the categories of Essence, have exhibited the gradual return of a still formal subjectivity. In Disjunctive Judgement the Universal was fully particularized, and the resultant Individual was developed through the phases of the notional Judgement, the *Denkbestimmung* which animates all our judgements of value.

We have seen that in a judgement of value our thought is no longer discursive: the predicate is no longer a 'what' outrunning a 'that' but coincides with the subject. To Kant, so far as he retains the position he reaches in his first *Critique*, this signifies that no judgement of value is cognitive.[1] To Hegel it signifies that intuition and discursion at length, so far as the form of Judgement permits, coincide.

But Judgement at once shows itself inadequate as a category of value. For value in general, the conformity of a thing to its notion, is not really a predicable character: value does not belong to but *is* the concrete individual. Value is the rationality of the concrete individual. In notional Judgement the actual is judged to be rational, but with that judgement we pass to a fresh form of Subjective Notion. 'In Apodeictic Judgement', says Hegel, 'we have an individual which through its qualities (*Beschaffenheit*) relates itself to its universal, i.e. its notion.'[2] But value, though we call it good*ness*, is not strictly a *Beschaffenheit*. We may call it, perhaps, a 'toti-resultant' character, but, as Kant rightly insisted in the case of beauty, we are mistaken if we suppose it predicable as a discursive concept is predicable in judgement. For logical subject and predicate have coincided, and in Apodeictic Judgement the subjective form of Understanding is, in Hegel's view, sublated in the subjective form of Reason: we pass from Judgement to Syllogism.

1·1. Value in general, then, is conformity to notion, and

[1] See, however, ch. xii, § 9·221 above.

[2] EL, § 181, *Zusatz*.

that is rationality. We have now to see how it is that rationality, within Subjective Notion, is Syllogism.

Hegel's general position is expressed in LL, ii, pp. 118–20. The traditional logic had held syllogizing to be the activity of Reason. Previous thinkers, who had accepted this traditional logic, had also maintained Reason to be the source of certain laws and eternal truths; certain absolute thoughts such as God, freedom, right, duty, the infinite, the unconditioned, the supra-sensuous. They had, however, through a perverse severance of form and content totally failed to reconcile these two aspects of Reason. They had remained at the level of Understanding, and treated the forms of Reason as a game, thereby reducing these absolute thoughts to negative abstractions. But in fact these thoughts of Reason, to which they paid mere lip-service, are concrete unities of their own determinate notional distinctions. That alone is why they are rational; and Syllogism is their form.

In other words, these thinkers[1] had not seen that the rational is that and only that which conforms to its notion, and that syllogism as a form of thought expresses precisely this. It is this severance of two aspects of Reason which Hegel supposes himself to heal by maintaining that when Judgement is sublated, (*a*) spirit defines itself as Syllogism, as Notion explicitly Individual through self-particularization: 'Alles ist ein Schluss'; and (*b*) conversely, any actual (*das Wirkliches*) is Syllogism: it conforms to its notion as 'an individual which through particularity rises into universality and makes itself identical with itself'.[2] This dual statement is inevitable because Syllogism still belongs to Subjective Notion; because the Notion has not yet developed its own proper object.

1·2. But even this subjective rationality of Syllogism is at first only implicit. Not only does the logician, when he illustrates Judgement, abstract a fragment from a continuous context of judging, but this continuous judging is itself a moment of inferential thought. We no more judge without by implication inferring than we 'entertain' concepts without judging; at whatever level we make a judgement, an inference at the same level is implied, and the higher the level the

[1] Hegel is clearly thinking chiefly of Kant.

[2] EL, § 181.

less merely implicit is the inference. Hence although it is only when notional judgement becomes apodeictic that Judgement, incapable of further development as Judgement, passes dialectically into Syllogism, yet the synthesis of Notion as such with Judgement develops gradually. The categories of Judgement are openly but gradually 'reviewed' in Syllogism, as were the categories of Essence in Judgement. The parallelism is closer, because Judgement is already Notion.

Yet, once again, this parallelism is not a matter of one-one correspondence. The main phases of Syllogism are (1) Syllogism of Quality, which treats the forms of Reason in that mere external immediacy beyond which formal logic does not rise, and may therefore be called the formal Syllogism of the Understanding; (2) Syllogism of Reflection; (3) Syllogism of Necessity.

At first sight this nomenclature, repeated from Judgement, is puzzling: the main phases of Judgement were, formally, four, whereas those of Syllogism are three, and there is no modal Syllogism to correspond with Judgement of the Notion. But the puzzle vanishes if we do not look for one-one correspondence, but remember that in the rationality of Syllogism the 'broken-backedness' of the Understanding is mediated and transcended.[1] If we do insist on pressing the correspondence we must say, I think, that Syllogism of Necessity 'corresponds to' notional Judgement as well as to Judgement of Necessity.

2. We shall get a clearer preliminary view of the Hegelian Syllogism if we compare it both with the the syllogism of formal logic and with Aristotle's conception of syllogism, from which formal syllogistic developed—or degenerated.

Hegel accepts from the Aristotelian tradition the three figures of syllogism and the principle of their differentiation according to the position of the middle term. Every main phase of the Hegelian Syllogism subdivides in accordance with them, although, as we shall see,[2] their original order is not preserved in this subdivision. Hegel rejects, however, not only the un-Aristotelian fourth figure but also the elaboration of valid moods, which began in Aristotle's *Prior*

[1] See ch. xii, § 5·4 above.

[2] See following section.

Analytics and culminated in Leibniz's application to syllogism of his calculus of combinations. All these distinctions are, on Hegel's view, totally irrelevant to the Notion. Of this calculus Hegel remarks that it

'connects with a pet idea of Leibniz, conceived in his youth and never surrendered despite its immaturity and shallowness, the idea of a "general characteristic" of notions, a vocabulary of symbols representing each notion as a relation derived from others or related to others; as though in rational connexion, which is essentially dialectical, a content retained those relations which it has if it is fixed by itself.'[1]

Hegel's point is that the application of any such calculus produces purely contingent quantitative differences which have nothing to do with the Notion—are not even further logical differentiations of the logical moments of Quantity.[2] Hegel further quotes the claim of Ploucquet,[3] the inventor of an equational calculus, that from his discovery it follows 'posse etiam rudes mechanice totam logicam doceri, uti pueri arithmeticam docentur, ita quidem, ut nulla formidine in ratiociniis suis errandi torqueri, vel fallaciis circumveniri possint, si in calculo non errant'. 'This recommendation', observes Hegel, 'is about the worst thing that could be said of an invention concerned with the presentation of the science of logic.'

2·1. Nevertheless between Aristotle's and Hegel's use of the three figures there is a great difference. Aristotle regards his first figure of syllogism as the proper figure of scientific demonstration. He conceives it as reflecting the inherence of a universal property, an essential accident, in a substantial *infima species*, which is, in Hegel's sense of the term, individual. This inherence has its cause in one among the substantial, definitory elements which go together to constitute the *infima species*,[4] and it is this cause which the middle term of scientific syllogism reflects.[5] This middle term is, in Hegel's sense, particular; it is a specification of the genus which truly grounds the conclusion, i.e. mediates the inherence of the property in the species. Thus the formula for

[1] LL, ii, pp. 146–7.
[2] Cf. ch. iii, § 4·1 above.
[3] Died 1790.
[4] See IH, ch. iv, § 3·1.
[5] In the primary, or basic, syllogism of a special science the middle term would reflect the differentia.

this figure is *I-P-U*; for example, 'Man (Individual), *qua* animal-specified-as-rational (Particular), is capable of laughter (Universal).' The middle term is here predicate in the minor premiss, subject in the major.

In the other two figures, on Aristotle's view, this natural order of terms exhibited by the first figure—natural because it reflects the real inherence of dependent, accidental property in substance—is distorted; i.e. in these figures the particular no longer occupies its proper central position as mediator. In the Aristotelian second figure the middle term is universal, and is predicate in both premisses. In Aristotle's third figure the middle is, in Hegel's sense, individual, and is subject in both premisses. Thus in Hegelian terminology the formulae for the three Aristotelian figures are *I-P-U*, *P-U-I*, and *U-I-P*.[1] Aristotle holds that the second and third figures are consequently imperfect, and that arguments couched in these forms require conversion to the normal, i.e. ideal, first figure.

2·2. The development of the Hegelian Syllogism is marked by each moment of the Notion in turn expressing the totality of the Notion, i.e. by each moment of the notion in turn occupying the position of middle term unifying the extreme terms. In the first phase of Syllogism the middle term will be the Notion as Particular; for, as we have already seen,[2] when Apodeictic Judgement passes over into Syllogism the copula becomes the middle term as Particular. Thus the formal expression of Hegel's first figure is *I-P-U*. He then takes *U-I-P* for his second figure, and *P-U-I* for his third. Thus Hegel has not, as we might perhaps have been tempted to expect, simply reversed the Aristotelian

[1] I set out these formulae on the assumption that in enunciating syllogism the minor premiss is to be put first; i.e. they represent the form '*A qua B* is *C*' rather than the form '*C* through *B* inheres in *A*'. I shall usually follow this procedure, as Hegel appears to do consistently in EL, although in LL he adopts the other order in treating his second and third figures. The point is of small importance. It is the nature of the middle term which matters. Its varying appearances as subject or predicate of the premiss are a mere corollary dependent on the grammatical form adopted. Neither to Hegel nor to Aristotle did this constitute the true *fundamentum divisionis* of the figures. That is why neither of them recognized the Galenian fourth figure.

[2] Ch. xii, § 8·61 above.

order (*I-P-U*, *P-U-I*, *U-I-P*) on the ground that in a dialectical order the perfect figure must come last. He has taken the formula of Aristotle's first and perfect figure for his own first figure, that of Aristotle's third figure for his own second figure, and that of Aristotle's second figure for his own third.

This radical reconstruction is grounded upon a fundamental difference between the metaphysical positions of Hegel and Aristotle.[1] To Aristotle *infima species* is real, self-subsistent substance; genus, considered in abstraction from its specification, is unactualized matter;[2] essential accident is real but dependent (inherent) entity. Hence Aristotle's ideal figure will show the *infima species* universally and commensurately united through the differentia, which grounds the conclusion, *not* with its genus but with its essential accident: the formula is *I-P-U*, but *U* is not genus but property. On the other hand, Hegel's ideal logical genus is not the Aristotelian genus, the nature of which entails a distinction between substance and accident belonging, on Hegel's view, only to natural genera. Hegel's own logical genus is fully commensurate with, exhaustively particularized and so individual in, its species.[3] Hence in Hegel's culminating figure Universal as a true system will unite within itself its particular and individual moments.[4] Its formula will, therefore, be that of Aristotle's second figure, viz. *P-U-I*, and *U* will signify not property but genus. Aristotle's first figure, meanwhile, will have supplied the formula *I-P-U* for Hegel's first figure, because Hegel regards the first phase of Syllogism as necessarily the attempt to mediate the Qualitative Judgement. The formula for Qualitative Judgement was 'Individual is Universal', and Syllogism begins as the effort to complete it in the form 'Individual *qua* Particular is Universal'.

2·21. There is here a further point of contrast between Hegel and Aristotle. Hegel's Qualitative Syllogism is a sublation of the formal syllogism of Understanding. It can, analogously to Qualitative Judgement, only be illustrated by the simple syllogistic inference of everyday experience, which subsumes a singular through a special under a general

[1] Cf. ch. xii, § 7·22 above.
[2] Cf. IH, ch. iv, § 1·2.
[3] Cf. ch. xii, §§ 7·21 and 7·22 above.
[4] Although not explicitly until we reach Disjunctive Syllogism.

quality: for example, when we wake in winter and hear the creaking of carriages in the street, and conclude that it is freezing.[1] But to Aristotle that operation would be 'induction',[2] not syllogism.

2·22. It should perhaps be said that while Hegel justly acquits Aristotle of attempting to apply the figures and moods of formal, subjective syllogism in his philosophical speculation,[3] yet it may be doubted whether Hegel fully recognized the intimate connexion between syllogism and its discoverer's metaphysical theory. Hegel was clearly more familiar with the *Prior* than with the *Posterior Analytics*.

3. Qualitative Syllogism

In Judgement the terms were sundered totalities of the Notion, at first linked barely by the copula. In the triplicity of Syllogism this distinctness remains, but in Syllogism the middle term has replaced the copula, and Syllogism in every phase is the explicit totality of the Notion. The conclusion of Syllogism is the explicit development of premisses which, taken by themselves in abstraction, are only Judgement; it is not a third Judgement. Nevertheless, in Qualitative Syllogism, which begins by sublating the formal syllogizing of the Understanding, these totalities of the Notion are in immediate external relation.

3·1. First Figure: I-P-U

Here the Qualitative Judgement seeks completion: e.g.

This rose is red (*I-P*);
Red is a colour (*P-U*);
∴ This rose, *qua* red, is coloured (*I-P-U*).

But the terms of this syllogism are related contingently. It may be a correct statement, but its form and content do not agree. For 'red' is any casually selected quality of the subject, and is only stated to be *de facto* a species of colour. Another selected property would have served to link the subject with another major term. The middle does not lock

[1] See EL, § 183, *Zusatz*.

[2] ἐπαγωγή; see Aristotle, *Posterior Analytics* 71ᵃ17 ff. and footnote in the Oxford Translation.

[3] Cf. EL, § 187.

the extremes together in a secure necessary connexion. And the fault lies in the form, not in the inadequacy of the content. To demonstrate the conclusion cogently prosyllogisms are required in order to justify each premiss; i.e. new middles must be inserted between the terms of each premiss until it be fully mediated. But such prosyllogisms, still taking the form *I-P-U*, would regress *ad indefinitum*. It is this, we may remark, which compelled Aristotle, who was unwilling to recognize that all reasoning within a special sphere is finite and for ever hypothetical, to postulate an immediate, infallible intuition of specific substantial natures and other first principles within each genus, an intuition apparently not subject to modification by metaphysical criticism.[1]

It follows that Qualitative Syllogism, which begins in the first figure, must mediate itself through a change of form. The truth which emerges from it is that Universal and Particular are mediated, though only through their coexistence in the mere qualitative Individual which the conclusion has stated to be Universal. This truth appears in

3·2. Second Figure: U-I-P

E.g. This rose is coloured (*U-I*);
This rose is red (*I-P*);
∴ Colour, *qua* qualifying this rose, is red (*U-I-P*).

The order in which we take the extremes is a matter of indifference, and this conclusion is more naturally put as 'Red, *qua* qualifying this rose, is a colour' (*P-U-I*).

Thus notional development has begun. For the minor premiss of this second Syllogism, *U-I*, is in a form which the first figure has already mediated, although the major premiss, *I-P*, is still immediate. Hegel observes that the second Syllogism thus presupposes the first, and that conversely the first presupposes the second.[2] He means that the first Syllogism presupposes the second because the form of the major premiss in the first Syllogism (*P-U*) implies mediation in the second figure.

In this second-figure Syllogism, even if the conclusion of the illustrative example, viz. 'colour is red', happens to be

[1] See IH, ch. iv, § 4·5. [2] See LL, ii, p. 133.

correct as a fact, this is not so because it is the conclusion of this syllogism. This contingency in the union of the genus with only one of its species (i.e. the contingency of their union by coexistence in mere qualitative individuality) is what the second figure makes explicit,[1] whereas in the first figure this was only implicit. The extreme terms, then, have failed to reach mediation, and remain at present in the immediate externality to one another of qualitative individuality.[2]

But in this relation of immediate mutual externality the extremes by their very failure to reach mediation are each intro-reflected, just as in Negative Judgement Individual and Universal were intro-reflected.[3] Thus the middle term, since it is intro-reflected individuality, is just as much the mere abstract qualitative Universal. As it were, mere contact at a single point is no really determining union, but mere coexistence. There is nothing to choose between such contingent contact and mutual independence, just as there is nothing to choose between bare identity and bare difference.

With the emergence of the truth that the middle term is abstract Universal Syllogism enters

3·3. Third Figure: P-U-I

E.g. This rose is coloured (*U-I*);
Red is a colour (*P-U*);
∴ This rose, *qua* coloured, is red (*P-U-I*).

Here the minor premiss, *U-I*, has been mediated by the first Syllogism, and the major, *P-U*, by the second. Thus this third Syllogism presupposes the other two, and conversely. In fact it now becomes obvious that the three Syllogisms reciprocally presuppose each other. Hegel's account in LL, ii, p. 137 is clear:

'What this reciprocal mediation contains is this, that each Syllogism for itself is mediation, but not in itself the totality of mediation: it has in it an immediacy whose mediation lies outside it.

[1] That is why in the Aristotelian third figure conclusions can only be particular.

[2] The reader must remember that the mutual relation of the extremes *is* the middle term, just as in Judgement the relation of notional moments *was* the copula. This follows from the very nature of the Notion.

[3] See ch. xii, § 5·21 above.

'The Syllogism *I-U-P* [in EL *P-U-I*], considered in itself, is the truth of formal syllogism. It expresses the truth that the mediation of formal syllogism is the abstractly Universal, and that the extremes in respect of their essential determinateness are contained not in the middle but only according to their universality. Therefore precisely that which is here supposed to be mediated is *not* bound together in the middle. Thus that in which the formalism of syllogism consists is here posited: the terms of this Syllogism have a content immediate and indifferent to form, or (which is the same thing) they are Form-determinations which have not reflected themselves so as to become Content-determinations.'

Thus the movement of Syllogism so far has been a dialectical advance, because the Universal has now become middle term linking its extremes as the genus systematically binds together its own individual and specific nature. Syllogism, synthesizing Notion as such with Judgement, has reproduced the movement of Notion as such from Individual through Particular to Universal. Yet with its purely qualitative content this Universal is no true system, but the mere coexistence of individuality with specification,[1] and in this aspect the dialectic has gradually exposed the mere formalism of the syllogism of the Understanding. Moreover, since the middle term is now the utterly abstract Individual, there can at this point be no notional distinction at all between the three terms. The question which term is to be taken as middle can only depend on which two of the terms are taken as immediately given, i.e. on a purely contingent external relation. Correspondingly all relation of content to form is now extinct. Quality lapses—there is neither inherence nor subsumption—and sheer Quantity remains. Hence arises the Mathematical, or Quantitative, Syllogism,

3·4. 'Fourth Figure': U-U-U

This is expressed in the formula: if two things are equal to a third thing they are equal to one another.

This 'fourth figure' is at first sight a little puzzling. Hegel is not introducing a fourth figure of notional Syllogism. Quantitative Syllogism is in effect no more than the negative form of third-figure Qualitative Syllogism. One

[1] That is why conclusions in the Aristotelian second figure can only be negative.

may take it, I think, that third-figure Syllogism of Quality and Quantitative Syllogism together constitute the synthesis of Qualitative Syllogism, and so correspond to the duality of identical and infinite Judgement which together formed the synthesis of Qualitative Judgement. But Hegel observes that such quantitative syllogizing 'is in no way a notional process: even, we must say, the Understanding has not so much as the formal and abstract determinations of the Notion before it'.[1]

Hegel here clearly has in mind equational logic,[2] which he regards as wholly nugatory, as making no contribution to the important natural history of thought-forms in which he takes the Aristotelian formal logic to consist. Hegel's 'fourth figure' would thus seem to be a criticism of equational logic from the point of view of the Notion, but a criticism which can contain no reconstruction; which cannot sublate because there is nothing to preserve. One must confess that this leaves it obscure why in that case Hegel allows it to appear in the dialectical movement; and what mere notionless calculation which a machine can perform really consists in. It is often difficult in Hegel—and in any philosophy of the Hegelian type—to be sure whether a hostile view is being criticized as totally false, or as erroneous because it claims to be completely true. Strictly speaking, criticism in a purely destructive form is inadmissible on Hegel's principles, but it is difficult for any philosopher to avoid sometimes giving the impression of sheer polemic.

4. Syllogism of Reflection

Whatever be the precise significance of Quantitative Syllogism, the Syllogism of Quality has this result. The reciprocal intermediation of its three phases signifies that Syllogism is now intro-reflected. For though each phase by itself fails in self-mediation and depends for mediation upon the others, yet as synthesized in the third phase they constitute an intro-reflected, self-mediating totality. The middle term is now the posited unity of the extremes; i.e. it is again Particular.

In this particular middle term Individual and Universal

[1] LL, ii, p. 140. [2] See § 2 above.

are united as each intro-reflected, as they were in Singular Judgement. Hence in any illustrative example the middle term cannot be merely qualitative: essential nature begins to emerge. On the other hand, the middle term unites Individual and Universal not in full notional identity but as still quite imperfectly mediated. The middle can be illustrated only as a totality of singular individuals: the inadequately mediated union of *I* and *U* is the thought of a class. Therefore the first phase of Syllogism of Reflection is

4·1. Syllogism of Allness: I-P-U

E.g. Gaius is a man (*I-P*);
All men are mortal (*P-U*);
∴ Gaius *qua* man is mortal (*I-P-U*).

Here, in a middle term which is not a quality but a totality of singulars, the Syllogism of the Understanding is completed.

But as it stands this Syllogism is an obvious *petitio principii*: the conclusion is presupposed already in the major premiss. The major premiss thus presupposes mediation, and that means that this Syllogism rests upon induction. The mediating Syllogism into which we pass is therefore

4·2. Syllogism of Induction (U-I I I, &c.-P)

The Syllogism of Induction falls into the second figure because the inference turns upon what precisely the individuals are; turns upon, as Hegel puts it, 'individuality posited as complete'. For example (putting the major premiss first),

Gold is a metal; silver, copper, &c., are metals (*I I I, &c.-P*);
Gold, silver, copper, &c., all conduct electricity (*U-I I I, &c.*);
∴ All metals, *qua* the totality of these species, conduct electricity (*U-I I I, &c.-P*).

But the conclusion clearly stands or falls with the completeness of the enumeration, and therefore entails indefinite regress. The middle term is an aggregate limited by experience up to date and by nothing else. If it is really universal it presupposes the truth of the conclusion, and the question is begged. If it is not, a fresh individual may upset the conclusion. Yet induction, though its conclusion be problematic, does at least both presume and suggest necessary and universal connexion. If it did not, there would be no such thing as empirical thinking. As synthesis of mere allness with singular individuality a more nearly concrete universality emerges, and we pass to

4·3. Syllogism of Analogy: P-U-I

Here the middle term is universal, but universal as the essential nature of a concrete individual. For example, the inference that the moon, because it shares with the earth the generic character of being a celestial body, is inhabited can be put in syllogistic form thus:

The moon is an earth (*U-I*);
The earth is inhabited (*P-U*);
∴ The moon, *qua* an earth, is inhabited (*P-U-I*).

The conclusion in this example is probably incorrect as fact, and the formulation is clumsy, but analogy is a genuine form of Syllogism, not *quaternio terminorum*. Analogy is 'the instinct of Reason', already implicit in induction, and it plays a vital part in empirical science. The difficulty of illustrating its genuinely syllogistic form is this: the nerve of analogical inference is a presumed necessity, which is more than the universality of the individuals aggregated by induction but less than strict necessity; i.e. the middle term falls just short of being true genus; it is, as Hegel puts it, only a moment of the genus. Yet analogical reasoning and, less explicitly, induction do operate by virtue of an inkling of necessary connexion; for this inkling is no more merely subjective in the sense of arbitrary than is the thought of Real Possibility separable from the thought of Real Actuality. In fact Real Possibility and Real Actuality is the category openly sublated in Syllogism of Analogy through Universal Judgement.[1] But the middle term, being thus something between

[1] See ch. viii, §§ 7–7·5 above. The middle term in all three Syllogisms of Reflection openly discloses the coupled moments which characterize any category of Essence.

I I I, &c., and true genus, is hard to illustrate effectively, because nothing we take as middle will convey naturally the special sense in which it is to be taken. Hegel puts the whole matter clearly:

'Analogy is still a Syllogism of Reflection inasmuch as Individuality and Universality are *immediately* [i.e. lacking mediation] united in its middle term. This immediacy accounts for the continued presence of that externality which belongs to the unity of Reflection: the Individual is only genus implicitly (*an sich*), not posited in that negativity which would make its determinateness the proper determinateness of the genus. Hence the predicate of the individual which constitutes the middle is not *ipso facto* also (*auch schon*) predicate of the other individual, although both belong to the same genus.'[1]

Thus because of this imperfectly mediated middle term Syllogism of Analogy still presupposes its own conclusion. But again, as in Qualitative Syllogism, the circle of reciprocally presupposed and presupposing mediations must constitute a synthesis. This synthesis, since it is a synthesis of intro-reflected mediations, transcends Reflection and shows itself to be Necessity. Or the transition may be expressed by saying that the middle becomes explicitly the objective universality of genus, synthesizing the allness of the first reflective Syllogism with the individuals of induction. The middle *is* thus the explicit totality of the three moments of the Notion. Inference is now truly grounded, and we pass to

5. Syllogism of Necessity

In the Syllogisms of Quality and Reflection inference passed through all three figures. But in Qualitative Syllogism the first figure was never really transcended. For the middle, whether exemplified as 'red', 'this rose', or 'colour', was always an unmediated compromise between Individual and Universal; it was never really more than the initial Particular. Analogously in Syllogism of Reflection the middle always really remained in the second figure. Whether as 'all men', or as an indefinite plurality of metals, or as 'the earth', it never really advanced beyond mere intro-reflected individuality. The Syllogism of Necessity, too, will pass through all three figures, but its middle will always really be,

[1] LL, ii, p. 158.

as in the third figure, universal. Its three phases are Categorical, Hypothetical, and Disjunctive Syllogism.

5·1. Categorical Syllogism: I-P-U

E.g. Gold is a metal (*I-P*);
Metals are elements (*P-U*);
∴ Gold *qua* a metal is an element (*I-P-U*).

Here the premisses are categorical judgements which neither demand mediation *ab extra* nor beg the conclusion. The middle is generic. It unites in itself as a totality the three moments of the Notion; they are what, in reference to the lower category here conspicuously sublated, may be called its substantial content. The major term, the universal, is not a mere quality. It conspicuously sublates the moment of Accident in which Substance is differentiated. It is also, analogously, the specific differentiation comprehended simply: in the example given it is metal-determined-as-an-element which functions as middle. The minor term is, correspondingly, concrete unity of genus with this determinateness.

But metal determined as an element is not fully determined, for element is 'wider'. The middle term, though generic, is only subgenus. The major term is abstract universal, and the minor term is only immediate unity of the subgenus with this still abstract determinateness. The middle term alone is explicit totality of the notional moments. Hence the middle term turns out to be individual, but an individuality which mediates its extremes only as an inner necessity.

With this we pass to the form which asserts only this inner, and therefore so far contingent and subjective, necessity:

5·2. Hypothetical Syllogism: U-I-P

Hegel in EL says almost nothing of this form. The account in LL is not always easy to follow. The doctrine is, I think, as follows.

Hypothetical Syllogism may be exemplified thus:

Gold is a metal (*I-P*);
If anything is a metal it is an element (*U-I*);
∴ Gold *qua* metal is an element (*U-I-P*).

The major premiss differs from the major of Categorical Syllogism in that it is an hypothetical and not a categorical judgement; i.e. the connexion of metal with element is here explicitly necessary connexion with an abstract universal, but it is explicitly not actual fact. That is why the middle is Individual: it openly fails to be Particular commensurate with Universal, and is accordingly connected with it by *mere* necessity. On the other hand, the minor premiss is a categorical judgement which does assert actual fact. Hence the conclusion, the syllogism as a whole, asserts the nexus of *U* through *I* with *P* (of element through metal with gold) to be at once and (in a notional sense) contradictorily both necessary and an actual fact.

The sublated category of Essence is primarily Cause and Effect; but it is also Ground and Consequent, or, again, Real Possibility and Real Actuality. But 'Condition', which covers generally categories of this type, serves well to express the situation in the conclusion of Hypothetical Syllogism. For (*a*) a condition is an indifferent existence (sc. in that it does not at once imply the actual existence of what it conditions as Cause does imply Effect), and (*b*) the relation of condition and conditioned is reciprocal. The major premiss is thus the condition, and the minor is what it conditions.

Hegel in LL formulates the Hypothetical Syllogism thus:

If *A* is, then *B* is;
Now *A* is;
∴ *B* is.

If we remember that necessity is never sheerly subjective but always, coupled with fact, a mode of essential being, this is not hard to follow. We may translate it in terms of our example as follows:

Metal-element being a necessary nexus, gold-element is also a necessary nexus;
Now gold is in actual fact metal;
∴ Gold is an element.

Here the 'is' which links gold and element expresses an actual fact and a necessity which are not in notional contradiction: until mediation is reached the fact is contingent and the necessity in suspension. But in the final categories of Essence the Correlation of moments already begins to express not mere issue of the first moment into the second, but the active return upon itself of the first moment in and through the second. So here this notional contradiction develops obviously to

5·3. Disjunctive Syllogism: I-U-P

Here the middle is the absolutely concrete genus, containing Individual and Particular completely determined, and no longer the mere internally necessary connexion of the extremes in substantial content. The subjective and formal factor in Syllogism all through has been the abstractness of the middle term, which remained still distinct from the extremes although it was their unity. But the middle is now as much mediated as mediating, and this subjectivity therefore disappears.

Disjunctive Syllogism, so far as it can be illustrated at all, requires two syllogisms. The middle term will be a genus distributed into all its species. Thus:

(1) A species of triangle is either equilateral, scalene, or isosceles;

But this species of triangle is equilateral;

∴ This species of triangle is neither scalene nor isosceles;

(2) A species of triangle is either equilateral, scalene, or isosceles;

But this species of triangle is neither scalene nor isosceles;

∴ This species of triangle is equilateral.

But since the middle is the explicit totality of the three notional moments, and as much mediated as mediating, therefore the same must be true of each of the extremes. In the examples given we cannot properly label the terms *I*, *P*, and *U*.[1] In fact we no longer have Syllogism. With the

[1] Hegel (see LL, ii, p. 168) gives no concrete examples but only the formulae:

(1) *A* is either *B* or *C* or *D*;
But *A* is *B*;
∴ *A* is neither *C* nor *D*.
(2) *A* is either *B* or *C* or *D*;
But *A* is neither *C* nor *D*;
∴ *A* is *B*.

disappearance of formal subjectivity inference is transcended. If there be thought without any defect of subjectivity it cannot be a discursive movement from premisses to conclusion.

5·31. If it here occurs to us to give such a thought the name of 'intuition' we must not think of intuition as the grasp of a self-evident premiss from which a conclusion is drawn.[1] Rather we must remember Kant's suggestion that an intuitive Understanding would create its own object. But before we discuss the transition to Objectivity, which now takes place, it may be well to sum up briefly Hegel's doctrine of Syllogism.

6. The index to the nature of Syllogism is the middle term, which takes the place of, or rather sublates, the copula of Judgement. The middle term purports to be, and eventually makes good its claim to be, the concrete totality of the extremes, i.e. the whole Syllogism. The movement of the three figures represents each moment of the Notion in turn as middle term. But at the same time the middle term is the Notion as an 'ought to be'; an unfulfilled ideal analogous to the copula of Judgement; a demand that itself, the mediating term, shall be the totality of the Notion. The three main types of Syllogism, whose subdivisions again reflect the three figures, are the three stages in this concrescence of the middle term. In Qualitative Syllogism the middle is totality of the Notion only in so far as each separate moment plays in turn the part of middle term. Their successive failure to fill the role leads to the Syllogism of Reflection. Here the middle does comprehend the extremes, but only externally; for, as in the Judgement of Reflection, the terms are all construed in extension, and the comprehension is mere class inclusion with just the hint of necessary connexion to come. In the Syllogism of Necessity this hint becomes explicit. The middle term is there the *unity* of the three notional moments, a unity which becomes fully developed and concrete in the Disjunctive Syllogism. Hence in Disjunctive Syllogism the *distinctness* of the middle term, which is the differentia of Syllogism, vanishes. Mediation becomes again immediacy, and Syllogism is transcended.[2]

[1] See IH, ch. iv, §§ 3–3·11.

[2] On the question why there is no form of Syllogism to correspond with Judgement of the Notion see § 1·2 above.

7. It is of importance to compare Hegel's doctrine that the middle as it develops through Syllogism is the Notion as an 'ought to be', an approximation to its norm, with Aristotle's conception of syllogism.

In the Aristotelian ideal basic syllogism of a special science the middle term reflects the cause which links those elements in the real which are reflected in the extreme terms. It is the specific differentia, and it is a partial definition of both the extremes. Inasmuch as it is the differentia it defines the minor term, the *infima species*. But it also partially defines the major term, the property or essential accident. This is because the being of accidents is their inherence in substance, and the middle term determines the precise mode of the property's inherence in the substantial *infima species*, and is consequently the differentia of the property as well as of the species.[1] Hence the middle term *qua* reflecting cause should, ideally, reflect formal cause. But, ideally, final and efficient causes coalesce in formal cause.[2] It is, however, impossible to formulate this coalescence, even as an ideal, for the Aristotelian syllogism. For its major term reflects not the genus of the minor term but a property which has a merely inherent and not substantial being. The middle term is thus differentia and partial formal cause of (*a*) the minor term and (*b*) the major term on, so to say, two different planes. It can never be the totality of the terms as an ideally concrete system. In other words, a special science is a closed system only on sufferance. Its separation from other special sciences marks it the object of Understanding, and its reasoning is hypothetical. Moreover, the fixation of the genus thus separated and taken as a closed system has an obvious consequence. When, within it, the *infima species* is taken as substance *par excellence* and the primary subject of demonstration, then the genus cannot be taken as fully actualized in *this* species alone: there remain other merely co-ordinate species. Moreover, the substantial *infima species* exhibits accidents which do not enter into its substantial, definable nature. In the Hegelian Syllogism, on the other hand, the middle term develops into the totality of the genus particularized to individuality. If the natural genus is to be used

[1] See my *Aristotle*, pp. 198–9. [2] See IH, ch. ii.

to illustrate Hegel's logical genus it must be imagined as actualized in two strictly contrary and contradictory species.[1]

Moreover, it follows further from Aristotle's conception of genus, species, and property that the premisses of his ideal syllogism must be grasped by immediate intuition and be true quite independently of the conclusions which they necessitate. The immediate and mediatory moments of thought are thus severed. *Per contra* the Hegelian Syllogism passes from qualitative immediacy through mediation in the Reflective to re-immediation in the Disjunctive Syllogism. The first immediacy is inference in germ, not the sheerly discrete flash of intuition which Aristotle is compelled to posit. The second immediacy is the result sublating the inferential process, and not the formal conclusion castrated by elision of its middle term.

8. Different as Hegel's Syllogism is from the syllogism of formal logic, it may yet strike the reader that in confining inference to syllogism he appears to ignore that distinction between syllogism and induction which even opponents of formal logic so different in their views as J. S. Mill and Bradley have not failed to draw.

A full answer would demand more space than it is here possible to afford. I can only indicate a few points of importance, and to begin with I must refer again to Aristotle.

That all inference is syllogistic may on the whole be said to have been Aristotle's view. The 'induction' (ἐπαγωγή) which he opposes to syllogism is not the induction which later logicians set up as the 'linear' converse of syllogistic deduction. His accounts of it are ambiguous. It is dialectical in the sense that it moves from potential to actual, but also in the further depreciatory sense of being merely the process by which the individual pupil passes by disputatious discussion with a master from the level of sense-perception and opinion to knowledge. 'Dialectic', says Hegel, 'has often been considered an art; as though it rested on a subjective talent, and did not belong to the objectivity of the Notion.'[2] This degradation from the position to which Plato had raised dialectic was due to Aristotle. The Aristotelian ἐπαγωγή is the mere shadow of 'the soul's conversation with herself'.

[1] Cf. ch. xi, § 6·1 and ch. xii, § 7·21 above.

[2] LL, ii, pp. 336–7.

It is on the whole conceived by Aristotle as a psychological process and not as a logical movement of inference.[1] Although it can begin and proceed only because in the act of human sense-perception the universal is given in germ, yet the insight into first principles to which it leads is not the grasp of a proven conclusion. It is the converse of syllogism, perhaps, in that it moves 'upward' to first principles, whereas syllogism moves 'downward' from them. But syllogism does not descend to the singular perceptible, and ἐπαγωγή and syllogism are not converse methods of proof. Rather, syllogism contrasts with ἐπαγωγή as expressing an articulated structure of, so to say, static public knowledge, which any man may with sufficient 'inductive' effort make his own. This structure derives its syllogistic form from the fact that it reflects the inherence of property in specific substance, and syllogism in turn determines the form of true thinking in the individual thinker who has mastered his subject. But the structure of syllogism does not as such reflect, is not determined by, the nature of thinking as a subject's activity. *Per contra* the dialectic of Hegel's Syllogism is an effort to restore the naïve unity of Plato's dialectic[1] at a higher level by resynthesizing these two shapes of thought, the 'private' psychological process and the 'public' structure of syllogistic truth which, long before Hegel's day, had lost its connexion with a real world of substance and inhering property and become a mere criterion of formal validity.

8·1. The theory of induction as a 'linear' method of proof, opposed in direction to syllogistic deduction and contrasting with it also as a logic of truth with a logic of validity, could not arise until formal logicians had taken the step of construing the terms of syllogism in extension. J. S. Mill boldly based inductive inference on a tie of unanalysed resemblance between singular and singular, without seeing that if syllogism involves a *petitio*, equally does induction, as he conceives it, fail to work without complete enumeration. Mill did not realize, as Aristotle in his theory of ἐπαγωγή had seen, that the singular can enter thought only in so far as it reveals the universal.

8·2. In my *Introduction to Hegel* I have given some account

[1] Cf. IH, ch. x, § 2·4.

of the conflict in Bradley's *Logic* between a 'private' and a 'public' aspect of thought.[1] In Bosanquet's *Logic* the same conflict is often apparent. In *Implication and Linear Inference* he opposes the 'linear' conception of inference, which he regards as common to traditional syllogism and traditional induction, with the notion of a single principle of implication. His contention is that on a 'linear' view of inference the terms remain discrete; they are self-contained, and logical process is not their continuous development. *Per contra* his conception of systematic implication carries with it the view that, as Bradley had held, in inference an ideal object develops itself. In chapter vii appears perhaps the clearest account in Bosanquet's works of the logical and psychological (what I have called the 'public' and 'private') aspects of thinking as he conceives them. But, moving as he does at a more or less empirical level, he does not go far beyond showing that in all thinking they are inseparable, and that any logical theory which simply discounts one or the other is ruinous. On the whole he treats thought as the activity of a finite, though certainly self-transcending, thinker rather than as the activity of spirit's self-definition. Although for him psychological process is but one aspect of thought, yet the complementary aspect of it is the self-development of an ideal object, not a self-manifestation of spirit only within which the distinction of thinker and object emerges. He shows his restricted conception of logic when he asserts that thought 'is in its essence an effort to define the universe by meanings adequately conditioned; to reconstruct the unity of the real in ideal or discursive form'.[2]

[1] See IH, ch. xiii, § 4 and ff.

[2] *Implication and Linear Inference*, p. 149.

XIV

TRANSITION TO OBJECTIVE NOTION

1. HEGEL's conception of Objective Notion may well prove difficult to a reader already somewhat wearied by the effort to distinguish the shades of meaning which Hegel in different contexts attaches to the terms 'subjective' and 'objective'.

At the risk of repetition we may begin by summarizing the two main senses of this contrast in Hegel.

The term *Subjektivität* always refers to the *activity* of the subject. (A) So far as the subject's activity is imperfect, it is subjective in the depreciatory sense of contingent or arbitrary. Its correlative object is then, for the subject, an independent object. If we accept as finally true the view which the subject, thus imperfectly active, takes of the 'detached' nature of its object—if, that is to say, we petrify this view into a theory of philosophical realism—then we find that upon this theory the only escape for the subject from purely capricious opinion to objective knowledge must lie in conforming itself to its 'detached' object-world, and that, nevertheless, contingency cannot be expelled from this object-world. Realism, even if it should maintain that self-consciousness is impossible apart from consciousness of objects other than the self, rests ultimately on the assumption that the mind in becoming the object of philosophic reflection becomes just such another 'detached' object as the mind at a level of incomplete activity takes its 'external' object to be. Realism is, in Hegel's view, the futile effort to stand detached from the mind and its object-world in order to contemplate their mutual relation, and to call realism philosophy is to confer no more than a courtesy title.

(B) In so far as the subject's activity has risen above this level, it recognizes itself in and as its object, and its objective knowledge is its own completed consciousness of itself. Its subjectivity is then not arbitrary caprice contrasted with the stable being of its object-world; it is an activity which, over-reaching its object and cancelling its detachment, returns upon itself therein.

As the dialectic of the Notion progresses beyond the pre-subjective categories of Being and Essence, the meaning of subjectivity moves gradually from (A) towards (B).

2. It has been already remarked that the self-particularizing Universal of Notion as such is best illustrated by the activity of the individual self-conscious subject.[1] This illustration may be elaborated to throw light upon the special sense which Hegel is now proposing to set on objectivity.

The individual experient is an *ego*, a subject, in so far as he enters whole into all his divers activities. It is by virtue of his unbroken complicity not only in his thinking but also in his feeling of pleasure and pain, in his action economic and moral, in his aesthetic appreciation or creation, in his religious life, that he is subject and can call himself 'I'. In every phase of his thinking—the form of his experience which here concerns us—he enters whole. Though his attention be concentrated and focused in one direction, and all other possible types of experience be forgotten, yet this wholeness is therein specialized and not partitioned. Even in dual personality and insanity it abides. Dr. Jekyll may not know himself for Mr. Hyde, and the paranoiac may believe himself to be Napoleon, but both—or should I say all three?—still experience as universal subject. This universality of the subject is further attested if we consider the object of his thought. The forms of his thinking can be distinguished from its object; i.e. the forms of judgement and inference in which he freely moves can be distinguished from that about which he judges and infers. But these forms of thinking, when thus considered in distinction from the object, are not subjective in the sense of arbitrary. If the thinker violates them, his thinking expresses not a free subjective activity by virtue of which he enters whole into all his thoughts, but a mere irrelevant idiosyncrasy and error which, if he is seriously trying to think, he is constantly at pains to suppress. That is to say these forms of thought are the forms of his thinking so far as that is genuinely active thinking. But further: that his thinking should embody these forms is a condition of his apprehending objective truth.

All this is no more than the familiar paradox that in

[1] See ch. xi, § 1·11.

asserting a proposition as true we are asserting it to be true irrespective of our *private* opinion of its truth, confessing that we must accept what we sometimes call the 'control' of the object. Hence these true forms of the subject's free activity are *eo ipso* forms of his object. In short, this paradox of servitude which is perfect freedom is soluble only if the object of true thinking is the *alter ego* of the subject; only if the object is that in the apprehending of which the subject realizes as content its own true universal nature as thought, not its phenomenal nature as a singular subject which fancies and opines. Or, to put it conversely, objectivity in the present context is the nature of a thinking whose object is *explicitly* identical with the content of the thinking, and so *is itself thought*.[1] True thinking is objective because between an absolutely true theory and its object there could be no difference. The difference between any current theory, scientific or philosophical, and its object is simply a function of its imperfect truth, and equally to its imperfect truth is due the appearance of this difference as sheer severance. This severance a special science must accept, because the very specialty which marks it as imperfectly true also constitutes the science. Philosophy is nothing but the effort to sublate this severance.

So, it might be said, Hegel interprets Aristotle's doctrine of the single actualization of subject and object in actual knowledge.[2]

3. The preceding account of objectivity may become clearer if we repeat it in the medium of logic, turning back to the categories from illustration in the individual thinker.

The forms of subjective thinking activity, the phases, that is, of Subjective Notion, develop directly from Essence, so that Subjective Notion is the proximate higher truth of spirit defined as Essence; and Subjective Notion is no more than the proximate higher truth of Essence. Yet as Subjective Notion spirit contains implicit the germ of itself—of its newly achieved notional self—as object. It is because this

[1] The reader may find an illustration from the practical sphere helpful. The object of true thinking is itself thought, just as the state or any other social institution is at once the creation of a spiritual activity and an objective fact.

[2] Cf. IH, ch. v, § 4.

germ is present that Subjective Notion develops through the forms of Notion as such, Judgement, and Syllogism, gradually reaching explicit definition of spirit as subjective thinking activity. These forms of thought *qua* subjective activity also define *implicitly* the subject of that activity: they are forms of the object as implicitly the *alter ego* of the subject. For there are here but two alternatives. If these forms of thought are not implicit forms of the object, then the universal is not *in re* at all, and all our judging and inferring is a meaningless gymnastic *in vacuo*. But if they are implicit forms of the object, then this object must itself develop and become explicit: it must become object-for-subject. Moreover, and this is the vital point, the object which is implicitly the *alter ego* of Subjective Notion, and must become so explicitly, must itself be a thinking. It obviously cannot be the mysterious alien thing which realism erects as the object of thought. But neither can it be merely the Actual defined in categories of Essence as Substance, Cause, &c. If it were no more than that, it would constitute no dialectical advance upon Subjective Notion. To entertain such a supposition would be to entertain in an analogous and aggravated form the error of supposing that Judgement and Syllogism, because they openly contain the categories of Essence which they sublate, are themselves no more than categories of Essence. The categories of Essence are not characterizations of the real *qua* object. 'Object', despite a loose current usage which tends to invade second-rate philosophy, does not mean Thing, nor even Substance; it means nothing whatever but object-for-subject. It therefore presupposes subject; it is dialectically posterior to subject. 'The Notion', says Hegel, 'is not describable as subjective previous to the subsequent contrast with objectivity.'[1] Consequently, unless we can—as I cannot—devise some fourth meaning whereby the object is neither an alien opposite of thought nor the already sublated self of thought, it must be itself thought in further development beyond subjective thinking.

3·1. In Disjunctive Syllogism, then, the unsatisfied movement of inference becomes free activity. Subjective thinking is at length fully systematic, and this systematic form is now

[1] EL, § 193.

explicitly the form of an object-for-subject, of an object which is itself thought, but no longer subjective thought. The original unity of thought and being has led inevitably to this doctrine.

If the nature of such a category seems still obscure, the reader may consider the teleological categories in which Objective Notion will culminate. An object thought as expressive of purpose is clearly not thought through categories of Essence. Yet, unless we follow Kant in holding that the human mind can have theoretical knowledge only of objects without value which are constituted and connected by no higher principles than the Kantian categories of relation, we cannot deny that when we recognize purpose we have objective knowledge.

4. I will end this chapter by illustrating objectivity, as Hegel himself illustrates it,[1] from the ontological proof of God's existence.

Anselm's original argument runs thus:

'Certe id quo maius cogitari nequit non potest esse in intellectu solo. Si enim vel in solo intellectu est, potest cogitari esse et in re: quod maius est. Si ergo id quo maius cogitari non potest, est in solo intellectu, id ipsum quo maius cogitari non potest, est quo maius cogitari potest. Sed certe hoc esse non potest.'

'Certainly that than which nothing greater can be thought cannot be merely in the intellect. For even if we assume that it is, it can still be thought to exist in fact too; and that is greater. Hence if that than which nothing greater can be thought is merely in the intellect, then the very thing than which nothing greater can be thought, can be exceeded in thought. But that is certainly impossible.'

4·1. Kant's attack on the ontological proof won a wide acceptance because common sense found his illustration highly plausible. He appeared to convict Anselm of exactly identifying a hundred actual dollars and a hundred merely possible dollars. But Kant's attack, Hegel argues, fails for two reasons. In the first place Kant, in accordance with his doctrine of modality, is assuming that the *Vorstellung*, the imaged presentation, of a hundred dollars can be held before the mind as a content judged merely possible—as conforming, that is, to the formal conditions of experience—without

[1] See LL, ii, pp. 172–6 and EL, § 193.

being judged real in any sense at all. That is to say, Kant takes as the final standard of reality for human knowledge actual existence as content of actually co-operant Understanding and sense, or necessary connexion with that content. Tested by this standard—i.e. by reference to my purse or my pass-book—the hundred dollars, judged merely possible, are not real at all. The *Vorstellung* obeys the law of contradiction and conforms to the formal conditions of experience, but the dollars are merely imagined, and merely imagined means wholly unreal.

What it signifies that the human mind should be capable of day-dreams and hallucinations Kant does not here stay to consider. In effect he is maintaining that a *Vorstellung* can simply float, suspended in the mind and cut off from all context, without any act of judgement at all.[1] Though the imaginary hundred dollars is supposed to be judged possible, Kant—as is obvious when he asserts that existence is not a predicate—really reaffirms the crude and ruinous Cartesian doctrine that, before we judge, and while we are still innocent of truth or falsehood, we can apprehend that identical content which we subsequently go on to judge. He forgets the essential connexion of that doctrine with the 'problematic idealism' of Descartes, which he gives himself such pains to refute. Kant's hundred dollars turns out to be a mere abstraction, more dead than any text-book example of judgement divorced from all context,[2] because he supposes that possibility can be thought apart from any sort of actuality, a view amply refuted by Hegel in the later categories of Essence.

In the second place Kant appears to miss the whole point of the ontological argument. If its purpose had been to prove that God's existence is the finite actuality lacked by the optimistic financier's day-dream, then no doubt Kant's trivial criticism would have served to refute a trivial piece of reasoning. You certainly cannot conjure actual finite existence out of a merely imagined content. But such finite actuality is not what the ontological proof was ever intended to vindicate for God. Anselm, neglecting the transitory

[1] Cf. IH, ch. ix, § 4·311 and xiii, § 4·3.

[2] Cf. above, ch. xii, §§ 2 and 3·5.

connexion of finite perishable things with their existence, their discrepancy with their notion in which their finitude consists, rightly pronounced that only to be perfect which exists not merely in a subjective but also in an objective mode. The 'existence' which the thought of God carries with it and guarantees is objectivity, the being of the supreme Good as object-for-subject.

4·2. The ontological proof has no bearing on the special attributes attached to the God of any particular religion—hence no doubt its common failure to satisfy the *croyant*—and Hegel points out its shortcomings. It is, he says, more objectively stated by Descartes and Spinoza than by Anselm and intuitionalists such as Jacobi, who were chiefly concerned with the inseparable nexus of our subjective thinking with existence. But in all the forms of this proof the unity of thought and being which is proclaimed to be the supreme perfection or the true knowledge is presupposed in the sense of assumed as merely implicit (*an sich*). It is merely asserted as an abstract identity, and when it is opposed by the equally true diversity of thought and being, it is dumb. Its defect is that it is formulated as self-subsistent and conclusive; as itself a result instead of what it is, namely, a mere beginning to be justified by development in and as a concrete speculative result. That is why it is defenceless against an equally true half-truth.

XV

MECHANISM, CHEMISM, AND TELEOLOGY

1. The general tenor of Objective Notion is the development of that immediate totality of Universal-Particular-Individual in which Disjunctive Syllogism collapsed, into a system possessing a unity of final cause which is only intelligible by reference to a subject.

This gradual return of the subject through Objective Notion is analogous to the approach towards subjectivity which the categories of Essence display to the philosopher. But the two movements must not be confused. (A) Essence emerges from Being, and comprises the higher categories of the Understanding, the categories, that is, of a thought which absorbs and yet contradicts its own rudimentary intuitional phases. In Notion as such subjectivity emerges as the beginning of a universal but *merely* subjective thought, and this emergence follows upon a development of spirit in Essence which is prior to the true distinction of subjectivity and objectivity. The Understanding, so far as its thought is expressed in the categories of Essence, is merely conscious. What it knows through the categories of Intro-reflection, Appearance, and Actuality is not for it the explicit work or product of self-expressive spirit, and from Reciprocity it advances as Subjective Notion only to reflect on its own thinking; that is, it passes back, so to say, to observe the detail of its own functioning, which it has hitherto taken for granted. It performs upon this the office of a natural historian, thus treating it as if it were *in pari materia* with what has hitherto been its object. But (B) Objective Notion is object-for-subject into which the completed form of subjective thinking has itself passed. It is not the 'detached' *Gegenstand* of Understanding, but an already theorized object: it bears the stamp of mind upon it. Explicitly it is the Universal developed to Disjunctive Syllogism, and it prefigures intrinsic value as the explicit union of subject and object. For the synthesis of Subjective and Objective Notion will be fully self-conscious thought.

1·1. The three main divisions of Objective Notion are Mechanism, Chemism, and Teleology. The dialectic of the first two is extremely curt in EL, and in LL extremely complicated. I am doubtful, particularly in the case of Chemism, how far I have understood Hegel's doctrine. My exposition must be taken as even more than usually provisional.

The terms 'Mechanism' and 'Chemism' give a first impression of direct adaptation from the sphere of natural science, but Hegel conceives these categories as true speculative thought-determinations, which are illustrated not merely in Nature but also in the sphere of Concrete Spirit. Hegel has, moreover, already used the term 'genus', which is commonly associated *par excellence* with Nature, in a purely logical sense. In this use of genus he follows the tradition of ordinary logic, and appears to regard Mechanism and Chemism as corresponding to their analogues in the world of Nature in much the same way as the logical corresponds to the natural genus. Thus we shall do well to attend even more closely to Hegel's spiritual than to his natural illustrations, but above all we must watch the dialectical development of these categories from Subjective Notion.

2. MECHANISM

The nearest clue to Mechanism is, I think, the monadic principle of Leibniz.

'The definition which states that the Absolute is the Object', says Hegel, 'is most definitely contained in the Leibnizian monad. The monad is supposed to be an object, but an object implicitly (*an sich*) representative, indeed a total representation of the world. In its simple unity all difference is merely ideal, not self-subsistent. Nothing comes from without into the monad: it is the whole Notion in itself (*in sich*), only distinguished by its own greater or lesser development. Nevertheless this simple totality parts into the absolute multiplicity of differences, each becoming an independent monad.'[1]

Wallace's comment[2] expresses admirably what Hegel finds significant in the Leibnizian monads:

'A monad is the simple substance or indivisible unity corresponding to a body. It is as simple what the world is as a multiplicity: it "represents", i.e. concentrates into unity, the variety of phenomena: is the

[1] EL, § 194. [2] *Logic of Hegel*, p. 428.

expression of the material in the immaterial, of the compound in the simple, of the extended outward in the inward. Its unity and its representative capacity go together. It is "the present which is full of the future and laden with the past"; the point which is all embracing, the totality of the universe. And yet there are monads—in the plural.'

In Leibniz's attempt to ground and realize the ideality of his non-interacting monads in a supreme monad which pre-establishes the harmony of their inner development, Hegel finds 'completely developed contradiction',[1] but the *Monadologie* very nearly reflects that phase of the dialectic which Hegel calls the mechanical Object. It is further to be noted that although Leibniz calls his monad, even his *monas monadum*, substance—as Spinoza had called his God—yet his monadic unity is clearly inspired by the notion of a subject which is one in the diverse totality of its consciousness.[2] That is the type and norm to which *all* sub-human monads approximate in varying degrees of clarity. It is clearly for this reason that Hegel draws upon Leibniz for his conception of Objective Notion in its first phase, whereas he enshrines the system of Spinoza, for whom he had a far greater respect, in a category of Essence.[3] In general I suspect that Hegel owes more to Leibniz than his rather rare references suggest. Leibnizian influence is very evident in his conception of Nature as a graded approximation of the pre-spiritual to Concrete Spirit.

2·1. In LL Mechanism divides first into (1) Mechanical Object, (2) Mechanical Process, (3) Absolute Mechanism. These subdivide in a complicated dialectic, (2) and (3) under definite sub-titles. I shall try to expound the movement so as not to obscure its main articulation.

2·2. Mechanical Object

(A) From Disjunctive Judgement results the Object as an immediate (i.e. re-immediated) totality of the notional

[1] EL, § 194.

[2] Incidentally I fancy that the Leibnizian monad had more influence on Kant's conception of the unity of consciousness than many of his commentators, preoccupied with Kant's attitude to the Leibnizian *a priori*, have observed; see Paton, *Kant's Metaphysic of Experience*, i, p. 183.

[3] Cf. ch. viii, §§ 4·3 and 4·4 above.

moments. Hence it differs from, for example, the categories of Matter and Form, and of Whole and Parts, in that it contains no opposite in itself: it is a plurality of Objects, but a merely inner plurality reflected only into its own universality and not into an other. Implicitly it has a ground outside it, but it is an aggregate *in se*, an aggregate or arrangement of monads rather than of atoms, because it is not determined for itself against an other.

Thus the various determinations proper to the Object are mutually indifferent and merely aggregated or ordered: they are not deducible from each other, nor does their aggregation or order constitute a system from which they can be deduced. Hence (B) the Object has its 'determinateness as totality in the form of a *Dasein überhaupt* [a There-being in a general, unqualified sense] outside itself in other Objects which are likewise externally determined, and so *ad indefinitum*'.[1] Since we are in the Notion, and the Object is therefore explicitly Universal, the return upon itself of this regress is also given. But it is only given as a universe, that is as universality enclosed in itself by virtue of an *indeterminate* individuality. *Self*-determinateness is still absent: each Object is a formal totality which is indifferent in its activity to its determination by other Objects. The determinism which makes this category its principle, the view of the world as a blind, natural mechanism, is a tautological explanation which regresses *ad indefinitum*.

Yet (C) the Objects, though indifferent and mutually repellent, are identical in their determinateness. And this contradiction gives us

2·3. Mechanical Process[2]

The originality and independence of the monadic Objects is now seen to be after all dependent on the common self-identity of them all, which is thus their negative unity. There *is* some affinity between them. Each is in fact only individual by virtue of this bare negative universality. This constitutes a dialectical criticism of Leibniz's windowless

[1] LL, ii, p. 183.

[2] Called in EL *Differenter Mechanismus*, which Wallace translates 'Mechanism with Affinity'.

monads, which, incidentally, by their very claim to represent the world with relative degrees of distinctness betray their dependence. We thus return in antithesis to that interaction which Leibniz sought to evade by his postulated harmony.

This 'interaction' is (A. i) at first bare universal 'communication'; it is not transition into an opposite. So in the spiritual sphere, laws, manners, and reasonable ideas are unconsciously communicated among men without encountering resistance. Heat, motion, magnetism, and electricity evince the same unhindered continuation of an identical determinateness from one body into another. Even if we do imagine them also as 'stuffs' or 'matters',[1] yet the physical bodies which conduct them do not provide a ground which individualizes them: they are imponderable agents.[2]

But (A. ii) this 'interaction' entails 'reaction', wherein the Objects *do* pass into an other as cause into effect, but yet retain their independence. What is communicated, that is to say, remains universal but is particularized. Moreover, since action and reaction are equal, each Object now actively restores the whole action communicated to it, but retains its own specific share. Each is thus in a sense individualized and in self-relation.

The Object thus reaches an equilibrium. It is (A. iii) the product of process, a product particularized against other Objects, but still universal only *qua* indifferent to them.[3] It is similarly indifferent to the process which determined it. For it is a merely aggregated system, a result relatively contingent and not, like the end of a teleological process, truly present from the beginning.

2·301. (A. i), (A. ii), and (A. iii) are grouped in LL under the heading Formal Mechanical Process, and in EL the first phase of Mechanism is given as Formal Mechanism. In EL, § 195, *Zusatz* (which every behaviourist should read) it is observed that Mechanism is the dominant category only in the sphere of Mechanics, which concerns the relations of

[1] Cf. above, ch. vi, §§ 9 and 9·1. [2] See LL, ii, pp. 187–8.

[3] I.e. although its activity is now action and reaction, yet it is still no more truly individualized through this commerce with other Objects than was the original windowless monadic Object.

masses. It is not fully adequate to explain even the phenomena of light, heat, &c. Yet even in the sphere of Concrete Spirit it has important illustration. There is an indispensable mechanical basis in memory, especially obvious in operations such as reading and playing an instrument. In LL, ii, pp. 180–1, this is clearly explained:

'A mechanical mode of imagining [*Vorstellungsweise*; Hegel clearly has the association of ideas in mind], a mechanical memory, a habit, a mechanical mode of action—all these mean that the peculiar permeation and presence of spirit is lacking in that which spirit apprehends or does. Though spirit's mechanical behaviour, theoretical or practical, cannot occur without its self-activity, without conscious impulse, yet the freedom of individuality is missing, and because this does not appear such activity seems to be merely external.'

Hegel points out, too, the obvious emergence of mechanism when the higher natural functions are hindered; for example the sense of pressure which accompanies indigestion.[1]

2·31. In LL the antithesis (B) to Formal Mechanical Process is Real Mechanical Process. The intro-reflected or self-related Objects belonging to the stage of equilibrium in action and reaction which we have now reached, exhibit a new form of self-dependence. Their intercommunication is now such that they are not merely particularized by it, but offer resistance to it. The very weak is untouched by communication with the stronger—e.g. the cloth freely suspended in air is not pierced by the bullet, and the dull mind is simply untouched by real intelligence—but the less impotent nature resists. In the terminology of Essence, 'communication' is the absolute necessity of Power,[2] but it acts as mere Force[3] upon the resisting Object, which perishes because it has not itself the power to absorb this communication; it cannot make it, in Hegel's phrase, 'predicate to itself as subject'. This Power is objectively universal, and is the Greek notion of Fate. In so far as it appears as mere Force to the resisting Object which it destroys, it is a blind mechanical fate. The abiding genus which living things perish to sustain may be called their fate; but they perish unresisting, and real fate pertains only to a self-conscious

[1] EL, loc. cit.

[2] Cf. ch. viii, § 8·1 above.

[3] Cf. ch. vii, § 6 above.

being. When a man or a nation strives to determine itself to an individuality alien to its own objective universality, then by this self-separation it excites Fate against it as a hostile force which crushes its resistance and snatches it away into the mechanical Process.[1]

2·32. The Product of this Real Mechanical Process (C) is the Object as a system which exhibits centrality; it is not, i.e., a mere aggregation, nor even a mere ordered whole, but a system with a centre which prefigures the return of subjectivity and recalls the middle term of Syllogism.

With this we pass in LL to

2·4. Absolute Mechanism

The communicated universality is now (A) a centre: an immanent mean or middle, which is the penetrating Essence of the Objects. 'In the material world it is the central body which is the genus but also the *individual* universality of the singular objects and their mechanical process.'[2] The meaning of this sentence and the passage which follows is, I think, that the peripheral bodies of a gravitational system, although they attract and repel each other externally, do not relate in that same manner to the central body, but receive from it a generic nature which individualizes each of them as a body with a centre of its own. The central body is the centre of a system of centred bodies whose nisus towards it is not the mere external determinateness which relates them to each other. The total system is thus not a mere aggregate.

Yet so far the central individual is a mean or middle without true extremes. For the other bodies which it individualizes nevertheless remain outside it as each a centre with its own dependent peripheral objects. It links these secondary centres with their peripheries externally, as the middle term of an objectified syllogism in the third figure, *P-U-I* or *I-U-P*. It is the objective universal nature manifested in, and mediating, the relation of the secondary centres to their dependent peripheral objects. But second- and first-figure Syllogism are also sublated within this system and integral to its nature. For the secondary centres mediate between the primary centre and the peripheral objects

[1] LL, ii, pp. 192–3. [2] Ibid., p. 195.

dependent on the secondary centres, and the dependent peripheral objects mediate, though merely formally, between primary centre and secondary centres.

Hegel also illustrates this first phase of Absolute Mechanism from the state:

'Like the solar system, so, e.g., in the practical sphere the state is a system of three syllogisms. (1) The individual (the person) through his particularity (his physical and spiritual needs which when fully developed for themselves give civil society)[1] is coupled with the universal, i.e. with society, law, right, government.[2] (2) The will or action of the individuals is the mediating factor which procures for these needs satisfaction in society, law, &c., and which gives to society, law, &c. their fulfilment and actualization. But (3) the universal, i.e. the state, government, and law, is the substantial mean in which the individuals and their satisfaction have and receive their fulfilled reality, intermediation, and persistence. . . . It is only by the nature of this triple coupling, by this triad of syllogisms with the same termini, that a whole is thoroughly understood in its organization.'[3]

2·41. This reciprocating movement through the syllogistic figures is (B) the free Mechanism of Law (*Gesetz*); not, i.e., the mere rule of dead, formal Mechanism. As Law the central unity is in explicitly external relation to the objects—the elements of the system—which tend or strive towards it. But it is in a degree spontaneous or self-moving;[4] it is the soul or the ideal unity of the elements. The system now, that is to say, is not mere process in which the elements, passive or resistant, perish and pass away: it is freely self-necessitating.

2·42. Yet the independence and externality of the objective elements is not cancelled altogether. We pass (C) not straight to a teleological system, but to a phase in which the single centrality is dissipated, and the elements each assume the character of the whole system, so that they tend not all to one centre but each towards another object opposed to it. The objective elements in this synthetic phase, which in LL is entitled Transition of Mechanism, have lost their indifference to one another. The external affinity of Mechanical

[1] i.e. the purely economic and social moment of the state.

[2] i.e. the state in its narrower sense.

[3] EL, § 198.

[4] Compare Leibniz's distinction between the spontaneous and the voluntary; e.g. Gerhart's ed., vol. iv, p. 519.

Process recurs as an explicit state of tension: the elements are now negative and *gespannt* against one another. With this result we now pass to the new category of Chemism.

3. Chemism

It is the tension between the objects which makes Chemism the antithesis of Mechanism. The objects are no longer peripheral about a single centre, for centrality has passed into temporary abeyance in this negative tension. No thinker has attempted to conceive the universe as a chemical system.

3·1. The first phase of Chemism in LL is entitled (A) Chemical Object. Tension is not indifferent determinateness, but the Universal particularized in the objects. It is their principle, their notion, which they tend towards realizing. Thus (i) chemical objects in tension are only intelligible each through another, for the being of the one is the being of the other. Yet (ii) this very tension holds them apart as individuals relatively external to one another. This tensional nature is therefore an immanent self-contradiction, a nisus in objects towards self-transcendence and realization of their notion in a neutral state of self-completion. It is not the mere common tendency to a centre exhibited by peripheral objects in Mechanism: it is a rudimentary self-movement or spontaneity of more or less individualized objects, which now openly prefigures the return of subjectivity.

This in Nature is illustrated by the tendency of elements possessing mutual affinity to combine in a neutral product in which their properties are changed. It is also the 'schema' of biological sex-relation, and the formal basis of love and friendship.[1]

3·2. Thus the antithesis in which this initial state of equal tension develops is (B) Chemical Process.[2] The distinctive character of this process is its duality. (i) The elements pass into a neutral product. This passage, syllogistically expressed, is the coalescence of the objective Universal [sc. the notion of the elements] through the particularity of the

[1] LL, ii, p. 201.

[2] Here I shall in the main follow EL. The LL version is not easy.

cognate elements[1] with the individuality of the products (*U-P-I*); but the second and third figures are equally involved in it. Yet the chemical self-movement is extinguished in this neutral product. It does not fully actualize the notion of the elements; in Nature, for example, not every property of the combining elements is involved. The product thus (ii) suffers contingent dissolution; i.e. it returns by a converse process to a state of tension. The two processes are dependent upon external conditions and stimuli, and go on externally to one another. In Nature chemical process has not the self-maintaining character which life has: its existence falls far shorter of its notion. This self-movement is not yet free, but essentially finite.

Yet these processes of combination and dissolution are both integral moments of Chemical Process. Their regular alternation shows them to be not wholly at the mercy of external stimuli. They cancel each other; but logically it is the externality of Chemism, the severance of the Object from its notion, which is sublated in their mutual cancellation.

3·3. In the synthesis of these two processes we have passed to (C) Transition of Chemism. The Notion has now become End (*Zweck*), and the system which has developed through Mechanism and Chemism has become teleological. Hegel observes that according to ordinary Chemistry there is an approximation in Nature to this teleology in the behaviour of some chemical substances. There are bodies which raise the degree of oxidation in one part of their mass and lower it in another, being thereby enabled to combine with bodies to which they would otherwise remain alien.[2]

[1] This middle term is, according to Hegel, illustrated in the spiritual sphere by language, or in general the symbol, as a medium of communication.

[2] The chemistry of Hegel's day has suffered a pretty complete transformation. Yet there is a modern theory of organic chemical reactions which seems to present some analogue to the doctrine in Hegel's mind. Professor Robinson accounts for many such reactions on the hypothesis that a slight shift of electrons takes place from one part of a molecule towards another. He suggests that the consequent change in electrical charge at the point from which or towards which the shift has occurred serves to initiate chemical reaction with another molecule, and so to produce a fresh compound. See 'Two Lectures on the Outline of an Electronic Theory of Organic Chemical Reactions', *Institute of Chemistry of Great Britain and Ireland*, 1932.

3·4. Hegel in LL, ii, p. 207 sums up Chemism in three Syllogisms, which are meant, I think, to correspond to (A), (B), and (C) respectively. The middle term is (1) mere formal neutrality (sc. the possibility, the unrealized notion, of particular chemical combination), which binds the Objects in tension; (2) the real neutrality (the combination which is the product of the first Syllogism), which binds the dissolving action with its indifferent product, i.e. with the elements again in tension; (3) the self-realizing Notion, which binds the combining and dissolving processes, and so 'posits for itself the presupposition by which its process is conditioned'. It is clearly implied by Hegel that these middle terms are successively *P*, *I*, and *U*, but it is not very evident how the notional moments are distributed among the extremes. Possibly in (2) the dissolving action is *U* and the indifferent product *P*, while in (3) the combining process may be *I* and the dissolution *P*. In (1) there seems to be no means of distinguishing. Probably, however, Hegel means to imply that (1), (2), and (3) each involve all three syllogistic figures. He observes that because of the relatively conditioned nature of Chemism these syllogisms fall apart.

Despite a certain obscurity of detail in the syllogistic expression of Objective Notion, it must not be forgotten that Syllogism is the category here perspicuously sublated. Thought when considered as subjective inference already displays the systematic nature which is objectified in Mechanism, Chemism, and Teleology. The middle term is developed through the abstract, external centrality of Mechanism to the self-moving unity of Chemism, and we shall watch it in the teleological categories approach more nearly the unity of a subject's activity.

4. It is worth while here again to consider generally Hegel's view that Mechanism and Chemism are categories explicitly determining reality as object-for-subject. Even after reading Hegel's own exposition of them it may perhaps seem difficult not to assign them to the dialectical level of Essence, and even questionable whether they are categories at all, and not, as Kant, for example, would have held them to be, *a posteriori* specifications of causal law. In what follows I shall attempt at my own risk to reconstruct Hegel's underlying

thought, and I shall assume that he had Kant's philosophy in mind to a greater extent than is at first obvious.

In the first place it is important to bear in mind that Hegel's categories of Absolute Correlation are no more than Kant's corresponding schematized categories when these are stripped of space and time and seen in dialectical connexion. The causality of Essence is precisely the Kantian conception of finite causality which begets an indefinite regress. Hegel's Reciprocity completes the development of causality, but it does not bring us to any genuine system.[1] And similarly Kant's 'world-whole' of phenomena which follows as a consequent from his category of Reciprocity[2] is not a genuine totality. It exhibits the phenomenal world as, so to say, homogeneous throughout an indeterminate extent; as unindividual and still lacking any centrality. It is *not* the thought of the universe as a system of reciprocating elements, for a system must have a centre. The schematized category of Reciprocity is particularized in systems of reciprocal causal connexion, but the centrality of, for example, a gravitational system is not given through the category.

4·1. Hegel's category of Reciprocity, then, differs from Kant's only in so far as it is a pure category and explicitly synthesizes the two preceding categories. But in the conception of centred system Hegel sees a problem demanding a very different solution from that offered by Kant. Inspired perhaps proximately by Schelling, but finding in Leibniz a far more precise expression of the thought, he did not doubt that this conception of centred system, obviously operative in physics and chemistry, and already offered as a crude philosophical theory by the Greek atomists, was quite meaningless save as an approximation to the nature of mind.[3] To the natural scientist Nature is not pre-spiritual but non-spiritual. To him gravitation, for example, and chemical combination are special principles which in respect of their general nature he must assume, and cannot justify or connect rationally with the special principles of other sciences. He

[1] Cf. above, ch. ix, § 5·1.

[2] See KRV, B, p. 265 note, and IH, ch. ix, § 4·11.

[3] I think there can be no doubt that Hegel would have named Aristotle as the real source of this view.

cannot modify them beyond certain limits without effacing the peculiar character of his own subject-matter. He cannot, that is to say, treat them as entirely provisional working hypotheses and as in no sense at all first principles exempt from criticism. And this acceptance by the special scientist of an inescapable brute element in his principles is enshrined in Kant's philosophy. But Hegel sees that upon an object recognized as centred system the subject, consciously or not, ὕπαρ or ὄναρ, has cast the shadow of its own self-conscious nature, as it has not done in ascribing to its object mere causal reciprocity.[1] Where Kant can find no more than *a posteriori* particularization, Hegel detects a higher category. An object construed as that which in its very nature is determined by being an object, belongs not to Essence but to categories which presuppose subjective thinking.

4·2. This higher category, then, cannot follow immediately upon Reciprocity. In Reciprocity we are upon the threshold of the Notion, because Substance fully developed passes at once into the Universal which is *eo ipso* Particular and Individual. But Notion as such is not a further direct characterization of the detached object-world of the Understanding, but the re-emergence of subject as at first merely formal and lacking its proper object. Throughout Subjective Notion spirit is defined as thinking, not as thought concrete in its own, no longer alien object.[2] Thus the thought of centred system falls naturally into its place after the categories of Subjective Notion which it presupposes.

5. It may serve to clarify further Hegel's position, and to facilitate transition to the categories of Teleology, if we recall again the dual nature of dialectical progress in Objective Notion.

(*a*) In Mechanism and Chemism the Object is becoming more and more a system *for itself*: from the external centrality of Mechanism, through the *quasi*-spontaneity of Chemism, it approaches teleological behaviour, viz. the systematic activity of that which has its end in itself. (*b*) The Object as a system is only present to a mind which construes it as approximating to the mind's own self-conscious nature. But

[1] The difference is of course in the end one of degree as well as kind.

[2] Cf. § 1 above, and ch. xi, §§ 2·3 and 3.

(*b*) is an assertion neither of theism nor of anthropomorphism: without (*b*) there is no meaning in (*a*).

5·1. This will become clearer in the teleological categories, and it is important to note the uneasy attitude towards teleology which characterizes both the critical philosophy, which finds human knowledge exemplified in natural science, and also modern biology.

On Kant's view teleological concepts have a merely regulative and heuristic value for the investigation of Nature, because they are essentially subjective. They cannot assist to constitute an object of human knowledge, because they cannot, like the categories, co-operate with sensuous intuition.[1] The categories are the indispensable, but also sufficient, intellectual condition of perceiving objects. If the scientist did not order his data causally, there could be no scientific observation at all, because there could be for him no observable object. But even if it be living organisms which the scientist is observing, no teleological concept which he employs as a means towards unifying his knowledge subjectively can contribute one iota of constitutive form to the content of that knowledge. Kant is here perfectly consistent. To him the object of human knowledge, although it is phenomenal, is the 'detached' object of Understanding. If the reflection of the mind's subjective activity falls upon the object, this borrowed light affords no aid to knowledge of what it is.

5·2. In modern biology the dilemma remains, and modern biologists have usually understood it less clearly than Kant. Some of them hesitate to discard teleology, lest the very conception of life be destroyed. Others—the majority perhaps—are prepared to risk the dissolution of the organism in its environment, because to them teleological interpretation appears to be an illegitimate advance upon observed data which can be quite intelligibly construed without it. These commonly call themselves mechanists. But the grounds upon which they reject teleology justify equally the rejection of mechanism. Unless the categories of cause and reciprocity are presupposed, there can be *no* intelligible construing of biological data, and there lies the strength of their

[1] Cf. IH, ch. ix, § 4·11.

position as empirical scientists. But that which behaves mechanically behaves as centred system, and no such system is guaranteed *a priori* through the categories of cause and reciprocity. If, whether as a first principle or as a working hypothesis, teleology is to be rejected in science as a mistake,[1] nevertheless mechanism is the first stage upon this path of error. Yet on the categories of substance, cause, and reciprocity alone no *special* science can be founded.

6. TELEOLOGY

Hegel's teaching in this section of the Logic is firmly rooted in Greek philosophy, particularly in Aristotle's doctrine of form as final cause[2] and Aristotle's rejection of external teleology.[3]

In LL[4] Hegel approaches the subject by pointing out that when we perceive design, that is adequacy to an end (*Zweckmässigkeit*), we always assume that an intelligence[5] originates it. The former (sc. the pre-Kantian) metaphysicians merely presupposed the world as they found it, and merely argued the question whether design or blind mechanism, which they assumed to be the two mutually exclusive and together exhaustive alternatives, afforded the true explanation of it. But neither mechanism nor design will serve by itself, and to view the world as a patchwork which here efficient and there final causes sufficiently explain, is equally futile.[6] Only through examining these Notions in themselves can we reach their truth, which is dialectical.

The difficulty was aggravated through the influence of a religious piety which imagined God as an extra-mundane intelligence.[7] It became obvious (*a*) that such a designing intelligence must be limited by a supposed material which

[1] As alien to the purpose of natural science; see ch. xxii, § 1·2 below.

[2] Cf. IH, ch. ii. [3] See ibid., ch. iii, § 6·2.

[4] ii, pp. 209 ff. What follows is partly a condensation, partly an expansion, of these pages. [5] *Verstand*; but the word is not used here in its narrower sense.

[6] Cf. IH, ch. iii, §§ 5 ff. above.

[7] Christian metaphysicians from Descartes to Leibniz were affected in their speculation by this piety in different degrees, but I think it may be said that not one of them was as free from anthropomorphism as Plato in his consciously mythical account of creation in the *Timaeus*. Spinoza, of course, is not here in point.

awaits intelligent fashioning; and (*b*) that the design must be quite external to the object upon which it is imposed, in no way the object's own nature and self-expression. By this crudely anthropomorphic conception of divine creation and conservation the very notion of teleology was doubly violated. Teleology is a universal and immanent principle of self-determination, and in this caricature of it Form and Content were displayed in ridiculous incongruity: (*a*) God's activity was reduced to a series of arbitrary and therefore contingent results, the acts of a petty Providence, each merely finite in its content. (*b*) The end attributed to the object showed itself to be equally contingent, and not a universal determination connecting the object systematically with other objects. The futility of so childish a teleology, and its uselessness in the investigation of Nature, seemed strong arguments in favour of mechanism.[1] For in Mechanism, and Chemism, too, the objects are at any rate determined each by other mechanical or chemical objects. The category does express the universal nature immanent in them, and even if it leaves them relatively indifferent to one another, yet this very mutual indifference preserves intact their further particular content:

> 'In Mechanism the objects become essential through the mere form of necessity, and their content remains indifferent, for they are meant to (*sie sollen*) remain external: Understanding alone as such[2] is meant to be satisfied by recognizing its own mode of connexion, which is abstract identity.'[3]

In this shallow teleology of external design the content of the object as an end is not shown to differ from its content interpreted mechanically. Design seems redundant, and mechanism then naturally appears to be the better principle of interpretation.

6·1. In LL, ii, pp. 213–16 Hegel praises Kant for distinguishing between external and internal design—in effect for recalling Aristotle's final cause[4]—and for distinguishing

[1] Which may be here taken to include Chemism.

[2] Sc. the apprehending subject: *für sich* is *für uns*.

[3] LL, ii, pp. 211–12.

[4] See the parallel passage in EL, § 204 and cf. Aristotle's definition of life in *De Anima*, 412a14: *ζωὴν λέγομεν τὴν δι' αὑτοῦ τροφήν τε καὶ αὔξησιν καὶ φθίσιν.*

the reflective teleological judgement from the merely subsumptive determinant judgement, so that the former becomes a link between the universal of Reason and the individual of intuition.[1]

But Hegel points out that Kant's advance upon the general position of the first *Critique* is incomplete. The conclusion of Kant's third antinomy (of necessity and freedom), which Hegel here analyses, is that final causality is a mere subjective maxim. In denying that the reflective teleological judgement is determinant Kant still halts in an uneasy half-way position. To recognize purpose in an object is not a mere '*reflective* judging which only considers external objects according to a unity *as if* some understanding had given them for *the benefit of our powers of cognition*'. It is a determinant judgement of objective truth.[2]

It will be remembered that Kant in his third *Critique* had attributed to the teleological judgement of purpose in Nature a subjectivity similar to that which belongs to his aesthetic judgement.[3] Both are universal but non-determinant. The teleological judgement plays a necessary part in the pursuit, through reflection on particulars, of empirical laws in Nature; for these cannot be derived *a priori* from the categories. But Kant, though conceding that through the categories and the unity of apperception mind contributes to constitute the object of its theoretical knowledge, is as reluctant as any out-and-out empiricist to conclude that mind must therefore in the last resort find in that object only its own free nature.

It is perhaps superfluous to remind the reader that although notional Judgement could be illustrated by any value-judgement, including the judgement of beauty, yet beauty, save in its general nature as value, yields no logical category.[4] For Hegel beauty—in its highest form, art—is the content of Reason in sensuous form, and revealed religion is this same content elevated to the form of imaginative myth. The distinction between art, religion, and philosophy belongs to the Philosophy of Spirit.[5] Great as are the difficulties of

[1] Cf. also ΦG, *Enc.* § 415.

[2] LL, ii, p. 216.

[3] See ch. xii, §§ 9·21 ff. above.

[4] Cf. ch. xii, § 9·26 and § 11 above.

[5] Cf. ch. xii, § 11 above, and also IH, ch. viii, § 6·2.

this doctrine, they do not belong to an exposition of Hegel's Logic.

7. The main phases of Teleology are Subjective End, Means, and Realized End.

Subjective End

External design, which Hegel so sharply criticizes when it is offered as a final interpretation of the world, provides him, nevertheless, with the first phase of Teleology. In order to understand this, we must remember that the return of explicit subjectivity, and its development through the teleological categories, will be two-sided,[1] taking the form of a gradual coalescence of object with subject. In Subjective End the subject, though formally infinite, 'has before it an objective mechanico-chemical world, to which its activity relates itself as to something already given'.[2] It is so far finite, and the further teleological categories will show the cancelling of this contingent external relation. But in this process the object, just as much as the subject, will develop; and it will, moreover, be developing its *own* subjectivity as a teleological system. These two moments of one process must throughout be held together in the reader's mind. Subject and Object will gradually conform each to its notion, and in the end the notion of each will turn out to be one and the same. On the other hand, when this occurs we shall have passed beyond Teleology, which in none of its categories can wholly transcend the opposition of means and end, and so passed beyond finitude. To activity which is an end in itself—even to the self-maintenance of a living organism—no category of Teleology is fully adequate.

7·1. The End of Subjective End may be illustrated by an agent's 'designs upon' an indifferent object which he proposes to use. But it may equally be illustrated by the urge of animal appetite, the impulse, that is, of that which has a rudimentary subjectivity to overcome the external relation between itself and its environing object by appropriating the object.[3] The tension of this urge, or rudimentary desire, shows precisely the transition from Chemism to a teleological level. The object appropriated to satisfy the subject is never

[1] See § 5 above. [2] LL, ii, pp. 219–20. [3] Cf. EL, § 204.

a *wholly* indifferent object. The satisfaction of eating may seem one-sided, but there is development of the food 'consumed' into the organism of the subject, and less rudimentary appetite is quenched in a common satisfaction.

7·2. Yet human purpose offers the clearest illustration of all the teleological categories, provided always we do not forget that purposive activity exemplifies as well higher categories with which we are not yet concerned.

If I do not misunderstand Hegel, Subjective End is the category exemplified in intention as opposed to will. I intend, let us say, to build a house. I am so far the Notion as a universal which is only potentially particular and individual. The as yet merely planned, only ideally conceived, house presents itself to me as a partial particularization of my universal self. In that I plan it, intend it, I am indeed particularized, and it is a potential final cause. But because it is only an ideally conceived self-realization, it stands over against and opposes itself as an object to my actual mere universal subjectivity; and it will continue more or less to do so until I have got it built. In this state of intending I am two selves; a universal self that is, and a particular self that is to be. Or it might be better to say that I am a single self at once in two discrepant phases. For as subject I am the Notion: I can never wholly lack any one of the three notional moments. Hence my two selves, or the two phases of myself, do not simply fall apart; I remain a single person. Because I only intend my house, the two phases or selves cannot coalesce in full individual self-realization; but even in my state of mere intention their unity is expressed in the fact that I criticize my present mere subjectivity as a defect which contrasts with the implicit totality of the Notion which I am. I tell myself that I can build the house, and that I ought to get on with it. I accept my unbuilt house as a motive, a final cause the operation of which I ought to permit because that operation would be my own self-realization. I am in fact a union of discrepant selves in tension.

7·3. If we express this category syllogistically we get a first-figure syllogism: the ideally conceived end is the particular which links the bare universality of the intending subject with its individuality. For this individuality, though not yet realized, is yet not nothing. A man is to some extent characterized by his intentions.

7·4. Thus in Subjective End the subject does *unite* its own discrepant phases; it is so far the intro-reflected totality of the Notion. But because these phases are discrepant and contradictory, the subject also at the same time turns outward, reflected into an other: the contradiction is, as always, an impulse.

This contradiction provides the antithetical phase of Teleology,

8. The Means (*das Mittel*)

In Subjective End individuality was present only as the universal particularized. I am as yet individualized only in so far as I am particularized in my ideally planned house. Only inasmuch as I have a plan have I achieved objectivity. I am an end or final cause only in intention. It is this formal intro-reflection, this defective individuality, which now seeks completion by turning outwards. It puts itself forth as power to mediate, to bridge the chasm which divides it from its still external object.

This power of mediation forthwith subjugates the external object to itself, cancelling its independent existence and appropriating it as a means. Even appetite reveals clearly this practical disproof of realism.

'The satisfaction of impulses restores the peace[1] between subject and object. The objective thing (*das Objektive*) which, so long as the contradistinction exists, i.e. so long as there is a felt want, stands on the other side, loses this one-sidedness by its union with the subject. Those who talk of the fixity and invincibility (*Unüberwindlichkeit*) of the finite, subjective and objective, may see the reverse illustrated in every operation of appetite. Appetite is, so to say, the conviction that the subjective is only a half-truth (nur einseitig ist und keine Wahrheit hat), no more adequate than the objective. But appetite in the second place carries out its conviction. It brings about the supersession of these finites: it cancels the opposition between the objective which would be and stay an objective only, and the subjective which in like manner would be and stay a subjective only.'[2]

The Object appropriated as Means is so far merely

[1] There is here a play on the words *Befriedigung* and *Frieden*.

[2] EL, § 204.

mechanical. Its relations to Subjective End and to the object to be achieved through its instrumentality are both equally external. The category of Means is thus expressible as a formal syllogism in the second figure. The subject is particularized in an object, as in Subjective End it was not; but this object is external to it.

But this externality of Means, as we have already seen in discussing appetite, is only a half-truth. When a mechanical object is appropriated as a means, its externality is in part cancelled, and just so far as this is so the Means is no longer mere Means but End partly realized. Thus we pass to the third phase of Teleology,

9. Realized End

The End is realized inasmuch as the Object appropriated as Means embodies the activity of the subject. Thus Means is now seen to be two-sided. It is (*a*) the external object appropriated and used (the popular sense of the word 'means'). But it is also (*b*) the impulse, or power, or action (according to the level upon which we choose to illustrate) embodied in this object by the appropriating subject. The means are in my power, but my power thereby becomes my means. Subjective agency and objective instrument are thus two moments inseparable within the Means as it now mediates between the subject and its object. Hence the Means is the concrete Universal, uniting Particular and Individual in itself, and so the middle term of a third-figure syllogism.

9·1. There is a defect in this syllogism which cannot be overcome within the limits of Teleology, but before we examine it some illustration of the major premiss—that is of the partial cancellation of externality in the Means—may be helpful. In the absorption of nutriment, and indeed in any process of adaptation to environment which preserves an organism, the innate impulse and the object which elicits it and is appropriated by it are together integral elements of the means to life. Again, the plough and the skill of the ploughman are distinguishable. But they are quite inseparable. The plough's independence as a physical object is cancelled, since it signifies nothing save as the ploughman's instrument. Analogously the nisus of the builder and his materials of all sorts are the two inseparable sides of his means to building the house.

9·2. We may now return to consider the syllogism as a whole. As middle term of a third-figure syllogism the Means, which we have seen to be dual, relates as follows to its extremes. (*a*) *Qua* subjective activity it connects with the major term, with the subject, that is, which is now particular in its state of intention. This major premiss is no longer unmediated, as were both the premisses of the syllogism of Means. (*b*) *Qua* itself an external Object it is externally and mechanically related to the minor term, that is, to the second Object upon which it is used as instrument; and this second, more remote Object is mechanical because, although a non-mechanical determinateness, a design or end, is impressed on it, yet this determinateness is not an element of its nature. So the plough, for example, is related to the field which it is used to plough, and an organism's digestive apparatus to that on which it feeds. This minor premiss is thus an external relation which lacks proper mediation.

9·3. Hegel's dialectic is not always easy to follow, because in concrete illustration the line to be drawn between appropriated, or 'subjectified', Object (Means) and external, more remote Object varies indefinitely from case to case. The digestive apparatus of an organism strikes one as an instrument which is, so to say, appropriate to it from the start; whereas the organism appears to appropriate its food as a quite external object. Yet 'the human soul has much to do before it makes its corporeal nature into a means',[1] and in the process of digestion some of an animal's food acts chemically upon the rest, and so functions instrumentally in a manner analogous to the digestive apparatus itself. So in conscious purposive action the means may comprise both instruments with which the agent works, and instruments which he sets to work for him, both tools and machines. Moreover, the extent to which the instrument itself realizes the subject's end, and the extent to which it remains a *mere* means, are contingent and not logically determinable. Yet activity is always to some extent an end in itself, and the means in which

[1] EL, § 208, *Zusatz*.

it is expressed is, therefore, never quite a mere means. And equally, as we have now to see, teleological activity is never completely self-realizing, and its means is, therefore, always a means to an end beyond it. The category of Realized End is just this two-sided truth.

9·4. Since the dual Means cannot fully mediate between Subjective End and its Object, it follows that that which the Means achieves is once again Means and not absolute End. The ploughman ploughs the field, but the ploughed field is a means for raising a crop, and so forth. Because no teleological working is a creation independent of a presupposed material the end it realizes is never self-sufficient.

Yet these successively appropriated means are in a measure the ends of the subject which appropriates them. The Subjective End uses mechanical processes for its own purposes. Man 'harnesses the forces of Nature', and here lies what Hegel calls 'the cunning of Reason'—of Reason, that is, manifest at the level of Teleology:

'Reason is as cunning as it is powerful. Its cunning, to speak generally, lies in the mediative action which, while it permits the Objects to follow their own [sc. finite or apparent] nature, and to act upon one another until they waste away, and does not itself directly interfere in the process, is yet only working out its own aims. With this explanation, divine Providence may be said to stand to the world and its process in the relation of absolute cunning. God lets men do as they please with their particular passions and interests; but the result is the accomplishment of—not their plans but his, and these differ decidedly from the ends primarily sought by those whom he employs.'[1]

Thus the remoter Object, which through the initial Means becomes itself a Means, has its external mechanical character cancelled thereby; it becomes one with the Subject's activity. Its mechanical externality, showing itself first as indefinite regress of means, is nothing but the distinctive externality of Objective Notion. Yet because the regressive means are *eo ipso* also ends this externality is not simply cancelled, but in it the Notion returns upon itself. The Notion is now that which has and retains overtly and explicitly *within* itself its externality *to* itself. The level of mediation is transcended, and we reach the unity of Subjective and Objective Notion

[1] EL, § 209, *Zusatz*.

in the Idea. That is, I think, the gist of the difficult dialectic of LL, ii, pp. 231–5.

10. This doctrine of Teleology has inspired Bradley's conception of the self-realizing practical idea. It is itself quite clearly inspired by Plato and Aristotle. The Greek word τέλειος, 'perfect', or perhaps 'consummate', is the adjective of τέλος, 'end', and exactly expresses Realized End. Aristotle's conception of the end of action which deliberation analyses into means[1] is here especially in point. On the whole, though with some wavering, Aristotle treats the means in the sphere of moral action as constituent of the end; so that in the activity which actualizes the successive means reached by deliberative analysis of the end, viz. the good, or apparent good, which operates as final cause, that end itself is coming to be embodied from the very start. This is the real strength of the view that, although any stick may do to beat a dog with, the moral end cannot justify evil means. It has sometimes been objected that means and end are of necessarily opposed natures: if, for example, I do work which is sheer drudgery in order to pay for my children's education, then my means cannot possibly be counted a constituent of my end. I doubt if this objection holds. At least where moral and not merely economic action is concerned, no means can, I think, fall wholly outside the end. Even my drudgery is a different thing because of the motive for which I do it; different, for example, from the drudgery of a slave. That I should at once abandon it for work more consonant with my other personal aims if I had the opportunity is merely symptomatic of the inherent defect of teleological working. In so far as the means remains contingent and external to the end, the end can be realized through alternative means. Moreover, even in economic action, in which the category of Means is specially illustrated, the means is not ultimately in total opposition to the end. For as the category of Means finds its truth in Realized End so, as both Aristotle and Hegel held, there is no meaning in the conception of economic action save as ultimately subordinate to moral action.

Yet these illustrations from the sphere of conscious pur-

[1] Cf. *Nicomachean Ethics* 1112b20 ff. and my *Aristotle*, p. 143.

pose must not deceive us. Conscious purpose, as we shall see, exemplifies higher categories than those of Teleology. Impulse or urge affords a nearer illustration, though even Life is a category of the Idea. Intrinsic value is clearly foreshadowed in Realized End, just as the last phase of Judgement was judgement of value; but only when external objectivity closes with Subjective Notion can intrinsic value come to overt expression. So long as the end is still also a means value is still relative.

XVI

THE IDEA: LIFE

1. THE Kantian Idea of Reason is conceived as a goal, a prototype set up as a maximum which we must approach, as it were, asymptotically, both in understanding the actual world and in transforming its condition. In respect of practical Ideas Kant even observes that

'nothing could be more harmful or less worthy of a philosopher than the vulgar appeal to an experience which is asserted to conflict with an Idea. Such an experience would itself never exist if, for example, political institutions were made at a fit moment in accordance with Ideas; if the place of Ideas had not been usurped by rough concepts which frustrate every good intention just because they have been drawn from experience.'[1]

Yet despite this admission, Hegel complains, Kant's Ideas are merely regulative. Most strangely, Kant denies them validity because no object congruent with them can be given in experience; because, that is, they lack precisely that which constitutes the appearance, the *untrue* being, of the actual world. But the Idea is not an unreachable beyond, a mere 'ought': it is truth, the union of the Notion and Objectivity. The Actual is not cancelled or contradicted but preserved in the categories of the Notion: 'Whatever is actual *is* only so far as it has in it and expresses the Idea.'[2] Even a bad thing, even a bad state, is only actual at all in so far as its reality still conforms in some slight measure to its notion, that is, in so far as the Idea is in it. Destroy all conformity, and its soul and body are parted; it is disintegrated into abstract thoughts on the one side, and an aggregate of individuals on the other.[3] Although Kant had full faith in the reality of spirit he could never quite possess the truth that, save as it is in the medium of spirit, nothing can be *or be known to be* real.

1·1. The Idea may be called the unity of ideal and real, of finite and infinite, of identity and difference. But these are mere formal modes of apprehending it, each designating

[1] Kant, KRV, B, p. 373, cited by Hegel in LL, ii, p. 238.

[2] LL, ii, p. 238; cf. also ch. xi, § 1·1 above. [3] LL, ii, p. 240.

some one stage of the determinate Notion. Idea in fact is the unity which every dialectical synthesis in truth is. 'We cannot begin now to ask for proof that the Idea is the truth. The proof of that is contained in the whole deduction and development of thought up to this point.'[1] The nearest clue to the Idea is the conception of pure activity, wherein the subject, its outward issue, and its return upon itself are three moments held together in the third moment in absolute triunity; a process which is result, and a result which is process.

Hegel, as we shall see, conceives this pure activity to be nothing but thought as thought truly is. Meanwhile the more particular transition from Teleology is as follows. Even in Realized End the externality of a presupposed Object confronting the subject's design is not overcome. In the Idea this externality does not simply collapse as resistance crushed; it persists as a moment embraced within the activity. For in the Idea thought overlaps and includes being; it does not nullify or neutralize it. The Idea, Hegel says in EL, § 215, 'is the course of movement (*Verlauf*) wherein the Notion, as universality which is individuality, gives itself the determination of objectivity *and of the antithesis thereto*;[2] and this externality which has the Notion for its substance finds its way back to subjectivity through its immanent dialectic'.

Yet this movement of the Idea has its own dialectical steps. Its three main phases are Life, Cognition (*das Erkennen*), and Absolute Idea.

2. Life

Hegel has attempted to show that the categories of Mechanism and Chemism are two phases in the necessary self-developing content of thought itself; that despite their titles they must be distinguished from the principles which give their names to the natural sciences of mechanics and physics on the one hand, and to chemistry on the other; that they are thus distinguishable because in Nature Mechanism and Chemism are illustrated imperfectly and, as they appear in Nature, presuppose certain peculiarities of their natural medium which are irrelevant to logic.

[1] EL, § 213, *Zusatz*.

[2] Italics mine.

In the main Hegel's case depends upon whether he succeeds in showing that these categories do inevitably emerge when the dialectic passes from Subjective to Objective Notion. But it is strengthened if we agree with him that Mechanism and Chemism are illustrated not only in Nature but also in the sphere of Concrete Spirit. If there is a mechanical behaviour of the human mind, subserving its higher functions and also constituting a level to which on occasion it may lapse, and if this mechanism of memory, association, and habit is something quite other than the mechanical functioning of a body, animate or inanimate, this would seem to be evidence for a distinct logical category of Mechanism. If we can suppress prejudice against the word 'chemical', and admit a peculiar aspect of 'chemical' affinity in human affection, then the case for Chemism receives a certain support. The point is not to be pressed so long as the whole question of 'illustration' remains *sub judice*, but the justification of Life as the first, immediate phase of the Idea depends on closely analogous considerations. We shall have shortly to examine its dialectical truth, but we shall do well to approach this examination by way of its 'illustrations'.

2·1. Nature as such is the self-external but pre-spiritual. It is the presupposition of Concrete Spirit, and the forms which it reveals to philosophic insight ascend dialectically from Space and Time to Life.[1] But life in Nature is Life 'expelled into external subsistence (*in die Äusserlichkeit des Bestehens hinausgeworfen*), and having its condition in inorganic Nature so that the moments of the Idea are a multiplicity of actual formations'.[2] Moreover, the philosophy of Nature distinguishes not one but two main forms of life, namely vegetable and animal; and the dialectical presupposition of these is a mineral world. But these distinctions are not logical: they do not issue directly from the Idea.

Nevertheless, natural life affords us the easiest initial clue to Hegel's logical category of Life, which it illustrates. Natural life is found only in a living body, which it animates as a 'soul' in the broadest Aristotelian sense of ψυχή; a term with which Aristotle covers the three main grades wherein

[1] Cf. IH, ch. viii, §§ 4·2 ff. [2] LL, ii, p. 245.

ψυχή relates as form to an ever more highly informed proximate matter, viz. vegetable, animal, and rational 'soul'.[1] That life is the body's form means that life is immediately one with its body. The body, that is to say, can be analysed physically or chemically only after its death, or by making deliberate abstraction from the fact that it lives. And in neither case is it then properly speaking a body. If its members, when severed by the knife or by abstractive analysis from their organic unity, are still called 'hand', 'heart', 'brain', &c., then these terms are equivocal. The members are what they are only for the life which animates them.[2] Correspondingly, the nature of life is not comprehended if life and body are conceived as two ingredients of a complex which death or analysis can sever. The puzzle as to how soul and body communicate is a wholly illusory problem, and at death neither does the soul perish as a physical structure dissolves, nor has it fled from the corpse to take up a disembodied but still temporal existence. These are crude misunderstandings which all equally reduce the living body to a mechanical level. Life, as Aristotle knew, possesses its body as *totum in toto et totum in qualibet parte*. It is not localized, but everywhere present and sovereign. The natural organism dies, and even while it lives there appear within the body degrees of 'organicity': some parts of it seem not to be alive as others are. But the relative 'deadness' of the callous parts, and the greater vulnerability of the more 'vital' portions, no more justify the localization of life in the body than death justifies the attribution of spatio-temporal position to a disembodied soul. The inorganic which conditions natural life, whether as a callous part or a mechanical environment, or again as its mortal fate, is not, *qua* inorganic, *for* life.[2]

2·2. It is this sovereign omnipresence of an informing principle even in natural living things which reveals the logical Idea. Hegel detects a further illustration of Life in the first phase of Concrete Spirit, which in the Philosophy of Spirit he entitles Soul (*Seele*). By Soul he there means, roughly, natural life become the explicit presupposition of consciousness.[3] At a far higher level Life is illustrated as a

[1] Cf. IH, chs. i, § 2·6, and iii, §§ 1–4.

[2] Cf. IH, ch. iii, §§ 5 ff.

[3] See ch. i, § 2·3, above.

moment of beauty.[1] Thus the category of Life finds illustration through a range of levels which rise from Nature into Concrete Spirit.

2·3. Teleology as illustrated in appetite does not exhaust the whole intelligible content of the living organism, its whole self-possessing and self-maintaining nature. Teleology expresses the organism's struggle to constitute itself at once out of and over against the merely physical level below it.[2] Life is thus more than Teleology, in which the object never quite loses the moment of presupposed externality which belongs to Objective Notion. In natural life the organic unity is sovereign and omnipresent; or, rather, its relation to its body is inadequately expressed as ubiquitous occupation, for its body is for it an object which it contains within its own immaterial nature, not that within which it is somewhere or everywhere contained.[3] So spirit as logical Life contains within itself its own external objectivity: the Idea 'gives itself the determination of objectivity and of the antithesis thereto'. Life vitalizes its Object.

2·4. But this complete possession in Life of the Object is only immediate. The phases of the Idea display the return of subjectivity in the final sense which that word receives in Hegel's Logic, namely, as the character of a subject coincident with an object which it has of its own nature put forth and posited. But in Life this coincidence is not yet mediated. Life is a subject one with its object, yet it is still 'subject' only in a proleptic sense. Its full possession of its object is not yet self-possession. Life is not a definition of spirit as explicitly self-conscious. It is more than the thinking of Subjective Notion, and it is more than the Object as thought; but it is not yet the developed coincidence of these in fully concrete thought.

3. Life subdivides into (A) Living Individual (*Individuum*), (B) Life-Process, and (C) Kind or Genus (*Gattung*). The dialectic in LL is to me highly obscure, and I find it often

[1] In the *Philosophische Propädeutik* (1809–11) Hegel had actually identified Life with the beautiful; see JE, iii, p. 142. In his early writings *Leben* is more or less equivalent to *Geist*.

[2] Cf. IH, ch. iii, § 5·3.

[3] In biology *für sich* and *für uns* are not so easy to equate as they are in more abstract special sciences.

impossible to decide where Hegel is drawing distinctions which he regards as logical, and where he is merely illustrating from natural life. I shall, therefore, take the EL version as a basis.

(A) The living agent as it emerges from Realized End is universal subject fully particularized in its immediate possession of its object. That is to say, it is immediate individual: Life is essentially something alive. Natural life in its first phase is a singular living organism which comes to life and dies, but we must endeavour to see clearly what Hegel means by this immediate individuality in logical Life. His point is that here the subject, spirit as living agent, is immediately one with its own external being, with an externality, that is, which is an explicit moment of its own spiritual nature, because we have passed from Objective Notion to Idea. This Unity cannot be thought save as a totality of the notional moments, a syllogism in itself, an *internal* realization of End in which Mechanism and Chemism play no part. Life to be thought at all must be thought as a living *being*. Although its Being—its internal externality, so to say—is so far not mediated, yet Life has not the abstractness, the defective individuality, which in varying degree all the categories preceding the Idea have revealed.

3·1. Hegel, however, analyses Living Individual into three subphases which are not altogether easy to distinguish from their analogues in Nature and Concrete Spirit. (i) Life as Universal may be called Sensibility; an indefinitely determinable receptivity which, when it is determined by impressions, merely reduces them back into the unity of self-feeling. It absorbs all externality, and brings it back to simple universality. (ii) As Particular, Life may be called Irritability or Impulse: it reacts upon its own externality, and is thus in reciprocal relation with it. But (i) and (ii) are mere abstract moments of the concrete vitality expressed in (iii) Reproduction. This is the self-renewal of Life, which in Nature is manifest as the vital agent's constant self-restoration from—or perhaps self-assertion as the unity of—the inner distinction of limbs and organs which are always producing and renewing themselves through a process of using each other as means. This process is competitive, but it is *eo ipso* co-operative, 'because nothing is thereby produced but the subject: in other words, the subject only reproduces itself'.[1]

4. (B) *Life-Process.* Life as intro-reflected, self-constitutive, Living Individual inevitably now presupposes what Hegel in EL, § 219, calls 'an inorganic nature confronting it'. The phrase is liable to mislead. Hegel means not a mechanico-chemical environment—that has no place within the Idea—but, as the rest of the section explains, an environment felt by the subject (*a*) as alien, but also (*b*) as a moment of its own nature in which it must complete itself. Life in this phase is a self-contradiction: it is and is not its own objectivity. In short it is 'pain' of 'need', and it could not be this if the confronting 'inorganic' nature were not within it as a moment of its notion.

4·1. This appeal to 'pain' and 'need' in the discussion of a logical category may seem strange, but Hegel's meaning is plain. That the tension of unsatisfied want is painful is the clearest indication that the wanted object lies within the subject. When Plato said that a man can only desire 'what is unprovided and absent, something which he has not and is not, and which he lacks',[2] he was right, inasmuch as the object of desire has no being as an external thing. This is obvious in the case of desiring a future event, but it is equally true in cases which we express loosely as desire for a presently existing thing. I say, 'I desire this apple', but in fact I desire no actually existent external thing, but a state of myself eating the apple, and this state is *ex hypothesi* not actual. But that is not to say that the object of desire has no being at all. It is not an external, 'realistic' thing, but it has being as an element within a world with which the desiring subject is continuous; a world with which in desiring he is already partially identical and in satisfying his desire will more fully identify himself. The external 'real' things which we say loosely that we desire, belong to the 'detached' object-world of the Understanding, not to the object of desire.

In respect of logical Life the pain of want illustrates the

[1] EL, § 218, and cf. LL, ii, pp. 251–2. I think we may here detect an analogue of the cunning of Reason; cf. above, ch. xv, § 9·4.

[2] *Symposium* 200 E.

beginning of mediation. The subject is at first immediately omnipresent; it has 'lost itself' in its object. Hence mediation brings no mere severance. The subject is now faced, not by a blank external other, but by something with which it still identifies itself. It is severed only from itself, and pain in natural life precisely illustrates this.

It is important to observe that this distinction in union of object and subject prefigures the analogous distinction in thinking and knowing, which falls for consideration in the next chapter. We must live before we can think and know, and we could not know if the identity of subject and object in Life were not the basis of our knowing.

4·2. Life is thus here a process of impulse to transcend the internal incompleteness of 'want'. The object of its want is within it, yet no longer one with its individual nature as were the members in the Irritability or Impulse of Living Individual. This self-contradiction of Life belongs to the living individual as such, and is to be reconciled only in a new phase of Life.

In this Process of want and impulse Life is Particular: the immediate Individual-Universal of Living Individual has broken down, because the individual has turned out not to be self-sufficient. But the object of its want, since this lies at once within and without it, can be nothing but another individual. That is to say, Life now emerges as (C) Genus or Kind (*Gattung*).

5. The defect and insufficiency of Living Individual has its truth in the thought of the universal Kind which manifests itself in individuals. This Kind is neither the genus of Nature nor the logical genus which emerged in Subjective Notion. The former illustrates it and the latter is a category presupposed by it. The Kind as final phase of the Idea in its immediacy is (i) 'the identity of the individual's self-feeling in what at the same time is another self-subsistent individual'.[1] The individual finds and feels itself (in Nature through sexual affinity) in another individual, and so far it realizes its individuality as Kind or Genus. But the individual is thereby universal genus only in germ and not explicitly, only *an sich* and not *für sich*. What is *for* it is still only another living

[1] LL, ii, p. 260.

individual. Hence (ii) this reciprocal relation between the individuals is again a contradiction. It is the germ of fresh living individuals, but it can further actualize the universality towards which it strives only through the process of the generations. In Nature the individuals sustain the genus through procreation, but themselves perish. In Logic there is so far no more than an indefinite regress of Living Individuals. But (iii) even the natural kind is more than this abstract universal of mere repetition, just as the life of a natural organism does not perish *as* its body perishes. And in Life, which is the Idea, the moment of individuality is internal to the Kind. The Kind, as it were, not merely creates individuals, but transcends them and returns upon itself from them. 'It is then the Idea which is related to itself as Idea, the Universal which has universality for its determinateness and its There-being.'[1] That is to say, the Idea is then universal subject which has for its inner moment of externality not anything particular which (though internally) conditions and limits it, but a fully commensurate universal objective self. It is concrete Universal-Individual. It is spirit as Life and nothing but Life.

5·1. But this is more than Life. In Nature life even as genus exists on sufferance of environing externality, even if this environment is not *for* life mechanico-chemical. In Logic the full mastery by Life of what I have called its internal moment of externality is what we must think as the truth of Life. But in this truth Life transcends itself, and spirit passes to define itself afresh as the Idea of Cognition (*das Erkennen*). Life's immediate self-possession in its 'body', its objective but internal *alter ego*, is now mediated in a phase of self-consciousness or, perhaps it would be better to say, self-thinking.

[1] LL, ii, p. 262.

XVII

COGNITION: THE IDEAS OF THE TRUE AND THE GOOD

1. In Life thought and Being are as yet immediately one. Life is only the germ of thought, although without this germinal form Hegel's conception of thought is unintelligible. In Cognition the Idea again puts forth from itself the moment of Being, and so mediates its living immediacy. Yet this newly released Being or objectivity is still explicitly a moment within the Idea itself; it is still explicitly identical with the subject.

This Hegel emphasizes by introducing Cognition with an illuminating criticism of Kant's attack on rational psychology.[1] The gist of it is this. Kant convicts rational psychology of illegitimately erecting the 'I think', the abstract mode of self-consciousness, into a substance qualitatively simple and independent of spatio-temporal existence. But he only succeeds by means of adopting an equally one-sided position. He argues in a Humian manner that if all empirical content is excluded, as the rationalists profess to exclude it, nothing but the empty unity of apperception remains. If, he says, we try to think what the thinking subject is, we are thereby trying to make it an object. But in thinking any object we necessarily presuppose the subject, and this case can be no exception: the subject, so to say, remains at the back of our heads, and we cannot get it before us as a known object. The subject cannot know itself as thinking subject, but only as phenomenal object; that is, as an empirical self which is not only a mere appearance but also quite innocent of subjectivity.

Hegel retorts that this is barbarous. Kant has wholly failed to grasp the nature of self-consciousness, which is in fact manifested even in empirical experience. He has not seen that the problem of the always presupposed subject, which is said to prevent our knowing the subject as an objective content, has its converse in the fact that equally in

[1] LL, ii, pp. 264–9.

assuming the subject we inevitably presuppose the object: 'The ego thinks *something*, either itself or something else.' That is to say, as Hegel so frequently elsewhere expresses the situation, the presupposing of the subject is not a mysteriously isolated necessity of experience, a mere form which waits upon sense-intuition for its object: subject and object, as Fichte saw,[1] equally posit and presuppose each other within an 'original unity'.

It is this original unity of thought and Being, developed through the whole Logic from Pure Being up to the level of the Notion as explicitly self-conscious thought, which constitutes the Idea as Cognition. To understand Cognition we must grasp the precise sense in which the object of Cognition is other than the subject and yet within it and identical with it.

1·1. Cognition, then, is the antithesis which begins to mediate the immediacy of Life. The subject again puts forth the object from itself as its own other, but the object already is, and still remains, within the subject and identical with it. Hence it is now put forth as explicitly both (*a*) the very self of the subject, as it already was *immediately* in Life; and (*b*) the object of the subject. As it were, the two moments of itself (*a*) as *ego* and (*b*) as *alter* are held together by the subject. The Idea now explicitly presupposes *itself* as an external object-world.

1·2. This will perhaps become clearer if we distinguish the object of Cognition from Objective Notion. The latter is known object presupposing knowing subject, but the former is the knowing subject's object *qua itself a knowing*. We might in fact summarize the three main phases of the Notion in Aristotelian terminology, and say that Subjective Notion is *νόησις*; Objective Notion is *νόησις νοητοῦ*; Idea is *νόησις νοήσεως*, although only in Absolute Idea is the nature of the object as itself a knowing fully consummated.

That in the Idea—that is, in thought which is explicitly in the form of thought, or conforms to its notion—the object as well as the subject is a knowing, can be illustrated in terms of individual self-consciousness. (A) The world which I know, I know as a world external to me; a world which

[1] Cf. IH, ch. vii, § 6.

I distinguish as object from myself as subject. But (B) the world which I know is the world of *my ideas*. Whatever I assert of it, claiming that what I assert is true beyond my direct awareness of it (however the limits of direct awareness are to be fixed), still qualifies it as *for me*. It is in that sense wholly within me. It is my idea. (A) and (B), which are together true, are equally false if either is insisted on to the exclusion of the other. (A) by itself leads to realism, to the philosophy which consists only in the seeking of an excuse not to philosophize. An external world not also internal could be the object neither of will nor of theoretical knowing. (B) by itself leads to solipsism, which is a mere stultifying persistence in contradiction. I cannot assert the world to be nothing but my own idea, because by that very assertion I determine its nature over against something else, which on my solipsist hypothesis does not exist.[1] In both (A) and (B) it is forgotten that in all self-consciousness the subject is individual only because it is essentially universal.

Cognition in its general nature is at once this recognition of the opposition of subject and object and the certainty of their ultimate identity. Cognition, as we shall see, divides into two phases, theoretical thinking and will; but both these activities deny the absolute, and affirm the relative, externality of their object. 'Reason', says Hegel, 'comes to the world with an absolute faith in its ability to make the identity (of subject and object) explicit, and tor aise its certitude to truth; and with the impulse to posit the nullity of that opposition which it sees to be implicitly null.'[2]

1·3. The two main phases into which Cognition as antithesis to Life divides are entitled in LL the Idea of the True and the Idea of the Good, in EL Cognition (sc. Cognition proper) and Will (*das Wollen*). In the first attitude the subject strives to nullify the opposition by admitting the object within itself. This attitude implies that for the subject the object is presupposed: 'The Idea at first merely gives itself a content whose foundation is *given* and in which only the

[1] I have expressed Hegel's position in what Dr. Ewing would doubtless call an 'epistemological' argument for idealism (cf. IH, ch. xiii, § 6·1), but the reader will easily see that for Hegel the reasoning is metaphysical, or if the word is preferred, 'ontological'.

[2] EL, § 224.

form of externality has been sublated.'[1] In the second attitude the subject strives to cancel the opposition by subduing the object to itself, by constructing and not merely construing it. Yet already in the first attitude 'the form of externality has been sublated'; i.e. I seem to accept the world, and to contribute nothing, but I am nevertheless construing the world as my idea. And in the second attitude, although I construct my world, yet I am only reconstructing what I have already construed. The second attitude is logically posterior to the first, but both are meaningless outside the antithesis which they constitute.

2. The Idea of the True (Cognition Proper)[2]

Truth is thought utterly coincident with its own Being. It is Reason fully concrete, and our philosophical thinking 'illustrates' it. Absolute Idea is this truth, but the Idea of the True is not. The Idea of the True is the True contrasted with the Good which is final and formal cause of volitional activity. Hence Cognition proper finds illustration in Understanding and not in Reason, and it may be called 'finite':

> 'The finitude of Cognition lies in the presupposition of a world already in existence (*vorgefunden*), and in the consequent view of the subject as a *tabula rasa*. . . . This Cognition does not recognize in itself the activity of the Notion—an activity which it is implicitly but not *for* itself. In its own estimation its procedure is passive. Really that procedure is active.'[3]

In short this category shows only the bare theoretical truth which for the Understanding is the full nature of truth, although it displays it not simply as it is for the Understanding but in process of sublation.

2·1. This becomes clearer when we examine the subcategories of Cognition Proper. Its two main phases are Analytic Cognition and Synthetic Cognition, and the latter subdivides into Definition, Division, and Theorem or Proposition.

The reader's first impression may be that this is mere

[1] LL, ii, p. 276.

[2] In both Logics Hegel's exposition in the sections under this head is fairly clear and straightforward. I shall therefore not often cite particular passages.

[3] EL, § 226, *Zusatz*.

repetition; that the thought of the Understanding has been already criticized and sublated in Essence, and then again in Judgement and Syllogism. Why, he may ask, do we at this stage come upon fresh categories attributed to the Understanding? The answer is this: The categories of Essence are those with which the Understanding operates *par excellence* in the special sciences to constitute its phenomenal objective world, and Judgement and Syllogism (in particular Judgement and Syllogism of Necessity) express this operation as subjective thinking. For the Understanding (*a*) the categories of Essence characterize the world which it experiences, but do not characterize it as explicitly object-for-subject; and (*b*) the categories of Judgement and Syllogism display the purely formal subjective side of the Understanding's industry. But Cognition Proper contains both these aspects sublated: it is Spirit self-defined as the world *qua* the subject's thinking, or as the subject's thinking *qua* construing a world which is for it its own. For, as we have already seen, Cognition in general is distinctively characterized as the duality of a world which is at once the object-of-the-subject and at the same time is within the subject. A category of Essence can be illustrated by a physical event, and a category of Judgement or Syllogism can be symbolized in letters; but of Cognition Proper the only possible illustration is a form of experience. Its subdivisions, that is to say, will be the *methods* with which Understanding operates. The contrast between Essence, Subjective Notion, and Cognition Proper may be thus briefly expressed: (*a*) The Understanding judges and syllogizes, operating with (*b*) the categories of Essence[1] upon (*c*) its object. But (*a*), (*b*), and (*c*) together, the categorizing Understanding together with its object, constitute Cognition Proper. At the same time Cognition Proper is the special analogue within the Idea of Subjective Notion. Its constituent methods, Definition, Classification, and Demonstration of Theorems, will recall respectively Notion as such, Judgement, and Syllogism more directly than they will recall the categories of Essence.[2]

[1] In mathematics only with the categories of Quantity.

[2] In the account of Cognition which Hegel gives in LL there persists an

3. Analytic Cognition

In Cognition Proper the subject, striving to overcome the opposition of an object implicitly identical with itself, admits the object into itself; or rather, perhaps, submits to being constituted by the object, viewing itself as inactive and non-contributory. In its first phase, Analytic Cognition, there are two inseparable moments each of which has sometimes been mistaken for the whole nature of analysis. Analytic Cognition is not (*a*) the mere extraction of determinations from a ready-made object, as the empirical realist must maintain; nor is it (*b*) merely the mind's positing of its own subjective forms in an object which is therefore not taken as a thing in itself, as the subjective idealist must hold. Because Analytic Cognition is the first phase of Cognition Proper, its inactive non-contributory character is marked; nevertheless both these moments can be detected in it.

3·1. This becomes evident, Hegel thinks, if we examine the actual procedure of the analytic method in special sciences. Analysis takes the individual concrete sensuous object as datum, and resolves the differences it finds in it into abstract general universals. The chemist, for example, analyses flesh into nitrogen, carbon, hydrogen, &c., and then tells us that flesh *is* these universal matters. Or else analysis keeps the concrete object as a ground, disregards its particular differences as unessential, and abstracts a universal which is still nevertheless concrete in the sense that it does not abstract from the concreteness of the given object. It elicits a genus, a law, a force, or a cause; a principle, that is, which classifies individual concretes or 'governs' their behaviour. In the latter case the datum has been a problem which the scientist has set himself to solve analytically. In either case the two moments mentioned above are present. For (*a*) the determinations reached by analysis, the constituents of flesh or the law or cause exemplified in the phenomenon, are taken as belonging to the object and not as any

undercurrent of exposition in teleological and syllogistic terms. This is natural, since the dialectic of the Notion, and *a fortiori* that of the Idea, is explicit development (cf. ch. xi, § 1·1 above), but for the sake of simplicity I shall ignore it. I think it presents no special difficulty.

contribution which the mind makes; but (*b*) these determinations are *abstract* universals. They have the form of sheerly subjective thinking, the mere formal self-identity of a general character or law divorced from objective differentiation *in re*, and so merely 'mental'. But this subjectivity is no active contribution by the subject to the nature of the object.

To any philosophy of the Understanding which takes Analytic Cognition for the full nature of thinking the relation of these two moments presents an insuperable difficulty. The empirical realist cannot, if he is consistent, allow that there is anything to be learned by thinking, and the subjective idealist inevitably turns thinking into arbitrary fancy.

3·2. As analysis proceeds its empty inactive character becomes more and more obvious. In carrying farther the solution of its problem it obeys the attenuated logic of Porphyry's Tree. The universals which it first reaches have still a vestige of that concreteness which belonged to the initial data, and from them analysis abstracts the yet more general determinations, the 'higher' generic character, the 'higher' law or cause. The essence of that which is analysed is sought in a more and more empty universal, and the goal of the search appears to be sheer tautologous self-identity without content. This seeming progress is the wholly undialectical repetition of the initial act of analysis. The universal thus elicited may be termed genus, which necessarily implies specification; or cause, which is essentially correlated with effect; or in general whole, which must imply parts. But in analytic procedure these logical couplings are still merely *given*: the only thinking in analysis is a dwindling towards blank identity.

3·3. This external formality of analytic thought reveals the problem which so painfully exercised Kant: the paradox by which Understanding transcends the sensuously given and yet must still accept sense as its co-operant partner.[1] Hence the most favourable field for analysis is to be found in mathematics, for the medium of mathematical thinking is what Kant called a *pure* manifold of sense-intuition.

Arithmetic and algebra are the purest illustration of

[1] Hegel's account of analytic thinking accords with Kant's; see IH, ch. ix, § 4·32.

analysis. Other special sciences begin with a concrete, sensuously given subject-matter. This offers a contingent manifold upon which all subsequent progress depends. But the subject-matter of arithmetic and algebra is discrete quantity, totally purged of all peculiarity of relation: its determinations are *ex hypothesi* purely external. The composition and separation of numbers depends wholly on an activity of the subject which is quite contingent so far as the method of mathematical operation is concerned: we manipulate what numbers we choose, and any man may set us a sum to do. When we do manipulate, our guide is the immanent principle of analytic identity, which appears as equality in the various.[1] Progress consists in the reduction of the unequal to ever greater equality. The procedure is wholly analytic; it solves a problem, but it never proves a theorem. If the operation were to be disguised as the demonstration of a theorem, the purely external distinction between the two sides of the equation would at once show up the proof as a trivial assertion of identity. Kant called '$5+7 = 12$' a synthetic proposition. It is not. The distinction between $5+7$ and 12 is founded on no category of Quality, Essence, or Notion; it depends upon nothing but the point at which we choose to break off an operation of adding which can be safely entrusted to a machine. If it were synthetic it would require a proof, but to prove it we could only once more count. On the other hand, the higher forms of algebraical analysis involve categories which reveal the return of Quality within Quantity,[2] and the method involved does begin to become synthetic.

4. SYNTHETIC COGNITION

This, speaking generally, is the opposite of Analytic Cognition. Yet it is to be remembered that in the Notion, and more particularly in the Idea, dialectic is development which preserves rather than cancels. Analysis works with synthesis in view, and there is no such thing as a purely analytic thinking.

Analysis started with the individual *datum*, trying to apprehend what *is* as a bare identity, not as a necessary connexion of differences in a unity. Synthesis, on the other hand,

[1] Cf. ch. iii, §§ 4·1 ff. above. [2] Cf. ibid., §§ 5·5 ff.

starts with the universal reached by analysis, and descends again to the individual. It does, moreover, endeavour to grasp the determinations of its object as connected and unified: it tries to form a notion of them. Hence analysis exhibits only the first moment of the Notion, sheer universality; but Synthetic Cognition moves through all three notional moments. Its three phases are Definition, Classification by Division, and Theorem or Demonstrated Proposition (*Lehrsatz*).

4·1. Definition

Synthesis as Definition strives to define the individual object by genus and differentia; that is, starting with the universal reached by analysis, it particularizes this to individuality, defining the object as *infima species*. It thus has for its content not the bare universal but the totality of the Notion. Yet mere analysis has supplied the material and the only ground (*Begründung*) for Definition:[1] the abstract universal of analysis was got empirically from the sensuously given, and no sure principle dictates its particularization. At any rate in Nature, and to some extent in Concrete Spirit, there is nothing to guard against the selection of a contingent character either as genus or differentia. For example, among animals only men have lobes to their ears, but this does not notionally distinguish man from brute. Thus Definition 'presents nothing but the form-determinations of the Notion upon a given content'.[2] Subject and object are not congruent. On the one side thinking makes an external beginning; on the other side the object is a given manifold of contingent qualities. Definition cannot determine which of these qualities are to be selected to fill the triple notional form, and consequently those actually selected are mere marks for subjective recognition. In Definition there is always an arbitrary element of convention.

4·11. The products of self-conscious purpose are comparatively easy to define, because the End purposed supplies a criterion for distinguishing between the notional and the merely contingent. Geometrical objects, again, are easily definable, because space, as Kant showed, is at once a pure

[1] See EL, § 229. [2] LL, ii, p. 296.

a priori form and a pure manifold, an *a priori* content, of sense-intuition. Hegel calls it *ein unsinnliches Sinnliches*.[1] 'Intuition', he says, 'is raised to its abstraction. It is a *form* of intuition, but still it is intuition. It is sensuous, the self-externality of sensuousness itself, the pure privation of the Notion (*Begrifflosigkeit*).'[2] When we determine geometrical space in figures, these are its only relevant, and therefore its essential, determinations. Geometrical figures are 'perfect'. Like the product of purpose, they are what they ought to be; or, as Hegel puts it, 'their general notion-determination and their more precise, specific difference have their simple unhindered reality in them'.[3]

The further properties of space do not affect geometrical definition. But in Nature and Concrete Spirit definition is never self-guaranteeing. The universal can only be selected for its relative permanence, or for its wider extension, its greater community. Moreover, a sport of Nature or a defective specimen, and in the sphere of Concrete Spirit a bad man or a bad state, are sufficient to upset the proposed definition: the actual specimen 'shows implicitly what it ought to be, but can equally show, according to the negative Judgement of the Notion, that its actuality corresponds only imperfectly with that notion'.[4] These defective individuals, characteristic of the transience and contingency which beset the Idea in its phenomenal externalization, must be regarded as conforming to the definition before they can be condemned as defective specimens. But their very defect consists in their failure to exhibit some determination which the definition contains. If natural science chooses to discount sports, it does so by virtue of an implicit principle which is beyond the principle of Definition. It appeals to an ideal

[1] So Aristotle assigns to the objects of mathematics a νοητὴ ὕλη, an 'intelligible matter'; cf. *Metaphysics* 1036a, 9–12. Aristotle's doctrine does not, I think, differ from Plato's. Paton observes the kinship of Kant's theory of geometry with Plato's; *Kant's Metaphysic of Experience*, i, p. 159.

[2] LL, ii, p. 313, an admirable summing up of Kant's doctrine. Hegel hastens to add that it is a pitiful error to suppose that geometry bases its proofs on intuition and for that reason ranks high as a science. Proof can rest upon nothing but thought, and its sensuous basis ranks geometry low as a science. Its merit is due to the high degree in which it abstracts from sense.

[3] Ibid., p. 291.

[4] Ibid., p. 295.

norm, in fact to the Notion; yet it does so not from any explicit knowledge of the Notion but through that instinct of Reason which is in the Understanding, and plays its part there as 'a dim feeling, an indefinite though more profound sense, an inkling of the essential, preceding the discovery in Nature and Concrete Spirit of genera to which the Understanding sought subsequently to give determinate externality'.[1]

4·12. Thus Definition as a self-definition of spirit is the thought of the objective world as the self-complete *infima species*. It is the thought which inspired Aristotle to proclaim the *infima species* substance, and to reject equally the claims of the genus and the singular. Hegel's whole treatment of Synthetic Cognition might be regarded as an effort to resolve dialectically the difficulties involved in Aristotle's theory of definition and demonstration.[2]

If Definition were a fully true category, then genus, species, and specimen would coalesce. But the objective world in Definition is neither the one specimen nor reducible to one species. The moment of particularization at once implies other species of the universal genus. Hence Definition develops to its antithesis in

4·2. Classification by Division (*Einteilung*)

'Division' here means the ordinary logical division by dichotomy, the διαίρεσις which Plato regarded as together with συναγωγή constituting διαλεκτική.[3] Its formula is as follows: Divide the genus *A* by some one differentia *B* into *A*-which-is-*B* and *A*-which-is-not-*B*. Then divide each of these halves by a further differentia *C*. The product will be (i) *ABC*, (ii) *AB*-not-*C*, (iii) *A*-not-*B* which is *C*, (iv) *A*-not-*B* which is not-*C*. So proceed until *infimae species* are reached. If now each differentia exhaustively divides its genus into two contrary species, the result will be a genus systematically articulated by disjunction into its *infimae species*. But, as Aristotle pointed out,[4] Division provides in itself no guarantee that the differentia is anything but a character casually

[1] Ibid., p. 294.
[2] See IH, ch. iv.
[3] Cf. *Phaedrus*, 265 c ff., where συναγωγή is an *analytic* process in Hegel's sense. Cf. also ch. xii, §§ 7·22 ff. above.
[4] Cf. *De Partibus Animalium*, i, ch. 2–4, and also 643^b, 10 ff.

selected and not essential. Hegel marks it as symptomatic of the impotent profusion of Nature that natural genera can never be thus systematically articulate.[1] While the natural scientist pursues the ideal of classification by dichotomous division, he is always being forced to begin all over again. He can seldom determine the negative half of his division as the one precise contrary of the positive. As in Definition so in Classification by Division an inkling of Reason is alone responsible for any progress achieved. In Division the notional form is still external to a content which has been abstracted by analysis from the sensuously given. As classification proceeds, other equally possible *fundamenta divisionis* occur, or—which is the same thing—the classified *infimae species* reveal their possession of universal characters other than those which have been taken as genus and differentiae. The effort at particularization fails, and the relation of Universal to Individual is still contingent and unmediated.

Hence arises the final phase of Synthetic Cognition:

4·3. Theorem, *or* Demonstrated Proposition

The Understanding must now attempt to mediate, i.e. to demonstrate a necessary connexion between an *infima species* and the universal character selected as its genus. The sphere *par excellence* of synthetic demonstration is geometry. The science of number, as we have seen, only approaches a synthetic method in its higher branches, and the natural sciences presuppose an object-world too concretely sensuous to permit much progress towards demonstrative proof. Hegel accordingly illustrates the category of *Lehrsatz* from the First Book of Euclid in a most instructive manner. We shall do well to follow him in some detail through LL, ii, pp. 306 ff. The axioms of Euclid are not subject to proof within the science of geometry, but they are not in themselves self-evident and so without need of proof. If they were, they would be sheer tautologies. The proof they demand is logical, a deduction from the Notion; and this belongs to another science (sc. the Philosophy of Nature, in which the nature of Space is criticized). The definitions of

[1] Cf. ch. xii, §§ 7·21 ff. above.

Euclid, on the other hand, are products of analysis. They contain a proximate genus and a specific differentia taken directly from the sensible object as immediately given; for example, the triangle is defined as a plane figure bounded by three straight lines. A series of further determinations is then demonstrated to belong to the triangle, until a fuller definition of triangle is reached in the theorem of Pythagoras. Euclid has always been praised for the orderly progression of these proofs, but though their formal consecutiveness is highly convenient, it is not notional development; its sole principle is the determining of magnitude in terms of equality. Since the demonstration starts from the sensuously given, the first theorem can only display equality through sensuous coincidence and not as a thought-determination. For thought, that is, for Understanding, the fixing of two sides and the included angle already gives the whole triangle, and the remaining angles and side required for the sensuous expression of the triangle are for thought a superfluity. Thus the purpose of the theorems contained in Euclid's First Book is to reduce the sensuous triangle to the simplest conditions, namely to determine its angles through the mutual relations of its sides until the right-angled triangle, the simplest and most regular triangle, is shown as determining its magnitude *in itself* through an equation of its hypotenuse with the sides adjacent to the right angle. The initial definition of triangle, which specified no relations of angles and sides, is thus completed, but the process has only been a passage from equality sensuously expressed to equality understood as immanent in the figure. Euclid ends Book I with the theorem of Pythagoras, and then proceeds in the same way to reduce other triangles to uniformity, closing Book II with the reduction of the rectangle to the square.

The defect, the notionless character, of this demonstration is clear if we examine the construction, which is the middle term of the proof. The construction is introduced externally; it does not flow necessarily from the universal as its essential particularization to individuality. The produced lines, the perpendiculars dropped, &c., are merely taken up out of a presupposed sensuous content. As they are first introduced, there is nothing to indicate whether the purpose of the construction is a theorem or a problem. Only when the proof is complete does the necessity of the demonstration through the construction emerge; and it then emerges as compulsion upon the subject, not as the expression of the subject's activity. Thus the defect of synthetic demonstration is apparent equally in object and subject. The details of the construction have *followed* from the nature of the object as given, whereas in the proof they become the *ground* mediating the object. We are thus concluding to the object's inner nature through its mere externals. That is to say, (*a*) the proof is no genesis of the object, but reverses the object's real nature; and so (*b*) the ground is a subjective ground in the sense of a mere compulsive *causa cognoscendi*. The reader will remember the observation that to exert and to suffer compulsion are both unfree.[1]

4·31. This account of geometry largely accords with Plato's description of geometrical procedure in *Republic* vi–vii. Aristotle took a more optimistic view of the synthetic method, basing syllogistic demonstration both in mathematics and natural science on no mere inkling of rationality such as Hegel holds to be in the last resort the sole salvation of all special sciences, but on indisputably self-evident rational intuitions.[2] To Plato as to Hegel the unquestioned presuppositions of ordinary mathematics show its defect and not its certain truth, and Hegel like Plato denies any validity to the synthetic method in philosophy, where Spinoza attempted to employ it. The brute necessity of a geometrical proof, which reverses the self-developing nature of the object and so merely compels thought, is precisely what Plato is emphasizing when he observes that διάνοια merely proceeds downwards from its given and unquestioned starting-point, whereas philosophical dialectic proceeds upwards to an ἀνυπόθετος ἀρχή, whence it again descends. Philosophy, that is to say, reasons upwards to a source which is the Good, the cause equally of the being and knowability of all things, the truth which is explicated in detail in the subsequent descent. Plato further implies—and this becomes the central point in Hegel's theory of knowledge—that the Good to which philosophic thought reaches up is at

[1] See ch. viii, § 7·4 above.

[2] Cf. IH, ch. iv, §§ 2 ff.

the same time the immanent source of its ascending activity. That is why the starting-point of philosophy is not a fixed assumption which it cannot question, but a presaging, a prophetic inkling.

5. The Idea of the Good

Upon the Idea of the Good, which Hegel calls alternatively Will or, again, the Practical Idea, depends his whole ethical doctrine. It has therefore to be considered in some detail. I shall draw mainly on the LL version, which is rather summarily telescoped in EL. Two preliminary points may perhaps help to orientate the discussion. In the first place the phrase 'Idea of the Good' may suggest Plato, but the Platonic Form of the Good—or the Good, as Plato more often simply calls it—is the object of a knowing which is at once theoretical and practical,[1] whereas Hegel's Idea of the Good, as its synonyms proclaim, is the expression of spirit only as will. Secondly it is important to remember that Hegel works largely with Kant in view, although in the relevant context of neither Logic is Kant's name mentioned, except in the *Zusatz* to EL, § 234.

5·1. In Cognition Proper, or the Idea of the True, the subject took up a non-contributory attitude: it was the bare indeterminate Universal accepting its content from a presupposed actual world. In Will, or the Idea of the Good, the subject reverses this attitude and imposes determination upon the world which confronts it. In short, for Will (i) itself, (ii) the world as it ought to be, and (iii) the world as it is which confronts the subject, are all actual; but the cognized determinations of (iii) are now held null and void—the realist attitude of the Understanding is cancelled—although (ii) lacks, as yet, immediate external Being. On the other hand, Will, although it is the antithesis of Cognition Proper, has developed out of it, preserving rather than simply cancelling it. Hence (*a*) the world which the subject confronts is an object cognized as determinate, and it is these complex determinations of the object, through which Cognition Proper has given itself content, that Will in its activity of

[1] Cf. my *Aristotle*, pp. 128–9. The Platonic Form of the Good corresponds rather to Hegel's Absolute Idea.

self-imposition counts as null and invalid. But also (*b*) the subject wills not as bare Universal but as actual determinate Individual. For it has got from Cognition Proper its content of necessary truth, which has turned out (in the transition from the Idea of the True to the Idea of the Good) to be its own free self-expression, the Good which it is and wills to impose. For the subject knows *itself* as good: knowledge of intrinsic value is self-consciousness, awareness of the real as not alien but one with the subject. For that reason Will posits the object-world of Cognition Proper as not after all self-subsistent. The active subject now takes its object as contingent and as determinable by the subject. For if the necessity at last discovered in the object by Cognition Proper turns out really to be the activity of the subject, then it follows that the object now becomes a contingent and determinable object, and that the gift of determination, so to say, now lies in the subject. It is now the subject which is to give the object-world its true nature, to make it what it ought to be, the expression, i.e., of that goodness with which the subject identifies itself.

5·2. The Idea of the Good is thus the Kantian good will.[1] It has the totality of the Notion in it. It is therefore absolute and universal as Kant held it to be. Yet it is not, as in Kant's hands it became, the abstract empty universal; it is an objective actuality, the concrete content of the individual self-conscious subject. What it lacks is not objectivity but mere external immediate actuality, which is just what the cognized world confronting it possesses. This confronting world must accordingly be forced, as it were, to yield up its external actuality by means of the subject's good actions; by actions, that is, wherethrough the confronting world of Cognition Proper shall at once and in one (*a*) express and realize the nature of the subject as good, and (*b*) make good its own nature. The Good Will is infinite, absolute, and non-contingent; it is intrinsically and not hypothetically good, and therefore does not wait upon external actualization for its validity. But it consists in no empty principle of non-contradiction but in the will to do this and that, to transform the detailed content cognized as actual into being

[1] Cf. also what was said of Fichte in IH, ch. vii, §§ 6·3 and 6·4.

intrinsically good. Thus the finitude which still infects the Good Will consists only in its own lack of immediate external being. The apparent *opposition* of the Good Will to an immediate confronting externality is for Will a *simple* determinateness of its *own* content: it is any particular good end.

Hegel is here[1] insisting that the Good Will implies that the Good must be real in the sense of rooted in the nature of Reality, with which the subject in Will identifies itself, *prior* to any particular realization of it in immediate external Being. If this were not so, the operation of an ideal in moral action would be inexplicable. Consequently the syllogism expressing the realization of Will in this or that good end differs from the formal syllogism of Teleology.[2] In both the content is finite, but in the teleological syllogism the end as Subjective End is not fixed from the start, and therefore when realized turns out again and again to be only means. The Good, on the other hand, is finite, but it is an absolutely valid and non-contingent end.

5·3. Nevertheless this finitude within the absolutely valid, intrinsically good Will infects it with contradiction. (A) If there is an intrinsically good Will, then the Good *is* real and has not to wait upon realization to be good: its goodness does not depend on its success. The Good is rooted in Reality, and 'There is no failure but low aim'. This is the half-truth in Kant's distinction between the categorical and the hypothetical imperative. Yet at the same time (B) the Good is that which ought to be realized, and the actual which confronts the subject is that which ought to be good. Hence the imperative, though categorical, is an essential moment of the Good Will; for the subject which *ought* to realize itself is so far not realized, and the confronting world which ought to be good is so far not good. The objective nature and intrinsic value which the Good Will possesses in itself does not render nugatory the lack in it of the moment of immediate external realization.[3] This lack—the fact, as

[1] LL, ii, pp. 321–2. [2] See ch. xv, § 7 above.

[3] The Good Will which lacks this moment in itself is of course not mere virtuous intention, but the will in concrete action:

'’Tis not in mortals to command success,
But we'll do more, Sempronius, we'll deserve it.'

Hegel puts it, that the Good Will is good *für sich* but not also *an sich*—appears in the contingency of its achievements. These are finite and perishing just because they are this and that particular good action, and so do not adequately correspond with the Idea. Again, because of this restricted content the Good Will manifests itself in various forms. It may perish not only through contingency and evil, but even through collision of good with good. Thus for all its absolute validity the Good Will is still subjective and finite in that it presupposes a defect in itself and an objective world which goes on its own way, hinders, and even prevents realization of good. Although it counts this opposing world as null, yet it remains an 'ought'. The Idea of perfected Good is an absolute postulate: it is absolute, but it is infected with subjectivity.

5·4. The Idea of the Good, then, is a contradiction. The Good is eternally realized, but ever being realized in response to the imperative. The external world of Cognition Proper is for Will null and void; it has become something which will only get its truth through the Will's particular transforming acts. Yet this external world remains an insuperable barrier. Moreover, Will, in order to be Will, *must* be realizing itself in the teeth of contingency, and indeed of evil. Evil, though contingent and unactual, is not illusory; it is the unrealized self which conditions the subject's self-realization in Will—just as error is the other-being of truth and a dynamic element in the self-conquest of the subject. Both, as it were, rise up to confront the finite subject with a *quasi*-positive power. But in the last resort this power is negative: it is conferred upon evil and error only by the subject, for evil and error are the subject's unrealized self. That is why, although they are not illusory, yet they have, if isolated from all context, no positive principle in them which makes them evil and error. There is nothing erroneous in a false theory if it is abstracted from the context of experience which it contradicts; taken by itself, it must be coherent in order to be advocated and believed at all. Equally, as Plato shows in *Republic* 352 B–C, the knavery of a gang of thieves, regarded by itself, is nothing but an internal principle of justice which binds them together, and it is the *sine qua non* of their nefarious activity. Hence (*a*) a man is responsible for his errors and sins; for they are himself. But (*b*) his errors are corrigible and his sins expiable. His rejection of error, if he finds the truth, cancels the error as such; his repentance and punishment cancel his wrong deed as such. But this cancellation is a turning of error into truth and of evil into good. Will thus inevitably stands in the way of its own realization. Its absolute success would cancel that discrepancy between what is and what ought to be which is of the very essence of Will.

6. To understand the transition from the Idea of the Good to Absolute Idea, we must first dwell a little longer on the characteristic defect of Will. The Idea of the Good, the Practical Idea, lacks the moment of immediate external Being *within itself*. It is not complete self-consciousness. There is wanting in it, says Hegel, 'the moment of real (*eigentlich*) consciousness, which would be consciousness that the moment of actuality had reached the determination of external Being for itself *in the Notion*. This defect can also be expressed by saying that the Practical Idea still lacks the moment of the Theoretical Idea.'[1]

6·1. A comparison with that modern obligationist ethic which claims descent from Kant, may here perhaps serve to make Hegel's doctrine clear. Hegel means that the good man does not simply desire that the external world shall become what *it* ought to be. That goodness could through action be made to attach to the finite existent as such is the mere suggestion of confused thinking, and the denial of this suggestion is the half-truth wrapped up in the obligationist doctrines that there is no 'ought-to-be-doneness', and that the rightness of an act does not consist in its productiveness of good. But what on Hegel's view the good man does desire to realize is the goodness at once of himself and of the external world which he will transform to a goodness, *possessing which it will be no longer external*. With this qualification, an act *is* right (or good, for the distinction now lapses) in so far as it produces good. Obligationism, on the other hand, must deny this unconditionally. It thus suffers in the end the nemesis awaiting all realism. H. A. Prichard was driven to maintain that a moral obligation is an obligation, not to do

[1] LL, ii, p. 323. Italics mine.

something, but to set ourselves to do something.[1] This can only mean that I fulfil my obligations within, so to say, my own head; that the good will is realized wholly inside the limits of a mind whereof the confronting objective world is independent. A realist may well shrink from the alternative view that in willing a mind causes an effect in a world independent of mind, but this subjectivist doctrine is even less plausible. Kant is no doubt responsible for some of these shortcomings, yet Obligationism founds itself on a fragment of Kant's ethic divorced from its context. It takes the categorical imperative and leaves the kingdom of ends, endeavouring to adapt Kant's preliminary formulation of his moral theory to a realist metaphysic. The result is not happy.

From Hegel's view it follows further that the good at which the good man aims is necessarily his own good, that is, his profit in that sense in which Plato maintains that virtue profits a man. For Obligationism this is simply false. But the bankruptcy of that shrivelled, legalistic ethic, with its Puritanical mistrust of human nature, becomes staring when its supporters are forced to the view that moral goodness and good in the sense of 'my good' are by some unlucky miracle of linguistic development purely equivocal terms. What on earth or in heaven a good may be which is nobody's good is not thought to need explanation.[2]

6·2. That the good man wills to realize the good at once of himself and of the world which in Cognition Proper confronts him externally, Hegel in the context last cited expresses by saying that Will lacks the actual consciousness that the universe with which as good it identifies itself is throughout of its own nature actually good. Will is manifested in finite particular acts, and the subject as moral agent cannot fully attain this consciousness. For the moral agent

[1] See 'Duty and Ignorance of Fact', *Proceedings of the British Academy*, vol. xviii. The Understanding's persistence in rigid antitheses is perfectly exemplified in this essay.

[2] See, e.g., E. F. Carritt, 'An Ambiguity of the Word "Good"', *Proceedings of the British Academy*, vol. xxiii. By assuming the existence of this astonishing equivoque Prichard contrived to prove Aristotle, and by implication also Plato and Butler, guilty of psychological hedonism! See 'The Meaning of ἀγαθόν in the Ethics of Aristotle', *Philosophy*, vol. x, no. 37, 1935, and also *Duty and Interest, an Inaugural Lecture*, Clarendon Press, 1928.

the perfected good is still a postulate, and so Will remains a contradiction.

6·3. The transition to Absolute Idea now becomes clearer. The contradiction and defect of Will are within Will itself. Will lacks the Idea of the True, out of which it developed as an attitude of spirit opposing Cognition Proper. It must now develop further as explicit synthesis with the moment of Cognition Proper, which *qua* Will it contains despite its relation to it of opposition. The self-transcendence of Will can be expressed in a syllogism analogous to the syllogism of Realized End.[1] In the major premiss the Will realizes itself in a particular act. This act is finite, and the achievement of it is one of an indefinite series of good acts, just as in the syllogism of Realized End there was still an indefinite regress of means. But as in that syllogism the middle term was end as well as means, so here the Good Will *is* realized in its particular act, although its achievement is finite and contingent. Thus in both syllogisms the middle term mediates as Universal which contains in itself the extremes: both syllogisms are in the third figure. In the syllogism of Realized End the externality of the object upon which the instrument operates turned out to be externality as a moment of the subject, externality wherein the subject returns upon itself. So in this syllogism the indefinite regress of finite achievement turns out not to cancel but to complement the absolute Good Will, to be its necessary expression, the moment of externality within and not without it. But with this conclusion Will is transcended. As even the final category of Teleology failed to express Life, so the Idea of the Good falls short of Absolute Idea. When the Good ceases to be a postulate it ceases to be a practical Good. When spirit comes to a full self-knowledge in which the contradiction of Will is sublated, it is neither Cognition Proper nor Will, but Absolute Idea.

[1] See ch. xv, §§ 9–9·4 above.

XVIII
ABSOLUTE IDEA

1. Absolute Idea plays a dual dialectical role. It is the synthesis of Life with Cognition, and also of Cognition Proper with Will. Moreover, it has itself no subdivisions. These consequences follow because the form of dialectical movement which is distinctive of the Notion, and still more distinctive of the Idea, becomes in Absolute Idea pure activity. There is no further transition within the Logic; not because in Absolute Idea dialectical movement ceases, but because it has become more than movement. If the synthesis of the Idea of the True with the Idea of the Good were different from the main synthesis of the Idea, it must have been followed by a new triad; development would not yet have become full activity. Correspondingly, the Idea of the Good can have no subdivisions, and Cognition Proper has only two phases, Analytic and Synthetic Cognition, which have no phase of synthesis within Cognition Proper, but pass at once to synthesis within Will.

2. As synthesis of the Ideas of the True and the Good, Absolute Idea is the full self-realization of Will in and as its object; a realization wherein also, conversely, the object coincides with its notion and is what it ought to be. Absolute Idea is the absolute self-definition of spirit. It is true beyond truth and error, good beyond good and evil; and yet neither true nor good as those intrinsic values are for Cognition, but real—or rather, perhaps, active—beyond truth and goodness. Yet this synthesis is, like any other dialectical synthesis, a return to immediacy, a re-immediation of its synthesis. Absolute Idea must be called a category of knowing rather than of willing, though of knowing in which willing is sublated. Absolute Idea *qua* absolute value must be called truth, though not the truth of Cognition Proper.

2·1. Hegel is thus at one with Plato and Aristotle in holding the activity of thought higher than practice and alone self-sufficient.[1] Hegel with the Greeks awards the palm

[1] Although he does not follow Aristotle in regarding the activity of thought and practical activity as the products of a partial bifurcation in spiritual activity; see IH, ch. v, § 4·2.

to thought over all other forms of experience, because thought alone can claim to judge, and thought must decide in its own favour, since a plea for the primacy or equality of any other form of experience can only be made and judged on rational grounds. Thought which confesses the superiority or even the equality of will contradicts itself: (*a*) It claims to know the inmost nature of will, a knowledge which clearly can be only possessed through the actual activity of willing; but (*b*) the very possession of this knowledge means that its thinking *is* willing and more than willing, implies that willing is sublated in it. In short, the only defect there can be in theoretical activity is ignorance, and only the attaining of knowledge can amend ignorance. No other form of experience can either supplement thinking or transcend it. If it be retorted that here speaks the egoism of philosophy, the answer is clear. If appeal be made against Reason, then either this is itself a covert appeal to Reason, or else it is an effort to overthrow Reason entirely—to deny, or rather to ignore, the very existence of truth. To set limits to thought in the sense of assigning a limited nature to thought as such is a mere failure to think. In *Republic* ix Plato argues (on much the same lines) the superiority of the philosophic life to the ambitious and apolaustic lives. Hegel's conception of Absolute Idea is in fact far closer in spirit to Plato's sketch of the Good in the *Republic* than to the views of any intervening philosopher.

3. The Absolute Idea is a singleness above distinction of subject and object, an absolute self-consciousness and not a grey neutrality. As subject Absolute Idea is absolute individuality, or, since it synthesizes Life with Cognition, it is absolute personality; but, again, as object it is its own absolute personality which it knows. If we start with the object, we may say that Absolute Idea as object is the whole content of the Logic, the whole dialectic of categories—that is what as subject it thinks or knows. But equally then we must say that this whole dialectic is that thinking or knowing, is Absolute Idea as subject. Inasmuch as the opposition of subject and object is not neutralized in Absolute Idea, we may still for want of a better language speak of subject and object in distinction. But we shall find that both terms of the

distinction we draw must fall on both sides of our distinction: subject is both subject and object, object is both object and subject. Absolute Idea is what every preceding category truly is, but it is what itself is only by preserving as well as cancelling all preceding categories. As final self-definition of spirit, Absolute Idea is spirit as a living dialectic, the culmination of which *is* its own process, the process of which *is* its culmination.

4. So far I have called Absolute Idea indiscriminately a knowing and a thinking; but it is both. As self-containing individual, or rather person, Absolute Idea may be called a self-knowing; as self-constituting it may be called a self-thinking. For it is both culmination or conclusion, and also process or method. But it is process and culmination in one; it is a singleness of conclusion and method such that in it either of these is both itself and the other. Hegel holds that it may be expressed for the imagination as a circle rather than as a straight line. For a circle has no sheer beginning or end, and it unites the extendedness of a line with the self-continence of a point. Within the 'circle' of the categories Pure Being is prior to Absolute Idea in the sense that it promises and prefigures it; but Absolute Idea is prior to Pure Being in the other sense that it is the full truth of Pure Being. Only for that reason could the Logic justifiably start with Pure Being, and Hegel meet the charge of derivation *ex nihilo*. In these two senses any two categories are both prior and posterior to one another.[1]

5. As a process or method Absolute Idea sums up and reconstitutes as itself all the processes which are its own developing phases. Not only is it that in which the categories of Being, Essence, and Notion are sublated with a progressive variation of emphasis between cancellation and preservation; it is also a final movement, or rather activity, of development, undispersed in its process, having for its prelude the seeming substitution of category for category in Being, for its intermediate phases first the procession of coupled moments in Essence and then the still not fully self-containing developments of Subjective and Objective Notion. Within the Idea itself the categories which are

[1] Cf. above, ch. ii, § 2·54.

explicit methods, namely, Analytic and Synthetic Cognition, are negated in Will and thereafter synthesized in the dialectical method of Absolute Idea. The method of philosophy, that is to say, is shown as against the methods of special science to be essentially one with the object-world which gives it content, and the object of philosophical thought is shown to sublate the worlds of Cognition Proper and of Will. Throughout the Notion dialectic has been a transparent play of development, in which the Actual has not been cancelled as in the Actual were cancelled all preceding phases of thought. But Absolute Idea is the perfectly luminous preservation of all earlier categories.[1]

The conclusion of the whole Logic—as it was also its presupposition—is that nothing but spirit is, and spirit is pure activity.

[1] Cf. ch. xi, § 1·1 above.

XIX

TOWARDS CRITICISM OF HEGEL: THE PERSISTENCE OF SPACE AND TIME

1. Hitherto this *Study* has been confined to sympathetic exposition. I have seldom directly criticized a phase or a transition of the dialectic. I have as a rule gone beyond as simple a statement or paraphrase of Hegel's doctrine as I could achieve only to illustrate it by reference to other thinkers; and I have on the whole frankly maintained the attitude of an advocate for the defence. A great thinker has the right to be heard in the first instance with sympathy and patience, and I might plead that in days when he is less often studied than denounced the mere attempt to restate Hegel simply and appreciatively was worth making.

Yet in the past I have perhaps been too anxious that Hegel should not continue to be condemned unheard. Already my *Introduction to Hegel* has misled one competent reviewer to infer that I regarded Hegel as *der unwiderlegte Philosoph* and accepted all his categories as they stand.[1] I have been warned, and the first chapter of this book will have suggested that I do not in fact find Hegel's dialectic quite so four-square and blameless. The remaining chapters shall be more directly critical.

2. The task of seriously criticizing Hegel's Logic is nevertheless difficult. To divide with a knife between what in Hegel is living and what is dead appears to me to be a far harder affair than Croce found it. The whole Hegelian system is so closely woven that its virtues and faults seem intermingled and ubiquitous. That is why the chief serious charges brought against Hegel's Logic have in effect concerned his entire system and not the Logic alone. Did Hegel, ridiculously, deny the law of contradiction? Did he equate the rational with actual present fact? Did he stuff his Logic with alien material? Do the categories, in his view, gain or lose by phenomenal manifestation? Is the transition from Idea to Nature a mere *tour de force*, a quite illegitimate

[1] J. Lowenberg in *Mind*, April 1942.

attempt to bridge the chasm between thought and sense? Does the conception of the super-triad, Idea–Nature–Spirit, accordingly set a mere sham finish on the system? Each of these questions in a different degree touches the whole system, but until they are directly or indirectly answered we cannot pass judgement on the Logic. In this *Study* I have expounded only the Logic and a small section of ΦG, and IH contains only the most meagre outline of Hegelian doctrine. I must therefore assume much without proper discussion and ignore entirely much that is relevant.

3. I shall begin by trying to restate very briefly so much of Hegel's doctrine as I think a critic must at least provisionally assume if it is to be worth his while to criticize Hegel at all. This minimum you may call as you will the general principle, the main elements, or the nucleus of Hegelianism. The exclusive choice of a term would depend on the view taken of logical structure within a philosophical system, and precision at this point would serve no end.

It might be held that to assume such a general principle or nucleus already implies a bias, that it is a too partial concession; but the critic who tries to concede less, even if in the case of Hegel the concession must cover monistic idealism and in some sense the dialectical principle, is likely to lose his author altogether and to find himself criticizing not this or that philosopher but all philosophy. If a critic's first duty is sympathetic exposition, his second is not, I think, to exchange sympathy for a spurious pose of detachment, but to press within his own thought the nucleus or main elements of his author's philosophy to as fair a conclusion as he can. Such a procedure would be a criticism of the provisionally assumed nucleus. No doubt it would still presuppose the central Hegelian doctrine that philosophic thought is self-critical, but there are non-Hegelian circles in which such a view is still held respectable. On the other hand, it is often so difficult to determine exactly Hegel's own views that I cannot hope to define rigidly the nucleus I assume.

4. I shall, then, first attempt to set out the bare nucleus of Hegel's system as I see it; but next, before asking how Hegel actually develops it, I shall venture to suggest in rough outline the limitations within which I think it is

capable of legitimate development. I shall, that is, before directly criticizing Hegel, try to discover in his own main principles a criterion by which he may be fairly judged, and only then endeavour to apply it directly to his system, in particular to his Logic.

I have again done no more than repeat the Hegelian doctrine that philosophical thought is self-critical, but at this point I cannot pretend to forget another charge which is commonly and not unplausibly brought against Hegel. He is said to have been so arrogantly self-confident as to regard his own philosophical system as not merely absorbing and completing all previous philosophical thought but as itself the absolutely final philosophy.

If this charge is just, Hegel would seem coolly to contradict his own doctrine that thought is self-critical, insolently to exempt his own philosophy from the criterion which it sets up to test all philosophy. This problem, however, I shall beg leave at present to postpone.

5. Hegel holds, and believes it to be the single task of philosophy to show, that reality is not a contingent aggregate, nor an endless generation and evanescence, but a necessarily ordered whole wherein the elements ordered are the phases of a single timelessly self-constituting activity which is mind or spirit.

This self-constitution is self-manifestation, and self-manifestation is the ἔργον and not any πάρεργον of spirit.[1] This manifestation is accordingly not only a complete and unreserved manifesting *of* itself but a manifestation *to* itself.[2] Self-constitution, in short, here means self-manifestation, self-manifestation means self-consciousness, and this alone is complete activity.

This activity is a dialectical thinking. Its self-manifestation, that is, is a progressive cycle of unreserved self-definition by thesis, antithesis, and synthesis, wherein each antithesis is the completely mediating and determinant

[1] 'Spirit's mode of being (*Bestimmtheit*) is manifestation. Spirit is not some one mode or content whereof the utterance and externality were a mere form distinct from it: spirit does not reveal *something*, but its very mode of being and content is this revelation.' ΦG, § 383.

[2] 'Der Geist is nur Geist, insofern er für den Geist ist.' Ibid., § 564.

negation, at once the contrary and contradictory opposite, of its thesis, and each synthesis is the coincidence of these opposites in a fuller definition.

This dialectic is not *explicit* self-definition except in its supreme form, philosophic thinking. For the forms through which, sublating them, spirit progresses comprise (*a*) forms which are explicit self-definitions of spirit, viz. categories; (*b*) forms of Nature which, although Nature is the dialectical opposite of spirit and a *sine qua non* of spirit's self-manifestation, are yet only real as progressively sublated in the activity of spirit; (*c*) forms of spirit which are not yet explicitly the philosophic thought in which they culminate but, so far like the forms of Nature, are real only as sublated in thought.

Yet this supreme form is not less than the totality of spirit by the lower forms which it sublates: it is the total activity of spirit. For the supreme form, the explicit self-definition of spirit in philosophical thinking, is not just philosophy *qua* the culminating phase of Concrete Spirit; nor is it philosophic thought self-explicating only in the categories. It is the whole self-explication of philosophy in and through the categories, the forms of Nature, and the forms of Concrete Spirit; it is the timelessly self-completing circle of the super-triad.[1]

It would appear to follow that if Hegel could have perfectly completed his task, his philosophy would not merely show reality to be the single active nature of spirit but itself be absolutely identical with that activity.

5·01. In attempting to express spirit's single activity of self-manifestation, which by a convenient abbreviation may be called the Absolute, Hegel frequently uses the language of theology. He was a theological student and writer before he became a professional philosopher, and he was a professing Lutheran throughout his life. His theological expressions are not mere metaphors; for though he conceives absolute

[1] Within the limits of Hegel's metaphor of the circle we must say that every triad of the dialectic is a circle in so far as in the synthesis the thesis returns upon itself through negation. But in any small-scale triad the synthesis is incomplete and the dialectic does not close but, so to say, advances on a wider curve. Only the super-triad is a perfect circle. It may be helpful to think of the super-triad as a spiral returning upon itself in a circle, but we should then have to imagine any given group of triads as approximating in a different degree to the circle of the super-triad.

self-manifestation as most truly a self-thinking or self-knowing, yet he regards the God worshipped in the Christian religious consciousness as a phase of Concrete Spirit already entitled to be called absolute.[1] In philosophy a metaphor is the expression by analogy of the whole in terms of the part, or of the more complete in terms of the less, and if Hegel's theological expressions are metaphors, no great distance separates the ratios in the analogy: God, we might say, is Hegel's proximate metaphor for the Absolute. The whole attitude of Hegel to religion, however, is ambiguous and difficult, and this nucleus of his system would not gain in clarity if it borrowed much from his philosophy of religion. It is none the less worth note that as the Absolute is nothing but the activity of self-manifestation, so Hegel's God *is* unreserved self-revelation. 'If self-revelation is denied to God there remains nothing to constitute his nature but to ascribe to him envy.'[2]

5·1. It is an old charge against the monistic idealist that any predicate with which he attempts to determine the nature of his Absolute at once denatures it, turning it from absolute to relative; that even if he be allowed to postulate an Absolute he can never show how it necessitates any special feature of its content. And it is an old corollary to this charge that the only true concern of philosophy is not any Absolute but the human experient and the world which he finds, interprets, and reacts upon.

Since the sole object of his philosophy is the Absolute, this accusation clearly touches Hegel, though it never seems greatly to trouble him. Viewed broadly, as in this context we must view it, Hegel's retort goes far beyond the counter-demand that the critic shall show some positive ground in the nature of human experience to validate his criticism; that he shall clear himself from the charge that he argues from mere impotence and privation, proving nothing but his own impotence to argue. Hegel in effect retorts that the sole subject of philosophy could not be the Absolute unless it were throughout also human experience.

5·11. The general meaning of this retort is clear. Hegel is maintaining that the Cartesian or any other defence against

[1] Cf. IH, ch. ix, § 1·1.

[2] ΦG, § 564.

total scepticism only holds good if human experience is that in which absolute experience constitutes and manifests itself. Man has no other ground than that for the trust which he finds himself forced to place in his own reasoning power. The position may perhaps be put thus. On the one hand, the subject of Hegel's Philosophy of Spirit is man's coming to consciousness of himself; his Philosophy of Nature shows Nature as the dialectical presupposition of the development of human self-consciousness; the dialectic of the categories explicates the culminating phase of human self-consciousness, viz. philosophic thought; and it is this explication of human self-consciousness which continues until the dialectical circle is complete, until man as philosopher has known Nature as the presupposition of that development which culminates in his own philosophic thought. On the other hand, this same whole dialectic is the single absolute activity which constitutes itself in self-manifestation. For Hegel's Absolute constitutes and manifests itself in and as human self-consciousness, and in and as Nature, which human self-consciousness presupposes. The Absolute is thus manifest to man by virtue only of its manifestation to itself; and, again, its manifestation to man is man's own self-consciousness.

5·2. To recall Hegel's doctrines of contradiction and of the unity of thought and being, which we must take as central within any nucleus of Hegelianism, may serve to throw more light on this unification of absolute and human experience.

On the one hand, the spring of the dialectic is contradiction, and the dialectic is the movement of absolute spirit through the coincidence of self-determinations which are at once contrary and contradictory. Yet contradiction has its source and goal in unity: the passage of spirit through contradictories springs from and expands the 'original' unity of thought (self-consciousness) and being,[1] which is the self-certainty of Reason that it is all the world. On the other hand, the dialectic is the struggle towards self-reconciliation of man, who comes to himself as a self-contradiction, as a being, that is, who experiences himself as at once constituted by the Absolute and at the same time distinct from it (so that

[1] Cf. ch. ii, § 1·1 above.

it is for him, as it were, lessened by his own self which he opposes to it) with a difference which is not mere discrepancy but contradiction.[1] Yet man's experience of all-pervasive contradiction presupposes and extends the original unity of thought and being. That unity, that self-certainty of Reason in man, he can assert categorically and not hypothetically because it constitutes him. It assures him against total scepticism, even if it also warns him that death is the only means of complete escape from thought and action which is not a proven failure.

6. It would thus appear that within this seamless, indivisible philosophy of the Absolute, at least in the elementary nuclear form in which I have tried to express it, the twin contradictory moments, which reflection abstracts in a vain effort to distinguish between absolute and human experience, persistently emerge together on both sides of the distinction. If the system is in fact flawless and the dialectic throughout utterly one with its content, and if as critics we now attempt, as I propose that we should, to stress the human point of view and press the implications of the system by examining self-contradiction as the distinctive character of human experience, our effort will be otiose but not illegitimate. For if the system is flawless, and if our criticism is fair, we shall find that in fact the Absolute alone has been its topic, and that the truth of our criticism was already contained in the system. But if the system is not flawless we may not be wasting our pains.

7. In this and the following chapter I propose to take certain familiar oppositions in terms of which not only Hegel but most European philosophers since Plato have discussed the contradiction of human experience, and ask whether, on the general Hegelian basis which we have agreed to assume, they can in human experience so completely coincide that a

[1] I assume that in calling man self-contradiction Hegel uses the term strictly; that he means, i.e., that whereas a man may experience elements in his consciousness as discrepant—e.g. particular desires—his experience of himself as over against, as excluding and opposing the Absolute, is essentially experience of contradiction. No doubt Hegel would hold that in the end all discrepancy has its truth in this contradiction, but that in so far as man *strives* towards a reconciling self-consciousness discrepancy and contradiction are differently experienced.

single and final philosophy of the Absolute, a flawless dialectic, is a real possibility; or whether when we apply them one by one to analyse human experience there emerges an obstacle to this consummation which is philosophically insuperable.

The main oppositions I have in mind are such as universal and particular, *a priori* and empirical, necessary and contingent, intelligible and sensuous. In general I shall be developing the doubts which I have already raised in Chapter I and Chapter II, §§ 2·4 and 2·55, but I shall probably appear to be reaching the same conclusion from various starting-points rather than presenting the steps of a single continuous argument. If I felt able either completely to destroy or completely to reconstruct Hegel's philosophy I should find my task far less hard.

7·1. These oppositions must, if we are to use them fairly in criticism of Hegel, be such as he would regard both as genuinely characterizing human experience and as genuine dialectical contradictories. I propose in this chapter to confine myself to two, namely, space and the supra-spatial, and time and the eternal, and they may not at first sight appear to pass the test. In the first place, it may be objected that if these oppositions are true dialectical contradictories in Hegel's sense, they ought each to reflect some relation of thesis and antithesis which appears *eo nomine* in Hegel's system. But they do not; each has rather the appearance of a thesis coupled with a synthesis. In the second place, I may be reminded that Space and Time are themselves in ΦN opposed as thesis and antithesis.

7·2. To meet these objections we must look again at the Hegelian doctrine of contradiction. In Hegel's system Contradiction is a category of Essence. This is Hegel's philosophical interpretation of contradiction as it appears to common sense and formal logic, viz. the relation between an *A* and a not-*A* which, mutually exclusive, divide the universe between them and cannot both be correctly predicated of any finite thing taken as self-identical. But contradiction in a wider sense, dialectical contradiction as such, characterizes every opposition of thesis and antithesis in the whole system, and the Contradiction of Essence, viewed within the system, is itself the synthesis of Variety and Contrariety.[1] How these two senses of contradiction relate we have already seen.[2] The contradictories of the Understanding are predicates competing to characterize one finite thing, which cannot accept them both. They are on the same level; neither develops the other by contradicting it. But the contradiction which belongs to every triad of the dialectic relates determinations of a developing activity which reconciles them as it produces them. The contradictory predicates are not on the same level; the negative in determining it develops the positive, the subject accepting both positive and negative because they do not compete to characterize it as it stands. It does not stand. It is activity. Dialectical contradiction is thus a negativity which varies its expression in every triad.

7·3. Yet to say that contradiction in every triad relates thesis and antithesis is to state the matter too simply. For every thesis, at any rate every thesis after Pure Being, has negative determination in it. It is a thesis only by virtue of being a synthesis in which negativity breaks out to make it thesis to a new antithesis. And every antithesis, at any rate every antithesis after Not-Being, has determined a positive and is so far itself, in the very performance of its antithetic function, a synthesis. Correspondingly, any synthesis, so far as it does not fully resolve contradiction, is still both a thesis because it still provokes negation, and an antithesis because it is a negation not wholly negated. The triadic form appears on many scales, and the larger the scale we consider the more obvious this is. Dialectical contradiction is not a relation of static opposites but negativity, viz. active contradiction moving towards synthesis and, because it is the self-determining of spirit, never wholly failing of synthesis. Thus contradiction and reconciliation together pervade every phase of the dialectic. The triad is the *minimum rationale*,[3] and whatever may be set down under the expository title of 'thesis', 'antithesis', or 'synthesis' is not intelligible save as both positive and negative and, further, as a unity of positive and negative.

7·4. It may seem to follow that every phase of the dialectic

[1] See ch. vi, § 5·4 above.

[2] Cf. ibid. §§ 5·42 ff. and IH, ch. xii, §§ 1 ff. [3] Cf. IH, ch. xi, § 3·2.

as Hegel states it, and *a fortiori* Hegel's system as a whole, is in principle an infinitely divisible continuum, or that as stated it is elliptical and subject to the insertion *ad indefinitum* of intermediating phases. This criticism shall be later considered,[1] but at present we are concerned with the question, Could Hegel accept the opposition between spatial and supra-spatial, and that between temporal and eternal, as partial but legitimate ways of expressing the contradiction which pervades human experience?

We may take first the more familiar opposition of temporal and eternal. The eternal, if man experiences it as the Absolute which constitutes him, is for him consummation, synthesis. But the eternal, if man experiences it as contradicting the temporal, is antithesis. Hence as contradicting the temporal in man's experience, the eternal is itself a contradiction, a synthesis which is yet still only antithesis.

That, I think, follows fairly from our analysis in § 7·3 of contradiction in the triad. Hence it would seem legitimate to apply the opposition, and I think that the opposition of spatial and supra-spatial is analogously justifiable.

7·5. We have still to consider the second objection, namely, that Hegel specifically opposes Space and Time as thesis and antithesis.

In ΦN Space develops certain determinations of its own (Point, Line, and Surface) before it begets Time as its antithesis,[2] but if the antithesis of Space is Time it does certainly follow that any element beyond these strictly spatial determinations which we offer as contradicting the spatial should, if we are to criticize Hegel fairly, contain Time. On the other hand, any such element must also, if the argument of § 7·3 is sound, contain Space as a moment sublated in it. My intention is not to attempt directly to trace, as Hegel's philosophy consists in tracing, the dialectical self-development of *Begriffs-* and *Denkbestimmungen*, but to examine a few of them severally as exhibiting contradictory opposition in an actual finite experience which 'illustrates' them. In particular I shall not try to follow and criticize the detailed dialectic of Space and Time as Hegel, suggestively but obscurely and perhaps arbitrarily, develops it in ΦN. This

[1] See ch. xxi, § 9·2 below.

[2] See ΦN, §§ 255–6.

procedure no doubt entails abstraction, but we shall not, I think, be opposing to space any element which is falsified because the temporal moment is provisionally ignored. Moreover, when we come to speak of time, I shall hope to some extent to make good the provisional abstraction.

7·6. I need scarcely remind the reader that our general idealist assumption entails two corollaries.

We are to take space and time as 'lived', as characterizing a total self-conscious experience. Hence we cannot view space as an independent receptacle in which things exist, nor time as an independent vehicle in which they change. Secondly, we shall not be presupposing a 'conceptual' spatial system and a 'conceptual' time order in which the experience itself is placed and dated. We shall be using as illustration a simple sense judgement, and we shall assume that the single spatial system and the single chronological order which we have, at any rate for practical purposes, in constant use, are a constructional extension of such judgement and not a ready-made presupposition of it. No doubt the 'here and now' of sense-judgement implies and presupposes within the *Erlebnis* a spatio-temporal context, and no doubt, too, the single spatio-temporal system which we construct for certain mainly practical purposes is perfectly legitimate. But the spatio-temporal context within the experience, and the single spatio-temporal system with which we work every day, are not the same thing. The latter, though an extension from the former, is also an abstraction from it.[1] If they were the same thing, space as 'lived' would be no more than geometrically measurable volume, and time within the experience would be just a section of 'geometrical' time; whereas, as we shall see, space and time within the experience are a good deal more than that.[2]

Thus we shall follow Kant in taking space and time as forms of experience and not things in themselves, but we

[1] An abstraction which need not, perhaps, in physics be always the same in structure.

[2] That not only the object of my sense-judgement but also my total experient act can be for practical purposes placed and dated within the single space and time system of everyday life is obvious enough. In what sense empirical psychology can profitably investigate experience as temporal process is another question; cf. IH, §§ 4 ff., and § 10·3 below.

shall go beyond him in that we shall assume (*a*) that the experience of sense-judgement is in a degree self-consciousness, whereas to Kant the empirical self is not genuinely experienced as a self at all, and self-consciousness is only present as a quite unparticularized awareness of subjective activity; (*b*) that space and time both characterize the whole experience; (*c*) that, as so characterizing the whole experience, space is not bare geometrical space, and time is not the abstract 'geometrical' time of classical physics.

8. It is an old paradox that we cannot state what we see without stating more than we see. If I say, 'I see a house', what I say is at least partly false; for I have judged as well as seen. 'That is a house' would better express my experience, but what 'that' was—what it was that I strictly and only saw—I should not find it easy to tell.

If we consider the opposition of space and the supra-spatial in relation to such a sense-judgement as 'That is a house', we may say, I suppose, that a man's experience is spatial in so far as it is for him an *extensum* of *partes extra partes*, and that this spatiality is contradicted in so far as the elements constituting human experience do not lie outside one another. Thus the supra-spatial would seem to be the character of concentration by reciprocal interpenetration of the constituent elements of an experience.

8·1. Having agreed to accept Hegel's general idealist position, we must reject any realist hypothesis upon which the experience could be analysed as a subject cognizing a 'detached' spatial thing, an absolute not-self. We have to take the whole experienced content as spatial, and the 'detachment' of a spatial object, its externality to me, as doubtless present for me as subject, but as nevertheless falling within my self-consciousness.[1] The self-externality of the object *qua* spatial and the relation of externality in which the subject stands to the object are not two quite different kinds of externality, and the point is worth a little attention. When I judge, 'That is a house', I certainly experience the house as an *extensum* of *partes extra partes*, but I also place it as 'there' within a context of extension centred

[1] IH, ch. iii, §§ 5–5·4 are here relevant. I was wrong in stating without qualification in § 5·4 that space can belong only to a purely physical level.

upon myself. In the first instance 'myself' is my spatially extended body, and within that—to go no farther—my eyes. I can in imagination—without which, indeed, I could not have extended my field of actual vision into a context of which I am the centre—go farther and place my eyes in relation to the house; and then, if I know something of physiology, I can go on to place my brain and possibly some special cerebral centre. But I do not see my eyes or brain. They are for me at once what I see the house with and a reference point whereby I place the house. Nor are they the only reference point I need. I cannot place the house 'there' merely by reference to my eyes (or my brain) 'here': I must —the metaphor is inescapable—go farther inward to myself as particular experient subject in order to reach the final centre of reference which I need. I myself as particular subject am in some sense localized in the experience.

8·2. A paradox perhaps. It may be objected that not I as subject but only my body, or some part of my body, is localized. But then what is meant by the pronoun 'my'? Why will not 'this' serve without 'my'? If it be granted that in order to place the house I must use 'my' eyes, even 'my' body, and not merely this and that other body which I do not own, the paradox is already accepted. Indeed, the counter-attack goes farther. The very dimensions which I discriminate in the house which I see (or better, perhaps, see and imagine), its length, breadth, and height, are determinations it possesses only in reference to a subject; for how could a non-dimensional object be 'there'? Finally, the house as a mere *extensum* can possess mutually external parts only for a subject: parts must be somewhere. In short, space without a subject has neither 'here' nor 'there', neither dimensions nor parts: it is nothing.

8·3. By this paradoxical localizing of the subject we may seem to have demeaned it preposterously. But we are not concerned to sustain what I might call the false refinement of a dualist metaphysics, and the paradox has its converse. If I as particular experient subject am localized, yet in this very localization my 'presence' as subject is precisely what characterizes the total experience as also supra-spatial. It is I as subject who give to my *Erlebnis* unity as a system centred upon the subject. To nothing else is due the concentratedness, the degree of self-internality, which the whole content possesses. The paradox lies not in any debasing of the subject but in the self-contradiction in which the very conception of spatial system seems to consist. For sheer extensity, the spatial moment of self-externality, is the absence of system, but it is absence as privation and persists within the system as positive complement. Concentration and interpenetration of elements so complete that self-externality were utterly annulled would have no meaning. Extensity persists as the room which the house and its context must have in order to exist. It is integral in the 'muchness' of the whole experienced content. It is sublated, but incompletely sublated. It persists to subserve that which sublates it as a *quasi*-positive and in some measure still by its own right. Neither the cancelling nor the preserving is perfectly achieved.

8·4. That we should reach this conclusion in analysing experience at the low level of the sense-judgement may not, since we are assuming Hegel's general idealist position, seem too surprising. But I would suggest, further, that it must hold true of human experience at any level.

Hegel might reply that the synthesis of any opposition, particularly of one which, as I have analysed it, does not exactly correspond to any opposition precisely stated in his own system, is necessarily imperfect sublation, but that in the whole system taken as a whole sublation is perfectly achieved. But is it? No doubt in self-consciousness fuller than is expressed in the illustration which I have taken, the moment of self-externality will not appear primarily, will not be *reell* in Hegel's sense of the term,[1] as extensity; but extensity will not, I think, ever vanish without trace. Even in philosophical thought, if that, as Hegel holds, be the highest form of human experience, there must remain, however insignificant it may have come to be within the content of philosophy, a moment of extensity. A ghost itmay be, but not a ghost so strengthless that it does no work. 'Concentration', 'interpenetration', 'inner and outer', when used at the higher levels of experience are metaphors—indeed, it is by meta-

[1] See IH, ch. xi, § 5·01.

phor that we speak of higher and lower levels of experience —and they are dangerous metaphors, not to be handled without asking ourselves how much in them is to be discounted. But if they wholly miss their mark, it is a miracle that we should so commonly select them.

9. If, as this rough analysis has suggested, that which contradicts the self-externality of space is the subject, we are not after all far from Hegel's position in ΦN. There Space appears as the first form of Nature's distinctively characteristic self-externality; it is *das ruhige Nebeneinander*. The second form is Time, the sheer 'vanishingness' of Nature, which negates the 'static' side-by-sideness of Space. But Time and Space in Nature are the first faint prophetic analogue, so to say, of subject and object.[1] Time is the sheer negative perishingness of the finite, but dialectically developed it is the negation of this negation, the negativity of spirit as freely self-determining thought, in fact eternity.[1]

This is not easy doctrine, and before we proceed to apply the opposition of temporal and eternal to human experience, an attempt to consider a little further Hegel's general view of both time and space may help to clarify both the oppositions which we are endeavouring to apply.

9·1. I take Hegel to mean that if you contrast time as the perishingness, the transience, of things with eternity, you have two poles, namely, sheer vanishingness and the abidingness of fully self-determining activity. Between these poles would lie all types of process, graded according to the degree in which change approximates to development, according, that is, to the degree in which that which changes is less and less merely cancelled, more and more really preserved. Thus time on this scale is the negativity of the graded phases, the developing contradiction of itself, the goal of which is the eternal. But this progression from fugitivity to eternity is by itself an abstraction. Negativity must have a positive to determine. If time is transience, something passes which is not mere time, and if time develops to absolute negativity, yet that which negates its own negation must be more than a negative. Space is this positive, and in ΦN the synthesis of Space and Time develops as Place (the synthesis of the

[1] See ΦN, § 258.

instant with the point), Motion (the flux of the 'here', as the line is the flux of the point), and Matter in Motion.[1]

It would appear to follow, though Hegel nowhere so far as I know draws this consequence, that if Absolute Spirit can be called eternal it can with equal significance be called supra-spatial, and that we have an equal right to apply either of our oppositions in provisional abstraction from the other.

10. Within the nucleus, then, of Hegelian idealism which we are assuming, the opposition of temporal and eternal will be the opposition between transience and activity. Applying it to human experience in provisional abstraction from other oppositions, we must take transience apart from any positive which passes away, that is, as sheer negative transience; and we must take activity as the full negation of negation, the complete negativity which activity is when abstraction is made from what is active.

Yet to maintain this opposition even in provisional abstraction from other oppositions, such, for example, as those between sense and thought, empirical and *a priori*, is not easy. Our best hope of success will perhaps be to concentrate so far as possible on the characteristic of order which human experience has inasmuch as it has irreversible direction. It is, I think, when we come to examine precisely how succession and simultaneity characterize experience that we come close to the opposition between transience and activity.

10·1. When I see and judge, 'This is a house', I experience temporal succession. By that, as I have tried to make clear in § 7·6, I do not mean that I can, if I wish, reflect upon the experience and date it as a sequence of events in one series with other events which, thus reflecting, I judge to have happened that day. I mean that for me in seeing and judging 'This is a house' there is an order in some sense temporal which qualifies my act as a whole. I live my total *Erlebnis* as in some sense a temporal lapse. The phases of it—roughly, my acts of sensating, selectively perceiving or intuiting, imagining, and judging, in and together with their

[1] I have not attempted to follow the detailed dialectic of ΦN, §§ 260–1, which, as I have said, I find obscure. I am not even sure that I have accurately reproduced its gist. The logical categories involved are those of Quantity; cf. ΦN, § 254.

content—are for me temporally successive. If I further expand the experience into explicit inference and express it as 'This house is so dilapidated that it must have long been uninhabited', it becomes obvious that my whole construction from sensation to inference is for me temporal lapse, even though I may be less distinctly conscious of the temporal order in the earlier than in the later phases.

10·2. On the other hand and contradictorily, these phases are not simply successional. Each phase does not terminate abruptly and vanish when its successor begins. I have not in inferring passed right out of judging, nor in judging ceased wholly to imagine, perceive, and sensate. These functions I somehow also perform simultaneously.

This does not mean that I perform them simply separately, as I might simultaneously but separately play a drum, a pair of cymbals, and a wind instrument with different parts of my body. The simultaneity to which I refer is the abstracted temporal aspect of the fact that my whole experience is a developing activity in which each persisting function is modified by the succeeding function which it subserves. Time, as in this experience I live it, is thus not a sheer transience of the content. The succession is cancelled, but it is also preserved in so far as its terms are held together in a simultaneity of function which does not abolish their order.

10·3. But order here begins to gain a new meaning. In such a sublated succession each phase, inasmuch as it is modified by its successor, is presupposed by it. That is to say that the order is no longer merely temporal but, also and further, logical. I am tempted to call it logico-temporal.

The hybrid epithet may horrify. Most of us were told in our philosophic infancy not to confuse logical with temporal order, and most of us have passed the warning on. Usually, perhaps, we have met the question whether this double use of 'before' and 'after' is an equivoque, by referring to difference of 'aspect'. Bradley attempted to distinguish logic and empirical psychology upon the basis of this difference of aspect.[1] Yet in our successional series from sensation to inference the difference is scarcely to be disposed of as merely one of 'aspect'. You may, I suppose, look

[1] Cf. IH, §§ 4 ff.

at it from one point of view and see nothing but temporal process, and then from another point of view and see only logical sequence. But provided that you are honest and make no covert *μετάβασις εἰς ἄλλο γένος*, from the first point of view you will not be able to see development at all, while from the second any contiguous pair of your logical stages will appear absolutely reciprocal in their mutual implication. You will, moreover, have missed the evident fact that the relation between phase and succeeding phase becomes more and more explicitly a logical relation as you pass from the beginning to the end of the succession. The immediate content of my sensation is presupposed by my sense-perception, that by my imagining, and that again by my judgement, but the transition between any of these earlier phases could at best be called *quasi*-logical or sub-logical; certainly it has not the explicitly logical necessity of the transition from the dilapidated condition of the house to the conclusion that it has been long uninhabited. The earlier the transition the more it approximates in character to a mere temporal succession of events,[1] and the more the persistence of the earlier in the later is a mere temporal simultaneity; but the premiss of the inference persists in the conclusion as an element in a systematic unity, as integral to the whole content of the inferring mind. The whole succession is continuous, but the inference is active self-development of thought, whereas the transition from sensation to perception and judgement is more nearly mere change.

10·4. Yet even the explicitly inferential phases of our succession are not phases of pure eternal activity. Obvious as that may seem at the level of our illustration, it is worth while looking to see why they are not.

The whole succession, even in its inferential stages, is still temporal lapse, and to say as we said in § 10·2 that I do not perform these experiential functions simply separately was only half the truth. Although each *is* a modification and development of its predecessor, yet in each stage—even in the inferential stages—I am also continuing to do what I was doing at the previous stage, because the synthesis is never complete. Perceiving is a developed sensating, judging a

[1] It is never simply this because it is an awareness, a phase of an *Erlebnis*.

developed imagining, and inferring a developed judging; yet I do still sensate while I perceive, perceive while I imagine, imagine while I judge, judge while I infer—even, I think, still premise while I conclude. The temporal simultaneity relates functions, not indeed simply separate, yet functions the later of which do not wholly and without residue absorb the earlier.

If we again examine our succession as a logical succession, the corresponding defect is patent. 'Once true always true' is a commonplace, and truth is not an event. Yet inference, any rate at the level at which we are here concerned with it, can never wholly clear itself of the charge of *petitio principii* by pleading that it is development. The conclusion, we may say, includes the premisses within itself and is their modification. Yet it is still a conclusion from and not only with its premisses, and the unity of the inference is not fully systematic: the premisses survive, imperfectly sublated, to support the conclusion. Inference—finite inference at any rate—has always a weak if not a broken back. It is never a complete synthesis.

In sum, inference, so far as it has this logical weakness in it, is still temporal transition, self-externality as evanescence; and logical and temporal passage characterize the inferential experience in inverse proportion to one another.

10·5. We have argued at a humble level, but I cannot see that on our general Hegelian assumption this hybrid logico-temporal character of experience can be wholly overcome at any level. The vanishingness of time is doubtless itself evanescent in the higher forms of human experience, but, as in the analogous case of space,[1] it cannot, I think, ever entirely disappear. For if time is, as Hegel holds, the vanishingness of things, it yet is also their duration. If we consider his first triad of Nature, viz. Space–Time–Matter in motion, and remember that to Hegel Nature *is* Space, *is* Time, *is* Matter in motion, then perhaps we may say that if we remove Space from the synthesis nothing but mere vanishingness remains. Yet within the synthesis the duration of matter in motion is surely the contribution rather of Time than of Space. If things must have room to exist,[2] they must also have time.

[1] See § 8·4 above. [2] See § 8·3 above.

Time, then, in any human experience, however insignificant a character of the experience it may have become, persists, as it seems to me, not only as vanishingness marking defect but also as an indispensable duration.

We appear bound to conclude that the spatio-temporal moment cannot be sublated wholly in a flawless dialectic, if that dialectic is in any sense to express human experience.

XX
EMPIRICAL AND *A PRIORI*

1. WE may next, in pursuit of our programme, turn to consider the opposition in human experience of empirical and *a priori*.

In the arguments of the last chapter concerning space and time, and in those concerning language in Chapter I, we have already reconnoitred in force for this operation. It might in fact be said, having regard to the main tradition of European philosophy, that all the oppositions of the type I proposed to discuss are shapes of the opposition between empirical and *a priori*. By tradition the empirical is the particular and the contingent, with which the spatio-temporal has been commonly identified; whereas the *a priori* has been held to be the universal and the necessary. The sensuous is traditionally the empirical and the intelligible is the *a priori*. The empirical is the immediately given, and that again is the sensuous, though not by all philosophical tradition confined to the sensuous.[1]

1·2. Thus to show that Hegel's philosophy—or any nucleus of it—cannot succeed in exhibiting the complete sublation of the empirical moment in human experience is a complex task in which we may easily lose our way. The shapes of this opposition are too closely akin to treat altogether severally and in separation, but the history of philosophy has not left their mutual relation perfectly clear. In an ocean where the charts conflict I shall try to steer a true course by attempting as we proceed to define more precisely the meaning which must be given to the empirical within our general Hegelian assumptions.

2. We must assume that in so far as our experience is to be called empirical the term 'empirical' qualifies the whole *Erlebnis*, not a mode of experiencing without reference to its

[1] The oppositions of this one general type which I have put forward for discussion of course form no exhaustive list. As we proceed the reader will see, I hope, that I might have worked out the same theme with, for example, the opposition of apparent and real, or of opinion and knowledge, or of subjective (in the sense of arbitrary) and objective, or again of Nature and spirit.

content nor a content without reference to the mode in which it is experienced. If the particular, the immediately given, the sensuous, the contingent, are shapes or aspects or moments of the empirical, then in an act of empirical experience they must be taken to characterize at once the experient subject and what it experiences. So far as what I experience is merely given and its 'what' and 'why' are questions still unanswered, so far, we must assume, am I myself particular, accidental, and immediately present to myself in my sensuous experiencing. If a clear and explicit distinction of subject and object is present in experience it must be taken as having emerged within experience, not as presupposed and so falling outside the inquiry, not as in its general nature to be assumed to hold between ready-made terms which themselves, too, in their general nature are taken for granted. For Hegel any such assumption of prefabricated data would wreck all hope of solving the problem of human experience.

3. The notion that a pain, or a red patch, or any other seemingly plain unequivocal matter of fact can be grasped as a purely immediate self-evident datum, determinate but determined by nothing beyond itself, is plausible to common sense, because at every turn of practical life we take as self-evident given facts what are really constructions so familiar and so well tested as reliable bases for action that we forget they are not pure of inferential construction. But upon reflection the sensible particular reveals readily a 'what' outrunning its 'that', shows qualities and relations which at once characterize it and extend beyond it. The universal was after all present in what seemed a sheer particular. The content was after all not just given, but in some sense constructed *a priori*. The truth of the fact is discovered to lie in its mediation, in its resolution into universal and necessary connexions; and with this discovery its immediacy is seen to persist only as a blind, potential phase, an Aristotelian *πρώτη ὕλη*, which mediation as such presupposes, and as an opaque residue—or rather, perhaps, as a patchy but still pervasive fog—of brute fact awaiting the further mediation of the content, the further informing of the *ὕλη*, in universal terms. There is no sheerly empirical experience. Without the *a priori* the empirical is nothing that as yet takes shape as the given, the

particular, the contingent, or even the sensuous. Only together with its opposite can it belong to human experience.

4. Yet the empirical is not a ghost to be exorcised by refuting the simple fallacy of self-evident matters of fact. Though apart from one another the empirical and the *a priori* are nothing, yet when they are linked as opposites the empirical becomes the apparently positive correlative of the *a priori* and not its mere presupposition, and each term seems unable to stand out against its opposite save by containing that opposite within itself. As experience develops, the universal emerges as merely abstract against the particular, which now by virtue of the contrast is real and individual. The former should be the essence, the truth, the real nature, of the latter, but it cannot fulfil the demand made on it. Each claims to be the whole reality of the situation, but only together can they express the whole reality, and they do so in unresolved mutual contradiction. For the universal as such exhibits necessary connexion of its own differentiations, and as identity in difference is truly individual, concrete and not merely abstract and general. But in its concrete self-differentiation it does not fully sublate the particular. Though it is implicitly *the* universal, single and indivisible, yet it is still one of an indefinite plurality of universals, a genus specifying itself in endless differentiations which are its own but not fully its own, and do not constitute it a genuine system. It still rests upon the particular for support, upon the indefinite multiplicity of logically indiscriminable singulars which it cannot absorb and must accept as its complement. And so far as it does so it is itself particular, an individual only as the mere singular is individual.

4·1. Again, the universal so far as it is not truly individual is contingent. It is determined *ab extra*, not self-differentiating. It exhibits necessitation, but only the necessitation of which the obverse is contingency. So far as its own nature is concerned it might have been otherwise than as it is. It is, paradoxically, contingent as the particular is contingent, viz. *against* the universal, and the whole experienced content, the particular universalized, now appears as contingent. Not the bare fact only but the reasoned fact, too, might have been otherwise than as it is. Yet we are forced to take this contingency as indispensable. This whole content of experience is after all as it is and not otherwise. The brute *de facto* presence of it as contingently determined does not merely indicate an opaque residue or a still pervasive fog—those metaphors for the persistence of the empirical were one-sided—for without it the content would not be real for the subject, and the subject would not find himself realized in experiencing the content. The universal takes shape as the intelligible system which somehow is to be the whole truth of what was given as mere fact, but its necessary connexion is throughout hypothetical, wholly in the air, unless brute fact somehow persists and contributes to the categorical basis without which hypothetical thinking can neither begin nor conclude. But even that is not the whole trouble: 'basis' is not an adequate metaphor because the moment of brute fact is all-pervasive and contingency characterizes the experience as a whole. Spirit is immanent in man not only as the criterion never fully formulable, the ideal never attained; it is also something that, so to say, wells up in him as that which he 'finds' and is by virtue of that criterion to shape towards that ideal.[1] The empirical and contingent everywhere sustains as well as lames the mind's activity, because what the mind empirically and contingently 'finds' it has externalized from within itself before it 'finds' it.

5. The sensuous may be thought not to be *in pari materia* and coextensive with the other shapes in which the empirical has been traditionally conceived. The oppositions of particular and universal, contingent and necessary, seem to be rooted in reality; without them no kind of universe appears thinkable. But the sensuous seems to be itself so particular and contingent that we may hesitate to call it an essential shape of the empirical. Sense, we may be tempted to argue, is a function of certain organic beings which we know to have existed for a limited period on one planet. Their origin is obscure, and there is no evidence for their existence elsewhere in the physical universe. How long they will

[1] Cf. Kemp Smith: 'Knowledge starts neither from sense-data nor from general principles, but from the complex situation in which the human race finds itself at the dawn of self-consciousness.' Cited by Bosanquet, *Implication and Linear Inference*, p. iv.

continue to exist is not predictable. Natural science has long ago shown that any geocentric hypothesis, and any corresponding suggestion that the nature of man offers a special and peculiar key to the nature of the universe, are mere superstitions of the human race, mere parochialisms begotten of its short sight and nourished on its vanity. How, then, can we accept the sensuous element in man's experience as contributing reliably to his knowledge of the universe? How can we take the sensuous as coextensive and *in pari materia* with the particular, the contingent, the empirical?

5·1. On the other hand, if man must trust his own reason, because only on a rational ground could he doubt it, he must also trust the sensuous basis of his reason so far as to deem the deliverance of his senses corrigible only within the development of his experience and not by some external criterion. For there is no external criterion. The whole physical universe, within which the perhaps transitory and narrowly local lodgement of sensuous beings appears as contingent, is a conception not given at all without sense with its spatio-temporal form. We cannot take the contingent as wider than the sensible, because there is no ground on which to base the possibility of a world in which there is contingency but not sensuous character. Any such speciously modest disclaimer of our own importance is based on nothing but ignorance, and ignorance is not a ground. Kant's argument that his pure categories are valid for any being endowed with understanding and a passive faculty of intuition whether sensuous or not, does not, even if it succeeds, afford any ground for the possibility of beings endowed with a non-sensuous passive faculty of intuition. In short, if we deny that the sensuous is an essential shape of the empirical, then we can no longer trust our reason. Thought sublates sense, but there remains between them a reciprocal relation of mutual dependence.[1]

5·11. Moreover and more positively, the particular and the contingent imply singular subjects of experience, each with his own point of view. Only what is in one aspect a singular subject can particularize its object, and what is for me contingent may be for you necessary. Thus the contrast

[1] The reader will see that the argument in this section is already involved in the assumption made in § 2 above.

of necessary and contingent is possible only for a subject in one aspect singular. But the notion of a singular subject without sensuous function seems nonsensical. Conversely, a purely intelligent subject, if pure intelligence be mind wholly without sense, could scarcely think the particular and the contingent.

5·2. Yet it may still be objected that even so we cannot take the sensuous *qua* an essential shape of the empirical as on all fours with the particular and the contingent. For the particular and the contingent, even if they are commensurate with the sensuous and meaningless without it, are forms of thought, which *is* form; whereas the sensuous as opposed to the intelligible is by virtue of the opposition not thought. The sensuous is not form but matter, a *πρώτη ὕλη* which we cannot name except proleptically by a forward reference to its 'illumination' by thought, calling it 'opaque' if we think of it as a potential content, 'blind' if we consider it as a potential function.

5·3. Hegel's reply to this more or less Kantian objection must, I think, be regarded as integral to that nucleus of Hegelianism which we are taking as a basis of criticism. It is a philosophical position of great difficulty, but we are bound to examine it at some length, because it contains a main crux of Hegel's system, viz. the transition from Idea to Nature, and because without it his doctrine of the original unity of thought and being has no meaning. I may perhaps express in advance the opinion that, although to some extent it meets the objection, it will not be found to justify Hegel's claim to have successfully overcome the opposition of thought and sense in human experience.

5·4. In face of the objection here raised Hegel remains a rationalist: in its full and true nature the self-manifesting activity of spirit is thought. But Hegel will not with Leibniz reduce sense to confused thought, nor will he with Kant accept their community of source as merely problematic. Thought, since it is self-manifesting activity, must contain its 'other' within its own nature. It must in an act of self-severance put forth this 'other' as the appearance in which it abides, and with which in its self-completion it is reconciled. This 'other', which, taken simply in the act of severance and apart from the process of reconciliation, may, I think, fairly be called a πρώτη ὕλη, is thus at once thought and the opposite of thought. *Qua* the opposite of thought it is utter privation of self-centred system, utter self-externality. For that reason we cannot, as we might be tempted to do, identify it with the first category of the Logic, with the Pure Being which is equally Not-being. Pure Being could be regarded as the utter opposite of the Idea only within the dialectical circle of pure thought, for Pure Being is a form of pure thought. But this 'other' of thought is beyond *pure* thought. It is the being to which the original unity of thought and being refers. Taken in abstraction from that unity and prior to the process of reconciliation, it is that which the category of Quantity, the negation of Being as Quality, manifesting itself as Space, informs.[1] As the reconciliation develops, as thought returns upon itself, it is the sensuous factor in spirit's self-manifestation through Nature and Concrete Spirit. Hegel's rationalism is thus an attempt to enrich rationalism by absorbing empiricism into it. The full nature of thought as containing its 'other' within itself is more than pure thought, and only Philosophy as the culmination of Concrete Spirit, the content of which is the whole circle of the super-triad, expresses this full nature of thought.

5·41. Yet thought both sublates sense and remains in reciprocal relation with sense, and Hegel does not unambiguously solve the problem. He cannot deduce the union of pure thought with its 'other'. To the question why Being as Quantity should be manifest as Space, neither he nor any

[1] It might at first sight seem that Nature, *qua* the antithesis of Idea, should in its first stages embody the categories of Quality, which logically precede those of Quantity. But Hegel is perfectly clear that they do not; see ΦN, § 254. His position, if I understand it, is that spirit in its self-diremption puts itself forth as utterly self-external, that is, as precisely the negation of Quality. In fact, although the logical thought of Quantity presupposes that of Quality, it is impossible to conceive Nature so abstractly as to exclude Quantity: Space is here the minimal abstraction.

The nisus of all natural science towards mathematics, its effort to grasp reality as quantitative (see below, ch. xxii, § 1·2), seems to lend support to Hegel's view. On the other hand, Nature exhibits qualitative determination, and one is entitled to ask Hegel how this is possible if the most primitive categories which Nature embodies are quantitative.

man can give a precise answer. He states that Space is the first unmediated determination of Nature, the abstract universality of Nature's self-externality.[1] But the formula does not clearly indicate how Space and Quantity differ, and indeed on Hegel's own premisses the difference between every form of Nature and Concrete Spirit on the one hand, and on the other the category of pure thought which it embodies, is something which cannot be expressed in terms of pure thought. The fundamental conviction, however, which operates in Hegel's doctrine of Nature and Concrete Spirit is his certainty that the 'other' which unites with pure logical thought is a total moment of the Absolute and is one in source with pure thought. 'In empiricism', he says in EL, § 38, 'lies the great principle that whatever is true must be in the actual world and present to sense-perception.' But he is clear that the shock of experience, the sense of confrontation by an *alien* other, is nothing but the negative moment of spirit's self-severance made manifest in human experience, and that it constitutes no ground for a realist philosophy. He takes it to follow that the progressive reunion of pure thought with its 'other' is no Kantian composite of thought and sense but the movement of a thought fuller and richer than the pure and abstract thought of the Logic. Yet he does not achieve without ambiguity the task of exhibiting this movement in detail and showing its difference from pure thought. We may hazard an attempt to reconstruct his procedure in stages.

5·42. In Hegel's philosophy the empirical has in effect two meanings. It is, as in all philosophy, a name for the sensuous and non-rational element or aspect of human experience. But to Hegel it signifies also an element in pure thought; for in sense the categories of Being are exhibited *par excellence*, and the coupled categories of Essence, exhibited in that uneasy union of sense and thought which constitutes natural science and everyday thinking, have each a moment expressive of contingency. There is, however, a difference between these categories and their manifestation in Nature and Concrete Spirit, and this difference is just the sensuous factor. Thus to the questions whether the empirical

[1] ΦN, § 254.

and the sensuous are co-extensive and *in pari materia* Hegel would reply that the empirical *qua* that diversity of *Denkbestimmungen* which is all there is of pure thought embodied in sense-experience, is co-extensive with sense; but that it is not *in pari materia* with sense, because sense-experience is more than the pure categories which it embodies.[1] Thus if we speak of the empirical as manifest in Nature and Concrete Spirit we ought perhaps to call it the sensuous-empirical. Hegel, in short, holds that although the sensuous-empirical is ultimately thought, it is not reducible to the pure abstract thought of the logical categories.

5·43. If the sensuous-empirical world embodies but is not reducible to categories, we must next ask whether the more concrete dialectic of Nature and Concrete Spirit is a more or a less clearly self-justifying development than the dialectic of the categories.

Hegel here wavers between two positions which it is necessary to set out at some length.

5·44. (A) Man's experience in its sensuous-empirical aspect wells up in him, so to say, as something which always shocks him with some degree of surprise. Indeed he is conscious of it as a temporal flow, which must by virtue of its very form present a content endlessly novel and in some measure unexpected. A temporal flow predictable *a priori* in all its phases would be a contradiction in terms. Moreover, the shapes of this endlessly novel content present themselves as positive or *quasi*-positive in their impact upon us. It seems to us that without their positive impinging quality there would be no reality for us. Colours and sounds, odours, tastes, and touches shock us with an unescapable cogency. They may even tempt us to assign them a source independent of thought and to embrace a realist philosophy. Hence it would seem that the dialectic in which this world of sensuous-empirical experience is revealed cannot be clearly and

[1] Sense-experience must here be taken to cover potential as well as actual, not merely, that is, the indefinitely regressing world of sense-experience radiating from the actual experience of a finite experient, but also all the forms of Concrete Spirit and Nature lower than sense-perception extending down to Time and Space. All the latter are for Hegel the *prius* and potentiality of a perceptible world.

distinctly self-justifying. Although in principle this dialectic is a thought richer and fuller than the pure thought of the Logic,[1] yet it can only exhibit itself in man and to man as a thinking disunited and irregular in its movement. The pure categories may be detectable embodied in it, but no perfectly clear and distinct difference can be shown between *Denkbestimmungen* and *Begriffsbestimmungen*, nor again between *Begriffsbestimmungen* and the partial regularities, the imperfect classifications, the empirical laws, in which the thinking of special science and common sense gains expression.

5·441. There is much evidence that Hegel accepts this view. His references to the embodiment of particular logical categories in particular phases of Nature and Concrete Spirit are frequent, but irregular in their incidence.[2] There is no attempt at precise correlation, and indeed it is hard to see how he could have set forth a precise correlation without presenting the categorics as a rigid framework of form unaffected by the content it supports.

5·442. Hegel states clearly that the Philosophy of Nature depends for its material upon the results of natural science. 'Not only', he writes in EN, § 246, 'must philosophy agree with the experience of Nature (*Natur-Erfahrung*), but natural science (*Physik*) is presupposed by and conditions philosophical science.' He goes on to point out that the fundamental principle (*Grundlage*) of philosophical science is the necessity of the Notion and not any historical genesis and elaboration, and that, therefore, philosophy cannot appeal to experience but, on the contrary, justifies experience. He does not, however, here suggest that philosophy can once and for all transform and justify the data provided by natural science. The passage must, I think, imply that although the Understanding and the *aperçus* of Nature which constitute its content are *Begriffsbestimmungen* on the ascending scale of Nature and Concrete Spirit, yet they are not sublated without residue in the dialectic of that scale, and so must

[1] 'The system of Logic is the kingdom of shadows.' LL, p. 57.

[2] *Sein*, *Dasein*, *An sich* and *Für sich*, Finite and Infinite, Substance, Notion, occur more often than most of the rest, and the levels of Nature and Concrete Spirit to which these are applied are by no means always the same.

appear as a *never ending* source of material for philosophy to reconstitute.

5·443. In the famous passage which closes the preface to the *Philosophie des Rechts* Hegel appears equally to renounce any claim to perfection and finality for his ethical philosophy. Pointing out that the philosopher cannot lay down beforehand for the would-be reformer the precise state of things which he ought to try to bring about,

> 'Philosophy', he says, 'cannot teach the state the shape it ought to take, but only how it, the ethical universe, is to be known. . . . As regards the individual, everyone is the son of his time; so philosophy, too, is its epoch apprehended in thoughts. It is just as foolish to fancy that any philosophy can extend beyond its present world as to fancy that an individual man can leap out of his time. . . . If a man's theory does pass beyond his own time—if he builds himself a world as it ought to be—then that world has an existence, but only in the man's opinion, only in that unstable element which gives room to any capricious fancy.'

And farther on he says that Philosophy always comes too late to teach the world how it ought to be:

> 'The world does not appear as thought until actuality has completed its process and constituted itself a finished product. The Notion teaches this lesson, and history can only repeat it: only when actuality is ripe does the ideal appear over against the real and, grasping that same real world in its substance, constitutes it in the shape of an intellectual world. When philosophy paints its grey monochrome, some shape of life has grown old, and it cannot by this unrelieved grey be made young again, but only known. The owl of Minerva takes wing only as the twilight falls.'

5·444. That Hegel regarded his Philosophy of History as provisional and not as any final perfection seems clearly indicated by the words in which he summed up his lectures on the subject: 'That is as far as consciousness has reached.'[1]

5·445. In an early work Hegel puts forward the view that every philosophy has a certain completeness just because it is the product, the consummation in thought, of its own

[1] JE, ii, p. 568. These confessions that his philosophy of Objective Spirit is an interim report imply that the Philosophy of Nature is not alone in depending on the ceaseless influx of empirical data.

time. But he does not imply that this completeness is absolute.

'The true peculiarity of a philosophy', he observes, 'lies in the interesting individuality with which Reason has organized itself a form out of the materials provided by a particular epoch. . . . Every philosophy is complete in itself; like a genuine work of art, it has totality in it. If Raphael and Shakespeare had been acquainted with the works of Apelles and Sophocles, they would have seen in them not mere exercises preparing the way for their own art, but a kindred spiritual force. Just so Reason cannot view its own earlier shapes as mere preliminaries instrumental to its [present] self-expression. And if Virgil had treated Homer as that sort of trial exercise for himself and his own more refined epoch, his work would have remained a mere exercise in imitation.'[1]

Hegel's own system was only in embryo when he wrote those words, but the whole implication of the passage runs counter to any possible claim of any possible system to finality.

5·45. (B) Hegel's conviction that thought and sense have a single source, and that form and content are inseparable, leads him sometimes to a less cautious position. Again we may hear some of the evidence.

5·451. Hegel, though he makes self-externality the distinctive character of Nature as such,[2] states that the philosophy of Nature depends upon the results of natural science. From that it must follow that the dialectic of ΦN is corrigible and at best approximate. In no triad which philosophically interprets scientific results, themselves liable to modification, can thesis and antithesis be perfect opposites coinciding in a perfect synthesis. But although Hegel's Philosophy of Nature shows considerable familiarity with contemporary natural science and considerable pertinacity in interpreting it, yet some sections of ΦN can only be viewed as the mechanical imposition of the triadic rhythm upon material which can by no stretch of anyone's imagination but Hegel's be conceived as the indubitable content of that form. To offer taste and smell as the antithesis of touch and to

[1] *Difference between the Systems of Fichte and Schelling*, JE, i, pp. 43–4. The work was published in 1801.

[2] Cf. IH, ch. vii, §§ 4·1 ff., where I have perhaps over-simplified the difficulty of the empirical factor in Hegel's Nature.

synthesize the opposition in sight and hearing[1] is at least to attempt to take account of an obvious progression in the development of the senses which is roughly analogous to the development of higher forms of spirit; but a dialectical deduction of a planetary system[2] at once lends itself to caricature. It may not be demonstrable error, but it is arbitrary; it lacks evident necessity either as an interpretation of scientific facts or as a link in the dialectic.

These more or less arbitrary impositions of the triadic structure are common in ΦN and also in certain parts of the Philosophy of Spirit where natural science plays no part, as, for example, the Philosophy of Art. Sometimes, too, Hegel the philosopher takes sides in scientific controversy, and so lays himself open to the charge of positive error; as when on philosophic grounds he prefers Kepler to Newton and Goethe's theory of colour to orthodox scientific doctrine. But the evidence seems on the whole to acquit him of the charge of claiming absolute finality for the Hegelian philosophy of Nature and Spirit.

5·452. On the other hand, it has been often alleged that Hegel was arrogant enough to claim absolute finality for the dialectical structure of his Logic. Certainly he never, so far as I know, disclaims it, but I can find only one passage which bears directly on the point.

'I could not of course imagine', he writes, 'that the method which in this system of logic I have followed—or rather which this system follows of itself—is not capable of much improvement, of much elaboration in detail; but at the same time I know that it is the only true method. This is evident from the fact that the method is not something different from its content and object. For the content is in itself, *by virtue of the dialectic which it has in it*, the source of its own forward movement. It is clear that no expositions can be regarded as scientific (*wissenschaftlich*) which do not follow the course of this method, and are not conformable to its simple rhythm; for that is the course of the thing itself.'[3]

5·46. It is hard to be sure of Hegel's meaning in this passage. Is he in respect of the Logic adopting position (B)? Is he maintaining that in pure thought, abstract but

[1] See ΦN, § 358. [2] See ibid., § 270.
[3] LL, i, pp. 51–2.

unsullied by phenomenal manifestation, form and content are so utterly one that pure thought reveals itself in his Logic as a flawless dialectical circle of ontological categories which abides no question? Or is he, on the other hand, tacitly accepting position (A) in respect of the Logic, too, and merely, as might be reasonably inferred from the context, insisting that, because thought is always both form and content, the method of formal logic, which erects empty thought-forms indifferent to their content, is for ever superseded in philosophy? May we interpret his assertion that dialectic is the only true philosophical method, not as a pretension to final truth but as at least a tacit recognition that the real claim of Hegelianism to immortality rests on the fact that it knows as a conclusion from its own premisses that it is destined to be superseded, that it is itself a thesis which must beget its own antithesis? Can we say that Hegel did not proclaim the provisional character of his Logic because to do so would have been to waste words on the obvious, and because what Bradley says of judgement must apply to any body of philosophical doctrine which its author allows to stand as his last word:

'Our last judgement, and that is our present judgement, must be taken or rather must be treated as infallible. This does not mean that a further reflection may not cause us to reject it. It means that, until that reflection comes, we must hold the judgement as true, and that we cannot, while making a judgement, entertain the possibility of its error'?[1]

5·47. I do not think it can be fairly denied that Hegel often does regard the circle of *Denkbestimmungen* as closed and finally complete. There is nothing in the Logic analogous to the passage in the *Rechtsphilosophie* describing the flight of Minerva's owl at twilight or to the closing sentence of the Philosophy of History.[2] There is nothing, that is to say, which suggests that the Logic is a product of retrospection eliciting the true logical nature of human thinking up to date as the *Rechtsphilosophie* and the *Philosophy of History* elicit the truth of man's social and political activity up to date. Rather he seems to think that the possibility of those latter interim

[1] *Essays on Truth and Reality*, pp. 381–2.

[2] See §§ 5·433 and 4 above.

reports depends upon the finality of the Logic.[1] The last words of the Preface to the *Phänomenologie des Geistes*, though they clear him of any charge of personal arrogance, seem to express an even wider claim to finality:

> 'At the present time spirit in its universal nature prevails strongly, and will not relax its claim to the whole compass of its rich accumulated culture. The mere individual aspect has become proportionately, and quite properly, a matter of indifference. Hence the share in the total work of the spirit which falls to the individual's activity can only be small. The individual therefore must—as indeed the very nature of science demands—be all the more oblivious of himself. Certainly he must make of himself, and achieve, what he can; but he has less to expect from himself, and there is less that he may claim for himself. Accordingly less must be demanded of him.'

These are not the words of a thinker who tries arrogantly to leap out of his epoch into eternity, but they may suggest that he stays within it because it seems to him to be almost all-inclusive, almost to reconcile time and eternity.

6. It may be doubted whether or not Hegel believed his Logic eternal, but it cannot be doubted that the nucleus of Hegelianism which we have tried to construct justifies no such view. If there be a fullness of thought which nothing less than the whole circle of the super-triad can express, then the circle of the pure categories is a lesser and an emptier truth. The *Denkbestimmungen* must in that case share in some measure the contingent, empirical character of the *Begriffsbestimmungen*. For when we compare *Denkbestimmungen* with *Begriffsbestimmungen* as two types of defective abstraction from the full truth of the super-triad, we find that *Denkbestimmungen* are the truer because (*a*) they contrast as pure abstract thought with the more crass and contingent *Begriffsbestimmungen*, and (*b*) by virtue of this purity their movement is more nearly the movement of a free self-developing activity in which content and form are so unified that we may even contrast the progressive synthesis of Being and Essence in the Notion with the movement of the *Begriffsbestimmungen* as in a special sense concrete and not abstract.

[1] That Hegel, for whom the speculative problem arose and long continued as a religious problem, came to subordinate religion to philosophy is perhaps further evidence that he believed his Logic final.

But as against the fuller thought of the super-triad the circle of pure logical thought must be defective; *Denkbestimmungen* and *Begriffsbestimmungen* are reciprocally dependent defective abstractions. Hence the Logic must not merely contain categories of contingency but be itself throughout in a measure contingent and empirical. Its empirical taint is not precisely the sensuous-empirical character of the *Begriffsbestimmungen*, but the categories of Being are manifested in sense-experience *par excellence*, and Hegel's categories as a whole are necessarily manifest in a world of experience based in sense.[1] For all the seeming sharpness of distinction between them, sense and thought for Hegel fall on one scale, and because *Begriffsbestimmungen* and *Denkbestimmungen* are reciprocally dependent, *Denkbestimmungen* cannot altogether escape contingency. If the Logic has no taint of the empirical Hegel's own principle is violated; for the unity of form and content is shattered. The categories become at best a framework for an alien filling, a prefabricated bed of Procrustes, at worst a congeries of sheerly transcendent forms, dead and disjointed because severed from their manifestation.

7. It might still perhaps be objected on Hegel's behalf to this argument, and by implication to all our previous criticism, that the super-triad is the complete and perfect synthesis, and that its elements, though *ex hypothesi* defective in abstraction from it, are not defective *in se* and are within the super-triad free from all defect.

7·1. To support this argument the objector might begin by maintaining that the Logic is not defective *in se*, because categories of the contingent are not contingent categories: they are the eternal and necessary thought-forms of the contingent.

This is plausible. There is certainly an important distinction between the contingent and its thought-form. But that distinction is not, as the objector implies, absolute, as the inevitable next step in his argument will reveal. For to preserve the final perfection of the super-triad, he must further

[1] Contrast Kant's pure categories, which he alleges to be valid for any being endowed with a passive faculty of intuition, sensuous or not. We should perhaps here distinguish a third meaning of the term 'empirical'; see § 5·42 above.

maintain that the *Begriffsbestimmungen* both of Concrete Spirit and of Nature are also eternally necessary. But we have seen that Hegel allows at any rate the philosophy of Nature to depend for material on the endlessly changing results of natural science. Hence the *Begriffsbestimmungen* of Nature, though they are thought-forms of the contingent, must have contingency in themselves. But if one element of the super-triad is defective *in se* the super-triad is not perfect, and the objector's position is at once undermined. Further, if the dialectic of Nature is defective *in se*, then the dialectic of Concrete Spirit can never fully sublate the residue of the natural in it, and is itself inherently defective. And the categories in effect become vulnerable from both sides. For (*a*) the categories are the first main phase in the development of Philosophy, in which Concrete Spirit culminates, and therefore must, if the dialectical circle is continuous, still for all their purity be tainted by a residue of that very Nature which, as the second main phase of Philosophy, is their antithesis; and correspondingly (*b*), if we place ourselves, so to say, at the point of transition from Idea to Nature and look backwards and forwards, we find the categories, as we contended before, in a relation of reciprocal dependence with the *Begriffsbestimmungen*.

7·2. Moreover, Nature is not the only sphere in which philosophy draws material from empirical observation and research. If one reads Hegel's Philosophy of Spirit, taking that to include the *Rechtsphilosophie* and the lectures on the philosophy of history, art, religion, and the history of philosophy, it is clear that at every step Hegel has used the results of empirical inquiry. Even in the field of logic, as he himself is aware, there is a substratum, so to say, of empirical inquiry into pure thought in the shape of formal logic.[1] It is equally clear that Hegel nowhere succeeds in perfectly sublating this empirical matter. In the transition from Idea to Nature thought is confronted with an 'other'. This 'other' is an *alter ego* which thought has severed from itself, but between thought and its 'other' there is an unbridged gap: to the question why quantity should be manifest as space there is no answer.[2] And the gap is never fully bridged. The 'other'

[1] Cf. ch. ii, §§ 2 ff. above, and IH, p. 122. [2] See § 5·41 above.

persists as the contingency and empiricality, the aspect of brute confrontation, which is present in every phase of Nature and Concrete Spirit. The categories of pure thought are by virtue of their abstractness less contingent than the forms of Nature and Concrete Spirit, but even in them there is contingency. The 'other' is not fully overcome in the final synthesis of the Philosophy of Spirit, and not only the products of formal logic but the whole history of philosophy contributes a material still in some measure empirical to Hegel's Logic.[1] At every phase one is forced to separate where there should in principle be no separation. One is compelled to ask the double question: Is this phase self-justifying within the dialectic, *and* does it give the truth of the 'facts'? At each point two currents meet but do not fully fuse. Although the original unity of its sources is not problematic but categorical, yet every phase is a sublation at once of its dialectical predecessors and of empirical material, and in no phase is there complete distinction or complete coalescence of these aspects. The dialectic is never a perfectly free movement. Philosophical thought can never sublate without residue the endless empirical flow,[2] and is therefore itself empirically tainted. Contingency differs in degree throughout the dialectic, but it is ubiquitous, and the super-triad is after all not complete and perfect.

8. Thus we conclude again that a flawless philosophical dialectic is not possible, and that its possibility is not an inference necessitated by that nucleus of Hegelianism which we have assumed. Whatever Hegel himself may have believed, no element of his system is exempt from the taint of the empirical.

[1] See below, ch. xxii, § 5.

[2] By calling the flow of empirical material 'endless', I do not so much mean that we believe it will go on for ever if the world, or the civilized world, does not come to an end, but rather that we recognize the empirical as extensible *ad indefinitum*. Our belief in an endless future rests upon the *a priori* category of the spurious infinite which makes empirical experience possible.

XXI

THE SCOPE AND LIMITATIONS OF A DIALECTICAL PHILOSOPHY

1. We attempted to formulate a nucleus of Hegelian doctrine, and we have found it to entail a fundamental dualism in human experience which precludes the possibility of expanding that nucleus into a finished system. Reality, we assumed, is a necessarily ordered whole, wherein the ordered elements are the phases of a single dialectical activity, phases of spirit's unreserved self-manifestation. But this assumption, we found, although its acceptance everywhere guarantees man against total scepticism, since it takes human experience to be an integral element in the self-manifestion of spirit, yet everywhere denies him the assurance of final truth.

We have now to consider whether or not with this dilemma we have reduced Hegel's system to absurdity. Have we, by presenting the traditional oppositions of speculative thought as each in each of its members all-pervasive of experience, confounded, as it were, the primary colours of philosophy in a fog of neutral grey? Or is our guarantee against total scepticism sufficient to let us hope that in the ordered blending of these colours before they fuse there is still some promise of dialectical construction? We have, in fact, to suggest in outline, as was proposed in Chapter xix, § 4, the limitations within which our nucleus of Hegelian idealism is capable of legitimate development.

2. Yet the task which I propose is a paradox. The inherent duality of human experience is the rock on which Hegel's system, if all or any part of it pretends to flawless finality, suffers total shipwreck. Yet this same duality is of the essence of Hegel's own thought, and it is, I think, the only possible basis of any dialectical philosophy. To clarify its nature, which was not, I believe, perfectly clear to Hegel, is so important that I shall weary the reader's patience by tracing it in a few more concrete examples before I try to outline the scope and limits of a less ambitious dialectic.

3. We may start with a very general reflection. The con-

flict of philosophic opinion is a scandal as old as philosophy, but if human experience is inherently dualistic, man's unresting oscillation between disbelief and conviction is at least an intelligible consequence of that dualism. The optimistic Hegelian may persuade himself that he possesses a finished system of eternal truth, while the despairing sceptic discards as insoluble or meaningless any question as to the source or ground of experience, and comes in the end to renounce all speculation; and the Spinozist, drunk with deity, may reduce appearance to illusion, although the phenomenalist can find in experience no content except appearance without correlative reality. Yet the spectacle of these conflicts is not on our present hypothesis merely ridiculous. For the criterion of truth and error is, as we see it, immanent in experience. It is also transcendent, but it does not fall right outside experience. Man's thought is, in fact, self-judging only because it is self-transcending. If the contingent and the necessary are characters which in human experience never absolutely exclude one another, then opinion and knowledge are not mutually exclusive. A philosophical (or for that matter an anti-philosophical) theory is never a pure, floating hypothesis which may or may not be assumed and may possibly have never been assumed by anyone. It rests always upon some categorically judged ground, and it in some measure commits even its most tentative propounder. Again, in the extremes of error spirit is somehow self-manifest and man somehow self-conscious. The logical positivist who denies metaphysics, holds philosophy to consist in linguistic manipulation, and charitably designs a therapeutic method to cure the illusions of the worried metaphysician, may be heading straight towards the denial of reason; but only reason links the steps of the falsest argument. Though error be perverted and not merely defective truth, a history of philosophic thought as degrees of partial truth and an historical treatment of philosophies as types of philosophical error would in principle coincide. For error, at any rate philosophical error, is a mistaking of grades, and a true grading of human experience would be the identical aim of both undertakings. Sharp discrepancies strike a professional philosopher when he considers his fellow workers first in the order of degree in which he respects the mental powers of each of them, and then again in the order in which he sympathizes with their several philosophic views. He might well be baffled if he did not recognize that what commands his respect without his sympathy is a clear insight into a partial truth in which, however, from his own point of view the error is more conspicuous than the truth. He might readily despair if he failed to understand that differences of philosophic attitude, individual, racial, historical, are at once necessary and complementary half-truths and at the same time contingent and conflicting idiosyncrasies of opinion, beneath which may be detected all the empirical diversities of talent, temperament, nurture, social and economic circumstance, and if he did not realize that the latter can never be sublated without residue in the former. Even the great landslides in philosophical opinion, the abrupt decay of long-accepted doctrines which collapse abandoned rather than refuted, do not simply accuse the futility of the human intellect. They justly excite ridicule only when the language either of the conservatives or of the revolutionaries betrays a more than ordinary ignorance of what is really going on.[1]

4. Nowhere is the conflict of theoretical opinion sharper, and nowhere is the ambiguous duality of human experience more evident, than in the sphere of action. The freedom of the will is a trite topic, and I shall be as brief as its complexity allows. I shall, for example, ignore the fact that no characterization of man's freedom or bondage in action is in the end independent of his modes of experience other than will, and I shall follow tradition by putting morality in the foreground.

If we bear in mind Kant's general formulation of the moral problem, as it is reasonable to do in discussing any problem with reference to Hegel, we may say that the ideal governing moral action is the full exercise of man's practical reason, the complete development of an autonomous will in

[1] The same contrast between the necessary and the contingent strikes us when we consider the two half-truths, (*a*) that it is the philosopher's function to sit back, as it were, and think out the implications of human experience as such, and (*b*) that the philosophy of an epoch is the product of that epoch, that the thinking of any philosopher is determined by and reflects the general attitude and temper of his time.

a kingdom of harmonizing ends: the essence of the good will is a freedom consisting in rational self-determination. But this freedom is never fully experienced, and, whatever be Kant's solution of the problem thereby arising, the reason seems to be that even at the highest level to which man's will reaches his nature is not wholly absorbed and integrated in his willing. He cannot fully transcend the lower levels of himself, although his essential nature lies in that transcendence. His morality never entirely synthesizes the opposition between (*a*) an inclination which, abstractly considered in a universe where there is no more fully developed consciousness, is merely a manifestation of the activity which constitutes man, and (*b*) a duty which does not indeed impel him mechanically, but does, in being experienced as obligatory, imply a still imperfect freedom in the fulfilling of it, a freedom which is still on the negative side partly a mere 'freedom from', and consequently on the positive side partly a mere choosing, and so is in part caprice. Many men, as Aristotle knew better than Kant, have willed the good with a freedom of activity sufficiently unhampered to be pleasurable with its own specific pleasure, but if we avoid the moral philosopher's common fault of attending too closely to actions in isolation from their context, and examine, so to say, the whole moral policy of a good man and its implementation over a period of time, we shall be safe in saying that this policy is not everywhere synthesized in an activity more free than can be pretty fairly described as the doing of a duty for the sake of doing duty. The desires and impulses are the essential material which the good will reconstitutes; without them there would indeed be no will at all. But in man they survive as a not fully absorbed residue. As language develops into thought, yet survives to subserve thought as its expression,[1] so the desires develop into a will which at the first stage of its emergence sets itself over against them and selects from among them, but can only realize itself by, as it were, descending again and satisfying its particular selected desire. The will emerging as choice, or subjective caprice (*Willkür*), is described by Hegel in ΦG, § 478. It is a contradiction because 'it actualizes itself in a particularity which at the same time it

[1] See ch. i above.

regards as a nullity [sc. as a cancelled lower self], and finds a satisfaction in what it has at the same time emerged from'.[1]

At a higher stage a man's residue of desire, rationalized but still imperfectly sublated, can conflict as an insubordinately arguing self within him, and that desire may survive to subserve as well as to conflict with the good will is implicitly admitted by anyone who believes that rewards and punishments can do anything to promote virtuous action.

4·1. Instinctive practical behaviour precedes self-conscious practice, but both must issue in physical change, even if the issue of the former differs as sharply from the issue of the latter as the speech of a small child differs from that of a grown man. Analogously, economic action survives in moral action. It is futile to argue that because an action is not morally good or bad according merely to its success or failure to produce the results at which it aims, therefore efficiency is not a phase sublated in morally good action. That at least may be learned from Croce if not from Plato and Aristotle, and if not from the philosophers then from the commonest practical experience. But the sublation is incomplete. A residue still survives, conflicts, and subserves. *Utile* and *honestum* clash often enough, but the less useful a man's conduct as a means to a good end the less it is moral. Some good intentions may serve to extenuate failure in duty, but with the rest Hell is proverbially paved, and only a sentimentalist regards as necessarily a mere cynic the statesman who regrets that prudence forbids the policy which is prima facie honourable.

4·2. Some thinkers, looking at the lower end of this scale of imperfectly transcended phases which go to constitute the human will (although perhaps not knowing where they looked), have called freedom an illusion. They have seen man's willing as no more than a mechanically causal succession of *sensa*, images, emotions, and desires. The Behaviourists have reduced it to a purely physiological causal series. Such views, until it becomes necessary to explain illusion, are plausible. If human consciousness constitutes itself out of a series of lower levels of itself which descends

[1] For a rather lengthy elaboration of this doctrine see T. H. Green, *Prolegomena to Ethics*, §§ 137–47.

into the pre-spiritual, we are bound in descending the scale to reach a level at which there is no principle to be seen at work beyond mechanical causation, and if the principle of cause and effect holds anywhere it holds everywhere—at its own level. Man has—nay, is—a physical body which is part of an environing physical world, and he is therefore subject to the same causality as the rest of that world. It is mere confusion of levels to suggest that in action man, so to say, taps in and exerts a 'free' control which in this special case modifies the nature of the causal current. But man's body—or man as his body—is, within his self-conscious self, a partly but never wholly transcended element, and so more remotely is the physical world of which for natural science (i.e. for a certain other level of experience) that body is a part. Because it is not fully transcended, it at once precludes Man from full freedom and at the same time subserves such freedom as he has. At the level of *sensa*, images, emotions, and desires there is nothing, I think, that can be viewed as sheerly mechanical causation, but one certainly can experience the impact of a sensation, even the urge of a desire, almost as an external cause which impels mechanically.

4·3. If we return now to the upper end of the scale and pass on from ethics to politics, the same theme is not less easy to illustrate.

The general conception of the state as organic is, I think, a corollary of the idealist position with which we are working; but it does not follow from that position that the transcendence of the practical individual at the higher level of the state is total and without residue. Rather we find that the relation between desire and will within the individual is here analogously repeated. The practical attempt to construct a perfectly organic state results inevitably in tyranny. It is possible to subordinate to the direct service of the state all the individual's practical interests—to say nothing of his aesthetic, religious, and purely intellectual activities—only by at once lowering and at the same time violently intensifying a community's level of experience, only by exciting or hypnotizing a community into a crowd. The function of government, of which a crowd is not capable, must then devolve upon a tyrant. Save by inducing a mass fanaticism which is below the level of individual differences, and by substituting tyranny for self-government, you cannot make the service of the state the sole direct motive of every citizen.[1]

4·31. But it does not follow that the singular individual alone is real and the state artificial. No doubt the organic state so constructed is artificial, if by 'artificial' in such a context is meant that which violates human nature; but to hold that in the life of the citizen the life of the private individual is sublated, it is not necessary to hold that the transcendence is total and without residue. One may hesitate to maintain that the partially capricious will of the individual —'private enterprise' is the modern name for it—must survive to subserve the state's activity, even if in principle the state transcends it. One may hesitate for fear of providing a ready excuse for purely selfish action. But all history forces on us the fact that, although the state exists to resolve individual conflict, yet the equilibrium of human society demands some clash of political opinion freely working, and beneath it some actual conflict of private interests, as necessarily as thought, which emerges through language, nevertheless requires language for the expression in which it gains completion.[2]

5. In Hegel's system Objective Spirit closes in World History, the thesis and antithesis of Absolute Spirit are respectively Art and Revealed Religion, and the synthesis of Absolute Spirit, Philosophy, begins to unfold itself as Logic. It is beyond the scope of this *Study* to offer detailed comment on Hegel's Philosophy of Spirit, but it may be worth while to indicate very briefly certain aspects of history and art which aptly illustrate the duality of human experience, and unless we can show that duality also in the movement of logical categories our argument must fail of its purpose.

5·1. We can at least by pressing our hypothesis of imperfect sublation reject several one-sided views of history

[1] Moreover, only the hatred of a real or imagined enemy, internal or external, can maintain the fanatical unity upon which the cohesion of a state so constructed depends.

[2] Plato in the *Republic* uses the divorce of power from wealth as one means to the solving of this problem. It is not, however, always remembered that in the Platonic state the 'profit motive' still does its necessary work in the souls of the δημιουργοί to create the economic basis of the state.

which in the past have provoked every type of irresoluble antinomy. We need not take history to be the fortuitous concourse of conflicting individual wills and indifferent natural events unshaped by any wider principle. But equally we need not suppose the principle of its movement to be either some impersonal law which works relentlessly in despite of particular wills, or some omnipotent and all-foreknowing deity whose predestinating plan for the progress or the destruction of the human race cannot fail. History is a form of human experience no less than sense-perception or moral conduct. In this historical activity of man natural events, we shall say, and the wills of individual men and states are transcended; the pattern of past history is sufficiently coherent to forbid any other conclusion. An external world of natural events, and again the conflicting and co-operating wills of men, are presupposed in history; they are the material of which it constitutes itself, the lower levels which are sublated in it. But very conspicuously they also persist in it as partially contingent elements, and they are also the indispensable media in which the phases of history gain expression.

5·2. Art yet more clearly illustrates our theme. Under stress of obscure feeling, a man potentially a poet struggles, developing his power of imagery and speech, until an emotion and a vision supervene, which are still incomplete until they are expressed in words. These words are not the half-articulate language of his struggle, but they still are words. That theoretical thinking can soar wholly beyond language is a faintly plausible doctrine, though, I believe, a false one; but poetry and all the other arts clearly must culminate, as they began, in sense.[1]

[1] The extent to which an artist can develop his creation purely imaginatively without resort to perceptible embodiment no doubt varies from art to art and artist to artist. Yet I doubt if any aesthetic creation is perfect if it does not become a work of art; it begins in direct perception and there, I think, it must end. The Crocean relegation of works of art to the world of practice, where they exist as mere physical stimulants of recollection, seems to rest on a false limitation of the externally existent to the practical. Doubtless a painting, a poem, or a statue has external existence as a practical means to recollection and communication, but it is not, I think, a lapse into realism to hold that it also exists externally as the necessary final externalization of aesthetic

5·3. We may now ask whether logic, too, illustrates the inescapable duality of human experience, and it may be well to begin by recalling an earlier discussion.

In ch. xix, §§ 10·1 ff. we examined the development from sense to thought with special reference to time, a form of sense. We were then considering what appears in Hegel's system as *Begriffsbestimmungen*, phases in the concrete self-manifestation of spirit, phases in particular of Subjective Spirit. But at that level of Concrete Spirit the emphasis fell upon the finitude of these phases as forms of human experience not highly developed, forms in which the immanence of spirit, coming to itself through the sublation of Nature, was far from fully explicit. Sense-perception, imagination, judgement, and inference, as we considered them, were little more than the generalized modes in which any finite subject experiences. On the one hand, because spirit is immanent in them they are in a degree universal; the content of each is totality. Sense-perception, though a subjective mode, is its subject's characterization of its world, and that world, however poor and abstract, however in one aspect narrowly private, is yet for the subject *the* world. On the other hand, that world is, as a whole world, not an actually perceived but a merely perceptible world. Similarly for imagination all the universe is not imagined but is imaginable. Again, although thought moves in universals, and judgement and inference claim all reality as the context within which they assert, yet judgement and inference are, on the other side, the act of a singular individual subject who asserts as his private opinion a particular content and can never fully specify the context upon which it depends. The subject in each of these cases is finite, though in a different degree.[1] His activity is still in some measure reaction to a stimulus which conditions it contingently. The imperfectly sublated factor is what in ch. xx, § 5·42 I have called the sensuous-empirical.

5·31. The logical categories are thought pure of sense. Their movement is therefore not temporal, and the empirical

experience. It is rather the copy of the work of art—the coloured print, the plaster cast, the gramophone record—which exists for a practical purpose.

[1] For example, the distinction between knowledge and opinion is not explicit prior to judgement.

factor in them cannot be any residue of sensuous function and content. But the categories possess their purity by virtue of abstraction, and although they are at once form and content of thought, yet their form has essential reference to the self-manifestation of spirit in and through a world of sensuous experience. Hence the empirical factor here appears at any rate in the fact that the categories of Being and Essence are themselves thought-forms of the contingent. But if it is true, as it clearly is, that we do think in categories of the contingent, it follows further that the whole movement of our categoreal thinking is tainted with contingency. To deny it would, if pure thought is both form and content, be to break the union of form and content within thought.[1]

5·32. We may now, in order to test this conclusion, examine in more detail the question what shape this pervasive contingency, this empirical factor, is likely to take in a logic of categories. If there be imperfect sublation in the movement of pure thought, how precisely will it compare with imperfect sublation in the transition from sense to thought? What residue will survive to subserve and eke out the higher level of thought which has failed to transcend it fully?

In the sphere of Concrete Spirit (*a*) the empirical factor was the sensuous-empirical, and this revealed itself as (*b*) an immediate brute presence of reality, which is therefore also (*c*) an unmediated indeterminacy. On the other hand, in pure thought (*a*) there can be no residue of sense; among the categories there can be no sensuous concept. Moreover, (*b*) in Concrete Spirit the brute presence of the real is that 'other' of thought, upon abstraction from which the purity of pure thought depends.[2] Yet pure thought must contain in itself the abstract or pure form of that brute 'other', since that 'other' is pure thought's other self and not any alien and indifferent matter. Pure thought, that is, must have its own moment of immediacy. And this immediacy will also develop as (*c*) an unmediated indeterminacy in pure thought, a presence there of categories of the contingent.

5·33. If we express this in terms of Hegel's Logic, it means

[1] This seems to complement the argument of ch. xx, § 6.

[2] Cf. ch. xx, § 5·4.

that the always unsublated residue in pure thought originates in the intuition of Pure Being with which the Logic starts.[1] Pure Being is the thought-form of that immediate brute presence of reality, of that 'other' which thought has severed from itself and in Concrete Spirit first encounters and reclaims as space.[2] Through the categories of Being this thought-form of brute immediacy develops in its own right, and already in its more emphatically antithetical phases (very obviously in the Spurious Infinite) reveals itself as a thought of unmediated indeterminacy. In the categories of Essence Being as the 'unessential' moment of Essence very clearly emerges in both these aspects. In fact Hegel's doctrine of Essence not only is his most brilliant achievement in logic and obviously integral to our provisional nucleus of Hegelian idealism, but also provides the very source and ground of such an hypothesis of imperfect sublation within pure thought as I have put forward. In the coupled categories of Essence the mind is clearly at once on two levels of thought; the 'unessential' is at once transcended in the essential and at the same time survives to subserve, eke out, and express the essential.[3]

5·34. Hegel does not, however, appear to accept the view that duality and imperfect sublation must persist *throughout* pure thought.

In general it would seem that for Hegel the duality in pure thought is (*a*) in the categories of Being not yet present, and (*b*) in the categories of the Notion transcended without trace. In more detail his position appears to be this. (*a*) The dialectic of Being presents itself as mere transformation or substitution without contradiction: there is only Being and not yet Essence. Yet in the internal dialectic of Being there is obviously an analogue of contradiction: without it there would be no movement at all. There is perhaps some ambiguity in Hegel's account of Being, but we need not press it until we have examined a more serious difficulty.

[1] Cf. ch. ii, § 1.

[2] Cf. ch. xx, § 5·41.

[3] No doubt the thinking subject in reflecting on the categories is conscious of this imperfect sublation to a degree in which the subject in empirical judgement is not, but that is not to say that in pure thought human experience overcomes its duality.

(*b*) The logic of the Notion culminates and closes in Absolute Idea. In Absolute Idea sublation is perfect, and there is no further onward movement of pure thought save in the sense that the dialectic of the categories is a return of spirit upon itself and may be metaphorically called circular. But Hegel further maintains that every category of the Notion is actual (*wirklich*), and that the entire movement of the Notion is perfect development above all contradiction, a mere transparent play in which there is no cancellation but only preservation of transcended categories.[1]

5·35. If we are here to assume that Hegel means what he says, we can scarcely escape the conclusion that the 'play' of notional categories is an illusion. It even becomes difficult to differentiate this perfect development from the transformation or substitution which characterizes the movement of Being. Hegel thus seems to defeat his own end. For his end was to make the sharpest possible distinction between the dialectic of Being and the dialectic of the Notion, and in pursuit of it he had perhaps already over-simplified the movement of Being. The general difference which Hegel intends between the movement in Being, Essence, and the Notion must characterize any dialectic of spirit, but that difference in human philosophizing remains a difference of emphasis; it cannot become absolute. If the movement of Being is quite innocent of contradiction, and the movement of the Notion has *ab initio* resolved contradiction in an actuality which is perfect self-development, then neither in Being nor in the Notion is there any genuine dialectic at all.[2] For there is no dialectic which has not contradiction for its spring, and no contradiction which has not its empirical moment. Certainly dialectic without the immanence in it of absolute activity is nothing, and Hegel is justified in making Pure Being the first, and Absolute Idea the last, category of pure thought. But neither is man's dialectical thinking anything without that contradictory duality which signifies that the immanence of spirit is incomplete. Hegel remarks in the Introduction to LL[3] that the content of the Logic may be expressed as the setting forth of God as he is in his eternal

[1] Cf. ch. xi, § 1·1.

[2] And if Being and the Notion vanish, Essence vanishes too.

[3] p. 46.

essence before the creation of Nature and of a finite spirit. There are times when he appears to be (*a*) supposing, as this metaphor strongly suggests, that his Logic displays pure thought as not in any sense human experience, and then (*b*) cutting the knot by forcibly identifying the empirical with the *a priori* moment in pure thought—and indeed in Concrete Spirit, too[1]—and asking us to believe that the phases of his own dialectic are final. He falls, we feel, himself a victim to the nemesis of our dual human experience. He seems to offer us the infinite and fob us off with the finite, and his system for all the vastness of its reach begins to excite in us an acute feeling of claustrophobia.

Thus there seems to be no reason why we should modify the conclusion of § 5·31 that the whole movement of our categoreal thinking is tainted with contingency. Logic, too, like practice, history, and art, reveals the inescapable duality of our experience.

6. Following Hegel closely, we have witnessed the failure of dialectic as a flawless system. We have seen that it can give us no final truth in any of the traditional branches of philosophy. Before we turn to consider the possibility of a modified Hegelian dialectic, we may first ask whether any other shape of dialectic which does not so closely follow Hegel is possible.

[1] Hegel frequently speaks as if all the phases of Objective Spirit were fully actual (*wirklich*). It is because of this seemingly intransigent insistence that the actual is perfect without degree or qualification in all its development that Hegel's famous identification of the actual and the rational has excited such violent opposition, and that his treatment of *Sittlichkeit* (Social Ethics; see Table II) has provoked ironic comment on the close resemblance of Hegel's State to the Prussian monarchy, and on the extreme tenderness of his *Weltgeist* for Germany. There is a point, however, which critics who contend that Hegel sacrifices the individual to the state might do well to recollect—or to learn, if they were never aware of it. Hegel may press the conception of perfect development so far that it almost collapses back into the cancellation, the seeming transformation or substitution, which characterizes the movement of Being; he may in his political theory tend to ignore that persistence of an unsublated residue for which I have contended in §§ 4·3 and 4·31 of this chapter. But his whole point in stressing the *Wirklichkeit* of Objective Spirit is to insist on the preservation as against the cancellation of the lower in the higher phase. He regards legal, moral, and social life not as cancelled but as fully preserved in the life of the state.

6·1. We should most naturally look first at Hegel's most brilliant and sympathetic modern critic, Benedetto Croce. For Croce's philosophy attempts ruthlessly to exclude from its structure all contingent, empirical differentiation, but remains dialectical.

In Croce's system the main difference—if I may be allowed to use the word without prejudice—lies between theory and action. By virtue of that main difference within spirit a great gulf is fixed between the nexus of 'distincts' and the synthesis of opposites on the one hand, and on the other the practical sphere of pseudo-concepts, which may be either representational or abstract, but are all empirical at least in the sense of indefinitely diverse.

This unconditional banishment of the empirical to the sphere of action, where there is no truth and error but only good and evil, success and failure, and no dialectic but only the endless classifications of the special sciences which are created purely for practical convenience, strongly suggests that Croce could countenance no such modified dialectic as we are seeking. Yet a glance at Croce's own conception of dialectic may nevertheless be helpful.

6·2. Croce, especially in his earlier work, sharply contrasts the dialectic of 'distincts' as a dialectic of degrees in which the terms are concrete, with the dialectic of opposites, which taken apart from their synthesis are abstract. His main criticism of Hegel is the charge that Hegel, who himself, interpreting Kant's *a priori* synthesis, discovered the dialectic of opposites, failed to distinguish from it the dialectic of 'distincts' and so came to treat 'distincts' as if they were amenable to the dialectic of opposition.

6·3. Croce's main 'distincts' are theory and action, which so relate that action presupposes theory but not vice versa. Each of these again subdivides into two concrete 'distincts' related in the same manner to one another. Theory is first art, which is individual intuition innocent of any contrast of fancy and fact, and then philosophical thought, which is the concrete universal. Action is first economic and then moral. In this developing series from art to moral action there is no sublation of abstract opposites; each moment is autonomous and concrete, although the succeeding moment is at once itself and its predecessor. Art, for example, is not thought, and, as a 'distinct' form of spirit, art owes nothing to thought; but the intuition which is (or was?) art is contained in the concrete universal of thought. And the same relation holds between economic and moral action, and again between theory and practice. The autonomy of these four 'distinct' forms does not, however, imply that each has its own peculiar content—if it had it would be a mere empirical differentiation; each form informs the whole content of experience.

6·4. I think it is fair, and for our present purpose sufficient, to exhibit the relation of opposites to 'distincts' as follows. We can express the concrete nature of the four 'distincts' as the beautiful, the true, the useful, the good. But each of these has its opposite, viz. the ugly, the false, the harmful, the bad. In each 'distinct' its opposite is present as the unreal in the real, but the 'distinct' is only concrete by virtue of containing its opposite. Thus the movement of spirit through the 'distincts' is not synthesis of opposites, but it is by synthesis of opposites that spirit moves within each 'distinct'. *Il concetto*, the Concept *par excellence* as opposed to the pseudoconcepts, is both synthesis of 'distincts' and synthesis of opposites, and knowledge of the Concept is philosophical knowledge.

6·5. Croce continues his criticism of Hegel from the basis of his own doctrine of error, which, so far as I understand it, I will try to outline.

The true as a concrete 'distinct' contains the false within it: it *is* the synthesis of true and false. Thought is thus in its own concrete nature incorruptible—'Man has in himself the fountain of truth'—and the false taken in abstraction from the synthesis which truth is has no content of thought. Hence no man can err in good faith. Logical error (for Croce all error is logical error) is a practical act. It is the substitution for thinking of a non-thinking act from another 'distinct', the practical act of substituting an aesthetic or practical content which is emphatically not a partial truth nor a degree of truth. The fault of Hegel was to mistake abstract negative opposites for particular concrete concepts exhibiting order of degree (i.e. for 'distincts'), and thus to incorporate in his Logic what are in fact philosophical errors with non-philosophical content.[1] Through this fault a mass of alien stuff found its way into the Logic, and further confusion was produced by Hegel's 'panlogistic' attempt to apply to Nature and Concrete Spirit his dialectical method which tries vainly to treat 'distincts' as opposites.

6·6. With the theory of error and the second part of Croce's criticism we need not yet concern ourselves. Unless we can accept his fundamental initial contrast between 'distincts' and opposites, we can hope for no solution of our problem from him. It might, however, be objected that the latest edition of Croce's famous *Essay on Hegel*, in which he puts forward these criticisms, appeared in 1927, and that since then his thought has moved towards a closer unity of spirit than is implied by his earlier doctrine of opposites and 'distincts'. That may be so, but at any rate the identification of philosophy and history is already present in the 1909 edition of the *Logica*, and in any case a position maintained by a great and already mature thinker possesses a right to be discussed for its own sake, whether or not its author later modify it.

6·7. At first sight the Crocean 'distincts' present themselves as a linear series in which the first term has no presupposition and each prior grade, although contained in its successor, retains complete autonomy. This is particularly so in the *Estetica*, where Croce is dominated by his sense that all possible content of human experience assumes in art the form of intuition and expression, which is something vastly different from (*a*) all the indefinitely multiple empirical differentiae by means of which arts and works of art can be classified, and from (*b*) intellectual, economic, and moral activity, no one of which has any claim whatever to dictate to art. Yet Croce holds that the 'distincts' are inseparable and in a certain sense reciprocally imply one another. They constitute a circle wherein spirit, traversing its ideal degrees, eternally returns upon itself.[2]

[1] According to Croce the task of philosophy in regard to error is (*a*) to determine the necessary forms of philosophic error in relation to the already distinguished forms of knowledge, to exhibit, that is, a phenomenology of error which is the critical moment of the whole philosophy of spirit; and (*b*) on the basis of this to trace in a history of philosophy the partially erroneous philosophies of various thinkers; see *Logica*, pp. 400 ff., and *Hegel*, p. 109.

[2] Compare Hegel's use of the circle metaphor.

But if the 'distincts' are fully autonomous they are too perfect; they are not degrees of spirit at all; their nexus cannot be conceived as synthesis; they are concretes immediate without mediation; spirit does not move dialectically through them.[1] In fact the ideal, eternal 'distincts' can hardly escape the charge of being, after all, the terms of an empirical classification.[2]

The 'distincts', then, cannot be fully autonomous. If they are degrees through which spirit moves by dialectical synthesis, then each taken by itself is abstract, and each is in synthesis mediated; as indeed seems quite obvious in the case at least of the transition from art to thought, for thought to Croce is the Concept, the universal which is concrete *qua* logical *a priori* synthesis of individual and universal, not merely *qua* synthesis of true and false. And with this the spring of spirit's movement through the 'distincts'—not merely within each one of them—becomes contradictory opposition. In short, if we attempt to conceive the distinctness of the 'distincts' without opposition, the unity of spirit is shattered.[3]

6·8. Thus Croce defies the empirical, and in the end his own ideal *a priori* distinctions turn out to be empirically tainted. Gentile and subsequent Italian thinkers have pressed this line of criticism, but in their construction they have for the most part pushed defiance of the empirical yet farther, and it would not serve our purpose to examine their rather tenuous idealism. On the hypothesis to which we are committed, we have far less to gain from them than from Croce.

7. We might in this predicament be tempted to look in a very different direction. We might consider the notion of a

[1] The movement of the 'distincts' presents somewhat the same sort of problem as the perfect development of the actual (*wirklich*) in Hegel's categories of the Notion; cf. §§ 5·34 and 5·35 above. Croce in the *Essay* pays rather little attention to Hegel's conception of the actual and to the varying character which opposition assumes in Being, Essence, and the Notion.

[2] The proffered infinite again turns out to be finite; cf. § 5·35 *ad fin.* above.

[3] In *Philosophical Method*, ch. iii, R. G. Collingwood presents a lucid and effective criticism of Croce without mentioning his name. On Collingwood's scale of forms the relation between terms is a difference at once of degree and kind and a fusion of opposition and distinction.

frankly empirical dialectic. But we have not to reflect long on dialectical materialism to see that it can afford us no refuge. Hegel believes dialectic to be in essence the self-manifestation of absolute spirit in human experience. We have stressed the limitations imposed on any dialectical philosophy by the inherent duality of human experience, but we have not abandoned Hegel's view of the essence of dialectic. Marx's inversion of Hegel is a flat denial of that view. He retains from Hegel little more than the triadic formula. To Marx the element of chief importance in Hegel's system is the philosophy of history,[1] and his accounts of economic and historical process contain a good deal of Hegelian terminology; but if in reading them one remembers that his view of development does not presuppose the immanent activity of spirit, meaning evaporates from his phrases. He holds the mainspring of his dialectic to be a real contradiction in things, but contradiction save between the phases of self-developing spirit is nothing but deadlock. Hegel 'denied the law of contradiction' only in the sense of transcending it; Marx violates it with no right at all. John Lewis fairly describes the movement of Marxian dialectic as emergent evolution without any teleological implication or postulate of a directive spiritual force.[2] It is entirely *a posteriori*, presented as purely a nisus from an underlying material basis and quite devoid of any element of *a fronte* attraction. But development so misconceived becomes not development at all but a mere succession of unpredictable emergent novelties. Nevertheless, Marx used the triadic formula to give the movement a quite spurious appearance of rigid necessity;[3] and so completely did the formula mesmerize him that, wholly ignoring Hegel's warning that

[1] A false emphasis which has hugely distorted the popular conception of Hegel.

[2] See *A Textbook of Marxist Philosophy*, Gollancz, undated, Introduction, pp. 12–14.

[3] No inquiry can be wholly empirical (cf. IH, ch. x, §§ 3·1 ff.), but in fact Marx's conclusions have no more validity than those of any other empirical thinker, ordinarily so called, in a special sphere of investigation. In his hands the triadic form is no more one with its content than is the rough decimal notation which, borrowing from Wittgenstein's *Tractatus*, I have used to divide the chapters of this book into sections.

the philosophy of history affords no basis for prediction, he indulged in a stream of prophecy which the event has by no means justified. Marx's determinism sorts no more consistently with his inversion of the Hegelian dialectic than it does with his indignant denunciation of capitalist morality.

8. Our discussion of Croce and Marx has not solved our problem, but it may perhaps help us to sum it up and restate it a little more clearly.

Dialectic, conceived as a cycle of triads synthesizing opposites which are at once contrary and contradictory, is the bare formula of a method. It is the formal outward reflection of that activity of absolute spirit, self-developing in human experience, which gives to dialectic its essential nature. If we accept as our hypothesis that nucleus of Hegelianism which we have been trying to elicit, we must regard as the primary task of philosophy the dialectical expression of this activity; but we have found good reason to think that a dialectical philosophy can express the activity of spirit only as human experience dual-centred and imperfectly self-transcending. From this it does not follow that dialectical philosophy is bankrupt; for manifestation in human experience is nothing otiose, nothing accidental to the activity of spirit. A simply single centred subject could not develop; it would be a sheer *caput mortuum*. An absolute self-developing activity, whose development were not its self-manifestation in the contradiction of a dualistic finite consciousness, would be nothing at all. It could not even, in Bradley's phrase, 'revolve its perfections like a squirrel in its cage'. Aristotle's God, if he is sheerly transcendent,[1] Plato's Forms, if they are not in any way immanent, not merely fail to explain the world of human experience, but themselves collapse into nonentity. The key to dialectic is the transition of the phases of human self-consciousness and the duality of activities which constitutes it. Held apart and considered each by itself in abstraction, neither the *a priori* nor the empirical moment of spirit's activity is dialectical; for dialectic is the interplay of these moments.

8·1. Yet the triad of dialectic might reasonably be called a major discovery in formal logic, a discovery greater than

[1] Cf. IH, ch. vi.

the syllogism. Both have a minimal reference to content. Whereas the syllogism reflects a world of substance and accident, or in its generalized form a mere classifiable multiplicity of things, the triad is the abstract reflection of the return of spirit upon itself in self-conscious activity, and the abstract symbol of that union of coherence and comprehensiveness which is the inherent demand of thought as it becomes self-conscious. Hence the triad at least has its methodological value as a kind of regulative idea, a formal abstract norm which we can use as a rough test of content. The question 'What are the limitations of a dialectical philosophy?' can, I think, be profitably be restated in the form 'How far can the phases of a dialectical philosophy conform to the triadic formula?' The attempt in the remaining sections of this chapter to answer it will recall the contrast drawn in IH, ch. x, §§ 3–6 between empirical thinking and Hegel's dialectic, but the emphasis will fall, as it there did not, upon the inevitable shortcomings of any human dialectic.

8·2. The thesis and antithesis of the triad are contradictory opposites, and contradictories divide the universe between them. They are also contraries. In short, in order to conform precisely to the triadic formula, the phases opposed in a dialectical philosophy would need to fulfil the three conditions of (*a*) universality, (*b*) contradiction, and (*c*) contrariety.

8·21. (*a*) In Hegel's system every phase is offered as the concrete relation of the subject to its object-world, which for the subject is the whole world, the universe;[1] or else as the higher or the lower analogue of that relation. This is perhaps most readily seen in the categories, and also in the subjective modes of human experience and in organic life.[2] But if Nature is, philosophically speaking, the pre-spiritual, then the phases of Nature below life are also, as philosophic concepts, *Begriffsbestimmungen*, universal in the sense of all-pervasive, of characterizing the universe.[3] Space, time,

[1] Cf. § 5·3, above.

[2] See IH, ch. iii, §§ 5·1–5·4, and also ch. viii, which the reader will do well to consult.

[3] Of course neither they nor any phase of Hegel's or of any other dialectical system are fully concrete universal. Only a whole philosophical system could

and the general characters in terms of which physics and chemistry define their subject-matters, do not express the universe as object for a subject nor as environing an organic centre, since they are nothing *für sich*, and what they are *an sich* they are only *für uns*.[1] Yet *für uns* they are universal in the sense of all-pervasive at their own level. The universality of phases above the subjective modes of experience (such as Hegel elaborates in Objective and Absolute Spirit) need on the assumption of our nucleus of Hegelian idealism hardly here be argued.

It would seem, then, that on our general asumption a dialectic of phases which are universal at least in the sense of all-pervasive and centred on a subject, or on a lower analogue of a subject, need not be ruled out as impossible.

8·22. (*b*) If dialectic expresses the self-developing activity of spirit, its phases are not only universal but also, so far as they are universal, opposed as contradictories. For the terms of a developing series, each of which at a different level characterizes the universe, must, if we abstract them from their development and take them at the same level, present contradiction.

8·23. But (*c*) if a dialectical philosophy can express the activity of spirit only as human experience dual-centred and imperfectly self-transcending, there can be no guarantee that its phases shall present perfect contrariety. Contraries exhaustively determine each other's nature. Within the limited system of an empirical judgement, they are the extreme species of a genus, or two intermediate species of it taken as extremes within a universe of discourse.[2] But within such a limited system the contrary terms are not universal in the strict sense of characterizing the universe as such. It is their empirical limitation which gives them their precise empirical contrariety. But a dialectical philosophy cannot meet the formal demand of the triad for true contrariety, for exhaustive mutual determination of opposites which are true universals. It will, so to say, fall between two stools. It will disclaim empirical limitation and with that lose precise empirical

even claim to be that, and we have already seen good reason to think that no philosophy could ever substantiate such a claim.

[1] See IH, ch. viii, § 4·3. [2] Ibid. ch. x, § 4·1.

contrariety, but it can never pass wholly beyond the empirical. Its phases will never be purely contrary, but always to some extent merely disparate; and their universality, which in § 5·21 we said that they could possess *at least* in the sense that they could be all-pervasive and centred on a subject or a lower analogue of a subject, will never quite escape that qualification. It will be always in a variable and not precisely measurable degree ideal and abstract; and this it will be, not because any two phases of a perfect and concrete dialectical whole—could there be one—would necessarily, if considered subjectively apart from it, be abstract, but because in human experience totality is a never fully realizable ideal.

8·231. It might also be urged that the phases or moments of human experience which offer the most serious claim to be called true contraries are opposites of which one is a value and the other a 'dys-value', such opposites, that is, as true and false, good and evil, beautiful and ugly; and these, though they are of the type of opposition which motives the dialectic within each of Croce's 'distincts',[1] do not lend titles to particular stages of Hegel's dialectic. But this further objection to any philosophical dialectic resembling Hegel's has, I think, no substance. On the assumption of Hegel's or any other dialectical idealism, it must be held that the content of error, evil, or ugliness is always and only an unsublated phase of spirit which persists at the higher level but, instead of subserving, dominates and perverts.[2] Hence error, evil, and ugliness have as such and *eo nomine* no place in a dialectical system, although such a system may be secondarily considered as a progressive overcoming of error.

We may proceed to consider a more real difficulty.

8·24. It was said in § 8·22 that the phases of a dialectical philosophy would, in so far as they are universal, be also opposed as contradictories. But here again is a qualification which cannot be wholly escaped. Where contrariety and universality vary, contradiction cannot remain unchanged in character. Within the abstraction of a limited empirical

[1] See § 6·4, above.

[2] That 'dys-value' and the persistence of unsublated residue go together in human experience is obvious enough, but I do not here venture to speculate further upon the connexion of these two aspects of finitude.

system, contrariety can be precise and can coincide with contradiction: within whole number odd and even are both precisely contrary and precisely contradictory. But if the phases of dialectic are both universals in some measure abstract and contraries in some measure merely disparate, then the contradiction which they present is also defective, is a never fully grounded denial.

9. The failure of dialectic tested by its own formal ideal shows once again that the human mind cannot move unbrokenly with the rhythm which its own activity demands. In fact this test in terms of the triadic formula does no more than sum up the results which we reached in previous chapters. This halting rhythm of the mind is nothing different from the imperfect sublation and the unabsorbed yet subserving residue from lower levels which met us so long ago as Chapter I. The abstract nature of the universal, the disparate character of contraries, the inadequate grounding of contradiction—each of these is nothing but the persistence of the empirical factor which we tried vainly to dispel in our discussion of opposites.

9·1. This repeated failure may suggest bankruptcy. It might be said that we have in effect fatally eliminated altogether the *a priori* element in experience. For if the sublation of phases in human experience is always and inherently imperfect, and if the triadic form has, as it seems, no better claim than the syllogism to be a test of valid thinking, then not only Hegel's but any other alleged developing series which professes to set out these phases, must be altogether empirical. Such a series, it might be argued, is bound to be implicitly a false infinite, since no limit can be assigned to the number of terms which might upon further reflection be inserted between any two contiguous and allegedly cohering, but in fact arbitrarily juxtaposed, phases.[1] And with that perishes utterly the possibility of any dialectic. All exactness of contradiction and contrariety is dispersed in a process *ad indefinitum* of mere contingent differentiation.[2]

9·2. But this argument, if it holds good, ruins far more

[1] Cf. ch. xix, § 7·4, above.

[2] This argument is analogous to Aristotle's contention that the number of terms in demonstration must be finite; see *Posterior Analytics*, i, chs. xix–xxii.

than dialectic. It ruins the humblest and most provisional body of empirical fact; for thinking cannot proceed at any level if the identity which it asserts has no stability in its differences. To urge this argument is to forget the positive side of our criticism. Certainly, if its negative side has truth, we have to admit that every phase of a dialectical philosophy must be established, as one might say, οὐκ ἄνευ ἐμπειρίας. The criterion of truth which governs it will still be relative in that the union of coherence and comprehensiveness will remain a never fully realized ideal. There will be a continual possibility, nay certainty, of alternative and partially discrepant statement in the formulation even of logical categories. Even in logic we could look to find no κτῆμα ἐς ἀεί of final truth. But, on the other hand, even in what is ordinarily called empirical thinking the shock of fact compels acceptance only in co-operation with the *a priori*. Only mind's own nature 'compels' it; only what mind has found within itself can it externalize and accept as if upon compulsion.[1] Moreover, the essential difference between empirical and philosophic thinking, viz. the self-consciously developing character of philosophy, is not abolished by the limitations which we have ourselves been time and again obliged to recognize. The least reflection on human experience at once develops it and at the same time reveals that its inherent nature *is* to develop actively from level to level.[2] And this reflection resolutely pursued is philosophy. Whereas empirical thinking achieves its precarious precision at the expense of accepting a hypothetical basis, philosophy is essentially the attempt to develop experience to self-consciousness by and in reflection which is without reservation; by and in a thinking which is categorical and not hypothetical.[3] For that reason it is essentially dialectical and universal, even if its full and real nature lies always beyond it. No doubt the universals in which it moves have in them

[1] See ch. xx, § 4·1 *ad fin.*

[2] So soon as we realize that to reflect on our experience is not just to stand apart, so to say, and watch it. H. H. Joachim in *Logical Studies*, pp. 143–52, has a most valuable discussion of this point.

[3] If even philosophy reflects upon what is in some sense a datum 'external' and 'found', yet this datum is the whole content of past philosophy.

an empirical element which the philosopher can never with full certainty distinguish, separate, and discard. Indeed, it is where the universal is most abstract and has least content that he can with the most confidence proclaim it to be pure *a priori* thought: its purity is in inverse proportion to its concreteness. Yet the universals of a philosophical dialectic, though the taint of the empirical be upon them, are not just the universals of empirical thinking. Their claim to be truly contrary and contradictory will always fail fully to justify itself, but they will not be wholly disparate, because they arise in human experience as explicit phases of its own developing activity.

10. I have tried to sketch the limitations to which, as it seems to me, any dialectical philosophy is inherently subject, and to indicate barely the positive scope to which dialectic might without arrogance lay claim. In the concluding chapter of this *Study* I shall attempt to carry this task a little farther by taking a last glance at Hegel's system, and try finally to sum up the general philosophical position towards which we have been moving.

XXII
CONCLUSION

1. HEGEL's conception of Nature as the pre-spiritual,[1] as the self-external which becomes intelligible only in so far as its self-externality diminishes in gradual approximation to the centrality and system of spirit, is vital to his whole position; and it is vital too, I think, to any dialectical philosophy. Moreover, in beginning his dialectic of Nature with space and time, matter and motion, and in stressing the growing implication of centred system as chemistry succeeds physics and the study of organism succeeds chemistry, Hegel merely followed the general lines which the study of Nature had accepted since its origin. On the other hand, no one would to-day attempt to defend in detail Hegel's Philosophy of Nature. A philosophical criticism of natural science was a part of his proper task, but the self-externality and impotent empirical profusion of Nature, emphasized by himself and reflected in the rapid obsolescence of all scientific theory, might have warned him that the more detailed his dialectic of Nature became the more provisional and transitory it must be.

1·1. Hegel held that the natural scientist provides the material which the philosopher must criticize and reconstruct dialectically, but he does not always conceive clearly the nature and scope of this co-operation.[2] The attitude and the purpose of the philosopher and the man of science respectively are, I believe, less akin than Hegel supposed.[3] It would not be true to say that the apparent tendency of the natural scientist to descend or, so to say, gear down his investigation, as when he passes from biology to biochemistry, or from chemistry to physics, and from physics to mathematics, constitutes a denial that Nature approximates to spirit in degrees. With that philosophic question natural science as such was unconcerned from the moment of birth (whenever we choose to date it) at which it severed itself from

[1] See IH, ch. viii, § 4·21.

[2] See ch. xx, § 5·442, above.

[3] In what follows I owe something to Oakeshott, *Experience and its Modes*, ch. iv.

philosophy. The scientific observer seeks precision where he can find it, and that is where he can measure. The assumptions which define his special subject-matter were in the first instance borrowed from outside it, and he has in his search for precision struggled to reduce their number and to make them ever simpler and more abstract. He has in effect tried, as the Pythagoreans tried, to modify them towards mathematics. This procedure is not an implicit denial that Nature approximates to spirit, but it does, so far as I can see, imply that the natural scientist produces no new universal determinations of Nature except in the course of breaking down and simplifying an assumption which he finds too concrete to permit the precision of measurement which he seeks. And when the need arises, he will throw over his simplified assumption for one more abstract still.

1·2. What, then, is the purpose of natural science? It is tempting to reply with Croce that science is concerned purely with practice and not at all with theoretical truth. Yet, while it is obvious that science elaborates that view of the world which we must first accept and render precise in order to act effectively, to hold that science offers no theoretical truth seems in the end to compel us, as it compels Croce, to take the less plausible view that mathematics, too, is purely practical. Moreover, the general definitory assumptions of the sciences clearly do contribute a 'knowledge' of Nature with which philosophical knowledge of spirit cannot dispense—even in the simple Cartesian antithesis the unextendedness of mind signifies nothing save in contrast with the extendedness of matter—and it can hardly be thought that this contribution is a quite accidental by-product.

The truth, perhaps, is that natural science, since its object is non-spiritual, must constantly tend towards conceiving reality as quantitative, and while without the urge of practical need natural science would not have originated nor diversified itself as it has, yet a purely speculative interest in an abstract quantitative universe arises not accidentally but necessarily, because there is no absolute severance between the forms of man's experience. Science is essentially impersonal, but men are essentially persons.

1·3. Natural science is essentially impersonal; its world is explicitly non-spiritual. It would seem, then, that a philosophical dialectic of Nature is bound to consist of positions which science has abandoned or will abandon in the pursuit of a purpose which is not philosophical. It is of value in so far as it succeeds in showing how the scientific assumptions of different epochs, or the assumptions which define the special sciences of one epoch, do in fact reflect the gradual approximation of Nature to spirit, although the process of science appears to be in the precisely opposite direction. Hegel's Philosophy of Nature loses much of the absurdity which at first scandalizes a reader conversant with modern science, if it is remembered that Hegel is reflecting on early-nineteenth-century science and not on science of the middle twentieth century. Yet Hegel, it must be admitted, does sometimes deprive himself of this well-grounded excuse for the obsolescence of his dialectic by indulging in what would seem to be an effort to reach scientific conclusions by independent philosophic insight. When he does so the result is sometimes a happy anticipation, but often a baseless construction of fancy.[1]

2. The ground covered by Hegel's Subjective Spirit is a realm which already in his day had been invaded by natural scientists striving less or more consciously to reduce their subject-matter to measurable quanta. The material upon which he here reflects is to some extent their product, despite his emphatic statement that Aristotle's *De Anima* is still far the best, perhaps the only, work of philosophic interest on the subject covered by his own Philosophy of Spirit.[2] His dialectic is often in consequence obsolete, and its oppositions seem sometimes arbitrary and susceptible of alternative statement. Yet these defects are far less conspicuous in the dialectic of Subjective Spirit than in the dialectic of Nature, because psychology as special science touches a minor aspect of its subject and has made no advance along 'the sure path of science' comparable to the progress of the strictly physical sciences. Moreover, Hegel's treatment of the modes of Soul, Consciousness, and Mind

[1] Collingwood, *Idea of Nature*, pp. 124–32, comments valuably on Hegel's Philosophy of Nature. His comparison of Hegel and Whitehead is of special interest.

[2] Cf. IH, Introd., p. xii.

as phases of a self-developing activity brings one to self-conscious realization of the developments within one's own experience, of one's self-transcendences, even of one's trivial everyday transitions from sense to thought, from feeling to emotion, from impulse to will, with a sureness and clarity which no other thinker since Aristotle has approached;[1] and this development of all levels of experience in philosophic thinking, not any measurable degree of conformity to a triadic pattern, is the essential moment of any dialectical philosophy.

2·1. Yet in the course of reducing the mind of man to measurable quanta, or of attempting to heal the diseases of singular individual minds, psychologists since Hegel's day have ἐν παρεργῷ thrown a dim but important light on the lower levels of spirit. Being in method and outlook natural scientists, they have not seriously concerned themselves with the relation of level to level, and frequently they have fallen into the error to which the specialist, because he is a man as well as a man of science, is always liable. They have often forgotten—indeed, they have seldom succeeded in clearly defining to themselves—the hypothesis under which they work, and they have regarded their results as interpreting not an abstracted level of mind but its full concrete nature. The consequences have been so grotesque that one is almost tempted to cry: 'In the realm of spirit give us superstition rather than science.' There is clamant need to interpret the results of modern psychological inquiry dialectically; not, that is, by the imposition of a rigid triadic formula, but in terms of levels of spirit and with due regard to the inevitably incomplete sublation of each level by its successor.

3. Since 1914, when the German people first attempted to dominate Europe, Hegel's doctrine of Objective Spirit has been subjected to a criticism which, since Germany's second attempt in 1939, has grown steadily more violent and more ill informed.[2] This is no place to defend its merits in detail.

[1] Even so little of the doctrines of Subjective Spirit as I have reproduced in the first half of ch. i and made use of in ch. xx, §§ 10·1 ff., has, I hope, done something to show this.

[2] In Dr. Popper's book, *The Open Society and its Enemies*, ch. 12, it becomes almost meaninglessly silly.

Suffice it to say that although here as in Nature and Subjective Spirit the empirical factor at once subserves philosophical reflection and denies it hope of finality, yet without the conception of political institutions as in some sense an objective and progressive embodiment of spirit, and without the notion of political history as in some sense a necessary movement of spirit's self-development, human life does not merely become unintelligible but is no longer there to be understood. If civilization again achieves the tolerably stable equilibrium of Hegel's later years, the dialectic of Objective Spirit will be rewritten. The practical agonies of these times, and the consequent chaos of moral and political emotions, permit man no very clear self-consciousness. The material offered by empirical observation is to-day too raw to suggest any immediate hope of a fresh philosophical analysis and synthesis.

3·1. Yet it may be worth while to suggest the direction in which a fresh dialectic of political history might move.

Any dialectical philosophy of political history must assume (1) that political history, in essence, concerns the will of man as it manifests the single activity of spirit, and not as it is outwardly manifested in temporal events which, viewed abstractedly as the whole and not as a partial moment of the whole, must appear merely contingent; and (2) that in consequence political history is history of freedom. Without these assumptions a dialectical philosophy would possess no criterion enabling it to detect direction and significance in events. If in the coming century man should embrace tyranny, and if the human race should decline through a period of unbroken darkness and perish from the earth, that would constitute no better ground for denying that history is the manifestation of spirit in human freedom than does the empirical fact that man had an origin in time. Moreover, if history is history of freedom its criterion must in some sense be progress; it must, that is to say, work in terms of better and worse. But to interpret this as meaning that either progress or degeneration is 'in the long run' inevitable would be absurd. The empirical material which the philosophic historian develops must present itself as a finite stretch within a false infinite of endless time, and he can never fully overcome this appearance; but for the very same reason 'the long run' must remain for him a purely relative term.

3·2. A future dialectical philosophy of history will therefore endorse Hegel's sober acknowledgement of the contingent factor which precludes the historian from prophecy. Nor will a veto on prophecy and the mere modification demanded by the passage of time occupied by fresh political action and fresh political researches be all that a new dialectic must concede to the empirical factor. Hegel's conviction that the world is a single rational process, though no dialectical philosophy can question that assumption, led him to overestimate his own grasp both of facts and values. Hence his often arbitrary selection of the significant fact,[1] and his tone of rather complacent ruthlessness when he upholds the claim of 'world-historical' heroes to override the lower ethical levels on which their lesser contemporaries move.[2] It is often when Hegel most passionately exalts the Absolute above the transitory and empirical that, by a nemesis not inexplicable if the duality of human experience is such as I have maintained it to be, his philosophical system most clearly reveals its temporal context and betrays its own empirical limitations. In human experience temporal and logical are never perfectly distinct,[3] and the posterior is never experienced as perfectly sublating the prior. That much of the good in a given social epoch depends on what is in principle obsolete is only a human half-truth, but it is a half-truth towards which Hegel failed in justice.

3·3. A new dialectic of history will be conscious that it reflects its own age in thought, and if it does so fairly it is likely to paint the past in a darker grey than Hegel's. Although it will assume a single activity of spirit, it will be less confident in its interpretation, and for a further reason, too, it will formulate itself in more diverse shapes than will any future dialectical interpretation of Nature. Man cannot make Nature, nor even the subjective modes of his own experience, as he makes history. Facts in natural science

[1] E.g. what we might call his erratic spiritual geography.

[2] Though he does what he can to preserve the values of individual conscience and religion; see ΦH, JE, pp. 63 ff.

[3] Cf. ch. xix, §§ 10 ff.

may be disputable, but they embody no values and they have a certain degree of impersonal hardness.[1] But the material of any professional historian, even the chronicler, is already spirit: it is the thought and will of men. This historical stuff was never fully intelligible to the actual enactors of it, and *res gestae* offer to every type of historian from the chronicler to the philosopher a far wider latitude of interpretation than that which scientific facts permit; and this interpretation is, further, subject to subsequent trends of human action as scientific theory is not. Natural science progresses because it envisages a non-historical Nature: the evolution of species is not history, because the biologist does not envisage it as a self-development of spirit. That is why the scientist commonly cares so little for the history of science. It is also the reason why in Hegel's Philosophy of History there is so much statement of historical fact at a pre-philosophic level; Hegel has to commit himself to interpretation at more levels than one.

4. The final triad of Hegel's Philosophy of Spirit presents problems upon which I can here only touch. In his Philosophies of Art and Religion the historical element remains prominent. It is clearly there a material more highly spiritualized than the data upon which the philosopher of political history must reflect, but it is the ineliminable empirical factor in those philosophies. Again, the content of Philosophy *qua* the final phase of Hegel's Philosophy of Spirit is in one sense the whole super-triad,[2] but in another sense it is the History of Philosophy as Hegel expounded it in his lectures under that title, one of his most permanent achievements. In the Philosophy of Art the empirical and historical factor is very conspicuously not, and could not be, sublated in the philosophical interpretation without a residue which at once lames and sustains the interpretation, and no doubt Hegel often, and to an extent beyond that which the limitations of his own epoch could excuse, forces the triadic form on a material too raw to accept it. Of his Philosophy of Religion the same is true, and even in Hegel's or any other possible History of Philosophy the series of doctrines presented in association with the names of men who lived and

[1] Cf. ch. xx, § 4·1.

[2] Cf. ch. xix, § 5 above.

died in particular epochs contains, and must contain, its contingent empirical factor, at once irrelevant and indispensable. It was perhaps in part the increasingly spiritual character of the historical material which awaits philosophic reconstitution in the higher forms of human experience which led Croce towards the identification of spirit with history (conceived of course far more widely than as political history) and of philosophy with the methodology of history. But no such historical industry could move save both hampered and helped in its movement by the empirical material upon which it must work. In its dialectic mere difference must masquerade as true opposition, and we have no criterion by which to detect the pretence but spirit self-developing in us as an ideal.

5. Hegel's Logic is not a homogeneous whole, but it might fairly be said to be in the main an attempt to discard an empirical residue from the history of philosophy, and to reshape and develop as a dialectic of pure thought the basic conceptions of what it is to be real which Hegel found in his predecessors. The history of philosophy, that is, on the whole relates to Hegel's ontological logic as an empirical material analogous to the historical elements in his Philosophies of Art and Religion, although still more spiritualized than they. Croce, I think, was right in holding that the logic of philosophy was the main goal towards which Hegel's effort was directed. But although the difference of pure thought from sense is perhaps the deepest difference in human experience, we have already seen enough reason to believe that even if we are prepared to pay the full price of abstraction we cannot achieve a world of pure thought quite untainted by contingency, and if we glance at the empirical material which Hegel struggles to reconstitute in the Logic we shall find this conclusion confirmed.

5·1. The attitude of Hegel to Kant, like that of Aristotle to Plato, is at first sight rather that of a critic than of a debtor. Both were too close to their masters to see them in a true perspective; or, to put it as Hegel might have expressed it, both were inevitably more conscious of antithesis than synthesis. Kant must nevertheless be counted the main contributor from the past to Hegel's Logic. Hegel was always a Kantian, though not quite to the extent to which Aristotle was always a Platonist. In the first place, although it was Hegel's outstanding achievement to develop the mere hints in Kant and show that pure thought is in itself both form and content, not a mere collection of principles but the phases of a unitary activity, and although Hegel vigorously combated Kant's view that the ascription of a single source to sense and thought is quite problematic, yet in Hegel's own treatment of the relation of thought to sense there persists, I think, a certain trace of that Leibnizian rationalism which Kant had not wholly overcome. Hegel concedes that logic is a realm of shadows, but he asks too much in return for this concession. He tends to conceive the purity of pure thought as a complete freedom from any taint of the empirical. In the second place, Kant had not, like Hegel and like no other thinker since Aristotle, deeply studied the whole history of European philosophy. He had taken up the quarrel between rationalism and empiricism as he found it developed in seventeenth- and eighteenth-century philosophers, and among them he had known little of Spinoza. Hence the critical philosophy, ample as was its scope, was not a medium in which the whole previous history of philosophic thought had been digested to serve Hegel as material. Inevitably those other constituents of the Logic which Hegel felt bound to include—for example, Greek philosophy, which always directly influenced Hegel, and the basic thought of Spinoza —do not perfectly synthesize with the Kantian contribution, more particularly because what Kant contributed to Hegel was as much a philosophic point of view as certain particular categories.

5·2. It is hard to be sure with what right Hegel's very detailed dialectic of Quantity appears in the Logic. Hegel connected mathematics with space and time in a more or less Kantian manner,[1] and his logic of Quantity in effect elaborates the Kantian categories of quantity by an attempt to elicit logical categories from the mathematics of his own time. What precisely is the subject-matter of mathematics is an agelong puzzle, but however it is solved[2] Hegel's dialectic

[1] Cf. ch. iii, §§ 1·1 and 4·3, above.

[2] The modern tendency to make order rather than quantity the subject

of Quantity must in principle be subject to modification with the advance of mathematics, just as his *Begriffsbestimmungen* of Nature are in principle subject to modification as natural science progresses.

5·3. Other constituents of the Logic, as I have from time to time observed in the earlier chapters of this *Study*, present at least the appearance of direct borrowings from the Philosophy of Nature, and sometimes, especially perhaps in the dialectic of Quality and of Show, Hegel seems to excogitate phases to bridge gaps of which the limits are clearer to him than to his reader.

Not only Quantity but any category of the Logic must in fact submit to modification in the light of a progressive research which is in different degrees empirical. Hegel's reconstitution of formal logic as a development from Notion as such was a solid achievement, but when the shouting and the tumult of as lightly ludicrous anti-metaphysical hostility dies from modern logic, it is very possible that these newer researches in the natural history, or the mathematics, of thought may yield material to a philosophical logic. Perhaps only the opening triads of Being, Essence,[1] and Notion are, by virtue of their extreme abstraction, their close approach to tautology, moments of pure thought which one can scarcely conceive as liable to be superseded.[2] The main triad of the Logic, the general conception of Being, Essence, Notion, seems to be indispensable to any dialectical logic, and Hegel, struggling to rethink his not fully homogeneous materials, his *impares materiae*, in an order from abstract to concrete, reaches a new stage in human self-consciousness. Anyone who has not blinkered himself by assuming that the triad is a rigid formula of perfect opposition and synthesis to which its contents must exactly conform on pain of unconditional expulsion, any student who has not, by attempting the futile task of correcting Hegel's Logic as if it were

of mathematics and to identify logic and mathematics is an interesting comment on Hegel.

[1] The opening triads of Essence, it will be remembered, are in the *Encyclopaedia* version simply a dialectical revitalizing of the traditional 'laws of thought'; cf. ch. vi, § 2 above.

[2] Yet if they connect dialectically with the categories which follow them their claim to eternity vanishes.

a faulty copy of Latin verses which do not always scan,[1] reduced himself quickly to despair, will find that, although difference may assume the guise of opposition and alternative statement seem often possible, yet there moves beneath these breaks and empirical patches a living activity of thought which no thinker but from time to time Hegel himself has had the power to bring home quite irresistibly to his reader. On every re-reading of Hegel the words of Bernard Bosanquet, which I quoted in IH,[2] recur to one's mind: 'Not that I can "explain" him any more than others can, but that when I do seem to understand he speaks to me as the only writer I can understand. What he says seems to come straight out of one's own heart and experience; everyone else seems distant and artificial beside it.'

6. At the end of the last chapter I proposed an attempt to sum up the general philosophical position towards which this *Study* has moved. Yet in the course of a painful struggle to criticize Hegel justly I have developed a philosophical policy rather than a philosophical position, a method of diagnosing rather than of solving philosophical difficulties. I have accepted Hegel's view that the unity of self-conscious thought with being is original, and that the real is the single self-developing and self-developed activity of spirit. But I have contended that the unity of thought and being, although it guarantees man against total scepticism, yet debars his thinking from any hope of finality; and I have urged that, because the single activity of spirit is of its own nature not only self-developed but also self-developing, self-manifesting in finitude, an ambiguous duality is omnipresent in human experience.

6·1. This is, of course, no new discovery. Hegel in the Logic of Essence brilliantly gripped and characterized this duality in its general nature, although he did not, as I believe and have tried to show, fully realize that the defect and limitation which it entails are inescapable at any level of human thought.[3]

[1] Which McTaggart in his *Commentary* seems often to be doing.

[2] Preface, p. xvii.

[3] See ch. xxi, §§ 5·33 ff. above. Under the title of 'the unhappy Consciousness' (see esp. *Phän.*, JE 2, pp. 167 ff.) Hegel characterizes this duality most subtly, but only as an historical phase of religious experience.

The same duality is central in the idealism of T. H. Green, who based his ethical theory on what he called man's 'double consciousness'. It pervades the thought of Bradley; and Bosanquet, applying to human experience the term 'dual-centred', stresses it strongly in *The Principle of Individuality and Value*.

6·2. To me it has seemed especially to reveal itself as an incompletely sublated residue, in different degrees empirical and contingent, which at once impedes and aids each successively developing phase of man's experience. This formula is doubtless no more than a partial aspect of the problem. In this book I have tried to show in a few concrete instances how one might apply it, and I have tried to use it in a very general way to criticize Hegel. It could be fairly tested only by applying it over wide and various fields, on a large scale and a small.[1]

6·3. I have thought that under the idea of this halting dialectic one might profitably try, on the positive side, to set in an order, not necessarily Hegel's, what seem to present themselves as the main forms of human experience, recognizing that in the main forms of human experience there is no order but that which expresses the immanence of spirit's single activity, but recognizing also, on the negative side, that man's passage through them is never sublation without residue. And it may be, I have thought, that this policy, or critique, if I may dare to dignify it with such a title, would serve often to bring out the positive merits of a philosophical system whereof it seems at first sight to be no more than negatively critical. That it has done so in so far as I have applied it to Hegel I can only hope, but a further word on Croce's philosophy may help to explain my point.

[1] The reader may ask why I have not applied it in more detail to Hegel's Logic. To do that, to try to show the precise degree in which its 'empirical' constituents help and hinder the dialectical movement of the Logic, would entail rewriting the history of philosophy, and, before one could deal adequately with some parts of the Logic, the history of natural science and mathematics too. My own incompetence and the scope of this *Study* precluded that. I have made what contribution I could by comparing Hegel from time to time with his greater predecessors, chiefly with Aristotle and Kant. To have tried to apply any such formula to Hegel's Logic triad by triad would have been to repeat the mistake of attempting to apply the triadic formula itself as a rigid yardstick to test the validity of its content. No formula will enable one to correct Hegel's dialectic like an exercise.

6·31. In the last chapter I suggested that under criticism Croce's dialectic of 'distincts', from which all taint of mere empirical difference is allegedly banished, cannot after all escape the charge of being an empirical classification. Yet if the view I have put forward has any truth, the elements of no philosophical system can wholly evade that charge, and I should not hesitate to declare Croce's comparison of economic and moral action admirable, and his conception of art a major philosophical achievement. Again, if one contemplates abstractly the Crocean system, it shows a frail neatness and a poverty of content which excites suspicion in any close student of the masters of philosophy. But Croce's main works include a wealth of historical material grasped and treated with a brilliant directness, and continual touches of wisdom and insight revealing the spiritual world in which he has lived and laboured intensely. If in the light of these one reflects again on the pages confined strictly to the exposition of his own theory, his system glows with fresh life. Yet this historical matter and these sudden flowerings of deep-rooted wisdom are in different degrees empirical. They are constituents of his system sublated in it, but they are constituents incompletely sublated and surviving to subserve.[1]

6·4. Some light, I have thought, might be thrown on the relation between philosophy and natural science by considering them in terms of this formula of incomplete sublation. At the beginning of this chapter[2] I have drawn a distinction between the attitudes of the scientist and the philosopher which it may be well to restate and perhaps to modify.

6·41. Natural science seems to determine its subject-matter ever less and less concretely. Philosophical thinking seems at first sight to move, or attempt to move, in the opposite direction. But if philosophical thinking is dialectical it is more than movement. It is, or it aims at being, an activity which takes up and carries its starting-point with it, transforms its initial into its final stage; so that if it is to be

[1] Croce himself has denied the finality of philosophic thought as vigorously as any man—in the concluding sentence of the *Pratica* he offers his work as 'an instrument of labour'—but he would not, I think, admit any degrees of the empirical.

[2] §§ 1·1–1·3.

called any kind of movement, it must be called a circular movement, and that is still a quite inadequate metaphor. The philosopher works under the ideal of this complete activity. Faced at each stage with imperfect sublation and an unabsorbed but subservient residue from the prior stage, he tends to neglect this residue and pass on, seeking to construct so true a scale of approximation to the active nature of spirit that his climax shall absorb without residue and luminously contain all the stages of his ascent. The natural scientist, on the other hand, whose purpose is not to comprehend the sublation of Nature in spirit but to grasp Nature as it is empirically given, finds himself, when he makes his empirical beginning, faced with what the philosopher describes as a level or reality with which is present an unabsorbed residue from a lower level, so that two categories—to use the term quite generally—which define the real at different levels seem both to claim to characterize it at the same level. But for the scientist there are no levels in the philosopher's sense, no degrees of approximation to spirit. To him this clash of categories is sheer contradiction, not contradiction resoluble in synthesis: one of them must go. The category which he discards is the more concrete of the two, because it is the more 'spiritual' of the two. It is the one which he cannot in the end as a scientist justify, because as a scientist his object is the non-spiritual, and he must therefore work always towards an explanation in quantitative terms; or rather, perhaps, he must always seek to reduce the number of his spiritual postulates, and quantitative explanation is at any rate a stage on his journey.

6·42. But this contrast of attitude is drawn, I think, too sharply. On the one side, if the philosopher neglects the problem of unsublated residue his result will be an abstraction bearing a spurious air of finality, a neat system which ignores the inherent defect of human experience. On the other side, the scientist does not, as his practice clearly shows, at each stage of his descent abandon the higher category instantly and without reluctance. If he did, natural science would lose at a blow all special differentiation. It would cease to be science of Nature and become, I suppose, some sort of mathematics. To take a familiar example of what is becoming a more and more complex *dégringolade*, biologists have for a long time tended to abandon teleological hypotheses, because they appear to lead to no *special* results,[1] and to substitute chemical explanation. But these explanations are not called simply 'chemical' but 'biochemical', and without any reference to 'function', an indisputably teleological term, would have no relevant meaning. An analogous lapse of chemistry towards physics, and of physics towards mathematics, has long been evident, and nowadays every special science tends to eschew any kind of causal explanation and seek refuge in statistics. But in every case this metamorphosis is incomplete and can never become complete. As the ascending philosopher cannot with impunity ignore the empirical residue, so the scientist cannot at each stage fasten upon nothing but the lower category and sink contentedly step by step into flat mathematics.[2] At each stage there is a spiritual residue which he cannot annihilate, although science has no language in which he can acknowledge it.

7. In the sphere of formal logic the conception of dialectic which I have offered would compel us to keep in mind, despite all temptation to forget them, two assumptions: that pure thought is itself both form and content, and that, while no principle or category of thought can signify in isolation, equally little can any principle or category of thought be held to be absolutely *a priori* and eternally exempt from criticism. But I could not, at any rate in this book, attempt to work critically with these assumptions upon the ever-changing products, so often mere programmes, of modern formal logic.

8. It would not serve the purpose for which I write to suggest further fields for the application of what I have confessed to be little more than a method of philosophical diagnosis. If it should prove a helpful clue to a few students of philosophy bold enough to read Hegel's Logic undeterred either by the extravagances of Hegel himself or by the hostility of modern critics who have scarcely troubled to open his works, I shall for the present be well contented.

[1] Cf. ch. xv, § 5·2 above. The problem is, of course, as old as Kant's *Critique of Judgement*; cf. ibid., § 5·1.

[2] If, indeed, there are no levels in mathematics.

INDEX

This Index is intended to supplement, not to cover, the Chapter and Section headings of the text.

PRINTED IN
GREAT BRITAIN
AT THE
UNIVERSITY PRESS
OXFORD
BY
CHARLES BATEY
PRINTER
TO THE
UNIVERSITY

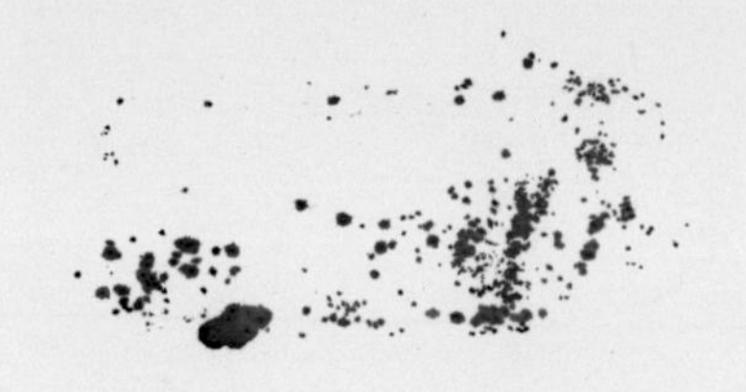